A·N·N·U·A·L E·D·I·T·I·O·N·S

DYING, DEATH, AND BEREAVEMENT 02/03

Sixth Edition

Editors

George E. Dickinson
College of Charleston

George E. Dickinson is professor of sociology at the College of Charleston in Charleston, South Carolina. He received a B.A. in biology from Baylor University, an M.A. in sociology from Baylor, and a Ph.D. in sociology from Louisiana State University. His research and publications focus on physicians' treatment of terminally ill patients, children and death, physician-assisted suicide, and health treatment for the elderly.

Michael R. Leming
St. Olaf College

Michael R. Leming is professor of sociology and anthropology at St. Olaf College. He holds a B.A. degree from Westmont College, an M.A. degree from Marquette University, and a Ph.D. degree from the University of Utah, and he has done additional graduate study at the University of California in Santa Barbara. Dr. Leming serves on numerous boards of directors, and he serves as a hospice educator, volunteer, and grief counselor.

McGraw-Hill/Dushkin
530 Old Whitfield Street, Guilford, Connecticut 06437

Visit us on the Internet
http://www.dushkin.com

Credits

1. The American Way of Dying and Death
Unit photo—© 2001 by PhotoDisc, Inc.
2. Developmental Aspects of Dying and Death
Unit photo—United Nations photo by John Orr.
3. The Dying Process
Unit photo—© 2001 by Cleo Freelance Photography.
4. Ethical Issues of Dying, Death, and Suicide
Unit photo—© 2001 by Sweet By & By/Cindy Brown
5. Funerals and Burial Rites
Unit photo—EPA-Documerica.
6. Bereavement
Unit photo—WHO photo by Marthelot.

Copyright

Cataloging in Publication Data
Main entry under title: Annual Editions: Dying, Death, and Bereavement. 2002/2003.
    1. Death—Psychological aspects—Periodicals. 2. Bereavement—Periodicals. I. Dickinson, George E., *comp.* II. Leming, Michael R., *comp.* IV. Title: Dying, death, and bereavement.
ISBN 0-07-247990-6   155.937'05   BF789.D4   ISSN 1096-4223

Sixth Edition

Cover image © 2002 by PhotoDisc, Inc.

Printed in the United States of America   1234567890BAHBAH5432   Printed on Recycled Paper

Members of the Advisory Board are instrumental in the final selection of articles for each edition of ANNUAL EDITIONS. Their review of articles for content, level, currentness, and appropriateness provides critical direction to the editor and staff. We think that you will find their careful consideration well reflected in this volume.

Editors/Advisory Board

Staff

To the Reader

In publishing ANNUAL EDITIONS we recognize the enormous role played by the magazines, newspapers, and journals of the public press in providing current, first-rate educational information in a broad spectrum of interest areas. Many of these articles are appropriate for students, researchers, and professionals seeking accurate, current material to help bridge the gap between principles and theories and the real world. These articles, however, become more useful for study when those of lasting value are carefully collected, organized, indexed, and reproduced in a low-cost format, which provides easy and permanent access when the material is needed. That is the role played by ANNUAL EDITIONS.

Though dying, death, and bereavement have been around for as long as humankind, as topics of discussion they have been "offstage" for decades in contemporary American public discourse. Indeed, dying in the United States currently takes place away from the arena of familiar surroundings of kin and friends, with approximately 70 percent of deaths occurring in institutional settings of hospitals and nursing homes. Americans have developed a paradoxical relationship with death: We know more about the causes and conditions surrounding death, but we have not equipped ourselves emotionally to cope with dying, death, and the bereavement process. The purpose of this anthology is to provide an understanding of dying, death, and bereavement that will assist individuals to better cope with and understand their own deaths and the deaths of others.

Articles in this volume are taken from professional publications, semiprofessional journals, and popular publications aimed at both special populations and a general readership. The selections are carefully reviewed for their currency and accuracy. On some issues, opposing viewpoints are presented. The current edition has changed approximately two-thirds of the articles from the previous editions through updating and responding to comments of reviewers regarding the earlier editions.

The reader will note the tremendous range of approaches and styles of the writers from personal, firsthand accounts to more scientific and philosophical writings. Some are more practical and applied, while others are more technical and research-oriented. If "variety is the very spice of life," this volume should be a spicy venture for the reader.

These articles are drawn from many different periodicals, thus exposing the reader to a diversity of publications in the library. With stimulated interest from a particular article, the student is encouraged to pursue other related articles in that particular journal.

This anthology is organized into six units to cover many of the important aspects of dying, death, and bereavement. Though the units are arranged in a way that has some logical order, one can determine from the brief summaries in the *table of contents* and the cross-references in the *topic guide* whether another arrangement would best fit a particular teaching situation. The first unit gives an overview of the American way of dying and death. Unit 2 takes a life-cycle approach and looks at the developmental aspects of dying and death at different ages levels. The third unit concerns the process of dying. Unit 4 covers ethical issues of dying, death, and suicide. In the fifth unit, the articles deal with death rituals and funerals. Finally, unit 6 presents articles on bereavement.

Annual Editions: Dying, Death, and Bereavement 02/03 is intended for use as a supplement to augment selected areas or chapters of regular textbooks on dying and death. The articles in this volume can also serve as a basis for class discussion about various issues in dying, death, and bereavement.

Annual Editions: Dying, Death, and Bereavement is revised periodically to keep the materials timely as new social concerns about dying, death, and bereavement develop. Your assistance in the revision effort is always welcome. Please complete and return the postage-paid *article rating form* at the back of the book. We look forward to your input.

George E. Dickinson
Editor

Michael R. Leming
Editor

Contents

UNIT 1

The American Way of Dying and Death

Five selections discuss definitions of death, focusing on alleviation of pain, various burial customs, and the medical aspects of death.

UNIT 2

Developmental Aspects of Dying and Death

Six articles examine how the experience of watching friends and relatives die can affect individuals at various periods of their lives.

The concepts in bold italics are developed in the article. For further expansion please refer to the Topic Guide and the Index.

UNIT 3

The Dying Process

Seven articles examine the various stages of the dying process, how physicians view dying, spiritual needs of the dying, and the dynamics of hospice.

The concepts in bold italics are developed in the article. For further expansion please refer to the Topic Guide and the Index.

Overview   90

UNIT 4

Ethical Issues of Dying, Death, and Suicide

Seven unit selections discuss active euthanasia, assisted suicide, and other ethical issues one may face at the end of life.

UNIT 5

Funerals and Burial Rites

Seven articles discuss the
American funeral, cross-cultural
burial rites, and cremation.

The concepts in bold italics are developed in the article. For further expansion please refer to the Topic Guide and the Index.

The concepts in bold italics are developed in the article. For further expansion please refer to the Topic Guide and the Index.

UNIT 6

Bereavement

Eight articles discuss the grieving process of children, young people, and adults and the loss of a significant other.

The concepts in bold italics are developed in the article. For further expansion please refer to the Topic Guide and the Index.

The concepts in bold italics are developed in the article. For further expansion please refer to the Topic Guide and the Index.

This topic guide suggests how the selections in this book relate to the subjects covered in your course.

The Web icon (⚫) under the topic articles easily identifies the relevant Web sites, which are numbered and annotated on the next two pages. By linking the articles and the Web sites by topic, this ANNUAL EDITIONS reader becomes a powerful learning and research tool.

DUSHKIN ONLINE

● AE: Dying, Death, and Bereavement

The following World Wide Web sites have been carefully researched and selected to support the articles found in this reader. The sites are cross-referenced by number and the Web icon (●) in the topic guide. In addition, it is possible to link directly to these Web sites through our DUSHKIN ONLINE support site at *http://www.dushkin.com/online/*.

The following sites were available at the time of publication. Visit our Web site—we update DUSHKIN ONLINE regularly to reflect any changes.

General Sites

1. Death, Dying, and Grief
http://www.emanon.net/~kcabell/death.html
There are many World Wide Web links to resources on death, dying, and bereavement at this site.

2. Death Related Weblinks
http://www.stolaf.edu/people/leming/death.html
This site contains links to some of the best Internet sites related to death and dying.

3. Social Issues & Social Services: Death and Dying
http://mel.lib.mi.us/social/SOC-death.html
Visit this site for resources regarding bereavement, death with dignity, euthanasia, and the funeral home industry.

4. Yahoo: Society and Culture: Death
http://dir.yahoo.com/Society_and_Culture/Death_and_Dying/
This Yahoo site has a very complete index to issues of dying and a search option.

The American Way of Dying and Death

5. Agency for Health Care Policy and Research
http://www.ahcpr.gov
Information on the dying process in the context of U.S. health policy is provided here, along with a search mechanism. The agency is part of the Department of Health and Human Services.

6. Brain Injury and Brain Death Resources
http://www.changesurfer.com/BD/Brain.html
Visit this site to investigate the debate concerning brain death. When is someone dead? Go to the philosophy of life, consciousness, and personhood page to get specifics.

7. Growth House, Inc.
http://www.growthhouse.org
Growth House is a nonprofit organization working with grief, bereavement, Hospice, and end-of-life issues, as well as pain, AIDS/HIV, suicide, and palliative care issues.

8. Mortality Rates
http://www.Trinity.Edu/~mkearl/b&w-ineq.jpg
This site contains a graphic representation of the U.S. death rates of different social groups to ascertain social inequities.

9. WWW Virtual Library: Demography and Population Studies
http://demography.anu.edu.au/VirtualLibrary/
A definitive guide to demography and population studies, with a multitude of important links, can be found here.

Developmental Aspects of Dying and Death

10. CDC Wonder on the Web—Prevention Guidelines
http://wonder.cdc.gov
At this Centers for Disease Control site, there are a number of papers on suicide prevention, particularly relating to American youth.

11. Children With AIDS Project
http://www.aidskids.org
This organization's role is to develop fuller understanding of children with and at risk of AIDS, including medical, psychosocial, legal, and financial issues. The mission of the organization is to develop local and national adoptive, foster, and family-centered care programs that are effective and compassionate.

12. Light for Life Foundation
http://www.yellowribbon.org
The Yellow Ribbon Program of the Light for Life Foundation provides educational material for American youth aimed at preventing youth suicide through the provision of easy access to support services.

13. National SIDS Resource Center
http://www.circsol.com/SIDS/
The National Sudden Infant Death Syndrome Resource Center (NSRC) provides information services and technical assistance on SIDS and related topics.

14. Palliative Care for Children
http://www.aap.org/policy/re0007.html
The American Academy of Pediatrics maintains this page, which gives a model for providing palliative care for children living with a life-threatening disease or terminal condition.

The Dying Process

15. American Academy of Hospice and Palliative Medicine
http://www.aahpm.org
This is the only organization in the United States for physicians that is dedicated to the advancement of hospice/palliative medicine, its practice, research, and education. There are also links to other Web sites.

16. As Death Draws Near
http://www.emanon.net/~kcabell/signs.html
Death—What You Can Expect is a list of signs that precede most deaths and is posted at this Web site.

17. Death in America, Project on: Death, Dying, Bereavement
http://www.soros.org/death.html
The goal of Project on Death in America is to help people understand and transform the dying experience in America. Headings include "Progress," "Issues in the News," and "Links."

18. Hospice Foundation of America
http://www.hospicefoundation.org
Everything you might need to know about Hospice and specific information on the foundation is available at this Web site.

19. Hospice Hands
http://hospice-cares.com
An extensive collection of links to Hospice resources can be found at this site. Try "What's New" to access the *ACP Home Care Guide*, a book whose goal is to support an

orderly problem-solving approach in managing care of the dying at home.

20. National Prison Hospice Association
http://www.npha.org
This prison Hospice association promotes care for terminally ill inmates and those facing the prospect of dying in prison.

21. The Zen Hospice Project
http://www.zenhospice.org
The Zen Hospice Project organizes programs dedicated to the care of people approaching death and to increasing the understanding of impermanence. The project also runs a small hospice in San Francisco. There are links here to related information on the Web.

Ethical Issues of Dying, Death, and Suicide

22. Articles on Euthanasia: Ethics
http://www.acusd.edu/ethics/euthanasia.html
This site covers biomedical ethics and issues of euthanasia in many ways, including recent articles, ancient concepts, legal and legislative information, selected philosophical literature, Web sites, and a search engine.

23. Kearl's Guide to the Sociology of Death: Moral Debates
http://WWW.Trinity.Edu/~mkearl/death-5.html#eu
An Internet resource on the ethics of biomedical issues that includes issues of dying and death, such as euthanasia, is found here.

24. The Kevorkian File
http://www.rights.org/deathnet/KevorkianFile.html
This Internet resource archive is devoted entirely to Dr. Jack Kevorkian, inventor of the controversial "suicide machine."

25. The Living Will and Values History Project
http://www.euthanasia.org/lwvh.html
Set up in response to the growth and proliferation of living will documents, this project works on a nonprofit basis and attempts to collate, analyze, and apply research in this area.

26. Living Wills (Advance Directive)
http://www.mindspring.com/~scottr/will.html
The largest collection of links to living wills and other advance directive and living will information is available at this Web site.

27. Not Dead Yet
http://acils.com/NotDeadYet/
Americans With Disabilities organization uses this Web site to mobilize Americans against euthanasia and mercy killing. Information about the Hemlock Society is also available here.

28. Suicide Awareness: Voices of Education
http://www.save.org
This popular Internet suicide site provides information on suicide (both before and after), along with material from the organization's many education sessions.

29. Suicide Prevention Advocacy Network
http://www.spanusa.org
SPAN, a nonprofit organization, offers a more political site on suicide prevention. The aim is to have suicide treated as a national (and global) problem that must be solved as a priority.

30. UNOS: United Network for Organ Sharing
http://www.unos.org/frame_default.asp
This Web site of the United Network for Organ Sharing Transplantation includes facts and statistics, resources, and policy proposals.

31. Youth Suicide League
http://www.unicef.org/pon96/insuicid.htm
International suicide rates of young adults in selected countries are available on this UNESCO Web site.

Funerals and Burial Rites

32. Cryonics, Cryogenics, and the Alcor Foundation
http://www.alcor.org
This is the Web site of Alcor, the world's largest cryonics organization.

33. Funerals and Ripoffs
http://www.funerals-ripoffs.org/-5dProf1.htm
Sponsored by the Interfaith Funeral Information Committee and Arizona Consumers Council, this Web site is very critical of the funeral industry and specializes in exposing funeral home financial fraud.

34. The Internet Cremation Society
http://www.cremation.org
The Internet Cremation Society provides statistics on cremations, links to funeral industry resources, and answers to frequently asked questions.

35. Funeral and Memorial Societies of America
http://www.funerals.org
The Funeral Societies of America is the only group that monitors the funeral industry for consumers regarding funeral guides, planning, and issues of social concern.

Bereavement

36. Bereaved Families of Ontario Support Center
http://www.inforamp.net/~bfo/index.html
The Self-Help Resources Guide at this site indexes resources of the Center along with more than 300 listings of other resources and information that are useful to the bereaved.

37. The Compassionate Friends
http://www.compassionatefriends.org
This self-help organization for bereaved parents and siblings has hundreds of chapters worldwide.

38. GriefNet
http://rivendell.org
Produced by a nonprofit group, Rivendell Resources, this site provides many links to the Web on bereavement process, resources for grievers, and information concerning grief support groups.

39. Practical Grief Resources
http://www.indiana.edu/~hperf558/res_prac.html
Here are a list of Internet and print resources available for understanding and coping with grief.

40. Widow Net
http://www.fortnet.org/WidowNet/
Widow Net is an information and self-help resource for and by widows and widowers. The information is helpful to people of all ages, religious backgrounds, and sexual orientation who have experienced a loss of a spouse or life partner.

We highly recommend that you review our Web site for expanded information and our other product lines. We are continually updating and adding links to our Web site in order to offer you the most usable and useful information that will support and expand the value of your Annual Editions. You can reach us at:
http://www.dushkin. com/annualeditions/.

Unit Selections

Key Points to Consider

❖ What can we learn from studying various cultures around the world as to how they relate to dying and death? Do you feel that Americans are really losing interest in memorialization of the dead?

❖ In a society where many people have limited resources, is it acceptable for some individuals to have access to better medical care than others? Defend your answer.

❖ Since socioeconomic status is related to death rates, should something be done to correct this inequity in our society? What do you suggest?

❖ Some health professionals argue that there simply is no room in the curriculum for thanatology. Yet, health professionals, especially physicians, have a high probability of relating to dying patients and their families. Should more emphasis be placed on presenting the topic of dying, death, and bereavement to health professionals? Why or why not?

❖ How can society help to reduce death anxiety? Do you personally see any relationship between religion and attitudes toward death? Explain.

 **Links**   **www.dushkin.com/online/**

5. **Agency for Health Care Policy and Research**
   http://www.ahcpr.gov
6. **Brain Injury and Brain Death Resources**
   http://www.changesurfer.com/BD/Brain.html
7. **Growth House, Inc.**
   http://www.growthhouse.org
8. **Mortality Rates**
   http://www.Trinity.Edu/~mkearl/b&w-ineq.jpg
9. **WWW Virtual Library: Demography and Population Studies**
   http://demography.anu.edu.au/VirtualLibrary/

These sites are annotated on pages 4 and 5.

Death, like sex, is a rather taboo topic. Socialization into the American way of life has not traditionally prepared us to cope with dying and death. Sex and death have "come out of the closet" in recent decades, however, and they now are issues discussed and presented in formal educational settings. In fact "end-of-life" issues are frequently discussed in the popular media as we move into the twenty-first century. Yet, we have a long way to go in educating the public about these historically "forbidden" subjects.

We are beginning to recognize the importance of educating America's youth on the subject of dying and death. Like sex education, death education (thanatology) is an approved topic for presentation in elementary and secondary school curricula in many states, but the topics (especially dying and death) are "optional" and therefore seldom receive high priorities in the classroom or in educational funding. With increased killings on school grounds across the country, an increased emphasis on this topic in the curricula may have a tremendous impact.

Death education in medical schools has also received limited exposure, though one might think that such instruction would be important for future doctors. Medical schools have not traditionally emphasized pain control in dealing with patients, as is pointed out in Adam Marcus's article on palliative care. Perhaps one of the best "teachers of dying and death" is someone who is indeed dying, as Chaplain Jane Dwinell notes in her article, "7 Final Chapters," in which she shares stories of death. Various therapies have recently come into vogue for helping dying patients deal with their situation. Not the least of these therapies is music, as Joshua Simon tells us in "The Harpist's Job Is to Ease the Pain."

The issue of determining when death has actually occurred is presented in "Is It Time to Abandon Brain Death?" The American way of death and how we handle the body after death is indeed changing, as the Baby Boomers want something different from the past. The funeral industry is adjusting accordingly, according to Judith Newman in "At Your Disposal: The Funeral Industry Prepares for Boom Times."

The American Way of Dying and Death

7 Final Chapters

Stories of death that teach us how to live

By Jane Dwinell

It was 1977. I'd just finished my first year of nursing school and was facing a few weeks of summer session when we would actually get to take care of patients all day. I was assigned to the oncology unit, which was frightening enough. Worse, Mr. Smith, my first and only patient for the day, was actually dying.

According to the charge nurse's report, Mr. Smith had been abandoned at the hospital by his family, which was unable or unwilling to care for him anymore. And like many dying people, he was constipated and had been put on a regimen of six different laxatives. On top of that, he couldn't speak or swallow. He'd lost his tongue and much of his esophagus to cancer, and a feeding tube snaked through his nose into his stomach.

My job was to give Mr. Smith his laxatives, administered through the tube and flushed with plenty of water. Before doing so, I questioned my hospital instructor about the dosage, only to receive a lecture on the dangers of constipation. When I returned to the room, Mr. Smith looked at me beseechingly.

"Are you in pain?" I asked.

He nodded.

"I'll see what I can do," I said, "but first I have to give you this medicine." I held up the cups of milk of magnesia and castor oil. I managed the tube and the medicine without too much trouble and then checked the chart to see what was prescribed for his pain. Tylenol. Liquid Tylenol. I dutifully gave him the biggest dose he was allowed to have, doubtful that it could touch his pain. Nevertheless, his face softened a bit, and he looked grateful that I had tried. But an edge of pain lingered in his eyes.

I left the room to do some paperwork and returned 15 minutes later to find Mr. Smith lying in a pool of diarrhea. I cleaned him, changed the sheets, and mopped the floor. No sooner was I done than a young resident came in and breezily asked Mr. Smith how he was doing with his constipation. Unable to speak (did the resident know this?), Mr. Smith just stared, obviously exhausted, embarrassed, and still in pain.

"Well, we'll keep up the medication, and you'll straighten right out," the resident said and turned to go.

"Excuse me," I said. "I think you should cut back on Mr. Smith's laxatives. He's been having diarrhea."

The resident seemed surprised by my audacity. He looked at me as if to say, "How dare you?" and walked out of the room.

I spent the remaining hour of my shift sitting at Mr. Smith's bedside, holding his hand. For a few minutes he and I held eye contact, but then, with a little smile, he drifted into sleep. He finally seemed comfortable, and I didn't dare move for fear of waking him. So I simply watched him breathe, slowly and irregularly, until the shift ended.

When I returned the next day, expecting to be assigned again to Mr. Smith, I was surprised to see my name on the roster next to another patient's name.

"Why can't I take care of Mr. Smith?" I asked the charge nurse.

"He expired," she said, using conventional nursing lingo.

"Expired? Oh, you mean . . . he died? When?"

"About 4 o'clock yesterday afternoon."

In other words, an hour after I left. I was stunned. But I was also proud that in some small way I had made his final hours more comfortable, that he had felt some love and connection to another human being before he left this earth.

It was my first experience with death. And though I didn't know it then, Mr. Smith's death helped prepare me for my work with the dying, first as a nurse and now as a chaplain. I continue to work with the dying because I don't want any more Mr. Smiths out there. I want people to be able to die comfortably and at peace in an atmosphere of love and caring.

I practiced nursing on and off for 18 years, from 1978 until 1996, when I became a chaplain. Over time, I have seen dramatic changes in the way society deals with the dying. In the 1970s, for example, few mechanisms existed to promote the comfort and quality of life of people facing life-limiting illness. With the emergence of hospice care, however, patients began receiving not only basic medical care but also an entire network of supports for themselves and their families that addressed their emo-

From *World,* The Journal of the Unitarian Universalist Association, July/August 2000, pp. 20-25. © 2000 by the Unitarian Universalist Association. All rights reserved.

tional, financial, social, and spiritual concerns. Major leaps have been made in controlling pain and its side effects: nausea, anxiety, and the ever-present constipation. Hospice also enables people to remain at home or go to a nursing home, rather than being shuttled in and out of hospitals. While hospice has traditionally assisted people in the last six months of life, a new movement known as palliative care is expanding service to include those with long-term, debilitating illnesses such as Lou Gehrig's disease and multiple sclerosis.

Had Mr. Smith been involved in a hospice or palliative care program, I believe he would not have endured such a painful and lonely death.

❖

I am often asked, "How can you do it? Isn't it depressing to be with the dying?" And I have to say, unequivocally, "No."

I learn from the dying how to live.

I found out about Jennifer's imminent death even before she was born. I was working as a maternity nurse in a small hospital and was briefed by the doctors that the birth I was about to attend would be a sad one. An ultrasound done a few days before had revealed that the fetus, a female, was anencephalic. She had no brain. Her head ended just above her eyebrows. She could not live outside the womb.

Before the cesarean, I talked with the parents about what they wanted. Did they want to see her? To hold her? They weren't sure. They worried about her grotesque appearance. "Cover her head," they said at last, "and show her to us."

So the baby was born, and they named her Jennifer. She tried to breathe once and didn't try again. Her heart continued beating as I wrapped her in a blanket, gently covered her head, and took her to her parents. Tentatively they touched her, and as they became more comfortable there in the operating room, they held her. They uncovered her head, and they held her until her heart stopped. Remarkably, thanks to the oxygen in her system, her heart beat for nearly an hour.

Jennifer taught me love and acceptance. She taught me to wonder about the nature of life and death. Had she ever really lived? When had she actually died?

❖

Charles was my father-in-law. For 30 years, he'd struggled with multiple sclerosis, a struggle he had borne with grace. Now he was dying from a mysterious infection that was shutting down his bodily functions.

Three grandchildren had been born that year, and each in turn had been placed in his arms, held up to his face. My six-week-old son was the last. That was in the months and weeks before the fast-moving infection had landed him, barely conscious, in the hospital early one

Saturday evening. Some family members kept an overnight vigil, and by morning 17 of us were assembled at the hospital. We hung out in his room—three babies, various parents and aunts and uncles, with the Sunday *Boston Globe* and *New York Times*, bagels, orange juice, and coffee. We talked and cried and told stories and played with the babies and walked the halls as we waited—waited for the inevitable—while Charles, now unconscious, lay in the bed.

Charles died that evening, his bed surrounded by people holding and touching him as he took his final breaths. His rigid, disease-worn body relaxed in death, and we were glad.

Charles taught me that a peaceful death can follow a tormented life lived with grace and acceptance. And he gave me my partner-in-life, his son, and for that I am forever grateful.

❖

Thomas, an eccentric fellow in his 50s, had lived here and there, done this and that, lived with several women, and somehow managed to have only one child. By the time his lung cancer was diagnosed, the doctors told him there was nothing they could do. They ordered hospice care, which meant he would receive various medical and volunteer services, and told him he had six months to live.

Thomas was furious. He said he would be fine. The doctors were wrong. He was living with his son temporarily but talked of finding his own apartment. He threw himself into megavitamins and shark cartilage.

Thomas's avocation was archeology. He was writing a book about a Native American tribe. When he wasn't taking vitamins, chewing out his son—with whom he had a troubled relationship—or ranting and raving about his doctors, he was passionately at work on it. The visiting nurses took him to the library to do research and found him an illustrator for the book.

Despite his attempts at self-medication, his disease advanced rapidly. His pain and weakness increased to the point where it was unsafe to leave him alone, and the nurses finally broached the idea of a nursing home. It had been nearly six months since his diagnosis. The book was finished. Thomas, by then extremely frail, reluctantly agreed. That was a Thursday afternoon. Arrangements were to be finalized the next day.

By 4:30 pm Friday, the paperwork was complete, and it fell to me, one of his hospice care nurses, to drive him to the nursing home. I phoned Thomas to tell him I was on my way. In the time it took me to drive across town, however, he had panicked and called an ambulance. It was there when I arrived. The ambulance driver told me that Thomas's blood pressure was low and insisted on taking him to the hospital. I said no. Thomas had already told his hospice care providers he didn't want to go to the hospital.

For seven miles I followed that ambulance, uncertain whether the driver would do as Thomas wished. I breathed a sigh of relief when we turned into the nursing home parking lot.

I arrived at Thomas's side as the EMTs were taking him out of the ambulance. His breathing was irregular and labored. The ambulance attendant had started an intravenous fluid line, and Thomas's body couldn't handle the excess fluid. I could tell he was close to death. We managed to get him to his room, I phoned his son, and for the next 30 minutes I held Thomas's hand as he lay dying, struggling to breathe, pouring out his life story, pouring out his regrets. I wished his son could have been there instead of me, listening to Thomas speak of his love for him, how he wished he had spent more time with him, been a better father. He turned to me and said, "I am really dying, aren't I? This is it, isn't it?"

Thomas, who had been in denial for the six months I had known him, squeezed my hand as I said, "Yes," closed his eyes, and died.

From Thomas I learned the importance of being present with my loved ones—and my self. Now. Today. While I'm alive. While they're alive. I learned not to wait until the last minute to tell them I love them. Not to wait until the last minute to face my own mortality.

❖

Fred was in his 30s when he was diagnosed with colon cancer. Unlike many people in his situation, he didn't seem frightened by the idea of hospice care. In fact, he struck me as courageous when he came to our office to inquire about our services. A charming, funny man, he wanted to go out with style, with grace, with the support of his New Age beliefs.

Several months passed. His condition quickly worsened. He grew emaciated. One day, despairing over his weakened body and his inability to take care of himself, Fred freaked out. He shut himself in a bedroom in the apartment he shared with his girlfriend and refused to communicate with anyone except the hospice staff, whom he began calling every hour in panic, over pain, over nausea, over fear, over his loss of control.

Some of the hospice workers went over for a while to help him. We did what we could, talking to his doctor, doing relaxation exercises with him, playing calming music, holding his hand. One nurse stayed until midnight, when he threw her out.

At 6 am our office got a call from his girlfriend. Fred had swallowed an entire bottle of morphine pills.

She wanted him out of there, she wanted him in a hospital, she no longer had the energy or the tolerance to care for him. Fred was whisked away in an ambulance, his guilt-ridden girlfriend in tears.

Fred didn't die that day. In fact, he remained in the hospital for three months, demanding that his girlfriend take him home, demanding higher and higher doses of pain medication. Gone were his New Age visions of a peaceful death. Gone were his openness and charm. Fred was angry. Fred was trapped. Fred was no longer in control.

It took those three months for his girlfriend to bring herself to tell him she had no intention of taking him home. Upon hearing the news, he did what the dying often do when they learn they won't be going home: he stopped fighting the inevitable. Within 24 hours, he was dead.

Why do I remember Fred? I remember his spirit change, I remember his anger, I remember him trying to stay in control. Always in control. And, in a way, he did stay in control—but not without alienating everyone around him. In spiritual pain, he could not find a belief that would bring him comfort, that would hold him in his sorrow and anger.

Fred is my reminder that death is not necessarily easy. And that we cannot know how we will behave until we are there, at that point.

❖

Suzanne was something else. A gregarious woman, she had spent her working life as a saleswoman of one sort of product or another: appliances, electronic equipment, furniture. She could probably sell you anything, whether you wanted it or not. She called to arrange for hospice care at home a week after her diagnosis with aggressive breast cancer. She had decided against cancer treatment, and the doctor had given her six weeks to live.

She had had difficult relationships with various members of her family. She called all her children and grandchildren—quite a number of them—to reconcile and say her good-byes.

She accepted her disease, was curious about it, discussed it openly. Even as her condition worsened, she faced the consequences without fear. In due course, she became too weak to stay home and chose to go to a nursing home. She endeared herself to the staff there with her stories, played mother hen to her roommates, and generally held court, all from the confines of her bed.

Eight months into her illness, when I came to visit, she began asking, "Why don't I die?" She'd say, "I want to die. I want to see the angels and go to God. Why am I still alive?"

It was then that I learned that she'd been estranged from all six of her siblings for years because of an abusive upbringing that had left everyone embittered. They were summoned to her bedside over the next several weeks, and Suzanne talked to them and reconciled. Finally, all was healed.

The day Suzanne died, nearly a year after her diagnosis, the room was filled with her family, all brought together because of her illness.

I remember Suzanne for the courage with which she accepted her condition, chose to live in a nursing home, and spoke forthrightly with her children and grandchildren, and finally, her siblings. For her courage, with which she continued to love in the face of great physical and emotional pain.

❖

Anna was elderly, a devout Catholic. I met her as she lay on her deathbed, surrounded by family in the room that had been hers for so many years, drifting in and out of consciousness, her body slightly restless and fidgety. Her children and grandchildren were restless, too. They paced about the house. She'd been near death for days, and they were exhausted and anxious to know when she might die. Her agitation and moaning scared them. I knew Anna was receiving the right amount of pain and anxiety medicine. I also knew from experience that she was very near death. It was early evening. I suggested they call her priest, Fr. John.

When Fr. John arrived, 20 minutes later, he took Anna's hand, and she opened her eyes. The three of us were alone in the room. "Let's say the rosary, Anna," he said. She nodded, and they held the beads together as he began the words. Anna stared at him and moved her lips along with the Hail Marys and Our Fathers. It was all she had the strength for. One by one, the family members came into the room. One by one, they began reciting the rosary with the priest, quietly, as if they didn't want anyone to hear. The only non-Catholic in the room, I watched and waited.

The rhythmic cadence of the prayer, now only a murmur, became all there was. Soothed by the familiar ritual, people relaxed, grew still. An aura of peace fell over the room. Anna's breathing slowed. She stopped moving her lips. She closed her eyes. With the final "amen," the priest and the family left the room. As they talked quietly in the kitchen, I watched Anna. Her face aglow and completely at peace, she took her last breath and died.

A devout woman, strong in her faith, Anna had opened her heart to her God and let go of this life. Having witnessed her utter serenity and the tranquility of her acceptance made hers the most powerful death I have seen. I remember Anna for her strong beliefs and the peace they brought to her.

❖

I have been a student of death for years, and I know I will never learn all the lessons it has to teach. These few will stay with me forever. Mr. Smith gave me the will to improve the lot of others in his condition. Baby Jennifer gave me the ability to wonder. Charles gave me my definition of dignity. Thomas gave me an appreciation of being in the moment. Fred gave me the knowledge of how not to die. Suzanne gave me the meaning of courage. And Anna gave me a look at the power of grace.

May they rest in peace.

The Rev. Jane Dwinell is minister of the First Universalist Parish in Derby Line, VT, and chaplain of the Orleans-Northern Essex Visiting Nurses and Hospice.

THIS HARPIST'S JOB IS TO EASE THE PAIN, SOOTHE THE SOUL

Abstract: Death and dying is a subject which often goes untouched within conversations until a crucial point is reached and the topic needs discussion. The dying process is examined through a harpist's view of how to care for someone on their deathbed. The position taken is that of midwifery as well as comforter for the patient while in the last moments. Music provides a familiar, gentle and often soothing atmosphere and helps the dying be at peace in one of the most frightening times of life.

Joshua Simon

Therese Schroeder-Sheker is at her best when most of us are at our worst: In the company of the dying, she gains strength and is able to pass courage back. She learned of her gift in 1972 during an encounter with a man she calls an angel, explaining, "An angel gives you something that changes your life, and he changed my life." She was, at the time, a classical harpist embarking on her professional career while moonlighting in the Denver nursing home. Mr. Lattimore, the most ornery patient on the floor, was dying of emphysema. "I went into his room and I could hear the death rattle," Therese remembers. "He was thrashing. It was frightening for both of us. I offered my hand. Rather than push me away, as he always had, he grabbed it. He was afraid, and more than that, he needed presence. He needed a witness." She cradled Mr. Lattimore and started to sing. "I sang my way through the Mass of the Angels and the Salve Regina. We began to breathe together. I sang Gregorian chants. Long after his heart ceased to beat, I held him.

"Walking home that night, I thought of three words—musical, sacramental and midwifery. Death is birthing into another realm. If a woman in labor is frightened, she fights her contractions. But if she's learned breathing—to go with it—there is less agony."

Therese acted on her epiphany immediately. As she continued to study music and, subsequently, to teach at Regis University, she developed a methodology and performed more vigils. She learned of similar work done in medieval France, and studied the music and instructions laid down by monks for achieving a "blessed death." By the mid-1980s, Therese was teaching a course in death vigils and participating in more and more of them, sometimes aided by her students. She gave her efforts a name: The Chalice of Repose Project. "A chalice is an empty vessel that can be filled with spirit," she says. "And repose means a place where we experience deep, intimate rest."

Music as therapy was nothing new: Traumatized soldiers returning from World War II were soothed with music in hospitals, and today there are more than 5,000 certified music therapists in the U.S. But from the start, the Chalice Project was about music for the dying. Therese considers herself a music-thanatologist—from the Greek Thanatos, meaning death—and says, "ours is a contemplative practice with clinical applications." She can seem esoteric, but stresses the science of her methods. Even with some unconscious patients, she says, "we can change heart rate and respiration. The entire skin surface serves as an extension of the ear."

Once Therese had organized her teachings and procedures for the vigils, she became an evangelist for music-thanatology, telling hospitals everywhere about its benefits. In April 1990 she gave a talk at St. Patrick Hospital in Missoula, a town of 50,000 in western Montana. Lawrence White, the hospital's president, recalls, "Therese did this presentation, and doctors were crying. You don't see that in this business. You can spend years studying,

 From *Life* magazine, December 1998, p. 108. © 1999 by Time Inc. Magazine Company. Reprinted by permission.

and out of the blue you encounter knowledge that is foreign but absolutely pertinent." White told Therese her mission could have a home at St. Pat.

In Missoula she met with some unease. "I was a skeptic," says Dr. Stephen Speckart, a 25-year veteran oncologist. "I wondered if this woman was a mystic. I thought, Aren't we proceeding a little quickly here?" Today, Speckart is the medical director of the Chalice Project. "I have seen nothing as effective as this. We can now reduce pain medications for the dying by a significant amount."

The vigils aren't meant just as painkillers, of course. "We try to work with the patient's pain," says Therese, "but also give the family a way to share. Sometimes they're the ones who need rest, or need to let go."

The Chalice of Repose Project has its detractors, among them ex-students who tired of Therese's philosophy or had problems with the program's focus. One complained in the local press last year that he thought he was joining a program based on Middle Ages infirmary song, but "I never saw any of that music in the year I was in the Chalice program." Despite criticisms, most folks in Missoula have taken Chalice to their hearts. They don't care what music is played if the result is solace. The late Michael Morris, who was a justice of the peace in town, turned to Chalice in the last stages of his cancer in 1996, saying the music "made a place for me to accept my death." That's all his fellow Missoulans needed to know.

The Chalice Project is now an institution. More than a hundred doctors have referred patients. Harpists are on duty from eight a.m. to eight p.m., 365 days a year, and teams of Chalice musicians make "mercy runs" out of town at a moment's notice. Foundations, private donors and the hospital support Chalice services—the Project has an annual budget of $600,000—and no individual seeking

comfort is denied. Chalice veterans teach alongside Therese in the Project's school, where a rigorous two-year program starts with study of the ancient Gilgamesh epic, travels through a medieval Latin death ritual and on to graduation. Then the students are ready for service—in Missoula, or wherever they spread their gospel.

Today, at St. Patrick, a vigil has been prescribed, and Therese herself answers the call. She hurries down the hospital's corridors, carrying her harp like a balsa-weight cross. She arrives at the room, composes herself and enters. She learns that the ill person is, as the physicians call it, "actively dying." As she sets up quietly in the corner, she hears a plea to the patient: "You said you wouldn't leave us!" Therese is in no way immune to the emotions of the moment, but she cannot be of assistance unless she maintains a sense of calm. She puts the harp to her left shoulder, fingers the strings and starts to play. Gently. The patient glides in and out of consciousness, eyes wandering, lingering for a time on Therese's face. She is careful to keep her countenance comforting. She plays an Irish air, "The Gartan Mother's Lullaby," at a slow tempo. The music seems to guide the patient away from the realm of beeping monitors, away from this antiseptic hospital room, toward something beautiful and restful. All conversation has stopped, and then the patient's spouse says, "It's O.K., it's O.K. You can go." There is an exhalation, audible to all. The patient has died. The music continues even as a doctor notes time and cause. Nurses switch off machinery. Harp song is a backdrop for soft sobbing. The harpist has helped as best she could.

FOR MORE INFORMATION Chalice of Repose is at 554 West Broadway, Missoula, Mont. 59802. Visit its Web site at www.saintpatrick.org or call (406) 329-2810.

Death Be Not Painful

Too many Americans spend their final days in the hospital and in unnecessary pain. Remedying that will mean changing the very way doctors and nurses are trained. At Hopkins, that process is already under way.

BY ADAM MARCUS (MA'96)

Medicine these days is enduring a highly publicized crisis of conscience. Patients in their final weeks of life seem more concerned about dying with dignity than extending their days. The notion almost has judicial fiat. When the Supreme Court in June upheld two state laws banning physician-assisted suicide, the justices raised the importance of palliative care, a testament to its increasing claim on the medical consciousness.

What's becoming increasingly clear, however, is how little we know about the dying process. In the past, doctors and nurses were educated with an almost warrior-like mentality: defeat disease before it defeats the body. Some are now re-examining such training and methods in an attempt to define the qualities needed to bring about the "good death." It's partly tilting at windmills. No death is good. But no death need be worse than another, and Johns Hopkins, a name for years synonymous with healing, has begun focusing on making its wards and wings a source of comfort to the dying.

Albert W. Wu's sixth-floor office at the School of Public Health overlooks the old Hopkins Hospital where, nearly a century ago, William Osler conducted the first study of pain in the final days of life. Wu's office may be more modern, but the associate professor of health policy and management is working on the same problem: trying to evaluate how patients die. Osler concluded that the majority of patients who died at Hopkins at the turn of the century did so without much "bodily pain or distress"—a finding most likely linked to the fact that infection, fever, and other complications did not give illnesses time to become chronic.

Indeed, Wu has turned up a much different picture. Wu collaborated with researchers from several other centers, including George Washington University and Beth Israel Hospital in Boston, on a study of some 9,000 individuals, known as SUPPORT (Study to Understand Prognoses and Preferences for Outcomes and Risks of Treatments). Their findings appeared last January in the *Annals of Internal Medicine*.

"The Death we fear most is the dying in pain, unnoticed and isolated from loved ones," the researchers noted in the *Annals* article. So it concerned the authors to learn that of the 46 percent of patients who died during the study, more than half spent their last moments in a hospital. Moreover, about 40 percent of those patients were in either severe or moderate pain for most or all of the last three days of life—pain, the authors argue, that could have been alleviated through medication.

SUPPORT, which was funded by the Robert Wood Johnson Foundation, began in the late 1980s in an attempt to describe the effects of Advance Directives (a terminal-care plan forged by patients in the event that they can't communicate their treatment wishes) and DNRs (a request not to be revived if their heart should stop). The data are so rich, however, that they are now throwing new light into nearly every corner of the dying process.

Patients qualified for the trials if they were over the age of 80, or had one of nine terminal illnesses—including certain cancers, congestive heart failure, coma, cirrhosis, and Multiple Organ System Failure. All patients in the five-center study were assigned nurse practitioners, whose role it was to give prognoses and improve communication among patients, families, and caregivers about end-stage care options.

Some of the participants had family members who agreed to be interviewed about their loved one's experience, and their thoughts formed the backbone of Wu's study. He found that most family members surveyed were pleased with the end-stage care their loved one received. Only one in 10 SUPPORT subjects received improper care, according to their families. Yet nearly half of the 4,100-some patients who died received "extraordinary measures" to keep them alive, including tube feeding, mechanical ventilation, and attempted resuscitation.

Here, according to Wu, arises a difficult paradox. Patient and family satisfaction might not be the most reliable measure of care in the case of terminal illness, he says. "That's part of this phenomenon of physicians and patients colluding in this vain attempt to defy death," he says. "They feel good about it because they did everything [they could]. The funny thing is, if we ask what a good death is, it's in a clean bed, with the family around, closing our eyes and drawing a last breath. And that's clearly not what's happening."

Although the nurse practitioners were specifically trained to be sensitive to end-of-life issues, including pain management, patient preferences about care, and how to convey patient wishes to physicians, their presence apparently did little to improve dialogue between the dying and their doctors, Wu says. Physician practices did not seem to change. In most cases, says Wu, patients and their loved ones should have been expecting death soon, but were not. Doctors continued to perform life-saving therapies even as their patients' prognoses worsened, sending the unrealistic message that survival was possible.

"I think that people did not understand that there were many things that they should have been beginning to attend to," says Wu. Calling key relatives and friends to the hospital, for example, is something that too often comes too late, although it can make a tremendous positive difference in a person's final hours or days, he notes.

Sometimes families debate about whether to summon relatives. Delay is a way of blocking out the reality of the imminent death, says Wu. This sort of denial is unfortunate, Wu says, because it deprives the patient of emotional succor. Even worse, pretending optimistically that death is not at hand may lead to treatment decisions that compound pain. Says Wu of the families in SUPPORT, "People were thinking about doing everything possible to prolong life to the exclusion of thinking about what impact that might have on the patient's comfort both physically and emotionally."

Wu and his co-authors believe that end-stage care is not given the respect it deserves in medical training. "It's interesting how we use language," he says. "We talk about heroic measures, extraordinary measures, but most of those words don't have negative connotations. We don't say that people were tormented until they died, but if we're to believe the results of this study, people were in pain until the end."

On Stuart "Skip" Grossman's desk sits a computer—a computer that offers him and his colleagues in the Oncology Center a digital means of evaluating the pain of each patient they treat.

"We are making pain control much more of a priority," says Grossman, an associate professor of oncology, medicine and neurosurgery, and the director of Neurooncology. By the time Grossman meets his patients—adults who suffer from primary brain tumors—they are already dying, so pain control is often all he can offer.

Each morning, a nurse on the ward presents to patients a plastic strip with a 10-cm line on it. Patients draw their own line to match the level of pain they feel that day, with 0 being none and 10 being the worst imaginable. The rating is then entered into a computer, and, as Grossman says, "any day before noon I can sit down behind the computer and get the pain ratings of all of the patients in the Oncology Center. It allows us to figure out which patients need some further attention or further evaluation." Getting patients involved is crucial, Grossman has found, because apparently even doctors aren't so good at eyeballing pain. "We did a study in the Oncology Center here looking at whether providers appreciated how much pain their patients had," says Grossman. "What you would hope is that the average of the pain rating from the providers would be similar to that of the patients, but it turns out that there is no statistical correlation between

the two." In fact, the only time the estimates matched was when patients reported no pain at all.

Grossman says that one explanation for this finding is that patients tend to hide the severity of their pain from doctors and nurses, who in turn don't pry as deeply as they should. Patients often feel that cancer by definition is painful, so there's no reason to be making a big fuss. They are also concerned that more pain equals more severe disease, and they don't want to distract their caregivers from treating their disease. Still others worry that taking too much medication will render them incoherent.

There are other barriers to providing adequate pain relief. Some physicians, aware that they are under the watchful eye of government drug regulators, have concerns about overprescribing addictive medication—particularly opioids like morphine. Their fears aren't unwarranted. In 1991, the Pain and Policy Studies Group at the University of Wisconsin surveyed state medical boards on their attitudes about painkillers. The group concluded that boards worried too much about the dangers of addiction and too little about pain management—findings that can explain why physicians have lost their licenses for prescribing narcotics to relieve pain in terminally ill patients.

Caregivers need to discuss with patients whether treating pain could bring death sooner, says Cindy Rushton, an assistant professor of nursing at Hopkins. "Many people are willing to accept that they may die sooner if they are able to die without pain. We know that one of the consequences of giving large doses of a pain medication is that life ends sooner, but in a terminally ill patient, that may be justified."

What's important, says Rushton, is knowing what a patient expects from palliative care, whether the goal is to obliterate pain completely, at the expense of lucidity, or simply manage it to the point of comfort.

Drugs today don't have to be incapacitating or mind-dulling, Wu notes, given recent advances in pain relief, such as patient-controlled anesthetics that can be self-titrated.

Grossman also pins some of the blame for poor pain relief on an institutional mindset that makes it a low priority. He finds a "gross imbalance" between the amount of attention devoted to palliative care in oncology, for example, and the attention given to the newest therapies. "It sends the message that it is more important to be researching a brand new drug than trying to make people more comfortable," he says.

Too often, the mental pain experienced by dying patients also goes unaddressed, Wu and his co-authors found. Dying patients frequently report feelings of intense sadness, depression, and anxiety—in fact, more than 60 percent of the SUPPORT participants had severe emotional symptoms like these, according to their family members. Wu says that those problems are readily treatable—as long as they are recognized.

Many people consider Hopkins's Debra Roter to be one of the nation's authorities on patient-provider communication. The professor of health policy and management at the School of Public Health has some ideas why the SUPPORT study uncovered muddled interactions between

Comfort from a Different Source

"I've been holding hands as they've gone from warm to cold many times," says Matthew Lascalzo, director of the Ocology Center's social work service. He and his staff of six social workers are on call around-the-clock to help oncology patients and their families cope with the emotional anguish that comes with dying.

When dealing with families, Loscalzo says that pragmatic issues often take center stage—like making sense of confusing insurance forms or finding the means to pay mounting hospital bills. Today we're not seeing "the acute deaths that we were so used to seeing 50 years ago," he says. "The impact on the family has changed dramatically. It may sound cold and harsh, but these are things that families have to manage.

Loscalzo, who serves on a national panel on assisted suicide, has found that terminally ill patients—particularly the elderly—can feel a strong obligation to die. They worry about being abandoned, about medical costs and their family's suffering. "They feel they're such a burden to themselves and others," Loscalzo says. He is pleased with the Supreme Court's recent ruling against physician-assisted suicide, describing the ruling as "a good thing for the elderly and for the vulnerable people in the U.S."

doctors and the dying. Crossed wires are especially troublesome with Advance Directives, she says.

Ideally, the process of working out an Advance Directive should allow a physician to explore what a patient is feeling about his or her imminent death, Roter says. Instead, physicians are often too uncomfortable to deal with the subject on an emotional level, so they resort to using a "legalistic script" with their patients. The result? Advance directives that don't accurately reflect patients' wishes, she says.

Roter is currently analyzing audio tapes of about 140 conversations between doctors and patients as part of a study to improve how the two parties communicate when death is imminent, so that patients will truly have informed consent when considering whether to terminate their own care.

"There certainly were a good number of [conversations] where it was clear that the doctor and patient were not on the same wavelength," she says. The physician end of the dialogue often consisted of overdoses of euphemism on the one hand and very technical medical jargon on the other. "It's confusing to patients," Roter says. "They're not sure what the doctor is telling them."

In her study, Roter hopes to identify the essential criteria of the end-stage-care discussion, a list that includes not only providing the cold facts (like what a defibrillator is), but how warm a physician's voice is in explaining what the device does. For, according to Roter, it's crucial that patients not only understand what their doctors are telling them, but that they feel comfortable hearing it. Early results of the study show that the most successful discussions of terminal care occur when doctors allow patients to express their fears, tell their stories, and explain their misgivings.

Part of the problem in communication can be linked to the fact that medical and nursing schools don't do enough to prepare their students to handle end-stage care issues, says Michael Williams, a neurologist and ethics committee member of the university's Bioethics Institute.

End-stage training ought to include hands-on experience, much the way students learn how to put in an IV or perform a surgical operation, Williams contends. He recently received a $200,000, two-year grant from the Kornfeld Foundation (to which the medical school added nearly $140,000 via the Bioethics Institute), to find out just how well he can teach good death etiquette. The study, which he plans to begin this fall with the help of other Hopkins colleagues, will look at two teaching paradigms for attending doctors and nurses: the traditional seminar model—the staple of Hopkins and other medical schools—and the more novel "standardized

patient" technique, which uses realistic situations and role playing.

Williams gives an example of how the latter technique can work. Two students, a nurse and a physician, meet with an actress portraying the wife of a comatose patient. In their first consultation, the students "break the bad news" to the distraught spouse. In the second round, the patient's condition has worsened and death is imminent. In this scenario, the patient is a young man, perhaps in his early 30s, and therefore unlikely to have a living will. The students must try to find out whether he had ever discussed his wishes vis-à-vis life support. In the final phase, the patient is diagnosed as brain dead and unrecoverable. The students must now guide his wife to the realization, if it's not already clear, that her husband will not survive, and then discuss the possibility of organ donation.

The process demands sensitivity, says Williams, since when to admit the end "is the sort of decision that many, many [families] are really afraid of."

Patricia Grimm is doing her part to help students at the School of Nursing deal more successfully with end-stage patients. For the last five years, Grimm, an oncology nurse with a PhD in nursing, has taught an elective course on Death and Dying. The seven-week class introduces students to issues ranging from dying young to differences in handling loss. "We don't limit [the discussions] to people who have died—a job, a relationship, moving, these are also losses," says Grimm, whose course usually has a waiting list. "We do a lot of talking about our own losses so that we can understand how we're reacting and hopefully put that aside so that we can be there for the patient."

"Being there" can also include a more metaphysical approach to caregiving. The scientific community is increasingly recognizing links between faith and good health. Several recent studies have shown that strong religious conviction correlates with healthier living and longer life. Still, it has been almost an anathema to teach medical students about spirituality, says Thomas Corson '77 (MD'80, MPH'82), an assistant professor in Pediatrics and Medicine. Corson has spent most of the last 22 years at Hopkins. Training in Asia and Africa, he learned that "it's very hard to care for people unless you have a good sense of what their religious tradition is."

"Traditionally, in a lot of heritages, the concepts of healing the body and the soul were not dichotomized," he says. "Priests were healers. There was an angelic conjunction between divinity and physician." Ignoring this relationship today is poor medicine, says Corson, who has prayed and read Scripture with his dying patients throughout his career. "As we care for people there is still a significant overlap be-

tween matters of the soul and matters of the body."

With that in mind, Corson began the first Religion in Medicine course at Hopkins in 1995. Created with the help of the Templeton Foundation, the five-week course—a version of which has now become part of the required upper-level curriculum—encourages future physicians to incorporate their faith into their art. Students learn how to take a patient's spiritual history along with the physical one, how to call on clergy for help, and what science is showing us about the link between religious faith and well-being.

I F SUPPORT uncovered some distressing aspects of dying, it also suggested a few ways to ameliorate them. Foremost, says Wu, is to make hospice care an integral part of end-stage care. Where hospital deaths can be lonely, painful, and sterile, dying at home in private comfort and familiar surroundings can help ease the trauma of life's final passage—and the pain, according to two physicians in the SUPPORT study. They reported that hospices relieved pain in at least 98 percent of cases.

In 1982, Medicare began covering hospice care as a billable service. Since 1985, the number of hospice programs in the United States has jumped from 1,400 to more than 3,000. Today, 20 percent of those near death will choose hospice care, according to the National Hospice Organization. From a financial standpoint, hospice care makes sense: A recent study showed that in the last month of life, the average cost of hospice care for a cancer patient is $3,200 less than traditional hospital care would be.

At Hopkins, hospice care is the dominion of Hopkins Home Health Services (HHS), which was established in 1995 and is jointly owned by the health system and the university. HHS has three subsidiary companies: one for pediatrics care, one for pharmacological and equipment supply, and an in-home care arm for adults: Hopkins Home Care.

Amy Rader, senior director of operations and clinical services for HHS, notes that treatment is purely palliative and is planned and performed by an interdisciplinary team. Rader rattles off the list. "We do nursing, medical social services, spiritual care, social work, home health aid. There's a pharmacist on staff to do pain and symptom management. We have a physician to guide in palliative medicine." HHS usually has 25 caregivers serving 30 to 40 patients.

Hospice nurses visit each patient three to five times weekly. Visits can last anywhere from 45 minutes to several hours, during which time the patient gets hospital-quality care—except extraordinary measures to keep them alive—without a hospital-like atmosphere. Nor does care end when the patient dies. HHS follows families for up to two years afterward.

Since its inception, the hospice company has seen marked growth. It served 130 patients in the first half of 1997, compared to 163 for all of its first year. Rader says that patients and caregivers alike "see the reliability and validity of providing care at home."

Bill Kilgour, 67, will attest to that. His wife, Eleanor, died last January at the age of 65, the same week that the SUPPORT study was released. Her death, while drawn out, was in the end a model of what hospice care can offer.

The first time he saw her in the fall of 1995, Michael Carducci knew that Eleanor Kilgour would die from her disease. She had bladder cancer that had invaded the vagina and lymph nodes. Carducci, an assistant professor of oncology and urology, later discovered tumor cells in her lung and bone cancer in one knee. "At that time I told her that she had a lot of disease, but little, if any, chance of [our] curing it," recalls Carducci. Like every doctor with terminally ill patients, Carducci had to make a choice. He could treat Eleanor Kilgour's tumors, or he could treat Eleanor Kilgour. The choice was clear, he says: "I knew that we weren't going to be able to cure this," he says. "But hopefully we could improve her quality of life."

Eleanor's health deteriorated for a year, and in the fall of 1996 Carducci recommended hospice care—an admission that there was nothing left to do but ease her pain. Eleanor, however, remained adamant that she did not want it. Her husband, ever the faithful nurse, obeyed, though he found himself increasingly overwhelmed by the demands of her disease, which had turned their home into a makeshift infirmary. Eleanor deteriorated rapidly, and around New Year's Day she finally accepted what her doctor and her husband knew signaled the end. "She could have been helped by hospice earlier, but she was very much clinging to life," Carducci says.

Bill Kilgour arranged for a nurse from Hopkins Home Care Group to come to the house. Karen Trageser arrived. "Pain management was the biggest issue in that home," she recalled recently. Eleanor, she says, "had a lot of pain in her bones, so we got her a hospital bed and an air mattress. She was placed on pain medication and we made her comfortable enough to the point where she peacefully passed away." Her husband was at her bedside.

"Hospice nursing isn't a skill that's easily taught," according to Trageser. She herself was never introduced to any terminal care issues in nursing school, and would have been completely in the woods but for a personal tragedy—her father's death from thyroid cancer 14 years ago. "He was not in a hospice program, and I wish he had been," says Trageser, who since has taken courses in hospice care. "He died in the hospital in a great deal of pain. We didn't know what to do. We weren't prepared." Trageser has imported that experience to her practice. "I don't want to see people suffer," she says.

At the Kilgour home, Eleanor's hospital bed is gone now, and Bill Kilgour has turned the living room into something of a small office. The dining room table is covered with bills, the paper trail of Eleanor's passing. "She used to say that she knew she was very sick, and that she wasn't afraid to die," he says softly and through tears. "But then the last three weeks she started telling me that she was afraid, and that I had to be with her. She wanted me to hold her hand all the time. If I had to go to the bathroom she wouldn't let me go. I'd have to pry her fingers off."

Bill Kilgour has nothing but praise for the doctors and nurses at Johns Hopkins who helped him take care of his wife. "They were very honest with everything they did," he says. "Dr. Carducci never said how long she would live or when she would die. 'I'm not God,' he said. Eleanor was grateful because he was so honest. I couldn't do enough for those people," Kilgour says. "I couldn't do enough for them."

Adam Marcus (MA'96) is a freelance writer who lives in Washington D.C.

AT YOUR DISPOSAL

The funeral industry prepares for boom times

By Judith Newman

Show me the manner in which a nation or a community cares for its dead and I will measure with mathematical exactness the tender sympathies of its people, their respect for the law of the land and their loyalty to high ideals.

—Motto appearing on funeral-industry paraphernalia

Now, here's what you do if you've tied their mouths too tight, or they have no lips and the family's not happy," says Dina Ousley, placing a stencil over the mouth of an audience volunteer. Using an airbrush, she gently sprays on a full, lush pout in vermilion. "And these lips stay on, even when people are kissing their loved ones good-bye!" Ousley, the president of Dinair Airbrush Makeup Systems of Beverly Hills, California, is a makeup artist for Hollywood stars, but occasionally she takes clients who are, well, less fussy. She is here, at the 115th annual convention of the National Funeral Directors Association (NFDA) in Cincinnati, to sell her system of airbrushed makeup for glamorizing the deceased.

"Hmm, sort of like detailing a car," murmurs a man behind me, as Ousley, a cheerful, birdlike blonde, demonstrates how easy it is to cover bruises and restore a "natural" glow to skin. At the end of Ousley's demonstration comes the *pièce de résistance*: airbrushing, compared with the application of conventional cosmetics, makes it much easier to beautify the client who suffered from jaundice; apparently, when a jaundiced corpse is embalmed, the chemicals can turn it green. Grabbing another volunteer from the audience, Ousley first airbrushes him the color of Herman Munster, then attempts to restore him to his natural hue by spraying him white, as a primer, and applying an alabaster foundation. When I finally fled the room, the volunteer was the shade of a buttercup. He would have looked perfectly natural had he been not a human but a suburban kitchen circa 1950. Ousley did not look happy.

Here's the thing about death that's hard to grasp: It's going to happen to you. Whether you are embalmed and entombed or your ashes are shot out of a duck blind, your loved ones will be spending a small portion of the $7 billion that every year is poured into the U.S. funeral industry. Since the average funeral costs about $4,600—not including the expense of the cemetery or mausoleum, which can add thousands more—disposing of their dead is, for many families, one of the most expensive purchases they will ever make, right behind a house or a car.

No matter when you go, you'll be in good company; approximately 2.3 million people in the United States die each year. But if you're a baby boomer who pays attention to the actuarial tables and plans to go obediently to your final reward in twenty-five to forty-five years, you'll have to muscle others out of the way for a glimpse of that white light: by the year 2030, the annual death rate will have increased by about 30 percent. So naturally, funeral directors must be nodding somberly about this news, then retreating into a small, quiet backroom office and doing the hora.

Well, not exactly. True, the nation's 22,000 funeral homes can look forward to a deluge of death—a certain consolation, since the average home handles about two deaths a week (fewer in sparsely populated rural areas). And since families have traditionally selected funeral homes based not on cost comparisons or value but on proximity—or, as Jim St. George, president and CEO of ConsumerCasket USA, a retail-coffin outlet, puts it, on "whoever can get Mama out of the living room fastest"—it would seem that the impending good fortune would be proportionally shared by all. But funeral directors are worried, because, as they see it, the baby boomers, who are now making decisions about how to dispose of their loved ones, are "under-ritualized." Religious observance is on a downswing, families are scattered around the country, and thus attendance at funerals has dropped significantly. "Baby boomers have developed a certain cynicism about what is traditional and what isn't," adds St. George. "And there's nothing traditional about getting ripped off."

On the other hand, this is also the Krups generation, a tidal wave of Americans who have had a passionate love affair with credit and a willingness to pay $3 for a cup of designer coffee. Many of us have ostentatiously lived the good life. Are we now going to choose—for ourselves and for our parents—the good death?

The funeral industry fervently hopes so. But, as I saw at the national convention last fall, they're not taking any chances.

My first seminar is entitled "Business Issues That Affect a Funeral Director's Bottom Line." "Service" is the buzzword in the industry, and speakers talk about the advantages—and profitability—of offering everything from catered lunches to grief therapy. Nobody could quite explain to me why I should be entrusting my mental health to guys whose favorite motto is "It ain't the dead who give you trouble, it's the living," but that's okay. Most directors are keenly aware that today's bereaved were raised on self-help books and support groups and are willing to pay a reasonable fee to unburden themselves to strangers.

The seminar quickly focuses around an ongoing source of anxiety: cremation, the increasingly popular and ostensibly inexpensive choice for disposal. (Fun fact: the average person takes an hour and a half to burn; the heavier you are, the hotter you burn, because fat acts as combustible fuel.) In 1963, only about 4 percent of the American population opted for the pyre; now, with cemetery space increasingly scarce and expensive, 21 percent nationwide prefer cremation, and more than 40 percent prefer it in such states as California and Arizona.

Of course, some segments of the population are still relatively unaffected by this disturbing trend toward cheap disposal. It's a not very well-kept secret that poorer families spend a disproportionate amount of their income on death. Dwayne Banks, an assistant professor of public policy at the University of California, Berkeley, who studies the economics of funerals and cemeteries, recently completed a paper on how the "Nike mentality" can afflict inner-city families making funeral arrangements. "In this society we're valued by our material possessions—not only by what we have but by our ability to purchase things," explains Banks. "So if you look at the cultural context of the inner cities, it makes sense: the way of showing you valued the deceased is by providing in death what you couldn't provide in life." And the fascinating thing, Banks adds, is that the community will rally around you. "You might not be able to get together the money for college, but death brings about this sense of communalism. For a funeral, a family will pull resources together and the church will contribute. It's what people dream of America being."

But even if poor and working-class families have not changed their spending habits in recent years, there remains the threat of middle-class baby boomers, who increasingly are opting for the simplicity of cremation. The emerging problem for the funeral directors is this: how to transform cremation from an event they dub "You call, we haul, that's all" to the payload of a full-blown ritual?

For years the industry line was that cremation was sacrilege, a cruel way to treat the body. Funeral directors lobbied state legislatures to ban ash scattering, painting pictures of a world where little Johnny out playing in a park would find recognizable bits of Grandma that had not been adequately incinerated. Despite the industry's campaign of disinformation, more and

more citizens were taking matters into their own hands and scattering ashes of their loved ones out at sea or over Wrigley Field. After a couple of decades, the industry realized that cremation could be every bit as profitable as traditional burial; all it took was a little ingenuity and a good deal of manipulation.

Brian Joseph, who runs a funeral home in Grosse Pointe, Michigan, advises the audience to "educate yourself to the 'disaster family' who comes to you and says, 'We just want nothing.'" They may *think* they want nothing, explains Joseph, but you, the sympathetic funeral director, know better. The family just doesn't understand its options.

And what options there are! Later that day, I watch a sales tape produced by The York Group, one of the largest casket-and-urn manufacturers in the United States. Actors apparently plucked from the Infomercial School of Subtle Emoting play a family trying to decide what to do with Dad in a few years—because Dad, although crotchety, is still very much alive and is arguing with his family about the future ceremony. "Just put me in a pine box," he says. "Better still, cremate me! Throw my ashes in my garden, and maybe I can raise better tomatoes when I'm dead than I could when I was alive." Clearly, the funeral director (played here by an oil slick with legs) must make the family realize how important a service ($300 to $650) would be to his family and friends; how embalming Dad ($300 to $600) would make everyone at the memorial service more "comfortable." And after his loved ones pick up his "cremains," his wife could then place a portion in a solid bronze "Eden urn" with a lovely garland design (about $1,400), and his daughter could preserve a sprinkle of him in a lovely limited-edition keepsake urn depicting dolphins frolicking in the surf (about $1,300). Finally, the remainder of his ashes could be sprinkled not only on his tomatoes but also in a cemetery scattering garden ($150 to $400), so "that way you'll always know where your husband's cremated remains are located."

By the end of the tape, the Jones family is smiling delightedly at the thought of what a splashy exit Dad is going to make. Dad is delighted, too. From a degrading $400 direct cremation to a deeply meaningful $5,000-or-so ritual—it's so easy!

If only this scenario were fantasy. It's not. Cremations, although still often cheaper than traditional burials, are climbing ever higher in price. And since scattering remains requires a permit that funeral directors encourage people to think is more difficult to obtain than it actually is, the demand for urns, and for final resting places to put them, is also going through the roof, as the sudden boom of high-rise mausoleums in Los Angeles attests. "Don't

forget about one additional product you can sell with cremation: the vault for the urn," says Brian Joseph at the end of his presentation. "We don't have some vault to put the vault in. We may someday," he adds wistfully.

A long habit of not thinking a thing wrong gives it a superficial appearance of being right.

—Thomas Paine.
Quoted by Bob Ninker, the executive director of the Funeral Ethics Association

Not until the late 1800s, when a more transient society began to require that someone other than the deceased's family or neighbors handle the body, was the funeral industry born. Undertakers originally were carpenters who built coffins on the side; sensing a profit center, they learned how to embalm. A typical late-nineteenth-century bill, quoted by Jessica Mitford in her 1963 groundbreaking indictment of the funeral industry, *The American Way of Death,* showed that embalming ran around $10; renting a hearse, $8 to $10; washing and dressing, $5. A few dollars were invariably thrown in for the embalmer being "in attendance." Embalming, the practice of replacing the body's blood with a chemical preservative became popular in the United States during the Civil War, when battlefield casualties had to be shipped home; before that, burials took place within a few days of death, and bodies were kept on ice. Arsenic was the embalming chemical of choice until the 1920s, when it became apparent that it was (a) carcinogenic and (b) confusing in murder cases: in several trials involving arsenic, guilt could not be proven because the chemical was already present in the embalmed body.

At any rate, embalming became perhaps the first service provided by the funeral industry that was almost always unnecessary and, because of its profitability, almost always performed. (In fact, modern embalming usually preserves the body only for a few weeks; the politico corpses that hang around for years—Marcos, Lenin, Evita—are preserved through careful climate control.) And thus began the industry's reputation for price gouging.

"People in the funeral industry have always had a bad rep," notes Mark Nonestied, a member of the Association for Gravestone Studies, who lectures on the history of the funeral industry. "First, you've got a group of people associated with death. There are some cultures where people who deal with dead bodies are shunned altogether, and in this culture there's certainly a stigma attached. Second, there's the fact that bad experiences are more memorable, because the average person connects with the funeral director at the time of his greatest vulnerability."

Such collective distaste is reinforced by stories like the one Nonestied tells next. "Did you hear about the guy in California? He wasn't even a funeral director, but *that's* what the public thinks of the funeral industry." Allan Vieira, a fifty-two-year-old pilot from Berkeley, had been contracted by local mortuaries to scatter the cremated remains of thousands of people at sea, for $50 to $100 a body. (That was the price fixed with the mortuaries; the bereaved paid hundreds, perhaps thousands, more.) Instead of scattering the ashes, however, Vieira stashed them in his airplane hanger and in a self-storage warehouse stuffed so full that the walls collapsed, which is how his duplicity was discovered. Several lawsuits have been filed against the pilot and the mortuaries that contracted him. (Vieira, however, has already paid the ultimate price. A few weeks after being caught, he drove to the woods and shot himself; his station wagon contained eleven more boxes of remains.) In 1988, a $31.1 million judgment was won against another pilot who had promised to scatter the ashes of 5,342 people but instead dumped them, in one nice big pile, on a ten-acre lot of land he owned in the foothills of the Sierra Nevadas.

What probably nettles the public more than such occasional tales of gross negligence is the velvet-pitbull tactics funeral directors routinely use to wear down traumatized consumers—not unkindly, not even with great calculation, but simply because this is the way the business has always been run.

"You see, there is usually only one thought going through the mind of a bereaved family when they walk through the doors of a funeral home, and that thought is, *Get me out of here,*" says ConsumerCasket's St. George, who for ten years worked at a mortuary in Erie, Pennsylvania. "Of course, every funeral directors knows this. Which is why the most expensive merchandise is always brought to their attention first—and why, for example, the less expensive caskets are always shown in the ugliest possible colors."

Then there are the markups. In most businesses, a 100 to 150 percent markup is common; in the funeral industry, says St. George, markups are 300 to 600 percent. "Where I worked, we'd sit around in meetings itemizing every single thing we used in the course of a funeral, right down to the ligature we needed per body to sew up incisions. Ligature—that's string for you laypeople. We'd triple the price of everything, including cold cream we used to rub on the deceased's hands. Naturally, we had to charge for the whole jar."

In part, markups are due to the way funeral costs are structured. Before 1984, the cost of a funeral was based on the price of a casket. There was all sorts of chicanery involved in getting a customer to purchase an expensive box, but in any case the cost of the coffin included the bare bones of a traditional funeral service: transportation of the deceased, embalming, staffing at the service, announcement cards, etc. In 1984, the Federal Trade Commission ruled that a funeral director had to agree to use caskets that the bereaved could buy from retailers such as ConsumerCaskets, but he could bill customers for allowing it into his mortuary—a practice the memorial societies refer to as a "corkage fee."[1] In 1994, the FTC again changed the rules and banned corkage fees. Yet what seemed like a slap on the wrist of the funeral industry has turned out to be a big wet kiss. Now all costs are billed separately, and although savvy consumers can find a cheaper casket, the funeral director can charge a "non-declinable fee," which is the cost of his overhead, however he chooses to define it.

At the Riverside Memorial Chapel in Mount Vernon, New York, for example (a home owned by the conglomerate Service Corporation International), the non-declinable fee is $1,495. The cheapest package costs $2,598; it covers moving the remains to the funeral home and an "alternative container" (read: cardboard box). Caskets, flowers, limos, embalming, cosmetology, announcement cards, flag cases, register books, shrouds, temporary grave markers, death notices in the newspapers, clergy—you name it, it's extra. (Did I mention the cost of refrigeration? If the body is in the funeral home for more than six hours, it costs an additional $550. At those rates it would be cheaper to put up your dear departed at The Plaza.)

In pursuit of profits, the funeral industry has demonstrated an unseemly propensity for capitalizing on public ignorance. In the 1980s, thousands of funeral homes started tacking on a $200 "handling fee" for people who had died of AIDS. When gay-rights groups complained, it was renamed a "contagious-disease fee"; then it was called a "protective-clothing fee," until, one by one, states began to enforce against the discriminatory fee.

"The thing is, the protective clothing embalmers have to wear is a throwaway 'moon suit' that costs ten bucks and surgical gloves that cost about ten cents a pair—and OSHA has declared this gear mandatory for every embalming," says Karen Leonard, the consumer representative for Funeral and Memorial Societies of America, an organization dedicated to providing dignified and affordable funeral services. "But lots of funeral directors justified the $200 to families by citing all the extra risk they were assuming." When

the required safety procedures were followed, however, there was no extra risk. "Think about it for a minute," says Leonard. "If you were in mortal fear for your life would $200 make a difference?"

You know what I've decided? I don't want to be cremated. I used to, but now I think it sounds just a little too much like a blender speed. Now I've decided I want to be embalmed, and then I want a plastic surgeon to come put in silicone implants everywhere. Then I want to be laid out in the woods like Snow White, with a gravestone that reads Gotta Dance.

—Lorrie Moore, "Starving Again"

As expensive as funerals may seem, when adjusted for inflation the price of an average funeral has risen only a few percentage points in the last twenty-five years. It's the creative introduction of all sorts of new services and accoutrements, says Berkeley professor Dwayne Banks, that has increased the range of prices.

I got a little taste for all those delicious extras during a tour of the exhibitor's floor at the NFDA. First I spotted the mahogany casket my grandfather had unfortunately test-driven into eternity a few years earlier. At the time, the funeral director was keen on selling my family a model with a special seal to "protect" the body from wildlife; I seem to recall a speech that featured a Hitchcockian vision of marauding gophers. The memory made me a little nauseous: I had recently discovered that, far from protecting the body, the expensive protective seal is the best way to guarantee that anaerobic bacteria will turn the body into goo in record time.

Moving on, I strolled through row upon row of caskets, burial vaults, embalming chemicals to plump up dehydrated tissues (my favorite: a disinfectant called Mort-O-Cide), and restorative waxes to fill in those pesky irregularities left by, say, feeding tubes or gunshot wounds. Burial clothing consists of loose-fitting pastel nightgowns for ladies and pinstripe suits for the gents; apparently, in the afterlife, all women are napping and all men are taking meetings. The dominatrix in me almost sprang for an "extremities positioner," a rope gadget for the proper positioning of the arms over the chest. The Cincinnati College of Mortuary Science was trolling for students, proudly exhibiting a life-size model of Uncle Sam in restorative wax ("Careful, his limbs come off easily!"), and the American Funeral Service Museum in Houston exhibited Victorian mourning jewelry made from the hair of the deceased and memorial cards of the rich and famous (some jokester had placed Bobby Kennedy's next to Marilyn Monroe's).

These days, you can buy blowup digital "memory pictures" of the deceased to leave at the graveside and solar-powered memorial lights to keep those pictures backlit into eternity. For the pious, the NFDA exhibitors offered urns with portraits of Jesus and Mary; for the sportsman, there were urns shaped like deer, cowboy boots, and golfclub bags; and for Zsa Zsa Gabor impersonators, an Aurora, Illinois, mortician has created a line of cremation jewelry—gold-and-diamond hearts, teardrops, and cylinders (from $1,995 to $10,000) that can hold a few precious motes of Mom and Dad.

Batesville Casket Company, the largest manufacturer in the United States, was introducing a coffin with a special "memory drawer" for personal keepsakes. Marsellus Casket Company featured "the Rolls Royce of caskets," a hand-polished model of solid African mahogany lined with velvet (retail: about $10,000) that had been the final resting place for such stiff luminaries as Richard Nixon, Harry Truman, and John Kennedy. "And don't forget Jackie O.," said the salesman excitedly. Marsellus may have had presidential cachet, but The York Group was drawing crowds with a new casket model it calls "Expressions": the light, ash-wood exterior is treated with a veneer that allows the casket to be scrawled on in Magic Marker. "We see this as a big seller in the inner cities, for the teenage market," a York salesman told me. "You know, a kid goes, his homies can wish him well."

Companies whose primary source of business is in more lively industries were scavenging for scraps of the death market as well. GeneLink, a Margate, New Jersey, company that deals in DNA testing and storage, was offering the bereaved an opportunity to save a bit more of a loved one than mere dust. The mouth of the dead is swabbed for a cell sample, which is sent to GeneLink's lab in Fort Worth, Texas, where the DNA is extracted and stored for twenty-five years. A kit costs about $100, and funeral directors will be charging about $295 for collecting a sample. I must admit, I never quite understood why anyone would want this service; after all, if you fear you are at increased risk for some genetically linked problem such as Alzheimer's, you could always test yourself.

Here's an idea that *does* make sense to me: cybergrieving. Jack Martin, president of Simplex Knowledge, an Internet production company in White Plains, New York, has come up with an idea that's bound to appeal to boomers too busy to hop halfway across the continent to weep over Aunt Martha's grave. Mourners will be issued a Website password; a camera will be set up at the funeral, and pictures of the service will be broadcast on the Internet every thirty seconds or so. "The family and funeral director can choose what will be

highlighted," says Martin. "The grieving family, the body, the minister whatever." About half of the funeral directors who have learned about Martin's concept see it as a valuable marketing tool, a service they could offer families gratis. The other half see it strictly as profitable: fees could be collected not only from the families (about $200) but *also from the mourners.* "They imagined that someone, say, in New Jersey without Internet access could drop by their funeral home and witness a service going on in California," says Martin. "And then the funeral director could charge each mourner ten or twenty bucks. But frankly I don't think this concept will go over too well. Making people pay to mourn isn't such great publicity for the industry."

Of course, it's possible to bypass the traditional burial altogether. You might want to be put on ice until medical science figures out a cure for what ails you (the first cryonically frozen man, James H. Bedford, just celebrated his thirtieth anniversary of "de-animation," as cryonics enthusiasts call it). Then again, you might want to have yourself mummified. On its Web page, Summum, a New Age, quasi-religious organization in Salt Lake City that practices modern mummification, offers this sales pitch: "Unlike the mummification techniques used by ancient Egyptians, which left the dead shriveled, discolored, and ugly, Summum's method is designed to keep you looking healthy and robust for millennia. The appeal may be to anyone who has labored to stay in shape. Why spend thousands of dollars in health-club fees while you're alive, then let everything go to pot just because you've died?"

Why, indeed.

You know what's real tough about this business? No one's real happy to see you.
—Bob Jones, Jones Funeral Home,
Altoona, Pennsylvania

At the end of the day, I was slumped at the hotel bar with a gin and tonic. The convention had no shortage of activities. I could have gone to hear Marvin Hamlisch give a command performance or had my picture taken with former astronaut Buzz Aldrin, who stood around in his flight suit looking a little confused; one funeral director solemnly shook his hand and murmured, "God bless America." But I wasn't up for merriment. I was exhausted. The worst thing about being at a funeral directors' convention was having to be around people who are so nice all the time; if I happened to be going through a door, four funeral directors would materialize from nowhere to open if for me. Despite their somber workaday attire, morticians are a jolly lot, and in a game effort to show they know how to

have a good time, everyone wore his snappiest neckwear: I spotted a few screaming eagles, dozens of ball-team logos, and at least one portrait of Larry, Curly, and Moe.

I forgot about the entertainment and instead eavesdropped on war stories. Two guys were fretting about a recent "situation" in which someone had mistakenly cremated the wrong body. Another guy was complaining about a woman who had sued for injury and negligence after she passed out and gave herself a concussion; he had warned her that her mother was in no condition to be viewed, but she had insisted on one last look. Still others were relating a tale in which a colleague had forgotten to take out a pacemaker before cremation—a definite no-no, since batteries explode during incineration.

When the barflies ran out of conversation, they'd inevitably turn to the legend of Larry Titemore, a funeral director in Vermont. In 1995, in addition to embezzling over $75,000 in prepaid funeral funds that were supposed to be placed in an escrow account, Titemore stopped embalming the bodies entrusted to him and left them to ripen.[2] He also practiced a necrological bait and switch, selling expensive caskets to families and then removing the bodies before burial and placing them in cheap models, or sometimes into no model at all: when investigators inspected his premises, they found the body of a local resident who had died earlier that winter stuffed into a broken-down hearse. After the service, Titemore had removed him from his pricey casket and then didn't seem quite sure what to do with him. Titemore's license was revoked. After completing his jail time, he found work as a used-car salesman.

A solidly built, bright-eyed man in a black polyester Elvis shirt and ruby jacket sits next to me, sipping Long Island iced teas with his wife. He notices me staring at his ensemble. "Don't get to wear this much around the home," he says. Ben Strickland's his name. Runs Seymour Funeral Home, sweet little operation in North Carolina. Knew he was right for the work when he embalmed a friend; knew nobody could do it better. "Don't want nobody to die, but I gotta eat," he says. Ben is a natural storyteller: we talk about gypsy funerals, where mourners throw money on top of the body; we talk about the fellow who was buried with his chihuahua's ashes. "He and his wife didn't have children. That was their baby," Ben explains. Ben loves everything about his business. Everything but the children. "Touches me real bad to have a child or infant die. Seventy-five, eighty, they lived their life. But a child?" Ben's eyes fill with tears.

Embarrassed, I look away; he thinks I'm looking at his watch. "Like that?" he says, playing with the thick gold band. "Took a lotta teeth to make this'un here."

I look up; Ben's still wiping his eyes, but he's grinning. "Gotcha!" he cries.

No question about it: Death care is becoming a hot career. According to the American Board of Funeral Service Education, since 1990 there has been a 45 percent increase in the number of students enrolled in mortuary-schools. And what used to be almost an entirely male-dominated industry is now increasingly estrogen-rich: in 1996, 33 percent of mortuary school grads were women. "There are several factors at work here," says Gordon Bigelow, ABFSE's executive director. "As we've gone through corporate downsizing, a number of adults looking for second and third careers have focused on funeral service as a recession-proof industry. And then, of course, there's the fact that the baby boom generation is beginning to, ah, terminate." According to the National Funeral Directors Association, the average funeral director makes about $49,000 a year (twice that in large, metropolitan firms). And considering that one needs no more than two years of college to get a funeral director's license, the Grim Reaper offers a pretty promising and secure future.

"It's becoming cooler to be a funeral director than it once was," says one young buck, whose perfectly tailored sharkskin suit suggests one too many viewings of the movie *GoodFellas*. We are shouting at each other over the din of an oompah band; Wilbert Funeral Services is sponsoring an Oktoberfest, complete with knee-slapping dancers in Tyrolean hats and leder-hosen. Y. B. scans the room, a trace of a sneer on his blandly handsome face. "This is still a very clip-on-tie-and-polyester crowd, though."

Maybe, but the clip-on set is what made this country great. The vast majority of funeral directors are solid citizens in their communities, overwhelmingly conservative and Republican. Rotarians and Kiwanis Club members, they believe in boosterism and practice it too.

We whine about how much money they make, how they capitalize on grief and loss. Our irrationality about death leads us to believe that no one has a right to make a living from it. But let's look at it this way: It's 2:00 A.M., and after a long and debilitating illness Nana has shuffled off this mortal coil. In your house. In the summer. Your air conditioner has broken down. By the time you find her, Nana is beginning to leak.

Do you want their job? I didn't think so.

Underneath the lingering scent of lilies and formaldehyde, however, there lurks the unmistakable stench of money. Three months after the Cincinnati convention, I'm sitting in on a seminar called "Death Care IV: An Undertaking in New York." It's for financial analysts and investors who track the rapidly consolidating funeral industry; the tacit theme of the day is "Stiffs: They're a Growth Market!"

Thinking I'm also an analyst, an impeccably groomed brunette—one of only about five women in the packed room—leans over and proffers some helpful advice. "Projections for the next quarter are looking good," she whispers. "The strain of flu that's hit this season is *really* virulent."

Thirty years ago, when she wrote *The American Way of Death,* Jessica Mitford accurately predicted just about every trend that has since come to pass in the funeral industry—most significantly, the rise of the giant funeral chain. Together, the Houston-based Service Corporation International (SCI) and The Loewen Group, headquartered in Burnaby, British Columbia, own about 2,000, or 10 percent, of America's mortuaries. (Smaller chains such as Carriage Services and Stewart Enterprises account for another 300 or so.) Traditionally, funeral homes were the ultimate mom-and-pop operations, run by legions of slightly creepy moms and pops whose business acumen was usually not the soundest. Jim St. George recalls how the funeral home where he worked tried to compete with lower-priced mortuaries: "We only had one person standing around to say hello to strangers at the visitation instead of three or four. Oh, and we didn't put candy in the candy dishes, mourners weren't allowed to use the coffee room, and we didn't fold the first paper on the toilet roll into a little triangle, like they do in hotels."

With Pecksniffian economies like these commonplace, it's no wonder someone would start taking a McDonald's-like approach to marketing and service. Quietly, relentlessly, SCI and Loewen have been coming into town and buying up homes and cemeteries, leaving the current management in place—at least for a while. One funeral director compares the takeovers to the movie *Invasion of the Body Snatchers.* "You think you're dealing with the same people you've always known and trusted. But they're not. They're pods. The business has nothing to do with community values anymore. Everything about the way they run their business now has to be decided from a headquarters that knows nothing and cares nothing about the community."

The big chains don't see it this way. They say they're leaving the funeral directors to do what they do best—caretaking—and letting the suits make the business decisions. They wax poetic about economies of scale. SCI, for example, will go into an area, buy up five or six funeral homes, and pool their resources—with one central-

ized embalming site, a roving staff and a fleet of hearses that can float from one home to another, caskets bought in volume, and so forth.

But if you think consolidation means that the cost of dying is suddenly going to become more reasonable, think again. The *Seattle Times* found that in Washington State where 49 percent of the funeral homes are owned by chains, the cost of funerals has risen by as much as 65 percent since 1992—because the real client is no longer the family of the deceased but the stockholder.

In fact, so bullish is Wall Street on death care that this year saw the introduction of the Pauzé Tombstone Fund, a mutual fund diversified across the death-care industry. The fund's prospectus is filled with exciting bar charts and graphs, showing how, if Tombstone had been around since 1986, it would have soundly beaten the performances of the Dow Jones Industrial Average, Standard & Poor's, and the Russell 3000 Index: "Population demographics indicate that the death care industry will continue to experience long-term expansion due to the aging of the U.S. population and the estimated growing number of future annual deaths." In a quiet moment, you can almost hear the sound of investors hyperventilating.

Back at the seminar, the senior financial officer for Stewart Enterprises, Ronald Patron, confidently quotes predictions that his company will see a 20 percent growth. Someone raises his hand and asks Patron the question on everyone's mind. SCI's recent attempt at a hostile takeover of Loewen had failed, thus preventing what one industry critic said was "the equivalent to Pepsi and Coca-Cola merging." But the FTC made noises about regulating prices and launched antitrust investigations in eleven states. "We don't see any problems in either of those areas," Patron said soothingly. "The FTC recently renewed its rules about full disclosure of pricing, but there's no *regulation* of pricing."

Perhaps I just imagined I heard a collective sigh of relief. It was sort of appalling. Naturally, I went home and bought stock in SCI.

The public backlash against funeral monopolies is in its infancy, but it will die young without some government intervention. Like health care, the funeral industry can't be run solely as an enterprise that responds to market forces, because none of us have a choice in being part of it.

Or do we? Can we opt out of the system? In California, home of bizarre trends that eventually become mainstream, a group of community activists have started the Natural Death Care Project, which teaches the bereaved to care for and bury their loved ones. "In all but eight states in this country, you don't need a funeral director at all," says Lisa Carlson, author of *Caring for Your Own Dead: The Final Act of Love.* "You have to learn how to do the paperwork, but it's certainly not that hard." And the body itself? "Care for people when they're dead is the same as when they're alive, except you don't have to feed them," she says. In fact, it's not much more involved than that—especially if the body is kept cold and disposed of within a couple of days.

Before Jessica Mitford died of brain cancer last year, she made a last request to Karen Leonard, the consumer activist who was also Mitford's researcher. "Decca [Mitford's nickname] wanted me to send her funeral bill to SCI. 'After all,' she said to me, 'look how much fame I brought them!'" Leonard sent the bill, $475 for direct cremation, to CEO Robert Waldrip, pointing out how much more expensive it would have been if Mitford had been cremated at an SCI-affiliated funeral home. "I wanted him to know he was in Decca's thoughts at the end," Leonard says. "Oddly enough, we never heard from him."

Unlike Jessica Mitford, I think we are the victims not of the funeral industry but of ourselves. A friend of mine, a former

flack at the public relations firm Hill and Knowlton, described a campaign for the National Funeral Directors Association she worked on a few years ago: "The idea was, we really had to create a cachet for death. You wouldn't cheap out on a wedding—why would you do it for a funeral?" The campaign never quite got off the ground, but it spoke eloquently to the guilt and desires of a generation that perhaps wasn't quite as kind to its elders as it should have been, a generation that trashed its parents' values and then tried desperately to acquire the things those values—respect, hard work, constancy, sacrifice—bought.

In some ways, we are more careful consumers than we used to be. But we are also terribly unsure of ourselves, unsure of our goodness, unsure of our souls. What a relief it is to be able to make up for our sins to the living by being generous to them after they're dead. When it comes to their future livelihoods, I'm quite sure the funeral directors of America may rest in peace.

Notes

1. *A number of cut-rate casket manufacturers have put up Web pages on the Internet; there's even a Web site (www.xroads.com/funerals)*

maintained by Father Henry Wasielewskil a semiretired parish priest and crusader in Tempe, Arizona, that details funeral-industry scams so that consumers can gauge their friendly neighborhood mortician's markup.

2. *In his 1948 novel* The Loved One, *Evelyn Waugh satirized morticians' eagerness to lock people into prepaying for their own funeral: "Choose now, at leisure and in health, the form of final preparation you require, pay for it while you are best able to do so, shed all anxiety. Pass the buck, Mr. Barlow; Whispering Glades can take it." Recently, a number of lawsuits have been filed against companies refusing to honor preneed contracts. The money is supposed to go into a trust or escrow account, and the interest accrued will compensate for the rate of inflation. But there are two major problems: (1) although the funeral director gets to control the money you have to pay taxes on the interest you'll never see; and (2) governmental oversight varies wildly. In some states, says Sue Simon, publisher of* Preneed Perspective, *preneed trust funds are required and carefully monitored, and in others—such as Washington, D.C., and Alabama—"the funeral director can take your $5,000, go to Atlantic City, and put it on red."*

Judith Newman is a freelance writer living in New York City. This is her first article for Harper's Magazine.

Is It Time to Abandon Brain Death?

Despite its familiarity and widespread acceptance, the concept of "brain death" remains incoherent in theory and confused in practice. Moreover, the only purpose served by the concept is to facilitate the procurement of transplantable organs. By abandoning the concept of brain death and adopting different criteria for organ procurement, we may be able to increase both the supply of transplantable organs and clarity in our understanding of death.

by Robert D. Truog

Over the past several decades, the concept of brain death has become well entrenched within the practice of medicine. At a practical level, this concept has been successful in delineating widely accepted ethical and legal boundaries for the procurement of vital organs for transplantation. Despite this success, however, there have been persistent concerns over whether the concept is theoretically coherent and internally consistent.[1] Indeed, some have concluded that the concept is fundamentally flawed, and that it represents only a "superficial and fragile consensus."[2] In this analysis I will identify the sources of these inconsistencies, and suggest that the best resolution to these issues may be to abandon the concept of brain death altogether.

Definitions, Concepts, and Tests

In its seminal work "Defining Death," the President's Commission for the Study of Ethical Problems in Medicine and Biomedical and Behavioral Research articulated a formulation of brain death that has come to be known as the "whole-brain standard."[3] In the Uniform Determination of Death Act, the President's Commission specified two criteria for determining death: (1) irreversible cessation of circulatory and respiratory functions, or (2) irreversible cessation of all functions of the entire brain, including the brainstem.

Neurologist James Bernat has been influential in defending and refining this standard. Along with others, he has recognized that analysis of the concept of brain death must begin by differentiating between three distinct levels. At the most general level, the concept must involve a *definition*. Next, *criteria* must be specified to determine when the definition has been fulfilled. Finally, *tests* must be available for evaluating whether the criteria have been satisfied.[4] As clarified by Bernat and colleagues, therefore, the concept of death under the whole-brain formulation can be outlined as follows:[5]

Definition of Death: The "permanent cessation of functioning of the organism as a whole."

Criterion for Death: The "permanent cessation of functioning of the entire brain."

Tests for Death: Two distinct sets of tests are available and acceptable for determining that the criterion is fulfilled:

(1) The cardiorespiratory standard is the traditional approach for determining death and relies upon documenting the prolonged absence of circulation or respiration. These tests fulfill the criterion, according to Bernat, since the prolonged absence of these vital signs is diagnostic for the permanent loss of all brain function.

(2) The neurological standard consists of a battery of tests and procedures, including establishment of an etiology sufficient to account for the loss of all brain functions, diagnosing the presence of coma, documenting apnea and the absence of brainstem reflexes, excluding reversible conditions, and showing the persistence of these findings over a sufficient period of time.[6]

Critique of the Current Formulation of Brain Death

Is this a coherent account of the concept of brain death? To answer this question, one must determine whether each level of analysis is consistent with the others. In other words, individuals who fulfill the tests must also fulfill the criterion, and those who satisfy the criterion must also satisfy the definition.[7]

 From the *Hastings Center Report,* January/February 1997, pp. 29-37.

First, regarding the tests-criterion relationship, there is evidence that many individuals who fulfill all of the tests for brain death do not have the "permanent cessation of functioning of the entire brain." In particular, many of these individuals retain clear evidence of integrated brain function at the level of the brainstem and midbrain, and may have evidence of cortical function.

For example, many patients who fulfill the tests for the diagnosis of brain death continue to exhibit intact neurohumoral function. Between 22 percent and 100 percent of brain-dead patients in different series have been found to retain free-water homeostasis through the neurologically medicated secretion of arginine vasopressin, as evidenced by serum hormonal levels and the absence of diabetes insipidus.[8] Since the brain is the only source of the regulated secretion of arginine vasopressin, patients without diabetes insipidus do not have the loss of all brain function. Neurologically regulated secretion of other hormones is also quite common.[9]

In addition, the tests for the diagnosis of brain death require the patient not to be hypothermic.[10] This caveat is a particularly confusing Catch-22, since the absence of hypothermia generally indicates the continuation of neurologically mediated temperature homeostasis. The circularity of this reasoning can be clinically problematic, since hypothermic patients cannot be diagnosed as brain-dead but the absence of hypothermia is itself evidence of brain function.

Furthermore, studies have shown that many patients (20 percent in one series) who fulfill the tests for brain death continue to show electrical activity on their electroencephalograms.[11] While there is no way to determine how often this electrical activity represents true "function" (which would be incompatible with the criterion for brain death), in at least some cases the activity observed seems fully compatible with function.[12]

Finally, clinicians have observed that patients who fulfill the tests for brain death frequently respond to surgical incision at the time of organ procurement with a significant rise in both heart rate and blood pressure. This suggests that integrated neurological function at a supraspinal level may be present in at least some patients diagnosed as brain-dead.[13] This evidence points to the conclusion that there is a significant disparity between the standard tests used to make the diagnosis of brain death and the criterion these tests are purported to fulfill. Faced with these facts, even supporters of the current statutes acknowledge that the criterion of "whole-brain" death is only an "approximation."[14]

Only 35 percent of physicians and nurses who were likely to be involved in organ procurement for transplantation correctly identified the legal and medical criteria for determining death.

If the tests for determining brain death are incompatible with the current criterion, then one way of solving the problem would be to require tests that always correlate with the "permanent cessation of functioning of the entire brain." Two options have been considered in this regard. The first would require tests that correlate with the actual destruction of the brain, since complete destruction would, of course, be incompatible with any degree of brain function. Only by satisfying these tests, some have argued, could we be assured that all functions of the entire brain have totally and permanently ceased.[15] But is there a constellation of clinical and laboratory tests that correlate with this degree of destruction? Unfortunately, a study of over 500 patients with both coma and apnea (including 146 autopsies for neuropathologic correlation) showed that "it was not possible to verify that a diagnosis made prior to cardiac arrest by any set or subset of criteria would invariably correlate with a diffusely destroyed brain."[16] On the basis of these data, a definition that required total brain destruction could only be confirmed at autopsy. Clearly, a condition that could only be determined after death could never be a requirement for declaring death.

Another way of modifying the tests to conform with the criterion would be to rely solely upon the cardiorespiratory standard for determining death. This standard would certainly identify the permanent cessation of all brain function (thereby fulfilling the criterion), since it is well established by common knowledge that prolonged absence of circulation and respiration results in the death of the entire brain (and every other organ). In addition, fulfillment of these tests would also convincingly demonstrate the cessation of function of the organism as a whole (thereby fulfilling the definition). Unfortunately, this approach for resolving the problem would also make it virtually impossible to obtain vital organs in a viable condition for transplantation, since under current laws it is generally necessary for these organs to be removed from a heart-beating donor.

These inconsistencies between the tests and the criterion are therefore not easily resolvable. In addition to these problems, there are also inconsistencies between the criterion and the definition. As outlined above, the whole-brain concept assumes that the "permanent cessation of functioning of the entire brain" (the criterion) necessarily implies the "permanent cessation of functioning of the organism as a whole" (the definition). Conceptually, this relationship assumes the principle that the brain is responsible for maintaining the body's homeostasis, and that without brain function the organism rapidly disintegrates. In the past, this relationship was demonstrated by showing that individuals who fulfilled the tests for the diagnosis of brain death inevitably had a cardiac arrest within a short period of time, even if they were provided with mechanical ventilation and intensive care.[17]

Indeed, this assumption had been considered one of the linchpins in the ethical justification for the concept of brain death.[18] For example, in the largest empirical study of brain death ever performed, a collaborative group working under the auspices of the National Institutes of Health sought to specify the necessary tests for diagnosing brain death by attempting to identify a constellation of neurological findings that would inevitably predict the development of a cardiac arrest within three months, regardless of the level or intensity of support provided.[19]

This approach to defining brain death in terms of neurological findings that predict the development of cardiac arrest is plagued by both logical and scientific problems, however. First, it confuses a prognosis with a diagnosis. Demonstrating that a certain class of patients will suffer a cardiac arrest within a defined period of time certainly proves that they are *dying,* but it says nothing about whether they are *dead.*[20] This conceptual mistake can be clearly appreciated if one considers individuals who are dying of conditions not associated with severe neurological impairment. If a constellation of tests could identify a subgroup of patients with metastatic cancer who invariably suffered a cardiac arrest within a short period of time, for example, we would certainly be comfortable in concluding that they were dying, but we clearly could not claim that they were already dead.

Second, this view relies upon the intuitive notion that the brain is the principal organ of the body, the "integrating" organ whose functions cannot be replaced by any other organ or by artificial means. Up through the early 1980s, this view was supported by numerous studies showing that almost all patients who fulfilled the usual battery of tests for brain death suffered a cardiac arrest within several weeks.[21]

The loss of homeostatic equilibrium that is empirically observed in brain-dead patients is almost certainly the result of their progressive loss of integrated neurohumoral and autonomic function. Over the past several decades, however, intensive care units (ICUs) have become increasingly sophisticated "surrogate brainstems," replacing both the respiratory functions as well as the hormonal and other regulatory activities of the damaged neuraxis.[22] This technology is presently utilized in those tragic cases in which a pregnant woman is diagnosed as brain-dead and an attempt is made to maintain her somatic existence until the fetus reaches a viable gestation, as well as for prolonging the organ viability of brain-dead patients awaiting organ procurement.[23] Although the functions of the brainstem are considerably more complex than those of the heart or the lungs, in theory (and increasingly in practice) they are entirely replaceable by modern technology. In terms of maintaining homeostatic functions, therefore,

the brain is no more irreplaceable than any of the other vital organs. A definition of death predicated upon the "inevitable" development of a cardiac arrest within a short period of time is therefore inadequate, since this empirical "fact" is no longer true. In other words, cardiac arrest is inevitable only if it is allowed to occur, just as respiratory arrest in brain-dead patients is inevitable only if they are not provided with mechanical ventilation. This gradual development in technical expertise has unwittingly undermined one of the central ethical justifications for the whole-brain criterion of death.

In summary, then, the whole-brain concept is plagued by internal inconsistencies in both the tests-criterion and the criterion-definition relationships, and these problems cannot be easily solved. In addition, there is evidence that this lack of conceptual clarity has contributed to misunderstandings about the concept among both clinicians and laypersons. For example, Stuart Youngner and colleagues found that only 35 percent of physicians and nurses who were likely to be involved in organ procurement for transplantation correctly identified the legal and medical criteria for determining death.[24] Indeed, most of the respondents used inconsistent concepts of death, and a substantial minority misunderstood the criterion to be the permanent loss of consciousness, which the President's Commission had specifically rejected, in part because it would have classified anencephalic newborns and patients in a vegetative state as dead. In other words, medical professionals who were otherwise knowledgeable and sophisticated were generally confused about the concept of brain death. In an editorial accompanying this study, Dan Wikler and Alan Weisbard claimed that this confusion was "appropriate," given the lack of philosophical coherence in the concept itself.[25] In another study, a survey of Swedes found that laypersons were more willing to consent to autopsies than to organ donation for themselves or a close relative. In seeking an explanation for these findings, the authors reported that "the fear of not being dead during the removal of organs, reported by 22 percent of those undecided toward organ donation, was related to the uncertainty surrounding brain death."[26]

On one hand, these difficulties with the concept might be deemed to be so

esoteric and theoretical that they should play no role in driving the policy debate about how to define death and procure organs for transplantation. This has certainly been the predominant view up to now. In many other circumstances, theoretical issues have taken a back seat to practical matters when it comes to determining public policy. For example, the question of whether tomatoes should be considered a vegetable or a fruit for purposes of taxation was said to hinge little upon the biological facts of the matter, but to turn primarily upon the political and economic issues at stake.[27] If this view is applied to the concept of brain death, then the best public policy would be that which best served the public's interest, regardless of theoretical concerns.

On the other hand, medicine has a long and respected history of continually seeking to refine the theoretical and conceptual underpinnings of its practice. While the impact of scientific and philosophical views upon social policy and public perception must be taken seriously, they cannot be the sole forces driving the debate. Given the evidence demonstrating a lack of coherence in the whole-brain death formulation and the confusion that is apparent among medical professionals, there is ample reason to prompt a look at alternatives to our current approach.

Alternative Approaches to the Whole-Brain Formulation

Alternatives to the whole-brain death formulation fall into two general categories. One approach is to emphasize the overriding importance of those functions of the brain that support the phenomenon of consciousness and to claim that individuals who have permanently suffered the loss of all consciousness are dead. This is known as the "higher-brain" criterion. The other approach is to return to the traditional tests for determining death, that is, the permanent loss of circulation and respiration. As noted above, this latter strategy could fit well with Bernat's formulation of the definition of death, since adoption of the cardiorespiratory standard as the test for determining death is consistent with both the criterion and the definition. The problem with this potential solution is that it would virtually eliminate the possibility of procuring vital organs from heart-beating donors under our present system of law and ethics, since current requirements insist that organs be removed only from individuals who have been declared dead (the "dead-donor rule").[28] Consideration of this latter view would therefore be feasible only if it could be linked to fundamental changes in the permissible limits of organ procurement.

The Higher-Brain Formulation. The higher-brain criterion for death holds that maintaining the potential for consciousness is the critical function of the brain relevant to questions of life and death. Under this definition, all individuals who are permanently unconscious would be considered to be dead. Included in this category would be (1) patients who fulfill the cardiorespiratory standard, (2) those who fulfill the current tests for whole-brain death, (3) those diagnosed as being in a permanent vegetative state, and (4) newborns with anencephaly. Various versions of this view have been defended by many philosophers, and arguments have been advanced from moral as well as ontological perspectives.[29] In addition, this view correlates very well with many commonsense opinions about personal identity. To take a stock philosophical illustration, for example, consider the typical reaction of a person who has undergone a hypothetical "brain switch" procedure, where one's brain is transplanted into another's body, and vice versa. Virtually anyone presented with this scenario will say that "what matters" for their existence now resides in the new body, even though an outside observer would insist that it is the person's old body that "appears" to be the original person. Thought experiments like this one illustrate that we typically identify ourselves with our experience of consciousness, and this observation forms the basis of the claim that the permanent absence of consciousness should be seen as representing the death of the person.

Implementation of this standard would present certain problems, however. First, is it possible to diagnose the state of permanent unconsciousness with the high level of certainty required for the determination of death? More specifically, is it currently possible to definitively diagnose the permanent vegetative state and anencephaly? A Multi-Society Task Force recently outlined guidelines for diagnosis of permanent vegetative state and claimed that

sufficient data are now available to make the diagnosis of permanent vegetative state in appropriate patients with a high degree of certainty.[30] On the other hand, case reports of patients who met these criteria but who later recovered a higher degree of neurological functioning suggests that use of the term "permanent" may be overstating the degree of diagnostic certainty that is currently possible. This would be an especially important issue in the context of diagnosing death, where false positive diagnoses would be particularly problematic.[31] Similarly, while the Medical Task Force on Anencephaly has concluded that most cases of anencephaly can be diagnosed by a competent clinician without significant uncertainty, others have emphasized the ambiguities inherent in evaluating this condition.[32]

Another line of criticism is that the higher-brain approach assumes the definition of death should reflect the death of the *person,* rather than the death of the *organism.*[33] By focusing on the person, this theory does not account for what is common to the death of all organisms, such as humans, frogs, or trees. Since we do not know what it would mean to talk about the permanent loss of consciousness of frogs or trees, then this approach to death may appear to be idiosyncratic. In response, higher-brain theorists believe that it is critical to define death within the context of the specific subject under consideration. For example, we may speak of the death of an ancient civilization, the death of a species, or the death of a particular system of belief. In each case, the definition of death will be different, and must be appropriate to the subject in order for the concept to make any sense. Following this line of reasoning, the higher-brain approach is correct precisely because it seeks to identify what is uniquely relevant to the death of a person.

Aside from these diagnostic and philosophical concerns, however, perhaps the greatest objections to the higher brain formulation emerge from the im-

plications of treating breathing patients as if they are dead. For example, if patients in a permanent vegetative state were considered to be dead, then they should logically be considered suitable for burial. Yet all of these patients

> Most people find it counterintuitive to perceive a breathing patient as "dead."

breathe, and some of them "live" for many years.[34] The thought of burying or cremating a breathing individual, even if unconscious, would be unthinkable for many people, creating a significant barrier to acceptance of this view into public policy.[35]

One way of avoiding this implication would be to utilize a "lethal injection" before cremation or burial to terminate cardiac and respiratory function. This would not be euthanasia, since the individual would be declared dead before the injection. The purpose of the injection would be purely "aesthetic." This practice could even be viewed as simply an extension of our current protocols, where the vital functions of patients diagnosed as brain-dead are terminated prior to burial, either by discontinuing mechanical ventilation or by discontinuing mechanical ventilation or by removing their heart and/or lungs during the process of organ procurement. While this line of argumentation has a certain logical persuasiveness, it nevertheless fails to address the central fact that most people find it counterintuitive to perceive a breathing patient as "dead." Wikler has suggested that this attitude is likely to change over time, and that eventually society will come to accept that the body of a patient in a permanent vegetative state is simply that person's "living remains."[36] This optimism about higher-brain death is reminiscent of the comments by the President's Commission regarding whole-brain death: "Although undeniably disconcerting for many people, the confusion created in personal perception by a determination of 'brain death' does not . . . provide a basis for an ethical objection to discontinuing medical measures on these dead bodies any more than on other dead bodies."[37] Nevertheless, at the present time any inclination toward a higher-brain death standard remains primarily in the realm of philosophers and not policymakers.

Return to the Traditional Cardiorespiratory Standard. In contrast to the higher-brain concept of death, the other main alternative to our current approach would involve moving in the opposite direction and abandoning the diagnosis of brain death altogether. This would involve returning to the traditional approach to determining death, that is, the cardiorespiratory standard. In evaluating the wisdom of "turning back the clock," it is helpful to retrace the development of the concept of brain death back to 1968 and the conclusions of the Ad Hoc Committee that developed the Harvard Criteria for the diagnosis of brain death. They began by claiming:

> There are two reasons why there is need for a definition [of brain death]: (1) Improvements in resuscitative and supportive measures have led to increased efforts to save those who are desperately injured. Sometimes these efforts have only partial success so that the result is an individual whose brain is irreversibly damaged. The burden is great on patients who suffer permanent loss of intellect, on their families, and on those in need of hospital beds already occupied by these comatose patients. (2) Obsolete criteria for the definition of death can lead to controversy in obtaining organs for transplantation.[38]

These two issues can be subdivided into at least four distinct questions:

1) When is it permissible to withdraw life support from patients with irreversible neurological damage for the benefit of the patient?

2) When is it permissible to withdraw life support from patients with irreversible neurological damage for the benefit of society, where the benefit is either in the form of economic savings or to make an ICU bed available for someone with a better prognosis?

3) When is it permissible to remove organs from a patient for transplantation?

4) When is a patient ready to be cremated or buried?

The Harvard Committee chose to address all of these questions with a single answer, that is, the determination of brain death. Each of these questions involves unique theoretical issues, however, and each raises a different set of concerns. By analyzing the concept of brain death in terms of the separate questions that led to its development, alternatives to brain death may be considered.

Withdrawal of life support. The Harvard Committee clearly viewed the diagnosis of brain death as a necessary condition for the withdrawal of life support: "It should be emphasized that we recommend the patient be declared dead before any effort is made to take him off a respirator . . . [since] otherwise, the physicians would be turning off the respirator on a person who is, in the present strict, technical application of law, still alive" (p. 339).

The ethical and legal mandates that surround the withdrawal of life support have changed dramatically since the recommendations of the Harvard Committee. Numerous court decisions and consensus statements have emphasized the rights of patients or their surrogates to demand the withdrawal of life-sustaining treatments, including mechanical ventilation. In the practice of critical care medicine today, patients are rarely diagnosed as brain-dead solely for the purpose of discontinuing mechanical ventilation. When patients are not candidates for organ transplantation, either because of medical contraindications or lack of consent, families are informed of the dismal prognosis, and artificial ventilation is withdrawn. While the diagnosis of brain death was once critical in allowing physicians to discontinue life-sustaining treatments, decisionmaking about these important questions is now appropriately centered around the patient's previously stated wishes and judgments about the patient's best interest. Questions about the definition of death have become virtually irrelevant to these deliberations.

Allocation of scarce resources. The Harvard Committee alluded to its concerns about having patients with a hopeless prognosis occupying ICU beds. In the years since that report, this issue has become even more pressing. The diagnosis of brain death, however, is of little significance in helping to resolve these issues. Even considering the unusual cases where families refuse to have the ventilator removed from a brain-dead patient, the overall impact of the diagnosis of brain death upon scarce ICU resources is minimal. Much more important to the current debate over the just allocation of ICU resources are patients with less severe degrees of neurological dysfunction, such as patients in a permanent vegetative state or individuals with advanced dementia. Again, the diagnosis of brain death is of little relevance to this central concern of the Harvard Committee.

Organ transplantation. Without question, the most important reason for the continued use of brain death criteria is the need for transplantable organs. Yet even here, the requirements for brain death may be doing more harm than good. The need for organs is expanding at an ever-increasing rate, while the number of available organs has essentially plateaued. In an effort to expand the limited pool of organs, several attempts have been made to circumvent the usual restrictions of brain death on organ procurement.

At the University of Pittsburgh, for example, a new protocol allows critically ill patients or their surrogates to offer their organs for donation after the withdrawal of life-support, even though the patients never meet brain death criteria.[39] Suitable patients are taken to the operating room, where intravascular monitors are placed and the patient is "prepped and draped" for surgical incision. Life-support is then withdrawn, and the patient is monitored for the development of cardiac arrest. Assuming this occurs within a short period of time, the attending physician waits until there

> The most difficult challenge for this proposal would be to gain acceptance of the view that killing may sometimes be a justifiable necessity for procuring transplantable organs.

has been two minutes of pulselessness, and then pronounces the patient dead. The transplant team then enters the operating room and immediately removes the organs for transplantation.

This novel approach has a number of problems when viewed from within the traditional framework. For example, after the patient is pronounced dead, why should the team rush to remove the organs? If the Pittsburgh team truly believes that the patient is dead, why not begin chest compressions and mechanical ventilation, insert cannulae to place the patient on full cardiopulmonary bypass, and remove the organs in a more controlled fashion? Presumably, this is not done because two minutes of pulselessness is almost certainly not long enough to ensure the development of brain death.[40] It is even conceivable that patients managed in this way could regain consciousness during the process of organ procurement while supported with cardiopulmonary bypass, despite having already been diagnosed as "dead." In other words, the reluctance of the Pittsburgh team to extend their protocol in ways that would be acceptable for dead patients could be an indication that the patients may really not be dead after all.

A similar attempt to circumvent the usual restrictions on organ procurement was recently attempted with anencephalic newborns at Loma Linda University. Again, the protocol involved manipulation of the dying process, with mechanical ventilation being instituted and maintained solely for the purpose of preserving the organs until criteria for brain death could be documented. The results were disappointing, and the investigators concluded that "it is usually not feasible, with the restrictions of current law, to procure solid organs for transplantation from anencephalic infants."[41]

Why do these protocols strike many commentators as contrived and even somewhat bizarre? The motives of the individuals involved are certainly commendable: they want to offer the benefits of transplantable organs to individuals who desperately need them. In addition, they are seeking to obtain organs only from individuals who cannot be harmed by the procurement and only in those situations where the patient or a surrogate requests the donation. The problem with these protocols lies not with the motive, but with the method and justification. By manipulating both the process and the definition of death,

these protocols give the appearance that the physicians involved are only too willing to draw the boundary between life and death wherever it happens to maximize the chances for organ procurement.

How can the legitimate desire to increase the supply of transplantable organs be reconciled with the need to maintain a clear and simple distinction between the living and the dead? One way would be to abandon the requirement for the death of the donor prior to organ procurement and, instead, focus upon alternative and perhaps more fundamental ethical criteria to constrain the procurement of organs, such as the principles of consent and nonmaleficence.[42]

For example, policies could be changed such that organ procurement would be permitted only with the consent of the donor or appropriate surrogate and only when doing so would not harm the donor. Individuals who could not be harmed by the procedure would include those who are permanently and irreversibly unconscious (patients in a persistent vegetative state or newborns with anencephaly) and those who are imminently and irreversibly dying.

The American Medical Association's Council on Ethical and Judicial Affairs recently proposed (but has subsequently retracted) a position consistent with this approach.[43] The council stated that, "It is ethically permissible to consider the anencephalic as a potential organ donor, although still alive under the current definition of death," if, among other requirements, the diagnosis is certain and the parents give their permission. The council concluded, "It is normally required that the donor be legally dead before removal of their life-necessary organs . . . The use of the anencephalic neonate as a live donor is a limited exception to the general standard because of the fact that the infant has never experienced, and will never experience, consciousness" (pp. 1617–18).

This alternative approach to organ procurement would require substantial changes in the law. The process of organ procurement would have to be legitimated as a form of justified killing, rather than just as the dissection of a corpse. There is certainly precedent in the law for recognizing instances of justified killing. The concept is also not an anathema to the public, as evidenced by the growing support for euthanasia, another practice that would have to be le-

gally construed as a form of justified killing. Even now, surveys show that one-third of physicians and nurses do not believe brain-dead patients are actually dead, but feel comfortable with the process of organ procurement because the patients are permanently unconscious and/or imminently dying.[44] In other words, many clinicians already seem to justify their actions on the basis of nonmaleficence and consent, rather than with the belief that the patients are actually dead.

This alternative approach would also eliminate the need for protocols like the one being used at the University of Pittsburgh, with its contrived and perhaps questionable approach to declaring death prior to organ procurement. Under the proposed system, qualified individuals who had given their consent could simply have their organs removed under general anesthesia, without first undergoing an orchestrated withdrawal of life support. Anencephalic newborns whose parents requested organ donation could likewise have the organs removed under general anesthesia without the need to wait for the diagnosis of brain death.

The diagnosis of death. Seen in this light, the concept of brain death may have become obsolete. Certainly the diagnosis of brain death has been extremely useful during the last several decades, as society has struggled with a myriad of issues that were never encountered before the era of mechanical ventilation and organ transplantation. As society emerges from this transitional period, and as many of these issues are more clearly understood as questions that are inherently unrelated to the distinction between life and death, then the concept of brain death may no longer be useful or relevant. If this is the case, then it may be preferable to return to the traditional standard and limit tests for the determination of death to those based solely upon the permanent cessation of respiration and circulation. Even today we uniformly regard the cessation of respiration and circulation as the standard for determining when patients are ready to be cremated or buried.

Another advantage of a return to the traditional approach is that it would represent a "common denominator" in the definition of death that virtually all cultural groups and religious traditions would find acceptable.[45] Recently both New Jersey and New York have enacted statutes that recognize the objections of particular religious views to the concept of brain death. In New Jersey, physicians are prohibited from declaring brain death in persons who come from religious traditions that do not accept the concept.[46] Return to a cardiorespiratory standard would eliminate problems with these objections.

Linda Emanuel recently proposed a "bounded zone" definition of death that shares some features with the approach outlined here.[47] Her proposal would adopt the cardiorespiratory standard as a "lower bound" for determining death that would apply to all cases, but would allow individuals to choose a definition of death that encompassed neurologic dysfunction up to the level of the permanent vegetative state (the "higher bound"). The practical implications of such a policy would be similar to some of those discussed here, in that it would (1) allow patients and surrogates to request organ donation when and if the patients were diagnosed with whole-brain death, permanent vegetative state, or anencephaly, and (2) it would permit rejection of the diagnosis of brain death by patients and surrogates opposed to the concept. Emanuel's proposal would not permit organ donation from terminal and imminently dying patients, however, prior to the diagnosis of death.

Despite these similarities, these two proposals differ markedly in the justifications used to support their conclusions. Emanuel follows the President's Commission in seeking to address several separate questions by reference to the diagnosis of death, whereas the approach suggested here would adopt a single and uniform definition of death, and then seek to resolve questions around organ donation on a different ethical and legal foundation.

Emanuel's proposal also provides another illustration of the problems encountered when a variety of diverse issues all hinge upon the definition of death. Under her scheme, some individuals would undoubtedly opt for a definition of death based on the "higher bound" of the permanent vegetative state in order to permit the donation of their vital organs if they should develop this condition. However, few of these individuals would probably agree to being cremated while still breathing, even if they were vegetative. Most likely, they would not want to be cremated until after they had sustained a cardiorespiratory arrest. Once again, this creates the awkward and confusing necessity of diagnosing death for one purpose (organ donation) but not for another (cremation). Only by abandoning the concept of brain death is it possible to adopt a definition of death that is valid for all purposes, while separating questions of organ donation from dependence upon the life/death dichotomy.

Turning Back

The tension between the need to maintain workable and practical standards for the procurement of transplantable organs and our desire to have a conceptually coherent account of death is an issue that must be given serious attention. Resolving these inconsistencies by moving toward a higher-brain definition of death would most likely create additional practical problems regarding accurate diagnosis as well as introduce concepts that are highly counterintuitive to the general public. Uncoupling the link between organ transplantation and brain death, on the other hand, offers a number of advantages. By shifting the ethical foundations for organ donation to the principles of nonmaleficence and consent, the pool of potential donors may be substantially increased. In addition, by reverting to a simpler and more traditional definition of death, the long-standing debate over fundamental inconsistencies in the concept of brain death may finally be resolved.

The most difficult challenge for this proposal would be to gain acceptance of the view that killing may sometimes be a justifiable necessity for procuring transplantable organs. Careful attention to the principles of consent and nonmaleficence should provide an adequate bulwark against slippery slope concerns that this practice would be extended in unforeseen and unacceptable ways. Just as the euthanasia debate often seems to turn less upon abstract theoretical concerns and more upon the empirical question of whether guidelines for assisted dying would be abused, so the success of this proposal could also rest upon factual questions of societal acceptance and whether this approach would erode respect for human life and the integrity of clinicians. While the answers to these questions are not known, the potential benefits of this proposal make it worthy of continued discussion and debate.

Acknowledgements

The author thanks numerous friends and colleagues for critical readings of the manuscript, with special acknowledgments to Dan Wikler and Linda Emanuel.

References

1. Some of the more notable critiques include Robert M. Veatch, "The Whole-Brain-Oriented Concept of Death. An Outmoded Philosophical Formulation," *Journal of Thanatology* 3 (1975): 13–30; Michael B. Green and Daniel Wikler, "Brain Death and Personal Identity," *Philosophy and Public Affairs* 9 (1980): 105–33; Stuart J. Youngner and Edward T. Bartlett, "Human Death and High Technology: The Failure of the Whole-Brain Formulations," *Annals of Internal Medicine* 99 (1983): 252–58; Amir Halevy and Baruch Brody, "Brain Death: Reconciling Definitions, Criteria, and Tests," *Annals of Internal Medicine* 119 (1993): 519–25.
2. Stuart J. Youngner, "Defining Death: A Superficial and Fragile Consensus," *Archives of Neurology* 49 (1992): 570–72.
3. President's Commission for the Study of Ethical Problems in Medicine and Biomedical and Behavioral Research, *Defining Death* (Washington, D.C.: Government Printing Office, 1981).
4. Karen Gervais has been especially articulate in defining these levels. See Karen G. Gervais, *Redefining Death* (New Haven: Yale University Press, 1986); "Advancing the Definition of Death: A Philosophical Essay," *Medical Humanities Review* 3, no. 2 (1989): 7–19.
5. James L. Bernat, Charles M. Culver, and Bernard Gert, "On the Definition and Criterion of Death," *Annals of Internal Medicine* 94 (1981): 389–94; James L. Bernat, "How Much of the Brain Must Die in Brain Death?" *Journal of Clinical Ethics* 3 (1992): 21–26.
6. Report of the Medical Consultants on the Diagnosis of Death, "Guidelines for the Determination of Death," *JAMA* 246 (1981): 2184–86.
7. Aspects of this analysis have been explored previously in, Robert D. Truog and James C. Fackler, "Rethinking Brain Death," *Critical Care Medicine* 20 (1992): 1705–13; Halevy and Brody, "Brain Death."
8. H. Schrader et al., "Changes of Pituitary Hormones in Brain Death," *Acta Neurochirurgica* 52 (1980): 239–48; Kristen M. Outwater and Mark A. Rockoff, "Diabetes Insipidus Accompanying Brain Death in Children," *Neurology* 34 (1984): 1243–46; James C. Fackler, Juan C. Troncoso, and Frank R. Gioia, "Age-Specific Characteristics of Brain Death in Children," *American Journal of Diseases of Childhood* 142 (1988): 999–1003.
9. Schrader et al., "Changes of Pituitary Hormones in Brain Death"; H. J. Gramm et al., "Acute Endocrine Failure after Brain Death," *Transplantation* 54 (1992): 851–57.
10. Report of Medical Consultants on the Diagnosis of Death, "Guidelines for the Determination of Death," p. 339.
11. Madeleine J. Grigg et al., "Electroencephalographic Activity after Brain Death," *Archives of Neurology* 44 (1987): 948–54; A. Earl Walker, *Cerebral Death*, 2nd ed. (Baltimore: Urban & Schwarzenberg, 1981), pp. 89–90;

and Christopher Pallis, "ABC of Brain Stem Death. The Arguments about the EEG," *British Medical Journal [Clinical Research]* 286 (1983): 284–87.

12. Ernst Rodin et al., "Brainstem Death," *Clinical Electroencephalography* 16 (1985): 63–71.

13. Randall C. Wetzel et al., "Hemodynamic Responses in Brain Dead Organ Donor Patients," *Anesthesia and Analgesia* 64 (1985): 125–28; S. H. Pennefather, J. H. Dark, and R. E. Bullock, "Haemodynamic Responses to Surgery in Brain-Dead Organ Donors," *Anaesthesia* 48 (1993): 1034–38; and D. J. Hill, R. Munglani, and D. Sapsford, "Haemodynamic Responses to Surgery in Brain-Dead Organ Donors," *Anaesthesia* 49 (1994): 835–36.

14. Bernat, "How Much of the Brain Must Die in Brain Death?"

15. Paul A. Byrne, Sean O'Reilly, and Paul M. Quay, "Brain Death—An Opposing Viewpoint," *JAMA* 242 (1979): 1985–90.

16. Gaetano F. Molinari, "The NINCDS Collaborative Study of Brain Death: A Historical Perspective," in U.S. Department of Health and Human Services, *NINCDS Monograph No. 24. NIH Publication No. 81–2286* (1980): 1–32.

17. Pallis, "ABC of Brain Stem Death," pp. 123–24; Bryan Jennett and Catherine Hessett, "Brain Death in Britain as Reflected in Renal Donors," *British Medical Journal* 283 (1981): 359–62; Peter M. Black, "Brain Death (first of two parts)," *NEJM* 299 (1978): 338–44.

18. President's Commission, *Defining Death.*

19. "An Appraisal of the Criteria of Cerebral Death, A Summary Statement: A Collaborative Study," *JAMA* 237 (1977): 982–86.

20. Green and Wikler, "Brain Death and Personal Identity."

21. President's Commission, *Defining Death.*

22. Green and Wikler, "Brain Death and Personal Identity"; Daniel Wikler, "Brain Death: A Durable Consensus?" *Bioethics* 7 (1993): 239–46.

23. David R. Field et al., "Maternal Brain Death During Pregnancy: Medical and Ethical issues," *JAMA* 260 (1988): 816–22; Masanobu Washida et al., "Beneficial Effect of Combined 3,5,3'-Triiodothyronine and Vasopressin Administration on Hepatic Energy Status and Systemic Hemodynamics after Brain Death," *Transplantation* 54 (1992): 44–49.

24. Stuart J. Youngner et al., " 'Brain Death' and Organ Retrieval: A Cross-Sectional Survey of Knowledge and Concepts among Health Pro-

fessionals," *JAMA* 261 (1989): 2205–10.

25. Daniel Wikler and Alan J. Weisbard, "Appropriate Confusion over 'Brain Death,' " *JAMA* 261 (1989): 2246.

26. Margareta Sanner, "A Comparison of Public Attitudes toward Autopsy, Organ Donation, and Anatomic Dissection: A Swedish Survey," *JAMA* 271 (1994): 284–88, at 287.

27. Green and Wikler, "Brain Death and Personal Identity."

28. Robert M. Arnold and Stuart J. Youngner, "The Dead Donor Rule: Should We Stretch It, Bend It, or Abandon It?" *Kennedy Institute of Ethics Journal* 3 (1993): 263–78.

29. Some of the many works defending this view include: Green and Wikler, "Brain Death and Personal Identity"; Gervais, *Redefining Death,* Truog and Fackler, "Rethinking Brain Death"; and Robert M. Veatch, *Death, Dying, and the Biological Revolution* (New Haven: Yale University Press, 1989).

30. The Multi-Society Task Force on PVS, "Medical Aspects of the Persistent Vegetative State," *NEJM* 330 (1994): 1499–1508 and 1572–79; D. Alan Shewmon, "Anencephaly: Selected Medical Aspects," *Hastings Center Report* 18, no. 5 (1988): 11–19.

31. Nancy L. Childs and Walt N. Mercer, "Brief Report: Late Improvement in Consciousness after Post-Traumatic Vegetative State," *NEJM* 334 (1996): 24–25; James L. Bernat, "The Boundaries of the Persistent Vegetative State," *Journal of Clinical Ethics* 3 (1992): 176–80.

32. Medical Task Force on Anencephaly, "The Infant with Anencephaly," *NEJM* 322 (1990): 669–74; Shewmon, "Anencephaly: Selected Medical Aspects."

33. Jeffrey R. Botkin and Stephen G. Post, "Confusion in the Determination of Death: Distinguishing Philosophy from Physiology," *Perspectives in Biology and Medicine* 36 (1993): 129–38.

34. The Multi-Society Task Force on PVS, "Medical Aspects of the Persistent Vegetative State."

35. Marcia Angell, "After Quinlan: The Dilemma of the Persistent Vegetative State," *NEJM* 330 (1994): 1524–25.

36. Wikler, "Brain Death: A Durable Consensus?"

37. President's Commission, *Defining Death,* p. 84.

38. Report of the Ad Hoc Committee of the Harvard Medical School to Examine the Definition of Brain Death, "A Definition of Irreversible Coma," *JAMA* 205 (1968): 337–40.

39. "University of Pittsburgh Medical Center Policy and Procedure Manual: Management of Terminally Ill Patients Who May Become Organ Donors after Death," *Kennedy Institute of Ethics Journal* 3 (1993): A1-A15; Stuart Youngner and Robert Arnold, "Ethical, Psychosocial, and Public Policy Implications of Procuring Organs from Non-Heart-Beating Cadaver Donors," *JAMA* 269 (1993): 2769–74. Of note, the June 1993 issue of the *Kennedy Institute of Ethics Journal* is devoted to this topic in its entirety.

40. Joanne Lynn, "Are the Patients Who Become Organ Donors Under the Pittsburgh Protocol for 'Non-Heart-Beating Donors' Really Dead?" *Kennedy Institute of Ethics Journal* 3 (1993): 167–78.

41. Joyce L. Peabody, Janet R. Emergy, and Stephen Ashwal, "Experience with Anencephalic Infants as Prospective Organ Donors," *NEJM* 321 (1989): 344–50.

42. See for example, Norman Fost, "The New Body Snatchers: On Scott's 'The Body as Property,' " *American Bar Foundation Research Journal* 3 (1983): 718–32; John A. Robertson, "Relaxing the Death Standard for Organ Donation in Pediatric Situations," in *Organ Substitution Technology: Ethical, Legal, and Public Policy Issues,* ed. D. Mathieu (Boulder, Col.: Westview Press, 1988), pp. 69–76; Arnold and Youngner, "The Dead Donor Rule."

43. AMA Council on Ethical and Judicial Affairs, "The Use of Anencephalic Neonates as Organ Donors," *JAMA* 273 (1995): 1614–18. After extensive debate among AMA members, the Council retracted this position statement. See Charles W. Plows, "Reconsideration of AMA Opinion on Anencephalic Neonates as Organ Donors," *JAMA* 275 (1996): 443–44.

44. Youngner et al., " 'Brain Death' and Organ Retrieval."

45. Jiro Nudeshima, "Obstacles to Brain Death and Organ Transplantation in Japan," *Lancet* 338 (1991): 1063–64.

46. Robert S. Olick, "Brain Death, Religious Freedom, and Public Policy: New Jersey's Landmark Legislative Initiative," *Kennedy Institute of Ethics Journal* 1 (1991): 275–88.

47. Linda L. Emanuel, "Reexamining Death: The Asymptotic Model and a Bounded Zone Definition," *Hastings Center Report* 25, no. 4 (1995): 27–35.

Unit 2

Key Points to Consider

❖ Since children are experiencing death situations at an average age of 8 years, what societal steps can be taken to help children better cope with the death of a person or a pet?

❖ Are the elderly in America "warehoused" and put away to die? Can you present evidence of such "warehousing"? How might the image of the elderly be improved in our society? Is growing old really "the best is yet to be," or is growing old really "hell"?

❖ What do you recall from your own childhood experiences with fairy tales and death? Do you remember any death themes in children's literature and how you reacted at the time? Describe.

 **Links**   **www.dushkin.com/online/**

These sites are annotated on pages 4 and 5.

Death is something we must accept, though no one really understands it. We can talk about death, learn from each other, and help each other. By better understanding death conceptualization at various stages and in different relationships within the life cycle, we can better help each other. It is not our intent to suggest that age should be viewed as the sole determinant of one's death concept. Many other factors influence this cognitive development such as level of intelligence, physical and mental well-being, previous emotional reactions to various life experiences, religious background, other social and cultural forces, personal identity and self-worth appraisals, and exposure to or threats of death. Nonetheless, we will discuss death and death perceptions at various stages from the cradle to the grave or, as some say, the womb to the tomb.

Research on very young children's conceptions of death still does not reveal an adequate understanding of their responses. A need exists to look more carefully at the dynamics of the young and to their families' relating to the concept of death. Adults, several decades later, recall vivid details about their first death experiences, and for many it was a traumatic event filled with fear, anger, and frustration.

In "Communication Among Children, Parents, and Funeral Directors," Daniel Schaefer, a funeral director, encourages parents to talk to their children about death. As parents, we need to recognize the insecurity often found in children at the time of a death and to deal with the situation accordingly. Children can generally accept a great deal of life experiences; the problem is that we adults are often inept in our dealing with dying and death, and thus we may practice avoidance in relating to children. We must remember that children, too, have feelings. They especially need emotional support during a crisis such as death. When children themselves are dying, our society has not done a very good job of addressing their pain. This topic is discussed in Joan Stephenson's "Palliative and Hospice Care Needed for Children With Life-Threatening Conditions."

Children's exposure to death may come through children's literature. In her essay, "Children, Death, and Fairy Tales," Elizabeth Lamers explores death themes in fairy tales and examines the evolution of these themes in children's literature.

As we enter into our college years, death does not disappear. College deaths are a rarity, like high school deaths, nonetheless, when they occur, it is especially difficult for individuals on

college campuses to adjust to the situation. Such deaths are out of the ordinary, and indeed are not supposed to happen. Deaths on college campuses are addressed in Carlin Romano's "When Death Breaches the Campus Walls."

As we move into "the autumn of our lives" and are classified as "elderly" (65 years of age and beyond), death surrounds us, and we are especially made aware that we are reaching the end of the tunnel, not the beginning, as is the case with children and adolescents. Though old age is often pictured as gloom and doom ("growing old is hell"), it can be viewed as "the best is yet to be," as poet Robert Browning said. Such a positive attitude is pointed out in "The Aging of America: Problem or Solution?" One should not go into the "senior years" unprepared, however, as Guy Halverson observes in "Coming to Terms With Long-Term Care."

Communication Among Children, Parents, and Funeral Directors

Daniel J. Schaefer

I have been a funeral director for the last twenty-five years. My family has been in the funeral service for one hundred and seven years. We have buried our friends; I have buried parents of my friends and children of my friends. Over the last ten years or so, I have found that something is missing: there have been fewer children attending funerals than I knew were in my friends' families. I began to ask parents, very simply, "What are you saying to your kids about this death in your family?" The replies of 1,800 sets of the parents of more than 3,600 children proved that they were basically unprepared to talk with their children about death and terribly uneasy about doing so, but not unwilling to say something once they were prepared by someone or given appropriate information.

The bits of information that I am going to present are not a standard message. They are building materials. The blueprint is individual to each family, so what we do is to take the family's blueprint, which has their particular death circumstance, then take the building materials, and build a message that parents can give to their children. For the families that I serve, I do this on an individual basis.

TALKING TO CHILDREN ABOUT DEATH

Thinking about talking to children about death is upsetting. It makes many parents anxious. It has been helpful for parents to know how many other parents feel. On Memorial Day two years ago, at three in the morning, I received a call that my brother had been killed in an automobile accident. I have five children, and I knew that four hours from then I was going to have to explain to them about their uncle. I said to my wife, "It's unusual—I've done this with hundreds of families, but I

have this thing in the pit of my stomach. I *know* what to say to these kids; I know exactly what I'm going to do. Can you imagine how it must be for somebody who doesn't know what to say?"

What do people say about speaking to children about death? Some are sure that they do have to talk to their children and some say they are not sure that it is necessary. Some parents who believe that something should be said are told by others that they should avoid upsetting their children. Parents naturally tend to build a protective wall around their children. What I say to them is "Let's look at the wall, let's see if it works, and if it does work, who is it working for? Is it working for you, to protect you from your child's grief? If we look over the wall, what do we see on the other side? Do we see a kid who is comfortable or do we see, in fact, a kid who is a solitary mourner?"

When parents plan to speak to their children about death, they have to understand that what they are about to do is not easy, that they are going to be upset and stressed, that they are probably going to lack energy, and that they are going to feel unable to concentrate. They are going to be afraid of their own emotions and the effect that these emotions will have on their children. They are not going to know what their children understand, and basically they have to realize that they want to protect their children from pain. It is important that parents know ahead of time that they are going to feel this way.

What do other people say to them? They say, "Your kids don't know what's going on," "Wait until later," "Tell them a fairy tale," "Don't say anything," "Send them away until the funeral is over," or "Do you really want to put your kids through all this?" implying that no loving parent would. It is almost frightening to talk with one's children on this subject, but I believe that it is dangerous not to.

Almost all parents will agree that children are surprisingly perceptive. They overhear conversations, read emotions and responses around them, and ask questions, directly and indirectly. They *will* receive messages; it is impossible not to communicate. No matter how hard parents try not to, they are going to communicate their grief to their children. Without some explanation, the children will be confused and anxious. What I say to parents is, "Since you're going to be sending a message out anyway, why don't you try to control the message?" A message is controlled by making sure that the information is true, geared for the age of the child, and, if possible, delivered in surroundings that make the child's reception of the message a little easier to handle.

For parents, feeling in control is important at a time when feeling out of control is routine and common, and when helping the child—the most dependent person in the family at that time—is also critical. The discussion between parent and child may be the child's only chance to understand what is happening. Sometimes, however, the pressure and enormity of this task, along with the advice of others, really proves too great for parents. They choose a short-term covering for themselves, without realizing the long-term effect on their children.

Explaining the How and Why of Death

Children have to know from the beginning what sad is. They have to know why their parents are sad and why they themselves are sad. So parents can begin with, "This is a very sad time," or "A very sad thing has happened," or "Mommy and Daddy are sad because. . . ." Children have to know that it is a death that has made the parents sad: with no explanation, they may think that they have caused the sadness. They also have to know that it is appropriate to feel sad.

The next stage involves an explanation of death and what it means. Death basically means that a person's body stops working and will not work any more. It won't do any of the things it used to do. It won't walk, talk, or move; none of its parts work; it does not see and it does not hear. This foundation is what parents feel comfortable referring back to when children ask questions like "Will Grandpa ever move again?" "Why can't they fix him?" "Why isn't he moving?" "Is he sleeping?" "Can he hear me?" "Can he eat after he's buried?" If parents come up with different answers to all of these questions, it becomes confusing, but when they have a foundation, they can come back to it repeatedly. The notion that something has stopped working is a firm foundation for children, and parents feel comfortable in not lying or deceiving in using this type of explanation.

Because death is a form of abandonment, the words "passed away," "gone away," or "left us," that many people use hold out to the child the hope that the deceased will return, which of course causes tremendous frustration while they wait for the person to return. Appropriate explanations to children of why a particular death happened might be, for example, in a case of terminal illness, "Because the disease couldn't be stopped. The person became very, very sick, the body wore out, and the body stopped working"; in a case of suicide, "Some people's bodies get sick and don't work right, and some people's minds don't work right. They can't see things clearly, and they feel that the only way to solve their problems is to take their own life"; in a case of miscarriage, "Sometimes a baby is just starting to grow; something happens and makes it stop. We don't know what it was—it wasn't anything that anyone did."

CHILDREN'S REACTIONS TO DEATH

When people start to take this information and relate it to their own family situations in preparation for confronting their families, they want to know what they need to be concerned about and what to look for. Even newborn infants and toddlers know when things are different. The smaller they are, the less likely it is that they will be able to figure out why. Children respond to changes in behavior; they sense when life patterns change. Infants may alter their nursing patterns; toddlers become cranky, and change their sleeping and eating patterns. Excitement at home, new people around, parents gone at odd times, a significant person missing, a sad atmosphere—children know that something is different and react accordingly. When parents expect these changes in their children, they can respond to them more sensibly.

Piaget says that children between the ages of three and six years see death as reversible. The way this translates for parents (and for children) is that people will come back, that dead is not forever. Parents have said to me, "How could a child think that somebody will return?" From a child's point of view, ET returns, Jesus and Lazarus returned, and Road Runner returns constantly. And children may misinterpret the rise-again eulogies often given by clergy.

Several years ago (1978), "Sesame Street" produced a program dealing with the death of Mr. Hooper. The program was written up in newspapers and other publications as being an advance for the education of children. The problem is that Mr. Hooper has returned in reruns of the show, so that children who experienced his death now find that Mr. Hooper is back again.

People may say, "My child isn't affected by his grandfather's death—he's only four years old." I say, "Why should he be affected? As far as he's concerned, Grandpa's only going to be dead for a little while." Knowing how children perceive death helps parents to understand their children better, so that they will not become upset when a child continues to ask questions. They know that children in that age range can be expected to ask more questions.

Children also tend to connect events that are not connected. Does this death mean that someone else is going to die? "Grandpa died after he had a headache. Mommy has a headache. Does that mean that she is going to die?" "Old people die. Daddy is old [he is thirty]. Is he going to die?" This means that we have to explain the difference between being very, very sick and just sick like Mommy or Daddy might be; the difference between being very, very old and over twenty; and the difference between being very old and very sick and being very old but not very sick.

Children ages six to nine know that death is final, but they still think about return. They need a more detailed explanation of why a person has died than younger children do. With these children, it is much more important to distinguish between a fatal illness and just being sick—to say, "It's not like when you get sick, or when Mommy or Daddy get sick." If a parent tells a child, "Grandpa had a pain in his stomach, went to the hospital, and died," what is the child to think the next time that Mommy has menstrual cramps? What are children to think when a grandparent dies from lung cancer after a tremendous bout of coughing and then find that their father has a cough? It is normal for children in that situation to start to cling to the father and ask, "Are you okay?"

Children of this age may not want to go to a house where a person has died because "it's spooky." They also have to deal with and understand their emotions, to know that crying, feeling bad, and being angry are all acceptable behaviors.

Children ages nine to twelve move much closer to an adult sense of grieving. They are more aware of the details of an illness and more aware of the impact of a death on them. Consequently, they need more emotional support. They need to know that their feelings are acceptable and that someone is supportive of those feelings.

Teenagers also need support with their new feelings. Parents may find it better to share their own feelings with their adolescent children. Teenagers also have to understand why a person has died.

At the funeral of a friend, I met a man I used to know, another funeral director. He said to me, "It's strange. When I grew up in Queens with my grandfather, we lived in a two-family house for ten-and-a-half years. When my parents had enough money, they bought a house on Long Island, and we moved there. That was in the summer. On my birthday, in October, Grandpa didn't send me a card. I was a little concerned about that, but when Grandpa didn't come for Thanksgiving, and then when he didn't come for Christmas, I asked my mother where Grandpa was. She said he couldn't come." My friend went on: "I couldn't think what I could possibly have done to this dear man that I had spent my childhood with that would cause him not to like me any more. Then it went on again. Grandpa never came in the summer, then it was another Thanksgiving and another

Christmas. It wasn't until I was thirteen that they told me that my grandfather had died. I thought that was bizarre until a woman came into my funeral home three weeks ago and when I said to her, as I say to everybody, 'What did you say to your kids about the death of your mother?' she said, 'I haven't told them. I just told them she went on vacation in Vermont.' " So the difference between ten years ago, or fifteen, or twenty years ago and today is not so great for uninformed parents.

Responsibility

People say, "How can a child feel responsible for the death of another person?" Yet, they will say to their children, "You're driving me crazy," "You'll be the death of me yet," or "Don't give me a heart attack!" Adults may say such things as figures of speech, but children do not always see it that way. "If only I had prayed harder," they may say. Children basically see God as a rewarder or punisher; He rewards good behavior and punishes bad. Therefore, if a child does a bad thing that only he or she knows about, God may punish the child by the death of someone in the child's family. If illness or death follows a misdeed, the child can feel really responsible for this. For example, when a parent leaves the home, a child may say, "If I had cleaned my room (done my chores, hadn't wet my pants, done better in school), maybe he (or she) wouldn't have left." This is what happens when no explanation is given to a child about why a person has died. When a grandparent stops visiting, the child again may say, "What did I do?"

Magical Thinking

Some children believe that by wishing that a person will die, they can cause the person's death. They sometimes also believe that if they think about the death of a person who is dying, they themselves may die.

Anger

This is a common response at the time of a death and one that is extremely damaging to families. Understanding it and anticipating its presence helps families deal with anger from both sides, the parent's and the children's. Children can be angry at parents for not telling them that the deceased was sick, for having spent so much time with the deceased and not enough time with them, for not allowing them to attend the funeral, or just because they need someone to be angry at.

I offer two examples of children's anger at parents. When my brother died, two days after the funeral there was a tremendous downpour. There were two inches of water in the back yard, and my ten-year-old son came to me and said, "I want to pitch my tent in the back yard." I said, "David, you can't pitch a tent. There are two inches of water in the yard!" He became angry, threw the tent down, and walked away. I said to him, "Look, I'll tell you why you're angry: you don't have anyone to be angry at. You can't be angry at your uncle because he was in an automobile accident. He wasn't drunk and he wasn't driving fast. It was a wet road, he didn't know it, and the car turned over and he was killed. You can't be angry at the doctors or the hospital because he was dead when he arrived there." I said, "There's nobody else to be angry at, so the next possibility is to be angry at me. As long as you understand that, it's okay." He came back a while later and said, "You know, after thinking about it, I don't know why I ever wanted to pitch my tent in the yard."

The second example came a few days ago when I spoke to a woman about coming to a funeral. She said, "You know, I was seven years old when they took me to my grandfather's funeral. I could go to the funeral, I could sit outside—my parents even bought me a brand new dress—but I was not allowed to go in and say good-bye to Grandpa. So you know what? I never wore the dress again and I never talked about Grandpa again."

Children can also be angry at themselves for wishing that a person would die or for not visiting or helping a dying person. One young boy had seen his grandfather walking down the street carrying some packages and noticed that his grandfather was not doing so well. But Grandfather did not do well a lot of the time, so the boy helped his grandfather take the packages inside, went on home, and did not say anything to his father about his grandfather. The grandfather died of a heart attack in the house. Later, the boy's father came to me and asked, "What am I going to say? My son said, 'If only I'd told you this time that Grandpa didn't look well, maybe we could have done something.' " Two weeks ago a mother came to me and said, "My daughter thinks that my mother may have died because she failed to send her a get-well card. She thought that maybe it would have saved her if she had sent it."

The driver of a car, the doctor at a hospital, the deceased for putting themselves in dangerous situations, even the event that caused a death—these are just a few examples of the legitimate targets of children's anger. When parents know that children are responding with anger or that they may do so, the parents will do best if they address it directly with the children. The important point for parents is that they feel much more in control when they can anticipate this kind of anger. They know the historical background of their old circumstances, their own blueprint, and if they consider these they can help their children through their anger.

Guilt

This is another aspect of grief and grieving. Knowing that a child may feel guilt, or having it pointed out, lets parents know that their children can, on one hand, be angry at the deceased and, on the other, feel guilty about being angry. Children may express their guilt in statements such as "I didn't do enough," "I should have visited him before he died," and "If only I hadn't gone to the movies last week instead of going to see Grandpa, I would have been able to say goodbye before he died." All of these "shoulds" and "if onlys" can have a tremendous impact on a family if they are not directed, if nobody anticipated them, and if nobody explains them to the children.

CHILDREN AND FUNERALS

People feel the need to know how to explain what is going to happen next: "After I've explained to my children that this person has died, what do I say to them about what's going to happen now?" I have some material in script form that I offer to families, but basically parents have to start from the beginning with a child. They can say, "Grandpa will be taken from where he died to a funeral home; it's a place where they'll keep him for a few days until he's buried. He'll be dressed in clothes he liked and put into a casket—that's a box we use so that no dirt gets on him when he's buried. People will come to the funeral home to visit and say how sorry they are that Grandpa has died. Because his body isn't working any more, it won't move or do any of the things it used to do, but if you want to come and say some prayers, you can."

The basic premise here is that people will ask whether or not they should bring a child to the funeral home. People are surprised when I say, "Never! Don't ever bring children to a funeral home if you're not going to prepare them for it ahead of time." My son had cardiac surgery a year and a half ago. Before his operation, they showed him the operating room, the recovery room, and the intensive care unit. He knew everything that was going to happen to him before he went into the hospital for the surgery. His doctor even drew a diagram of the operation for him and made a model of the surgical repair out of clay for him. But people will still waltz children into a funeral home and say, "We're just going to see Grandma." Then they wonder why the children are upset when they walk in and find out that Grandma is lying down in a casket and not moving.

Children should be treated like people and given the same concern we give anyone else. They should hear an explanation of what will happen and then be given the opportunity to come to the funeral home or not, but they cannot make that decision without information. If children decide to come, they should be prepared further. They should be told the color of the rugs and walls, whether there are plants or paintings, whether there are flowers, what color the casket is, what color clothing the deceased is wearing, and that the deceased is lying down and not moving. The children should be informed so completely that when they walk into the funeral home it is almost as if they have been there before. Does it work? Children have walked into my funeral home and checked off exactly the points that I covered with their parents three hours before—"Oh, there's a green rug, there's the painting on the wall, there are the flowers." When this happens, I know that the parents have used the information I have provided, and I know that the children are comfortable because the place is not strange to them. All of this draws a child into the family support network on the same side of the wall, rather than putting the child alone on the other side of the wall.

We cannot assume that parents speak to their children about death or that they know how to do so. We cannot assume that if a death occurs suddenly in the middle of the night the parents will be prepared to talk to their children about it at seven o'clock in the morning when they get up. We cannot assume that "user-friendly" information is available, that if parents were given a booklet it would apply, or even that they would read it. I used to think that talking to children about death was only the concern of parents, but another funeral director who is using my program told me that a senior citizen came to him and said, "I'm here because I want to make sure that when I die my children will provide my grandchildren with this type of information."

We cannot assume that children are not talking or thinking about a death, that they are not affected when a family pet dies or by the deaths they see every day on television, or by the death of a neighbor or classmate. We cannot assume that children are prepared in any way to come to a funeral. We cannot assume that their parents have answered their questions or that the children have asked questions. For example, I have found that about 85 percent of the children between the ages of four and twelve who come to a funeral home and see a half-closed casket do not realize or believe that the deceased's legs are in the bottom of the casket. How do I know? Because I have said to parents, address that issue with children: Walk into the funeral home and up to the casket, and say, "You know, some kids think that the whole person isn't there, so if you want us to, we'll show you the rest of the person." Some parents respond by saying "No, I don't want to do that, I don't want to deal with that." But I have found that their children will accept my invitation to have the bottom part of the casket opened so that they can look inside. I have been putting a family into a limousine and heard a child ask, "Why did they cut Grandma up?" and heard the mother say, "What do you mean they cut Grandma up?" So I have said, "She only saw half of Grandma; let's go back inside." We have gone back in, opened the bottom of the casket, and the child has said, "Oh, yes, she is all there."

Children constantly ask for this type of information. A mother said to me, "Why does my child ask if that's a dummy inside the casket? And why does she ask me how they got the dummy to look so much like Grandpa?" And I say, "What did you say to your child? And she says that she told the child that her grandfather had died and gone to heaven. So I say, "If Grandpa died and went to heaven, who's inside the casket?"

A psychiatrist told me that he had one patient, a five-year-old boy who had been very close to his grandmother. When she died, the boy was told that Grandma had gone right up to heaven. His mother later found the boy standing on the windowsill of the apartment, about to jump out. After the boy was safely on the floor again, his mother asked him why he had been going to jump and what he thought would happen if he did. The boy said, "I would go up, just like Grandma."

So many of the points that seem like separate, discrete bits of information are actually the building materials to be fitted into a family blueprint. When I present this information to parents, they ask, "How do you expect us to put all of this together in our grief? How do you expect us to do that?" I say, "I don't expect you to do that; I expect your funeral director to do it."

Daniel J. Schaefer is a funeral director, Brooklyn, NY.

Children, Death, and Fairy Tales*

Abstract

"Children, Death and Fairy Tales" examines the evolution and transformation of themes relating to death and dying in children's literature, using illuminating parallels from historical demographics of mortality and the development of housing. The classic fairy tale "Little Red Riding Hood" is used to draw these trends together.

Elizabeth P. Lamers, M.A.

Malibu, California

Historical Background

There is a history behind each of the familiar stories that parents read at their children's bedsides. Many of what have now become common fairy tales had their origin in an oral tradition intended as adult entertainment, replete with ribald humor and sensational events. As these tales began to be transcribed and considered more specifically as material intended for children, they began to contain incidents and behavior that reflected the customs of the place and period in which they were written down and that were intended to provide children with a moral education. Especially in the earliest versions, death had a place in children's stories because of its ubiquity and drama. There have been significant transformations to fairy tales, and to the content of children's stories in general, since a literature for children first appeared. Until recently, topics that have come to be considered disturbing to young people, concerning issues that adults would wish to protect them from, have been diluted, softened, and removed from the literature for children. In our modern generations, children have been insulated from an awareness of mortality.

Particularly in the last hundred years, a significant movement away from issues of morality and mortality has taken place. This has reflected the tremendous changes in attitudes concerning children and death over the last century. These changes have coincided with the shifting of the demographics of death in this time period and with the changing of attitudes toward children and their upbringing.

Up to the end of the nineteenth century, the highest mortality rate was to be found in children under the age of fifteen; today the highest rate is found in adults of far more advanced years. In the past, children were exposed to dying because it occurred almost exclusively at home after a short illness; death now occurs almost exclusively in some sort of health care institution following a prolonged illness. Although in recent years hospice programs have sought to return dying to the home, the majority of elderly persons still die either in a rest home or a hospital. As a result, children and even young adults today are commonly separated from the reality of death.[1] This isolation is reinforced by a paucity of material that would introduce children to the universal experiences of dying and death.

The changing composition and structure of the modern family has also had an isolating effect on the young person's awareness of mortality. At the end of the last century, it was common for children to grow up as a member of an extended family consisting of parents, grandparents, aunts and uncles who all lived in the same rural area. A child today is more likely a member of a "nuclear" or one parent family, living in an urban area, often separated from relatives by hundreds of miles. Children in rural areas once were exposed to dying and death in their families, in their communities, and among farm animals. They had repeated opportunities to be close to death, to ask questions about death, and to participate in healing religious and social bereavement ceremonies and rituals.

While once the loss of a relative was an occasion for ceremonies that emphasized and reinforced family coherence, today the death of a relative, especially an elderly or distant one, may pass with little or no observance. Many parents have come to believe that children should be shielded from dying and the facts of death, and it is common today for children to not attend funeral services.[2]

Although children may be exposed to literally hundreds of deaths in television programs and cartoons, these are a different kind of death, typically of a "bad" person, who, because of some evil actions, "deserved" to die. Children's cartoons consistently present a distorted view of mortality, even fostering the especially erroneous conclusion that death is somehow "reversible." With little contradiction, beliefs like these can continue to influence and pervade perceptions of death.[3] They come to stand in place of substantial experiences with dying and death, giving rise to difficulties and misunderstandings in later years, when the child, as an adult, has real experiences with mortality. Beliefs like these have been fostered by the isolation of the child from the experience of death as a part of life, an isolation that can be traced in the transformation that has occurred in the stories and fairy tales that have been read to children since such tales first appeared in written form in the early 1700s.

Books about Death for Children

The removal and glossing over of incidents of dying and death from material that children are exposed to has been occurring regularly since about the 1920s. At the same time religion was being removed from school books. It is only in the last twenty years that this tendency has begun to be reversed, and children's books now often contain topics that were previously taboo, including, feelings, divorce, sex and even death. Religion is still taboo in school books.

From the early 1800s until the 1920s, American children were commonly taught to read with a series of textbooks, such as those by Lyman Cobb, Worcester, Town, Russell, Swan or McGuffey. In *McGuffey's Eclectic Readers,*[4] the subject of many of the selections and poems was the death of a mother or child. These deaths were typically presented as a tragic but an inevitable part of life. The manner in which death was portrayed can be found in such representative examples as William Wordsworth's poem "We Are Seven,"[5] in which a little girl describes her family as having seven children, even though two are dead and buried in the churchyard near their house. The experience of the death of an older sister is also described in this poem. Other selections from the Readers in which death is a theme are: *Old Age and Death*[6] by Edmund Waller, The *Death of Little Nell*[7] by Charles Dickens, Elegy in a *County Churchyard*[8] by Thomas Gray, and *He Giveth His Beloved Sleep*[9] by Elizabeth Barrett Browning.

A selection in the Fourth Reader by an anonymous author, entitled "My Mother's Grave,"[10] provides an emotional account of a young girl's experience with her dying mother. The story aims to make children polite and obedient to their parents, by giving the example of a young girl who didn't realize how fleeting life can be. The author of the story recaptures her thoughts while revisiting the grave of her mother, who had died thirteen years previously. She remembers how she had been unkind to her mortally-ill mother after coming home from a trying day at school. Realizing her lapse in manners later in the evening, she returns to her mother's room to ask forgiveness, to find her mother asleep. The little girl vows to awaken early to "tell how sorry I was for my conduct," yet when she rushes to her mother's room in the brightness of morning she finds her mother dead, with a hand so cold "it made me start." The author relates how, even thirteen years later, her remorse and pain are almost overwhelming. This is not the type of subject matter and emotional content that is generally considered appropriate for today's basal readers.[11] The basal readers commonly used today in classrooms rarely contain any references to death or dying. They might contain a chapter from a book such as *Charlotte's Web,* by E. B. White,[12] but the chapter would not be the one in which Charlotte dies.

Insight into the fashion in which scenes of death and dying were typically portrayed in the nineteenth century can be found in the book *Little Women,* written by Louisa May Alcott in 1869, and still widely read by young readers today. Alcott wrote of the death of young Beth in a straightforward manner that was especially uncommon for her day. Recognizing that her depiction was at odds with the melodramatic scenes that were current in more romantic literature, Alcott added in the paragraph following Beth's death: "Seldom, except in books, do the dying utter memorable words, see visions, or depart with beatified countenances. . . ."[13]

The elements that Alcott took exception to were all common in death scenes in the literature of 1830 to 1880, where they reflected the expectations of an audience that was accustomed to being given a romanticized picture of death and its consequent "final reward" in what was known as "consolation literature." A preoccupation with death and a glorification of the afterlife was evident in popular literature from both England and America in this period. Much of this literature was written either by Protestant clergy (especially Congregationalists and Unitarians), their wives, or other pious women of the congregation.[14]

Between 1940 and 1970 only a few children's books contained references to death. Two that have become classics are *The Dead Bird* by Margaret W. Brown[15] and *Charlotte's Web* by E. B. White.[16] White's publisher initially refused to publish *Charlotte's Web* unless the ending was modified to allow Charlotte to live. White refused.[17] The book was criticized by reviewers who said that death was not "an appropriate subject for children." *Charlotte's Web* is still a best-seller, and often is one of the books which second or third grade teachers choose to read to their classes.

The separation of children from death has diminished somewhat in the last twenty years. Elizabeth Kubler-Ross'[18] early work helped make death a subject that could be discussed and studied. Children's books in the late sixties began to discuss subjects that had previously been neglected, such as death and divorce. During the nineteen seventies and eighties over 200 fiction books were written for children with death as a major theme. Unfortunately very few measured up to the standard set by *Charlotte's Web, Little Women, The Yearling* or *The Dead Bird*. During the same period some very good non-fiction books about death were written for children of various ages. (See resource list at end of chapter.)

This cornucopia of books on death has helped to begin to make death a more acceptable topic for discussion. The hospice movement has also helped by reintroducing home care for dying persons to many communities. Even so, many children are still insulated from death and often are discouraged from attending funerals. It is not unusual to find adults in their forties who have never attended a funeral.[19] The diminished awareness of mortality that begins in childhood is often carried on into adulthood.

The Development of Children's Literature

Prior to the development of a literature intended specifically for children in the middle of the seventeenth century, there were two characteristic ways in which children were considered. The first was a holdover from the age of the Greeks and Romans, in which children were perceived as miniature adults. Another manner of perceiving children, as something infra-human, was distinguished by Michel de Montaigne, the French humanist and essayist of the sixteenth century. It is difficult, however, from a modern perspective, to be sympathetic to Montaigne's assertion that children possessed "neither mental activities nor recognizable body shape."[20]

Authors writing children's literature in the eighteenth century were primarily interested in educating children and assisting them to become socially acceptable human beings. Beyond providing just a certain amount of book learning, they also sought to teach the correct ways to behave. For this reason, all the tales of Charles Perrault had an emphatic moral at their end. They were cautionary tales of what could happen to a child if he or she didn't act in a proper fashion. Some of Perrault's titles were: La Belle au Bois Dormant (Sleeping Beauty),[21] Le Petit Chaperon Rouge (Little Red Riding Hood)[22] and Les Fées (Toads and Diamonds).[23] As pointed out by Maria Tartar in Off With Their Heads!:

> From its inception, children's literature had in it an unusually cruel and coercive streak—one which produced books that relied on brutal intimidation to frighten children into complying with parental demands. This intimidation manifested itself in two very different forms, but both made examples of children. First, there were countless cautionary tales that managed to kill off their protagonists or make their lives perpetually miserable for acts of disobedience. Then there were stories about exemplary behavior which, nonetheless, had a strange way of also ending at the deathbeds of their protagonists."[24]

In 1658, John Amos Comenius's Orbis Sensualium Pictus (A World of Things Obvious to the Senses Drawn in Pictures), a Latin school book, was published. This teaching device was the first picture book for children,[25] and it was also the first to respond to the recognition that children needed their own literature because they were not scaled-down adults. It was still almost a century later, however, before children's literature began to come into its own. In 1744, John Newbery wrote A Little Pretty Pocket Book[26] for children. This book is credited as signifying the "real" start of children's literature in England.

Fairy Tales

Fairy tales provide an excellent example of the fashion in which themes that came to be considered distressing to chil-

dren have been moderated over time, and insulation of children from an awareness of mortality can be traced through the progression of different versions of typical stories. A generalization can be made about fairy tales as they came to be thought of specifically as children's stories: the sexual content was diminished, and the amount of violence tended to be increased. This process can be seen in successive editions of the Brothers Grimm's Fairy Tales. To understand this evolution, it is necessary to have a picture of the environment in which it took place. According to the perception of children's needs current at the time that the Brothers Grimm were writing, children did not need to be protected from portrayals of violence.

William Jordan in Divorce Among the Gulls provides a dramatic context for the state of life that was not untypical for children in London a mere one hundred years after the time that a children's literature came into being:

> "I doubt that any of us can comprehend how brutal the fight for survival has been throughout evolution. We ignore our prehistoric, evolutionary legacy, a world in which most children died in infancy or childhood, where teeth rotted out by the age of twenty, where gangrene took the lives of the injured, where thirty-five was foul old age. Even as recently as 1750 in London, the toll of disease staggers the mind: of 2,239 children born that year, only 168 were still alive five years later."[27]

From its inception, literature for children has been motivated by a belief that children needed written material, not so much for entertainment, but to prepare them for life. The majority of books published and intended for children up through the 1800s can be compared to James Janeway's A Token for Children: Being an Account of the Conversion, Holy and Exemplary Lives, and Joyful Deaths of Several Young Children (1671–72).[28] The London Bills of Mortality for the period shortly following the publication of Janeway's book show that the mortality rate of children age five and under was running as high as 66 percent.[29] Writers of this era commonly concurred with Janeway's position that they held a sacred duty to salvage the souls of those who were "not too little to go to Hell." The exemplary stories in A Token for Children were also designed to provide comfort to children faced with the tragedy of a sibling's death or confronted with their own mortality when visited by some dread disease.[30]

The violence and death in stories written for children takes on a different light when put in the context of such high rates of mortality. The practice of abandoning unwanted children either at the Foundlings' Hospital or on church steps was increasing in the seventeen hundreds. It was not just the poor but all classes who contributed to the ranks of abandoned children. The foundling institution was established to make it possible to dispose of infants without leaving any record. Buffon noted in 1772 that about one-third of all children born in Paris that year were abandoned. Jean-Jacques Rousseau (1712–1778) claimed to have turned his five children over to the state, leaving them at the Foundlings' Hospital at birth.[31]

A high mortality rate for children was reflected in children's literature. As Freud noted in The Interpretation of Dreams, half the human race failed to survive the childhood years.[32]

The characteristically romanticized depiction of an afterlife, that was superior to the life of this world, was seen as a way to help children cope with the brutal facts of the life they had no choice but to lead. In the seventeenth and eighteenth centuries, children were routinely required—not just encouraged—to attend public executions so that they could see the price of criminal behavior. This says much about the methods of child rearing believed appropriate in this era.[33]

The Brothers Grimm's story "Aschenputtel," or "Cinderella," shows an emphasis on punishment that was lacking in the earliest oral versions, and that increased in intensity in subsequent editions. In the early version, taken by Perrault from the oral tradition, Cinderella forgave her stepsisters for mistreating her and introduced them at court. Grimm's first version has Cinderella's sisters turning pale and being horrified when Cinderella becomes a princess, but in the second edition the sisters are punished by being blinded by pigeons that peck out their eyes.[34]

In the Brothers Grimm's "Hansel and Grethel" there is a description of how horribly the witch howled when Grethel pushed her into her own oven and how "... Grethel ran away, and therefore she was left to burn, just as she had left many poor little children to burn."[35] The use of violence as punishment for bad behavior is typical in fairy stories. And violent occurrences were frequently shown to be the result of even minor misdeeds. This tendency is evident in the collection of stories found in *Struwwelpeter*. In these short tales Little Pauline plays with matches and goes up in flames, and Conrad the Thumbsucker gets his thumbs sliced off. As Tartar observes the interesting point here is that "... the weight is given to the punishment (often fully half the text is devoted to its description) and the disproportionate relationship between the childish offense and the penalty for it make the episode disturbing."[36]

The removal of sexuality from books intended for children was a development that paralleled the evolution of housing in Europe. In the Middle Ages houses were rarely more elaborate than was necessary. Few homes had more than one room. The poor had hovels which were little more than a shelter for sleeping. Family life tended to be compromised. Because there was no room for children, only for infants, the older children were commonly sent away to work as apprentices or servants.

The living quarters of the bourgeoisie would typically be above a store or artisan's shop. It generally consisted of a single, large room in which the household cooked, ate, transacted business, entertained and slept. Households of up to twenty-five people were not uncommon. Privacy was unknown,[37] and children were not sent to bed in their own rooms so that racy stories could be told to adults only. Beds were generally large because they were intended to hold more than one or two people. Children lived and worked alongside adults and listened to the same stories. Since children were in the company of adults who were not their parents, but were employers or other servants, there was not the same concern then about what children were exposed to that parents of today have.

By the seventeenth century, living arrangements had evolved so that there tended to be greater segregation between quarters allocated to working, food preparation and sleeping. There still tended to be a main room used for dining, entertaining and receiving visitors, but servants and children began to be separated into smaller rooms adjacent to the central, common areas.[38] It was at this time that fairy stories began to be transformed into works intended more strictly for children. This transformation of living spaces coincides with other changes that had great impact on children, including attitudes about how children should be taught about proper behavior, and about death and dying.

By looking at the changes in one fairy tale, Little Red Riding Hood, we can observe the changes in attitudes toward death, children and their education. The earliest known oral version of the tale of Little Red Riding Hood, for example, would not generally be considered suitable entertainment for children today. In the version of the story traditionally told in Brittany, Little Red is unwittingly led by the wolf to eat her grandmother's flesh and drink her blood, and she performs a provocative striptease for the disguised wolf before climbing into bed with him. Little Red later escapes from the wolf when she goes outside to relieve herself. As this tale was originally told, its primary purpose was to entertain adults, so it was not as heavily encumbered with the admonitions and advice that later came to distinguish versions of this tale intended for children.

The earliest written version of Little Red Riding Hood was recorded in French by Charles Perrault in 1696–97. The title of the story in French was 'Le Petit Chapeon Rouge.' The 'chapeon' was a hat worn in the Middle Ages, which suggests an even earlier oral tradition.[39] One of the fullest texts faithful to the traditional, oral versions of "Little Red Riding Hood" was also recorded in France at the end of the nineteenth century.[40]

Perrault's first version of the tale was published in *Histoires ou Contes du Temps Passé* (Stories [Tales] of Times Passed), subtitled *Contes de Ma Mère L'Oye* (Tales of My Mother Goose). Perrault included seven other tales along with the tale of Little Red Riding Hood. Each of these tales had a moral in verse at the end. In this version of Little Red's tale, the grandmother and Little Red are both eaten by the wolf, and both perish. Although Perrault did not have Little Red's mother giving her any initial warnings before she departed for her grandmother's house, he did conclude the story with a moral suitable for the intended audience of children: Do not speak to strangers or you, too, may provide a wolf with his dinner. The violence of this story is later moderated in the Brothers Grimm's retelling, by the introduction of an additional character, a hunter or woodcutter, who is able to rescue Little Red and her grandmother by slicing open the wolf and letting them out.

The version of Little Red's tale as told by the Brothers Grimm also gives an expanded role to Little Red's mother, who gives Little Red many warnings and much advice before sending her off through the forest to her grandmother's house. Little Red is admonished to "make haste ... go straight ... behave prettily and modestly ... do not run ... and do not forget to curtsy and say 'good morning' to everyone who knows you."[41] These initial admonitions served to educate the young audience of the story in the manners that were expected of them, and they provided a framework in which the resulting action of the story would be played out. The Brothers Grimm vividly portrayed the consequences of not heeding mother's advice. Interestingly, in this version, the hunter refers to the wolf as "old sinner,"[42] perhaps as an oblique reference to risqué incidents excised from the children's version but remembered from the oral tradition.

In a popular nineteenth century retelling of Little Red's tale the grandmother still gets eaten by the wolf, but Little Red survives and learns to pay closer attention to her mother's words: "For she saw the dreadful end to which/ A disobedient act may lead."[43] This version of the tale has an interesting emphasis on avoiding any unnecessary suffering of the characters. Here is the depiction of the wolf putting an end to the grandmother:

> "He jumped up on the bed, and ate her all up. But he did not hurt her so much as you would think, and as she was a very good old woman it was better for her to die than to live in pain; but still it was very dreadful of the wolf to eat her."[44]

The editor of *Old Favorite Fairy Tales* was apparently undecided about whether the grandmother's fate was good or bad. When the woodcutter arrives on the scene to rescue Little Red, he advises her that one shouldn't "tell one's affairs to strangers, for many a wolf looks like an honest dog,"—an interesting way of warning a young girl that looks can be deceiving!

In later versions, the hunter arrives in time to shoot the wolf before he eats either Little Red or her grandmother, and in still other versions, even the wolf is spared to escape through an open window, or to become Little Red's pet. The moral or message of the story also evolves with the transformation of the events depicted in the tale. In the traditional, oral version of Little Red Riding Hood, Little Red was not forewarned by her mother about the dangers of talking to strangers, therefore Little Red cannot be seen as naughty or disobedient. In Perrault's original written version, the mother does not give Little Red any cautions, either, while in later versions the mother often gives many instructions and admonitions to her daughter. Upon rescuing Little Red from the dire misfortune she brings upon herself, the hunter/woodcutter inevitably gives her a lecture on obedience and points out to her that she now knows what can happen if she disobeys her mother's warnings. The role that mortality plays in the changing tale of Little Red Riding Hood is seen to diminish as the tale evolves. Rather than being the graphic and unmourned event as Perrault depicted it, it becomes unrealistically softened in the later versions, eventually being banished to the periphery of the young audiences' attention.

What Is a Fairy Tale?

To better understand the significance of the place that fairy tales, and other tales told to children, have in determining the formation of attitudes relating to death and dying, it is helpful to become familiar with some of the different definitions that these tales have been given. Fairy tales have been defined in various ways by different people. Rollo May considered fairy tales to be " . . .our myths before we become conscious of ourselves."[45] Bruno Bettelheim wrote,

> "The figures and events of fairy tales . . . personify and illustrate inner conflicts, but they suggest ever so subtly how these conflicts may be solved, and what the next steps in the development toward a higher humanity might be . . . presented in a simple homely way. . . . Far from making demands, the fairy tale reassures, gives hope for the future, and holds out the promise of a happy ending."[46]

Madonna Kolbenschlag writes:

> "Fairy tales are the bedtime stories of the collective consciousness. They persist in cultural memory because they interpret crises of the human condition that are common to all of us. They are shared wish fulfillments, abstract dreams that resolve conflicts and give meaning to experience."[47]

Edwin Krupp makes a distinction between fairy tales and the rest of children's literature:

> "The term 'fairy tale' is sometimes used for all children's stories, but the fairy tale really has its own special character. It involves or takes place in another realm or world, not in the one in which we usually reside. Fairy tales are really stories of the supernatural. Other laws prevail in them, and the creatures that inhabit them do not belong to ordinary reality."[48]

All of these definitions are good and even have merit in their own context, yet they are unsatisfying in their failure to consider the origin of these tales in adult entertainment and the purposeful manner in which they were converted into tales intended for children.

There is an easily confusing overlap between fairy tales, folk tales and myths. Myths are the most easily distinguishable, as they are mainly stories intended to provide explanations for the occurrence of natural phenomenon, generally by personifying a natural effect as an animistic or anthropomorphic deity. The depiction of the sun in its course as Apollo driving his fiery chariot, and winter being caused by Demeter mourning for the six months of Persephone's captivity in Hades, are typical of mythological stories. Even though, in their later elaborations, myths might come to deal with models of behavior and other topics commonly found in fairy tales, their origins can be found in the earliest explanations of natural phenomena. Broad definitions like Rollo May's seem to apply more clearly to myths than to fairy tales.

Folk tales and fairy tales are not as easily distinguished, as indicated by the fact that published collections of folk tales and fairy tales may very well contain some of the same stories.

A characteristic of fairy tales is the flexible way that they have been perceived by authors. Authors in different times and places have recognized that fairy tales are capable of carrying a message that can be tailored to fit their particular needs. Existing as they do in the common domain, fairy tales and their characters provide an easily accessible medium for both writers and their audience. The task of the audience is eased by the familiarity of the characters and situations with which they are presented, and the writer's burden is lightened as he brings stories from an earlier time into conformity with the standards he is trying to represent. The subtle or obvious manner in which a fairy tale departs from its audiences' expectations, while still fulfilling their desires, is a measure of its successful telling. A current example of this phenomenon is the bestseller *Women Who Run With the Wolves*,[49] in which many fairy tales are retold with an emphasis on their pertinence to the modern female experience.

Fairy tales are also significant in the wide range of characters and situations that may be found in them. Children are presented characters that they can identify with in fairy tales—commonly in the guise of a child not unlike him or herself—who is faced with an adverse situation in which he or she is called upon to make new judgments and exhibit mature behaviors. Children can be exposed to a range of novel situations through the fairy tale, and exposed to models for their own behavior to fit a variety of needs. The most popular fairy tales, especially, have always adapted as adult perceptions of children's needs have changed, and adult needs to communicate various lessons to children have changed.[50]

In distinction to fairy tales, folk tales often concern the actions of pseudo-historical or typical personages who are engaged in activities that represent cultural standards that children are expected to aspire to. The unerring accuracy of William Tell is related in a folk tale, as is George Washington's chopping down of the cherry tree and his precocious, unwavering honesty. The adventures of Paul Bunyan and his gigantic blue ox, Babe, are folk tales that recast popular stories from the era of the westward expansion of the United States as "tall tales" with a common, main character.

It cannot be maintained, as Bettelheim's definition suggests, that a fairy tale invariably holds the promise of a happy ending. The Little Mermaid, which is a definite fairy tale, has been subjected to a great of distortion, or "artistic license," to produce a happy ending. At the conclusion of the tale as Hans Christian Andersen originally wrote it, the Little Mermaid chooses death for herself rather than murdering the Prince, which would have enabled her to regain her form as a mermaid. The only consolation for the Little Mermaid, who had already sacrificed her home, family, and voice to pursue her love for the mortal, human Prince, is, that after performing deeds of kindness for three hundred years as a "daughter of the air," she might gain a human soul and join the Prince in heaven. The very morning that the Little Mermaid sacrifices herself and spares the Prince, he marries a princess from another land whom he mistakenly believes had rescued him from drowning, when actually the Little Mermaid had saved him. Only in Disney's version does the Little Mermaid manage to displace the "other woman" and marry the Prince. Disney justifies this alteration by casting the evil sea-witch in disguise as the other princess.

The classic fairy tale "Bluebeard" also presents a problematic ending. In this fairy tale, one of three sisters marries a wealthy but mysterious man, distinguished primarily by a beard of blue color. After the wedding, the wife is given access to all Bluebeard's possessions, but she is forbidden to use one small golden key. When she inevitably opens the door the key unlocks, she discovers the bloody bodies of Bluebeard's previous wives. When Bluebeard discovers his wife's transgression, he prepares to add her to his collection. At the last moment, the wife is saved by the sudden appearance of her brothers, who hack her husband into pieces before her eyes. The happiness of the ending of this tale must be considered more one of degree; although the latest wife did not meet the fate of her predecessors, is it really a happy ending to have your brothers murder your husband? This tale also leaves unresolved the dilemma of the wife's part in the action. Her disobedience is a necessary part of the story, yet there is no clear resolution to this issue. The fast and easy way to conclude a fairy tale is to recite "and they lived happily ever after," yet when one takes a close look at fairy tales there are many which do not have a "perfect" ending.

The Future of Fairy Tales

When folk and fairy tales existed solely in an oral medium, every storyteller was able to tell a version of a story that was personalized by the demands of his or her time, place and audience. When stories came to exist more exclusively in printed form, they began to reflect more enduringly the nature of the time and place in which they were recorded. For this reason, it is especially odd that we continue to read to our children—often without the slightest degree of critical reflection—unrevised versions of stories that are imbued with the values of a different time and place. L. Frank Baum, the originator of the tales of the Land of Oz (1900), recognized this predicament, and recommended that it was time for a new set of 'wonder tales,' and that previous fairy tales should be classed as 'historical.'[51]

There is a growing perception that children are capable of having an understanding of dying and death as natural processes, and that the lifelong relationship a person has to dying and death is based in no small measure on the experiences of childhood. In the last twenty years, there has been a revolution in the practices and perceptions surrounding dying and death, yet little has been effectively done to transmit these changes to children. Adults are beginning to recognize the difficulties they have experienced as a result of being sheltered from an awareness of mortality and the need is felt for a way to transmit a realistic awareness of mortality to children.

Denoting traditional fairy tales as 'historical' would help distinguish the changes in values and behaviors that have occurred in the many years since they were recorded, and would encourage parents and teachers to more critically examine just what they are presenting to children. Modern editions of fairy tales have enormous appeal, demonstrated by the lavishly illustrated editions that have been offered recently by some of the large publishing houses. It is interesting to note that reviews of these books have concentrated on the beauty of the illustrations, the size of the book, the quality of the paper . . . in other words on everything but the content. The assumption seems to be that the buying public already knows what the content is and that no explanation is necessary.

But it is important to consider the implications of fairy tales in our modern world. Perhaps it is time to begin transforming them to reflect the tremendous changes that have occurred in a world increasingly forced to accept the limits of medical technology, where death is being acknowledged again as a necessary and inevitable counterpart to life.

Reading with a child is a wonderful activity; introducing someone to the world of books is to offer them the promise of a greater and better world. Fairy tales can be an important part of this process, because their "real" existence is in the imagination of a child. Through the action of a fairy tale a child can learn that he or she can confront circumstances that are new or frightening and be able to do the right thing. It is important that the tales we tell to our children reflect what we ourselves believe. Rather than continuing to insulate children from the realities of death and dying—especially by providing the unsuitable types of messages that Saturday morning T.V. provides—fairy tales can provide a medium for children to be introduced to the types of situations that they will encounter all their lives.

One of the few activities that haven't changed since the eras of our parents and grandparents is tucking a child into bed with a story, even down to the story we might choose to read. There is a comfort in this nostalgia, and a sense of continuity to this activity that can make all involved believe in the truth of the final " . . . and they lived happily ever after." A cartoon in a recent edition of *the New Yorker* magazine illustrated this, while also showing the capacity fairy tales have to portray facets of the world that are not necessarily easy to explain. The cartoon showed a mother reading a bedtime story to her daughter with the caption, "She married and then divorced, and then she married and divorced, and then she married and lived happily ever after."

Although this cartoon was certainly intended to be ironic, it still points out the purpose of providing moral instruction that fairy tales can fulfill. With the expanding use of hospice programs and the corresponding increase in opportunities for children to be exposed to meaningful death experiences, and the increase of the awareness of the lethalness of AIDS, it is important that even the tales told to children come to reflect current perceptions of dying and death.

Notes

1. De Spelder, Lynne A. & Strickland, Albert L. 1983. *The Last Dance.* Palo Alto, CA: Mayfield Publishing.
2. Lamers, E. P. 1986. The dying child in the classroom. In G. H. Paterson (Ed.), *Children and Death* (pp. 175–186). London: King's College.
3. Lamers, E. P. 1986. The dying child in the classroom. In G. H. Paterson (Ed.), *Children and Death* (pp. 175–186). London: King's College.
4. *McGuffey's Eclectic Readers* (Vols. 2–6) (1920). New York: Van Nostrand.
5. Wordsworth, William. We Are Seven, *McGuffey's Eclectic Readers* (Vols. 2–6) (1920). New York: Van Nostrand, Third Reader, p. 163.
6. Waller, Edmund. Old Age and Death, *McGuffey's Eclectic Readers* (Vols. 2–6) (1920). New York: Van Nostrand. Sixth Reader, p. 95.
7. Dickens, Charles. The Death of Little Nell, *McGuffey's Eclectic Readers* (Vols. 2–6) (1920). New York: Van Nostrand. Sixth Reader, p. 96.
8. Gray, Thomas. Elegy in a County Churchyard, *McGuffey's Eclectic Readers* (Vols. 2–6) (1920). New York: Van Nostrand. Sixth Reader, p. 108.
9. Browning, Elizabeth Barrett. He Giveth His Beloved Sleep, *McGuffey's Eclectic Readers* (Vols. 2–6) (1920). New York: Van Nostrand, Sixth Reader, p. 195.
10. Anonymous, My Mother's Grave. *McGuffey's Eclectic Readers* (Vols. 2–6) (1920). New York: Van Nostrand, Fourth Reader, p. 253.
11. A basal reader is a text with which reading is taught. There are many different series, each usually having one book per grade level.
12. White, E. B. 1952. *Charlotte's Web.* New York: Harper & Row.
13. Alcott, Louisa M. 1947. *Little Women.* New York: Grosset & Dunlop, (originally pub. 1869), p. 464.
14. Douglas, Anne. 1988. *The Feminization of American Culture.* New York: Anchor Press. "The Domestication of Death," p. 200–226.
15. Brown, Margaret W. 1965. *The Dead Bird.* Reading, MA: Addison-Wesley.
16. White, E. B. 1952. *Charlotte's Web.* New York: Harper & Row.
17. Guth, D. L. 1976. *Letters of E. B. White.* New York: Harper & Row, p. 531.
18. Kubler-Ross, E. 1969. *On Death and Dying.* New York: Macmillan.
19. Newton, F. I. 1990. *Children and the Funeral Ritual: Factors that Affect Their Attendance and Participation,* Masters Thesis, California State University, Chico.
20. Encyclopaedia Britannica. 1976. Children's Literature, Macropaedia, Vol. 4, p. 229.
21. Perrault, Charles. *La Belle au Bois Dormant* (Sleeping Beauty). In Mulherin, Jennifer (Ed.). 1982. *Favorite Fairy Tales.* London: Granada Publishing, p. 12.
22. Perrault, Charles. *Le Petit Chapeon Rouge* (Little Red Riding Hood). In Mulherin, Jennifer (Ed.). 1982. *Favorite Fairy Tales.* London: Granada Publishing, p. 22.
23. Perrault, Charles. *Les Fees* (Toads and Diamonds). In Mulherin, Jennifer (Ed.). 1982. *Favorite Fairy Tales.* London: Granada Publishing, p. 52.
24. Tatar, Maria. 1992. *Off With Their Heads! Fairytales and the Culture of Childhood.* Princeton, NJ: Princeton University Press. p. 9.
25. Johnson, Clifton. 1963. *Old-Time Schools and School Books.* New York: Dover (reprint of the Macmillan 1904 edition), p. 16.
26. Newbery, John. 1744. *A Little Pretty Pocket Book.* Encyclopaedia Britannica, (1976), Children's Literature, Macropaedia, Vol. 4, p. 231.
27. Jordan, William. 1991. *Divorce Among the Gulls,* New York: Harper Collins, p. 169.
28. Janeway, James. *A Token for Children: Being an Account of the Conversion, Holy and Exemplary Lives, and Joyful Deaths of Several Young Children.* (1671–72). In Tatar, Maria. 1992. *Off With Their Heads! Fairytales and the Culture of Childhood.* Princeton, NJ: Princeton University Press, p. 14.
29. Tatar, Maria. 1992. *Off With Their Heads! Fairytales and the Culture of Childhood.* Princeton, NJ: Princeton University Press, p. 14–15.
30. Tatar, Maria. 1992. *Off With Their Heads! Fairytales and the Culture of Childhood.* Princeton, NJ: Princeton University Press, p. 87.

31. Boorstin, D. J. 1992. *The Creators.* New York: Random House, p. 573.
32. Freud, S. The Interpretation of Dreams, Vol. 4 of the Standard Edition, trans. James Strachery (London: Hogarth, 1953), p. 254. In Tatar, *Off With Their Heads! Fairytales and the Culture of Childhood.* Princeton, NJ: Princeton University Press, p. 46.
33. Tatar, Maria. 1992. *Off With Their Heads! Fairytales and the Culture of Childhood.* Princeton, NJ: Princeton University Press, p. 46.
34. Tatar, Maria. 1992. *Off With Their Heads! Fairytales and the Culture of Childhood.* Princeton, NJ: Princeton University Press, p. 7.
35. Owens, L. 1981. *The Complete Brothers Grimm Fairy Tales.* New York: Avenel, p. 57.
36. Tatar, Maria. 1992. *Off With Their Heads! Fairytales and the Culture of Childhood.* Princeton, NJ: Princeton University Press, p. 34.
37. Rybcznski, Witold. 1987. *Home: A Short History of an Idea.* New York: Penguin, p. 28.
38. Rybcznski, Witold. 1987. *Home: A Short History of an Idea.* New York: Penguin, p. 38.
39. Mulherin, Jennifer (Ed.). 1982. *Favorite Fairy Tales.* London: Granada Publishing, p. 22.
40. Tatar, Maria. 1992. *Off With Their Heads! Fairytales and the Culture of Childhood.* Princeton, NJ: Princeton University Press, p. 37.
41. Owens, Lily. (Ed.) 1981. *The Complete Brothers Grimm Fairy Tales.* New York: Avenel Books, p. 109.
42. Owens, Lily. (Ed.) 1981. *The Complete Brothers Grimm Fairy Tales.* New York: Avenel Books, p. 112.
43. Tatar, Maria. 1992. *Off With Their Heads! Fairytales and the Culture of Childhood.* Princeton, NJ: Princeton University Press, p. 39.
44. 1933. *Old Favorite Fairy Tales,* National Publishing Co., p. 20.
45. May, Rollo. 1992. *The Cry for Myth.* New York: Delta, p. 196.
46. Bettelheim, Bruno. 1977. *The Uses of Enchantment.* New York: Vintage Books, p. 26.
47. Kolbenschlag, Madonna. 1981. *Kiss Sleeping Beauty Good-Bye.* New York: Bantam, p. 2.
48. Krupp, Edwin C. 1991. *Beyond the Blue Horizon: Myths and Legends of the Sun, Moon, Stars, and Planets.* New York: Harper Collins, p. 11.
49. Estés, Clarissa P. 1992. *Women Who Run With the Wolves.* New York: Ballantine Books.
50. Tucker, Nicholas. 1982. *The Child and the Book.* New York: Cambridge, p. 80.
51. Tatar, Maria. 1992. *Off With Their Heads! Fairytales and the Culture of Childhood.* Princeton, NJ: Princeton University Press, p. 19.

Books about Death for Children and Young Adults

The following list of books is a sample of general books (fiction and non-fiction) about death available for children.

Non-fiction:

Bernstein, Joanne, & Gullo, Stephen J., *When People Die,* New York: Dutton, 1977.

Le Shan, Eda J., *Learning to Say Good-by: When a Parent Dies,* New York: Macmillan, 1976.

Richter, Elizabeth, *Losing Someone You Love. When a Brother or Sister Dies,* New York: Putnam's, 1986.

Rofes, Eric E. & The Unit at Fayerweather Street School, *The Kids' Book About Death and Dying,* Boston: Little, Brown & Co., 1985.

Segerberg, Osborn, Jr., *Living With Death,* New York: Dutton, 1976.

Stein, Sara B., *About Dying,* New York: Walker, 1974.

Zim, Herbert, & Bleeker, Sonia, *Life and Death,* New York: Morrow, 1970.

Fiction:

Alcott, Lousia M., *Little Women,* New York: Grosset & Dunlop, 1947. (originally pub. 1869) (sister—illness)

Alexander, Sue, *Nadia the Willful,* New York: Pantheon, 1983. (brother—accidental)

Aliki, *Two of Them,* New York: Greenwillow, 1979. (grandfather—old age)

Bartoli, Jennifer, *Nonna,* New York: Harvey House, 1975. (grandmother—natural death)

Blume, Judy, *Tiger Eyes,* Scarsdale, NY: Bradbury, 1981. (father—murdered in robbery)

Brown, Margaret W., *The Dead Bird,* Reading, MA: Addison-Wesley, 1965. (wild bird—natural death)

Bunting, Eve, *The Empty Window,* New York: Frederick Warne, 1980. (friend—illness)

Coerr, Eleanor, *Sadako and the Thousand Paper Cranes,* New York: Putnam, 1977. (Hiroshima—leukemia caused by radiation)

Craven, Margaret, *I Heard the Owl Call My Name,* New York: Doubleday, 1973. (young priest—illness)

de Paola, Tomie, *Nana Upstairs and Nana Downstairs,* New York: Putnam, 1973. (great-grandmother and grandmother—natural death)

Douglas, Eileen, *Rachel and the Upside Down Heart,* Los Angeles: Price, Stern, Sloan, 1990. (father—heart attack)

Gerstein, Mordicai, *The Mountains of Tibet,* New York: Harper & Row, 1987. (reincarnation)

Hermes, Patricia, *You Shouldn't Have to Say Good-bye,* New York: Harcourt, 1982. (mother—illness)

Hickman, Martha W., *Last Week My Brother Anthony Died,* Nashville, TN: Abingdon, 1984. (infant brother—congenital heart condition)

Kantrowitz, Mildred, *When Violet Died,* New York: Parent's Magazine Press, 1973. (pet bird—natural death)

Mann, Peggy, *There Are Two Kinds of Terrible,* New York: Doubleday, 1977. (mother—illness)

Miles, Miska, *Annie and the Old One,* Boston: Little, Brown, 1971. (Navajo Indians—grandmother—natural death)

Paterson, Katherine, *Bridge to Terabithia,* New York: Crowell, 1977. (friend—accidental death)

Saint Exupery, Antoine de, *The Little Prince,* New York: Harcourt, 1943. (death—general)

Smith, Doris B., *A Taste of Blackberries,* New York: Crowell, 1973. (friend—bee sting allergy)

Talbert, Marc, *Dead Birds Singing,* Boston: Little, Brown, 1985. (mother, sister—car accident)

Tobias, Tobi, *Petey,* New York: Putman, 1978. (gerbil—illness)

Varley, Susan, *Badger's Parting Gifts,* New York: Lothrop, Lee & Shepard, 1984. (personified animals—remembering someone after death)

Viorst, Judith, *The Tenth Good Thing About Barney,* New York: Atheneum, 1971. (pet cat—natural death)

Warburg, Sandol Stoddard, *Growing Time,* Boston: Houghton Mifflin, 1969. (pet dog—natural death)

White, E. B., *Charlotte's Web,* New York: Harper & Row, 1952. (death as a natural consequence of life)

Wilhelm, Hans, *I'll Always Love You,* New York: Crown, 1985. (pet dog—natural death)

Williams, Margery, *The Velveteen Rabbit,* New York: Holt, Rinehart & Winston, 1983 edition. (life and death—general)

Zolotow, Charlotte, *My Grandson Lew,* New York: Harper & Row, 1974. (grandfather—remembering him)

---

*This article also appeared as a chapter in *Awareness of Mortality,* J. Kauffman (ed.), Baywood, Amityville, New York, 1995.

Palliative and Hospice Care Needed for Children With Life-Threatening Conditions

Joan Stephenson, PhD

WHEN CHILDREN IN THE UNITED STATES ARE STRICKEN with a serious illness or injury, few question the medical community's focus on aggressive intervention aimed at curing or extending young lives. But what is all too often overlooked, say experts, is that children who die—along with many others who ultimately triumph over life-threatening conditions—often suffer needlessly because of lack of palliative and hospice care.

Such care not only addresses the physical needs of the child, such as managing pain and other symptoms, but also brings together a team of physicians, nurses, social workers, therapists, clergy, volunteers, and others to provide psychological, social, and spiritual support for children and their families.

Although pediatric palliative care is more generally accepted in some industrialized countries, seriously ill children in the United States often are not offered this kind of help. The United Kingdom, Australia, and Canada have done a better job in providing such services, says Marcia Levetown, MD, of the University of Texas Medical Branch, Galveston.

But there are encouraging signs that the issue is gaining new prominence in the United States.

A few months ago, the American Academy of Pediatrics (AAP) issued care guidelines for children with life-threatening and terminal conditions (*Pediatrics.* 2000;106:351–357) that include a number of recommendations to help make palliative care and respite programs more widely available to children and families who need them. And earlier this year, for the first time, Congress allocated $1 million to develop children's hospice care demonstration programs in Florida, Kentucky, New York, Utah, and Virginia.

"Not Doing A Good Job"

The need to improve the delivery of palliative and hospice care for young patients was underscored by a recent study of end-of-life care for children dying of cancer (*N Engl J Med* 2000;342:326–333).

Based on a review of medical records and interviews with parents of 103 children who had died of cancer, the research team concluded that 89% of the children suffered "a lot" or "a great deal" from at least one symptom in their last month of life—most commonly pain, fatigue, or shortness of breath.

Parents also said that attempts to manage such symptoms left much to be desired. Of children who were treated for specific symptoms, treatment was successful in only 27% of those with pain, 16% of those with shortness of breath, and 10% of those with nausea and vomiting.

"We know that we're not doing a very good job of caring for these children," notes Lovetown.

Part of the reason children's suffering goes unheeded is that in Western countries such as the United States, the death of a child is a relatively uncommon event, and the medical system concentrates on seeking cures and extending lives. (About 53,000 children die annually in the United States, compared with about 2.5 million adult deaths per year.) Because of the perception that palliative and hospice care are synonymous with giving up and accepting death, many people assume such care is incompatible with trying to save their children.

New Eligibility Rules Needed

That's one reason that the rules for adult palliative and hospice care don't fit the needs of children, say advocates of palliative care for children. Current federal regulations for Medicare hospice benefits—the model on which most state Medicaid hospice benefits are based—limit the availability of hospice services to patients whose life expectancy is 6 months or less.

While predicting which patients will die within 6 months is difficult in adults, the challenges in children can be even greater. The kinds of conditions that claim children's lives differ from the common killers of adults. And children and their families need the kind of support hospice care offers much earlier in the course of illness, says Anne Armstrong-Dailey, founder and director of Children's Hospice International (CHI), a nonprofit organization based in Alexandria, Va.

"What we've been hearing from parents for 18 years is that the real time of crisis is the time of diagnosis of a life-threatening condition," explains Armstrong-Dailey.

In addition some hospice programs may require those seeking care to agree to forgo potentially curative or life-prolonging therapies. Hospice benefits also may not cover therapies

From the *Journal of the American Medical Association*, November 15, 2000, pp. 2437-2438. © 2000 by the American Medical Association. Reprinted by permission.

aimed at improving a child's quality of life, such as long-term ventilator therapy for children with neuromuscular disorders or surgery to alleviate symptoms.

"Sometimes it's hard to draw a line between what is life-prolonging and what is symptom management," says Levetown, who helped develop the new AAP guidelines. Playing by adult rules simply does not well serve children with a life-threatening or terminal condition, according to the AAP guidelines.

"Palliative care is not a substitute for curative or life-prolonging therapies," she says. "It's needed from the time of diagnosis, and it should not be implemented only when we've exhausted all other options."

For example, some 80% of children with acute lymphoblastic leukemia are curable, but that means that one of five children dies from the disease. What often happens is that because of the perception that a child with this cancer has a good prognosis, health care providers don't acknowledge a legitimate fear of death that arises from the moment of diagnosis.

"What we're advocating for is acknowledging that there is fear from the time of diagnosis that a child has a potentially life-threatening condition—and in acknowledging that, providing the psychosocial support, spiritual support, symptom management, and community-based support that is needed to make those lives as good as they can be for as long as possible," explains Levetown.

In short, say the AAP guidelines, the goal should be "to add life to the child's years, not simply years to the child's life," although physician-assisted suicide or euthanasia for children "should not be supported."

Other Barriers

Other barriers to providing pediatric palliative care include the limited availability of such services. While there are about 2500 hospice programs aimed at adults, there are only 247 geared toward children, according to a 1999 survey by CHI.

"Only 1% of children with life-threatening illnesses are getting hospice care, which is shameful," notes Armstrong-Dailey. The group hopes the new federally funded demonstration projects for children's palliative care will help change that.

"The PACC [Program for All-inclusive Care for Children and their Families] model will allow the application of the hospice concept of care from time of diagnosis—with hope for cure—but with bereavement follow-up if cure is not obtained," she says.

Another barrier is the lack of physician training in pediatric palliative care. The new AAP guidelines note that educational efforts are needed to educate pediatricians, family physicians, pain specialists, and pediatric surgeons about pediatric palliative care practices, including aggressive symptom management and psychosocial care for children and their families. One document to help address this gap, the *UNIPAC on Pediatric*

Palliative Care, will be available next spring through the Academy of Hospice and Palliative Medicine.

Perhaps the greatest obstacle to providing pediatric palliative and hospice care, just as for adult patients, is financial. Reimbursement for such services—typically less than $100 per day—is based on the level of reimbursement and type of care given to adult patients with terminal illnesses.

"Physicians are typically reimbursed for procedures more generously than for medical management, multidisciplinary care, and counseling," said Levetown. "It needs to be recognized that with this kind of work, there is a lot of professional time spent talking separately with the family and with the child, listening to the family, and grieving with the family."

To break down such barriers to care, the AAP guidelines say that fundamental changes need to be made in the regulation and reimbursement of palliative care services. Such changes include broadening the eligibility criteria concerning the predicted length of survival, permitting simultaneous life-prolonging and palliative care, providing respite care and other therapies not currently mandated, and offering adequate reimbursement for palliative and respite care.

Need for Research

Even while asserting the need to increase the availability of services, the AAP guidelines urge increased funding for research into effective pediatric palliative care.

Levetown notes that while controlled trials of pediatric palliative care practices are needed, there is a body of evidence concerning effective measures that can be implemented now. These practices have been developed by hospice programs with years of experience in delivering such services.

To make such information more widely accessible, the Children's International Project on Hospice/Palliative Services has assembled a compendium of pediatric palliative care, including protocols and other materials developed by successful programs, which will be available this fall through the National Hospice and Palliative Care Organization, in Alexandria, Va.

Advocates for palliative care for children hope that some answers will emerge from the demonstration model programs that Congress agreed to fund earlier this year. According to CHI, which will provide oversight of the project, the hope is that the programs "will provide tangible evidence of how cost-effective and efficient children's hospice care is in meeting the needs of children with life-threatening conditions and their families."

The cost of offering this type of care is not exorbitant, and the number of children involved is not large, insists Levetown.

"It's important for us to advocate for regulatory and financial changes that will allow people to provide the appropriate care for these children," she said. "Not only will the children and their families be better served by these changes, but society will be as well."

When Death Breaches the Campus Walls

By Carlin Romano

COLLEGE SEEMS a life-or-death matter to students, professors, and staff scurrying about campus, but it isn't. It's a matter of life.

Every aspect of college and university existence promotes life. On the shelves of the main library, thousands of writers and thinkers and eras past, dead to most of the world, come alive again at a student's touch. Every semester at registration time, the wealth of possibility, of new beginnings, overwhelms student and teacher alike. Deans may carp about "deadwood," but the timber stands tall, if inert, in the hallways and faculty club.

At older colleges like Williams, complete with actual graveyard, the sepulchral setting is tucked away from campus consciousness. At universities with a medical school, the "health sciences" campus—where

> The wise men and women of academe are right to offer death no welcome, and only the occasional memorial service.

patients die, where the pale horse pulls up—is conveniently distant from undergraduates, the better to ignore death's sting. Even the chief

ritual of departure and loss on a campus is called "commencement"—a venerable triumph of spin that we'd punish as false advertising if attempted by a funeral home or hospital.

That's why death on a campus, like vulgar sacrilege in church or insipid banter during true life-and-death surgery, strikes with maximum force. Like the names chiseled on hallowed academic buildings, campus life is a commitment to immortality, a promise that the dead shall be raised.

At its most brutal—in the murder of two Dartmouth professors loved for their generosity to others, the murder of two Gallaudet students slaughtered in their dorm rooms—death can be an incomprehensible cataclysm exploding the norms of everyday life. When students die, one recalls Erich Fromm's thought that any death is "poignantly bitter," but dying "without having lived is unbearable." At its numbingly accepted yet painful norm, as in the memorial services recently for University of Pennsylvania English professor Lynda Hart, who died of breast cancer at 47, death is comprehended yet privately opposed, silently resisted.

But every death challenges the limitless optimism of the campus. If every institution, as Emerson wrote, is the lengthened shadow of a person, the college or university is a brick-and-marble Emerson himself: a reified fortress of buoyancy, ambi-

tion, and looking forward rather than back.

Because no matter who else walks the campus—the crotchety college president overdue for removal, the midlife-crisis professor rethinking career decisions for the umpteenth time—the ethos of the campus is that of the 18-to-22-year-old, to whom death is usually and thankfully a stranger.

In 1999, a Bennington College colleague of mine died toward the end of the fall semester. It was a peculiarly awful and ironic death. Tony Carruthers, an artist and professor of video and film studies, suffered a fatal heart attack while sitting on a train in Manhattan, waiting to head back to Vermont. He'd been teaching a course about depictions of death—Bergman and the like. The last time I spoke with him at the college post office, he'd cheerily invited me to one of his class screenings.

When I returned to campus the day after it happened, I wasn't sure whether students knew. Within moments, one of my undergraduate advisees saw me and called out, "Carlin, is it true about Tony?"

She came closer and I explained what had happened. She broke into tears and started sobbing, her whole body heaving. I put my arm around her to comfort her. At the same time, I felt awkward—because I wasn't crying.

Much as I'd liked my colleague, I didn't know him very well—certainly not as well as his students did.

More significant, the death of a man over 50 didn't shock me. People die at that age, and especially off campus. I'd seen lots of people die.

But my student hadn't. So I stood there, moved by her unabashed grief, sad myself at Tony's death, yet also uncomfortably detached, clinically conscious that I was comforting her with an embrace though I'd never so much as patted her on the shoulder before.

It was a moment suffused with a sense that something utterly foreign to the campus—too much reality— had entered. If troops had suddenly marched past the security gate, the intervention would not have seemed odder.

Whether one experiences such moments personally on campus, or witnesses them in vicarious pain while reading about devastated parents and siblings—so proud of their loved ones, so suddenly cut off— you inevitably think, at some point, like an academic.

Is there another side to it? Is there, if not a silver lining, at least the small rationalization that no one gets a pass on life's horrors, that students, too, must experience fate's dull-witted cruelty, the vicious crimes of pathological personalities, if they're to understand life?

HERE is where the magic of the campus asserts itself. Because every instinct in one answers, "No."

"This is not the place, and this is not the time," you hear yourself whispering to whoever hears such things. Like Wordsworth, we think of the blessedly young child and ask, "What should it know of death?" There will be time enough for murders, and cancers, and hatred.

Admissions offices are powerful, but not powerful enough to keep out death. It crashes in when it will. But the wise men and women of academe are right to offer it no welcome, no nomenclature to encourage it, and only the occasional memorial service. Like the young Emerson, who still wanted to play every part in life even after the death of his beloved young wife, Ellen, the college snaps back after each invasion of its cheerfulness. Its spirit is the spirit of Donne—that death shall be no more, that death shall die.

Camus wrote that there could be no lasting peace in the hearts of individuals until death is outlawed. On campus, we outlaw it from our minds whenever possible—knowing it to be the destroyer of worlds—and rightly so.

Carlin Romano, critic at large for The Chronicle *and literary critic of* The Philadelphia Inquirer, *teaches philosophy at Temple University.*

The *aging* of America: Problem or solution?

By Eric R. Kingson, Alejandro Garcia and Susan Taylor-Brown

Should we fear or welcome the aging of America? Are the old burden or opportunity?

"Talking heads" often falsely present the graying of America as demographic catastrophe, potentially overwhelming public and private pension and health insurance systems, drawing needed resources away from the pressing needs of children and nearly everyone else.

To this way of thinking, the old are an unproductive lot, and today's young are the "Gypped generation." Supporting tomorrow's burgeoning elder population threatens to bankrupt Social Security and Medicare, indeed the entire nation! Or as the Third Millennium, a group of affluent young advocates opposed to the traditional Social Security program, puts it, our society is "robbing our children in order to indulge ourselves in the luxuries of a time gone by."

Reading recent issues of the AARP's Modern Maturity, you might conclude that the aging of America is best understood as an entrepreneur's dream.

Seeking to appeal to aging baby boomers, Modern Maturity has had a face lift.

One article ("Who's Sexy Now?") shows us that Julie Christie, Harry Belafonte, Dolly Parton, Paul Newman and Tina Turner are among the sexiest 50 over 50. AARP's post-Viagra survey tells us that today's and tomorrow's old can have "great sex." Reading between the sheets—that is, the "pages"—you'll find advertisements and articles appealing to the needs (prurient and otherwise) of the "fifty-something" to "hundred-something" sets—from a titillating refresher course in intimacy to advice on impotency, from cruises to memory enhancers, from sports cars to mobile homes, from money market funds to long-term care insurance.

But defining the "age wave" as a demographic tsunami or treating the old primarily as an emerging market overlooks the rich diversity of and potential contributions of today's and tomorrow's old.

That more people are reaching old age and living better and longer is a great success of the 20th century—a result of investments in sanitation, education, public health, medicine, Social Security and the economy. Certainly public and private challenges—including the financing of retirement, health, and long-term care—must be addressed as the over-65 population increases from 13 percent today to 20 percent by 2030 and the over 85, from 1.6 percent today to 4.6 percent in 2050.

But aren't these the challenges we want—better than the many childhood deaths during the 1900s, the Flu Epidemic of 1918, economic collapse of the 1930s, loss of life in World War II, Korea and Vietnam, legal segregation of the 1950s, and threats once posed by the Iron Curtain. We can't turn away from the real challenges before us; neither should we term a major national achievement a failure.

The increasing numbers of older Americans provide opportunity to strengthen society, and the activities of many of today's old provide guidance for harnessing this resource. Old-age is being redefined. It's good that sexuality in old age is "out of the closet." But there's more.

Work and retirement patterns are changing. It's increasingly common for older workers to change careers, to move in and out of full and partial retirement.

Lifelong learning and skill development may well be the new norm for tomorrow's workforce. And today's old make numerous contributions to community and family. To wit:—Twenty-five thousand low-income Foster Grandparents provide social service to 80,000 children with special needs and 13,000 low-income Senior Companions serve 40,000 disabled elders, mostly homebound.

- Nearly half a million Retired Senior Volunteers tutor children, assist disabled elders and provide other needed services on a weekly basis.
- Baltimore's "Experience Corps" is successfully building on the best practices of the Foster Grandparent Program, Retired Senior Volunteers Program and other volunteer efforts to engage low-income elders as tutors, teacher aids, mentors for children (and in some cases their parents), and in roles that encourage parental involvement and facilitate service-learning for students.
- In Philadelphia and elsewhere, a Temple University program called Across Ages links older, inner-city residents as mentors to at-risk youth.

- Elsewhere elders join with youth to jointly respond to degradation of the environment and other pressing community problems.
- And 4 million children are being raised in households headed by grandparents; while millions of other elders provide needed child care and other support to younger family members.

These are the pioneers of tomorrow's aging society. A growing older population presents many opportunities to use the gift of added life to transmit a legacy of hope and opportunity.

ABOUT THE WRITERS Alejandro Garcia, Eric Kingson and Susan Taylor-Brown are professors at Syracuse University's School of Social Work. Readers may write to them at: School of Social Work, Syracuse University, Sims Hall, Syracuse, N.Y. 13244.

Coming to terms with LONG-TERM CARE

Planning to provide for seniors

By Guy Halverson
Staff writer of The Christian Science Monitor

You could call it "sticker shock" of the worst type.

A few months ago, Ann Bollinger and her brother set out to find assisted-living housing for their father, who has good health but is in his 80s.

The cheapest plan, at a pleasant complex in Quincy, Mass., started at $32,000 per year.

But that would have been just for their father. If their stepmother accompanied her husband into the complex, the cost would jump to $39,000.

For a studio apartment.

A one-bedroom apartment started at about $37,000 for one person, or $44,000 if both husband and wife moved in.

"And that was just for basic services," says Ms. Bollinger, who lives just outside Boston and works for a nonprofit organization. "Anything extra involved much more money."

After a family discussion, her father and stepmother decided to stay where they currently reside, in a senior-citizen complex that costs a little under $500 a month.

Moving to an assisted-living situation would have likely wiped out her parent's assets within a couple of years, says Bollinger (not her real name).

Her situation is far from unique.

Thousands of families in the United States—and throughout the industrial world—are struggling to find appropriate and affordable long-term care for senior citizens unable to take care of themselves.

Some social scientists say an "elder-care crisis," now looms, especially for baby boomers with older parents.

In 1994 alone, for which the latest definitive records are available, some 7.3 million Americans required long-term care. That number is expected to jump to between 10 million and 14 million people by 2020, according to the US General Accounting Office.

Despite the increasing need for assistance, elder care remains a largely hidden issue, in terms of the national political agenda, says Neal Cutler, director of survey research for the National Council on the Aging, in Washington.

But that will change dramatically, he believes, as the baby-boom generation ages, and more boomers discover that they must not only support their children, many of them in costly college programs, but also provide care for their parents.

Dr. Cutler notes his own situation: He is in his 50s, with a mother—who recently moved into an assisted-living facility—in her 80s. Cutler says that he was able to put the financial resources together to pay for the needs of his parent. "But many families will unfortunately find that they just can't afford to do it," he says. "What will they do?"

Many adult children of elders looking for assisted-living or special-care facilities have already discovered costs can be enormous, exceeding discretionary income, and, too often, directly threatening family savings.

Home care alone can run between $12 and $25 an hour. Nursing-home care is more expensive, running up to $40,000 a year. Assisted living can run from $20,000 a year in some locations to a more typical $35,000 to $40,000 in large metropolitan areas.

The elder-care challenge calls out for greater action on three fronts, experts say:

> Some early, inclusive planning can help ease the financial task of caring for elderly family members.

The making of a more elderly America

The aging of America is a success story by almost any measure. At the start of this century, the average American, according to the US Census Bureau, would have been fortunate to reach age 50. Today, thanks in part to advances in health care and better living conditions, Americans can be expected to live well into their 80s.

Currently, 12 percent of the US population, some 34 million people, are over the age of 65. But those numbers will soar in the next century, demographers say. More than 80 percent of all Americans will live past 65. Many of them—perhaps as many as 50 percent of the total, according to Na-tionwide Insurance Company—will need special elder-care living arrangements.

Women will be the main recipients of such care. More than 70 percent of all nursing-home residents are women. And since women already tend to outlive men, they have a greater likelihood of needing elder-care help at some point in their lives. Yet, few women have long-term health-care insurance.

Another aspect to the assisted-living equation: Many of those now receiving long-term care are not elderly people at all, but adults under the age of 65.

The bottom line is that many adults in their 30s and 40s are finding that they must not only meet the needs of their own families, while fulfilling their own work responsibilities, but must be caregivers as well.

Perhaps the most sobering statistic of all: According to a study by the Consumer Federation of America and Primerica, a member of Citicorp, one-half of all American households have accumulated less than $1,000 in net financial assets. For these families, helping an elderly parent can become very problematic.

—G.H.

1. Making affordable elder-care insurance more widely available.

2. Providing adequate financial help for elder-care needs.

3. Ensuring that there are affordable assisted-living or extended-care facilities in most metropolitan communities.

Total outlays for elder care in the US now run well in excess of $90 billion annually, and probably in the $100 billion range, say most studies.

Federal programs help cover some of the cost. Medicaid kicks in about one-third of the funding (about $29 billion). But to obtain Medicaid, elderly parents, or their families, must use up virtually all their savings.

Medicare pays about one-fourth of costs, about $23 billion. But that means that out-of-pocket payments by the elderly and their family members amount to roughly 40 percent of total costs, in excess of $39 billion.

Insurance is available to cover elder-care/nursing-home needs. But it can be expensive, especially for people in their 60s or older. That means you should "start buying when you are younger," says Don Kaufman, a vice president of the DeWitt Stern Group Inc., an insurance brokerage firm in New York.

He recommends people pick up a long-term health-care policy by the time they turn 50. A policy that pays about $200 a day in elder-care benefits costs about $540 a year for a 50-year-old, compared with about $930 a year for a 60-year-old, he adds.

If you buy insurance, make sure the policy has a low "waiting period," the number of days you have to be under care before benefits kick in. Mr. Kaufman says 20 days is a sound choice.

Also, get the longest-possible benefit period. Typically, a nursing-home stay runs under three years, he says. Also, buy through an insurance broker, he suggests, since they tend to deal with many firms, and you can find lower prices. More than 100 firms underwrite such policies, he says, although just a handful dominate the market.

Kaufman believes such policies are particularly important for boomers sandwiched between generations and having many obligations.

While in 1940 only 13 percent of persons aged 60 or over had an elderly parent still alive, today 44 percent of persons 60 or older have an elderly parent living, he says.

So far, "we're just seeing the tip of the iceberg," says James Hughes, dean of the Edward J. Bloustein School of Planning and Public Policy at Rutgers University, in New Jersey. Much of the elder-care challenge is now being faced by adults who were "war babies"—born during World War II, he says. But just around the corner, he says, will be the baby boomers. The oldest boomers are now in their early 50s. Many of the boomers' parents, moreover, were teenagers when they married, which means they are still relatively young.

But in four or five years, there could be a confluence of more elders needing care, just as the boomers move into their mid-50s and toward their 60s—in other words, the very years in which the boomers should be salting away savings for their own retirement.

Those most caught up in the elder-care dilemma tend to be the adult daughters of aging parents. Studies show that they most often become the primary caregivers. The majority of these women also hold down jobs. Thus, they juggle long hours, seeking to balance the needs of their employers, children, spouses, and parents.

Some sociologists worry that this balancing act puts too much strain on homes and marriages.

For now, the elder-care debate remains largely dormant compared with issues such as reforming Social Security and Medicare. But elder care "could be an issue in some congressional districts in next year's elections," where there are concentrations of older people, says Cutler.

The biggest push for better elder care is coming from the private sector. In New Jersey, for example, assisted-living complexes are being built for the state's relatively high number of retirees.

Early planning can help prepare for personal elder-care needs

Individuals can take a number of steps to anticipate future elder-care needs, experts agree:

● Talk the problem out with the entire family, and especially the elderly members who may need the care, says Dr. Neal Cutler of the National Council On The Aging. Make certain that elderly family members actively participate in making the final decision as to housing or care, he says.

● Contact as many national or local elder-care groups as possible. If your city or state has an office dealing with the aging, check with them for possible resources.

● Consider buying elder-care insurance as young as you can, to keep costs down over time. But make certain the insurance company has a solid financial record (if in doubt, check with your state insurance commission), and that the policy is adjusted for inflation over time, according to Don Kaufman, vice president of DeWitt Stern Group, Inc., an insurance brokerage firm in New York.

● If they don't already have it, ask your company to consider setting up an elder-care program. At the least, ask to have the company fund a counseling office that a person providing elder care can call if he or she feels intimidated by the conflicting demands of job and home.

● Write your local congressman to urge the exploration [of] the long-range ramifications of elder care on the nation's well-being.

● Make elder care part of the total financial plan that you put together early in your business and home-making experience.

In the 21st century, breadwinners (both husband and wife, or single parent) will have to consider it as much a component of family planning as providing for their children.

—Guy Halverson

Still, the main policy thrust for elder care comes from the private sector, if what is happening in New Jersey—which has an elderly population perhaps a tad larger than most states—is a guide, Hughes says. "In a number of cities, assisted-living complexes are being built," he says.

Nationally, some large blue-chip companies such as Boeing and AT&T offer elder-care programs, including hot lines where workers can seek help or counseling.

But corporate America has a long way to go. Fewer than 1 percent of all US companies now offer such programs.

Unit Selections

Key Points to Consider

❖ In an environment of advanced technology that has altered the ways in which we die, how are we to change our understanding of the dying process, enrich our engagement with those who are dying, and find a basis for our own growth toward death?

❖ How do we address the profound challenges raised by the questions of how and when we die and who decides?

❖ With the impressive experiences of the hospice movement to guide us, how can we improve our community witness to good care so that we can be present to the dying in ways that enrich their journey?

 **Links**   www.dushkin.com/online/

These sites are annotated on pages 4 and 5.

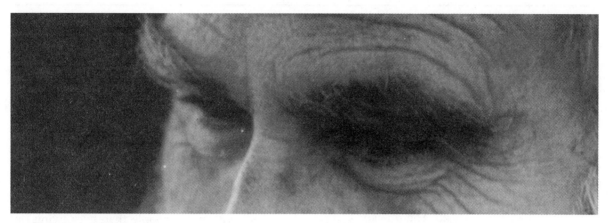

The Dying Process

"Death is the final stage of growth," as Elizabeth Kübler-Ross suggested in the title of one of her books. Death is the final stage of life; it is the "last act" of the play. While death comes at varied ages and in differing circumstances, for most of us there will be some time to reflect on our lives, our work, our relationships, and what our expectations are for the ending of that life. This is called the dying process. In the past three decades, a broad range of concerns have arisen about that process and how aging, dying, and death can be confronted in ways that are enlightening, enriching, and supportive. Efforts have been made to delineate and define various stages in the process of dying so that comfort and acceptance of our inevitable death will be eased. Awareness of approaching death allows us to come to grips with the profound emotional upheaval that will be experienced. Fears of the experience of dying are often more in the imagination than in reality, as the articles in this unit will demonstrate.

There are many and varied social, religious, and psychological responses that constitute and inform the process of dying, and the supports sought can be studied and used to the benefit of all. Spiritual questions and dilemmas are significant issues as life comes to a close and must be focused on as we learn to care for others. Key players in the drama that will unfold are physicians and nurses who attend the dying. Their personal attitudes and their professional roles are being examined by their professions, by the courts and legislatures, and by the public as increasingly serious attention is paid to the dying process. How do we decide on the care of the incompetent person who is dying? How do we delegate authority for end-of-life decisions and provide the comfort and assurance so needed as the end of life comes? The process of dying can be profoundly influenced by the compassion and the support of those trained to be with and for the dying. It is important for professional caregivers to learn the ways of comfort and compassion; it is also a challenge for family and friends to learn to be attentive to the demanding needs of those who are dying. Sensitivity to the needs we all have for love and consolation, awareness of the exquisitely personal nature of death, and willingness to attend to the difficult tasks at hand will greatly enhance and enrich the experience for all. There is also the rich reward we receive when the dying teach us about the richness of living for others.

The care of dying persons has always been difficult and demanding. The relatively recent use of the hospital as the place of death raises concerns about its appropriateness. Many persons are seeking to regain control of the process of dying—how, where, and with whom are valid questions to be considered. The high technology of the hospital and the lack of sensitivity of some caregivers to the personal aspects of dying have fanned the demands of many to die at home within their own defined environment. In former times, people died at home with family and friends in attendance. Many fear the abandonment of being left to die in an isolated room down a long corridor in a large hospital. For many, death is accepted for what it is—a time of transition or of ending. The thought of dying alone can be terrifying.

Neglected aspects of the care of the dying are the spiritual, the psychological, and the quality-of-life dimensions. The intensely personal aspects of spiritual issues, and commonly observed ignorance of them, can produce uneasiness in caregivers, both professionals and friends. It is important to be informed and alert to this profound support for those who suffer, are in pain, and coming to the end of life. Treatment—psychological and pharmacological—and attention to daily living needs can modify and often relieve the depression and sadness that so often darken the closing days of a life. Another aspect that is often ignored is the effect of ethnic and cultural factors on our care and on our understanding of the significance of death on people from widely disparate traditions.

The development of the Hospice movement in the United States over the past 30 years offers an alternative to the impersonal aspects of hospitalization. Hospice offers both home care and institutional care for the dying in a quiet environment with personal attention to the extremely intimate process of dying and assurance of the relief of pain. Though hospice had its conceptual origin in the Middle Ages, the present-day model is St. Christopher's Hospice in London, developed in the late 1960s by Dame Cecily Saunders.

Planning to Die

Jeanne Guillemin

Thirty years ago, in *The American Way of Dying,* Jessica Mitford roundly criticized Americans for their obsessive denial of death and their equally obsessive fixation on immortality. To the puritanical American sensibility, a miasma of shame surrounds the event of death. The quicker one died and the less the family and community were troubled, the better. Funeral directors, a uniquely American profession, assumed all responsibility for the corpse, including its embalmed, cosmetic display and its rapid dispatch to the cemetery or to the crematorium. Denial of death was also the theme of Philippe Ariès' work *Western Attitudes Toward Death* (1974). He credits early twentieth-century America with the invention of the modern attitude toward mortality. Death, once so banal a presence that Renaissance markets were held in graveyards and so communal that relatives and friends crowded the bedchambers of the dying, lost its tame aspect. Under the influence of urban industrialization, it became detached from domestic traditions, not the least of which was a religious understanding of the appropriateness and even the banality of the self's demise. In our times, Ariès argues, death became wild and obscene because we cherish an individualism that cannot be relinquished without extreme anguish. As with sex, death was not to be talked about in front of children or in polite company.

Today the American public is confronting mortality in ways that were unthinkable when Mitford was writing and improbable even to Ariès. The emphasis now is on rational planning for one's death that goes far beyond buying a burial plot. Topics such as traversing the emotional stages of dying, how to compose a living will to instruct final medical decisions, and the merits of rational suicide are ordinary fare on television and radio talk shows and in popular magazines. The head of the Hemlock Society, Derek Humphry, has a bestseller in *Final Exit,* a how-to book on "happy death." Jack Kevorkian, another book author, has gained notoriety for his "mercitron" devices, recently used by three women to end their lives. Despite his subsequent indictment for homicide, the public is far from outraged by the idea of physician-assisted suicide. In 1991, the state of Washington gained national attention with a popular referendum on the issue. The voting public there ultimately balked at granting it legal status, but polls had already revealed widespread support for the option of medically supervised suicide. In 1992, the state of New Hampshire initiated the nation's first legislation that would authorize physicians to write prescriptions to hasten the death of terminally ill patients.

This new frankness concerning death is due in part to changing demographics. The population of the United States has aged, with more people than ever living out a seventy-two year life span. Many are surviving decades beyond it. Perhaps aging alone would shift any society's focus to the end of life. Yet death itself has become unexpectedly familiar because of the AIDS epidemic, which has brought grief to hundreds of thousands of young victims, their families, and friends. Add to this the fact that the United States has the highest homicide rate of any industrialized country, with a disproportionate number of casualties among young minority males, and the difficulties of denying death and its repercussions become clear. Old or young, one thinks, "This could be me."

Still, death is far from tamed; it is now newly wild and familiar. The current discussion of how to die gives evidence of terrible fears that those final circumstances are beyond one's control. In a culture that prizes individual autonomy, there is a no more degrading scenario than the gradual diminution of physical and mental powers, the prolonged and painful helplessness, with mental lapses preceding and even obscuring the experience of dying. American anxiety about dying centers on how the individual can avoid dependence. Unfortunately, the two environments where death is likely to happen are poorly prepared to reduce this anxiety and are, in fact, increasing it. Neither the hospital, where 80 percent of Americans die, nor the home, where growing numbers of patients are being cared for, can be counted on to alleviate fears about death as a scenario of degradation.

Hospital Care and Uncare

In pondering the phenomenon of shameful death ("la mort inversée"), Ariès sees the modern hospital as the environment where depersonalized efficiency and order quell the fears of the dying. As a cultural instrument of repression, the hospital guarantees that the graceless, physically repulsive facts of expiration are hidden from view and that the emotional climate at the bedside is restrained. The sheets are clean, the meals regular, and the staff professional. Replacing family and friends is the hospital team, led by the physician. "They are," wrote Ariès, "the masters of death—of the moment as well as of the circumstances. . . ."

From *Society,* July/August 1992, pp. 29-33.

In the last two decades, hospital-based medicine has undergone radical changes and Americans have largely lost confidence in its protective guarantees, as chill and repressive as they have been. Hospital organization, once able to guarantee benign order for both birth and death, has been altered not with reference to the social or spiritual needs of patients, but in reaction to market incentives that favor large hospitals selling progressive medicine. The hospitals that survived the fierce competition of the 1980s did so by heavy investment in new and experimental technologies and by the build-up of centralized facilities offering a profitable mixture of specialized and acute care services. Small community hospitals closed by the hundreds. Public hospitals, burdened with welfare patients, are foundering. Private mega-hospital chains, like Humana, thrive because they serve only privately insured patients.

Far from being beneficent institutions, most hospitals today are businesses that serve clients. Linked to proliferating technological options and required to support high-priced professionals, their main incentive is to maximize returns on their investments. They are only unlucky if they do not. Cost control measures to cap procedure charges, such as Diagnostic Related Groups (D.R.G.'s), have merely succeeded in moving patients more quickly out of their hospital beds to make room for more. Costs for hospital medicine and services continue to rise and inflate health insurance coverage, which growing numbers of Americans cannot afford.

The progressive technologies being marketed through American hospitals fall into two categories. Both affect how we die. One kind addresses the diseases of the growing numbers of patients fortunate enough to survive past youth, at which point they become vulnerable to cardiac disease, cancer, stroke, kidney and liver failure. When Aaron Wildavsky coined the phrase, "doing better and feeling worse," in reference to modern American health care, he aptly summarized its major problem. The important determinants of health and illness—life style, genetics, and the environment—are outside the scope of medicine. Its principal technologies, geared toward an aging clientele, must be of the patch-and-mend variety, lacking the "magic bullet" efficiency of penicillin and sulfa drugs. Success with these "half-way technologies," as Lewis Thomas called them, is difficult and uncertain. Very sick patients do much more than lose faith in medicine. They take it on, they wrestle with it, and often they feel defeated by it. They are not just disappointed consumers. They engage their bodies and souls in a battle for life.

The role of the physician in treating the very sick patient is problematic, in part because doctors are only apparently disinterested in advising about medical treatment options. Many patients fail to understand that physicians like car dealers, will promote their products, if asked. Not that physicians are necessarily driven by profit motives, but they are integrated into the hospital reward system, now heavily invested in high-technology

Hospitals were organized, not for the patients' social and spiritual needs, but in reaction to market conditions.

resources—machines, laboratories, consultants—that must be used to get a return. Perhaps unwittingly, physicians often inform seriously ill patients about therapy in ways that encourage it. The use of statistical odds, for example, is a commonplace, as when a doctor refers to scientific studies to inform a patient about survival rates for cancer, using surgery or drugs or some combination of both. When cancer or any other disease is in an advanced stage, this tactic is little better than offering a lottery ticket to someone who is destitute. What even educated patients often do not know is that many clinical studies are poorly executed—without controls and on small samples—and yield only the most tentative results. Or, if they are well conceived and implemented, the patients researched may share none or few of the characteristics—age, gender, medical history, and so on—of the patient being informed. There is little or nothing in their training that prepares physicians to develop a posture of integrity and more genuine disinterest or new words of counsel for the seriously ill who should perhaps not venture any therapeutic course.

For a very sick patient, surgery, chemotherapy, or organ transplant might work. Then again, it might not. It will certainly be a physical and emotional ordeal, causing pain that is especially alienating because it is impossible to know whether it is part of recuperation or a sign of further degeneration. The patient cannot know, nor can the therapist, until test results come back. Even then, many therapies require years of monitoring, especially in the case of cancer, during which one simply does not know if a true cure has been effected. Starting with Susan Sontag's *Illness As Metaphor* to the essay on resisting chemotherapy by the anthropologist Susan DiGiacomo, the patient-as-survivor literature constitutes a searing criticism of how physicians mishandle patients confronting death.

The really bad news is that medical technology can offer multiple sequential therapeutic options for the same fatal disease. This creates uncertainty and uncertainty in medicine, as Wildavsky and others have noted, is often resolved by doing more. If drugs and surgery fail, other drugs or more surgery are substituted. The more advanced the disease, the more the desperate patient will value inclusion in an experimental trial of some new therapy, whereby she or he is diminished to a statistic and risks more physical devastation. This way of progressing toward death—by hopes raised and dashed, by technological assaults on the body, followed by periods of incomplete and

Subjection to experimental medicine is the pathway of everyone's last cure.

uncertain recuperation—is, of course, not the road traversed by people who are cured. Many people overcome blocked arteries, for example, or cancer because the therapy works. But subjection to experimental medicine is the pathway of everyone's last cure. No matter what the patient's age or how advanced the disease, or even if it is considered incurable, the options for more tests and treatment exist, in refined or experimental form, appropriate or inappropriate, as the physician advises.

The intensive care unit is the other important kind of technology that hospitals market. It has revolutionized the way Americans die, but not for the better. The concept of high-technology life support took hold in the early 1970s in response to a perceived need, public and professional, for emergency medical services. The argument for emergency medical units was and is based on the reduction of waste in human lives. Immediate aggressive intervention, not unlike that of a M.A.S.H. unit, would save victims of accidents, of heart attack and stroke, as well as premature infants, and post-operative patients. The key was vigorously sustained intervention with the maximum resources of a large central hospital. Emergency and intensive care facilities, costing billions of dollars, became part of the expansion of central hospitals throughout the 1970s and 1980s. Patients *in extremis* are always in good supply and treating them quickly in high-use beds has often helped hospitals underwrite less profitable services. Such heavy investment in acute care emphatically denied a preventive and more cost-efficient approach to health problems and to the general social problem of death by violence. Nor did emergency care enthusiasts predict that many whose lives were saved would not be able to resume normal lives or even a conscious existence, and would be passed off to chronic care facilities or to their families.

Even less concern is being expressed for the I.C.U. patient's experience of having to live attached to machines or dying that way. From the perspective of the conscious patient, experiencing what it means to be "worked on" by teams of strangers, to be coded for resuscitation (or not), to lie among others near death or already dead, to be dependent on and surrounded by wires and machines, intensive care imposes the most feared scenario: prolonged helplessness, often in pain. For years, hospital staff have known about "I.C.U. psychosis," the severe and not uncommon disorientation of patients reacting to the windowless, mechanical environment. For years, the only remedy has been to set a clock where the patient could see it.

The impact of the intensive care unit on the American way of dying has been profound, for it is there that contemporary medicine routinely eliminates the primary actor, the patient, from the ritual of dying. This is done by first selecting uncommonly passive patients in crisis. Medicine then perfected the way of artificially sustaining the clinically (if not legally) dead patient and replacing the old rituals of professional-patient interaction with emergency medical intervention, that is, professional team management of machines and bodies. Dying in this context is not something the individual patient, potentially a living corpse, really does, since it is a matter of the staff's withdrawing life supports. It has also become increasingly unclear what responsibility the once "masters of death" assume in hospital death scenarios. With few exceptions, modern physicians are revolted by death, leaving to nurses the "dirty work" of interacting with grieving families, the actual release of the patient from support machines, and ministering to the dead body.

Dying at Home

Recalling a time, long gone, when people died at home, Michel Foucault describes the family's gaze fixed on the sick person as full of "the vital force of benevolence and the discretion of hope." The contemporary alternative of dying at home guarantees no such comfort. Yet many households, prepared or not, must accept the prospect of such caretaking, even though the patient's death at the last minute takes place in the hospital.

Since the introduction of D.R.G.'s in 1983, the allowable length of hospital stay for Medicare patients has been sharply decreased. Growing numbers of chronically ill and elderly people are being cared for by relatives. But the family context has its problems: emotional ambivalence, instability, isolation from the larger community, and even violence. Hospice care, once hailed as the humane alternative to dying in the hospital, provides only minor support in terms of supplies and service. Family members, especially women, are left with the daily responsibility for patient care, which now often includes complex regimens of infusion drugs, intravenous feeding, oxygen support, and physical therapy. For most of the elderly, long-term nursing home care is economically not feasible. Hospitals have no room for those who are dying slowly—but then who does?

The toll of rejection may be seen in the increasing rate of suicide among the elderly. Between 1981 and 1986,

The choice to refuse medication or food may be rational if one truly believes it is time to die.

suicides among people over sixty-five rose sharply, from 12.6 per 100,000 to 21.8. Starvation, refusal of medication, and guns were the principal means. How such private decisions are reached or even if they can count as rational, we do not know, although fear of being a burden is frequently reported in anecdotes. Such a fear itself is not irrational. Government and professional support for home care is minimal. Home-care providers receive scant training for the technical tasks they perform, no provision for relief, and no credit for the round-the-clock time they give. Having little or no reimbursement incentives, physicians generally ignore patients cared for at home. Cost coverage for home care varies with the insurance carrier. Even under private insurance plans, many items must be paid for out-of-pocket. In the last ten years, unregulated commercial agencies have taken over the growing, multi-billion dollar home-care industry and have inflated the retail cost of everything—needles, gauze, plastic tubing, rubber sheets, bed rentals, and drugs—in ways that parallel hospital charges for aspirin and the price of Pentagon coffee pots.

As death re-enters the American household, it is tamed only by the resources a family or perhaps only a single relative or friend can muster. Maybe the community has a free slot in the hospice program, maybe the physician will do more than telephone, maybe a member of the clergy will visit. But there are no guarantees. If the scenario of hospital death is daunting, so too is the vision of a drawn-out, painful expiration, resented and uncomforted by those intimates or the intimate to whom one is a burden. The choice to refuse medication or even food may be rational, if one truly believes it is time to die. But the rationale "I am only a burden" threatens all of us, for we are all at some time in our lives completely dependent on others.

Confronting Death

The present controversy surrounding physician-assisted suicide and rational suicide in general may be all to the good, if it promotes change in our institutions. How many people would be interested in a quick (six minutes), painless death in a parked van (the scenario for Janet Adkins, the first user of Kevorkian's mercitron machine), if hospitals and homes provided a more humane context for dying? Or is it that Americans, Puritans still, ask for nothing more than clean sheets and a morphine drip? This may be true. The rational suicides reported in the media all have a tidy, pain-free aura about them.

Critics, such as Mitford and Ariès, accurately identified our cultural denial of death as a serious aberration. We want death to never happen, to be a non-experience, or an event that cannot threaten our dignity. Yet, as the philosopher Paul Ramsey used to say, there is nothing at all dignified about dying—one might add, nor happy either.

Death must be seen for what it is—cruelly inevitable, a painful rendering, our finitude—if we are to understand the human condition and even begin to ask about the meaning of life. Death is momentous, in the general and in the specific. For the dying person, spirit and body are inescapably involved in a final reckoning. No witness can be untouched, except by a distortion of the most fundamental truth, that we are mortal. The distance between us and the dying person is only an accident of time.

It is this sense of mortality we try to hide from and the reason we have created institutions of denial. Oddly enough, we even deny the extent to which these institutions contribute to our problems. In the innumerable debates and discussions about death, the focus remains on individual strategies, as if, for example, one person's choice of suicide over protracted terminal illness constituted a justification in itself, prompted by psychology, legitimated by one's will, and with no social consequences or meaning. Yet our hospitals are strange and alienating environments to the extent that they obfuscate this truth of mortality by therapeutic experimentalism, intensive care, and also the "harvesting" of organs from living corpses. Our homes are threatening to the extent that people are left in isolation to deal with life as a burden and death as an obscenity. The quick-fix suicide machine or the plastic bag method described in *Final Exit* might relieve the individual of woe and suffering, but what about the rest of us, who will dutifully attend to our living wills and then await the worst? We know that death is not obscene; it cannot by itself deprave us. But it is frightening in its familiarity and cannot be simply planned away. Rather, we should envision institutional reforms. We need physicians educated to say more to the dying patient than "Have a nice trip" (Kevorkian's farewell to Janet Adkins). We need hospitals with staff motivated to give humane attention, not overtreatment, to the dying. We need compensation for families that give home care so that they can afford to be kind and old people can die in relative peace. Death is indeed a wild beast of sorts. These are ways to tame it.

READINGS SUGGESTED BY THE AUTHOR:

Philippe Ariès. *Western Attitudes Toward Death.* Baltimore, Md.: Johns Hopkins University Press, 1974.
Susan DiGiacomo. "Biomedicine in the Cultural System: An Anthropologist in the Kingdom of the Sick," in *Encounters with Biomedicine: Case Studies in Medical Anthropology,* Hans Baer (ed.). New York: Gordon and Breach Science Publishers, 1987.
Susan Sontag. *Illness as Metaphor.* New York: Farrar, Straus, and Giroux, 1988.

Jeanne Guillemin is professor of sociology at Boston College. She has published widely on questions of medical technology and is co-author (with Lynda L. Holmstrom) of Mixed Blessings. Intensive Care for Newborns.

Placing Religion and Spirituality in End-of-Life Care

Timothy P. Daaleman, DO
Larry VandeCreek, DMin

IN 1995, THE SUPPORT (STUDY TO UNDERSTAND PROGnoses and Preferences for Outcomes and Risks of Treatment) trial stimulated a reexamination of systems of care for seriously ill and dying patients.[1] This study has indirectly promoted a rapprochement among religion, spirituality, medicine, and health care.[2] The goal of a quality comfortable death is achieved by meeting a patient's physical needs and by attending to the social, psychological, and the now recognized spiritual and religious dimensions of care.[3,4] This perspective is highlighted in a recent consensus statement that includes the assessment and support of spiritual and religious well-being and management of spiritual and religious problems as core principles of professional practice and care at the end of life.[5] Yet multiple ethical and pragmatic issues arise. For example, should physicians identify patients' spiritual and religious needs and intervene in clinical settings? The roles and responsibilities of patients and physicians in this scenario are unclear. An understanding of religion and spirituality within the context of end-of-life care, quality of life, and patient-clinician interactions may illuminate the problems and potentialities for both patients and clinicians.

Religion: The Provision of Belief and the Establishment of an Ethic

The distinction between religion and spirituality is an important and nuanced one. From its Latin roots (*religio*), religion has been associated with various connotations: the totality of belief systems, an inner piety or disposition, an abstract system of ideas, and ritual practices.[6] In end-of-life care, religion and religious traditions serve 2 primary functions: the provision of a set of core beliefs about life events and the establishment of an ethical foundation for clinical decision making.[7] Religious doctrine and belief systems provide a framework for understanding the human experience of death and dying for patients, family members, and health care professionals. Intuitively, strong religious beliefs, whether expressed or privately held, should be associated with a decreased fear of death and greater acceptance of death. However, research that has examined the interaction between religious belief and attitudes toward death has produced controversial results that generally do not support this assumption.[8]

In addition, religious traditions include substantial normative and ethical issues in end-of-life care.[7] Ethics in this context spans a wide range of human interaction from interpersonal to organizational levels and represents the moral response to approaching and encountering death. Religion-based ethics provides a point of reference for clinical decision making and many religious groups, such as the National Conference of Catholic Bishops,[9] the Unitarian Universalist General Assembly,[10] and the Conservative Movement's Committee on Jewish Law and Standards,[11] actively participate in public discourse about issues that accompany the end of life (eg, palliative care, withdrawal of advanced life support, advance care planning). Although these sources provide an ethical framework for decisions at the end of life,[12] religion-based ethics can both facilitate and impede clinical decision making,[13] which reflects a dynamic interplay among patients, family members, clinicians, and institutions.

The issues of physician-assisted suicide (PAS) and euthanasia exemplify the complex interaction between religious belief and ethical decision making in end-of-life care. Recent studies have found an inverse association between measures of religiousness and attitudes toward PAS. A survey of physicians, nurses, and social workers in New York City found that respondents who had lower levels of religious belief were more willing to endorse assisted suicide than those who reported higher levels of belief.[14] This finding is consistent with a national study by Emanuel et al[15] who found that oncologists who report high or moderate levels of religious belief were

From the *Journal of the American Medical Association*, November 15, 2000, pp. 2514-2517. © 2000 by the American Medical Association. Reprinted by permission.

less likely to perform euthanasia or PAS than those who reported no religious belief. In a national survey of US physicians representing specialties most likely to receive patient requests for assistance with suicide or euthanasia, Meier et al[16] reported that physicians who have no religious affiliation were more likely to be willing to provide assistance and to have complied with a patient request for PAS than those with a religious affiliation.

These findings parallel those from patient populations as well. A study of patients with amyotrophic lateral sclerosis living in Oregon and Washington found that respondents who scored higher on a scale measuring the importance of religion were less likely to consider assisted suicide than those with lower scores.[17] In 2 studies of older adults, the degree of self-reported strength of religious beliefs or role of religion in life was inversely proportional with more permissive attitudes toward assisted suicide.[18,19] For both patients and physicians, these studies suggest that religious belief may have a significant effect on ethical decision making at the end of life.

Spirituality: Resources for Personal Meaning

Spirituality may or may not be linked to religious beliefs, religious practices, or communities that support those practices and beliefs.[20] Terminally ill patients acknowledge a greater spiritual perspective and orientation than both nonterminally ill hospitalized patients and healthy patients.[21] Although there are multiple interpretations of spirituality within health care settings,[22] constructs of meaning or a sense of life's purpose have been suggested as primary components.[23] For example, in women with advanced breast cancer, maintaining a purpose or meaning in life has been identified as an important aspect of self-transcendence and spiritual well-being.[24,25] The coping literature delineates 2 forms of meaning: implicit meaning and found meaning.[26] Implicit meaning is an appraisal process that involves the gathering and processing of medical information.[27] Found meaning, or meaningfulness, interprets and places this information into a larger life context.[26] Antonovsky[28] describes this generally positive, pervasive way of seeing the world, and one's life in it, as a "sense of coherence," lending comprehensibility and manageability.

Psychological states and quality-of-life outcomes have been the primary end points in end-of-life care studies that have incorporated a measure of spirituality. For example, among oncology patients, modest correlations have been found between spirituality and lower levels of anxiety and psychosocial distress.[29,30] Additional studies suggest that spirituality is also positively associated with subjective well-being[21] and quality of life to the same degree as physical well-being.[31]

Quality of Life

In clinical and research settings, quality-of-life assessment examines the social, physical, and psychological influences on patient illness, health, and well-being.[32] Measures of religiousness and spirituality that are specific to end-of-life care vary in their content, validity, and reliability, which reflect the developmental state of work in this area. The McGill Quality of Life Questionnaire[33] incorporates items to assess achievement of life goals and personal meaning, while the Functional Assessment of Chronic Illness Therapy-Spiritual Well-Being[31] scale contains questions that measure the comfort and strength derived from religious faith, in addition to a sense of meaning, purpose, and peace in life. The Systems of Belief Inventory,[34] which was designed for use in quality-of-life and psychosocial research examining illness adjustment, measures religious and spiritual beliefs and practices and the social support that accompanies those beliefs and practices.

Religion and spirituality potentially can mediate quality of life by enhancing patient subjective well-being through social support and stress and coping strategies. Theoretically, religious and spiritual beliefs may enhance subjective well-being in 4 ways: promoting a salubrious personal lifestyle that is congruent with religious or personal faith traditions, providing systems of meaning and existential coherence, establishing personal relationships with a divine other, and ensuring social support and integration within a community.[35] Social support has been suggested as an intervening factor between quality of life and religion and spirituality. The positive impact of social support and support groups on survival in cancer patients generated considerable interest in the early 1990s,[36] although follow-up studies have failed to replicate earlier findings.[37] Religious and spiritual beliefs have been found to be beneficial when examined within theoretical models of stress and coping.[38] Research on religious approaches to coping and problem solving have been predictive of successful psychological adjustment to stressful life events.[39] For example, Jenkins and Pargament[40] report that cancer patients who attribute more control over their illness to God have higher self-esteem and are more adjusted to their disease state than those who do not attribute such control to God.

Patient-Clinician Interactions and Interventions

Assessment of quality of life raises some practical and ethical issues regarding the clinician's role in spiritual and religious support during end-of-life care. How do physicians and nurses frame religious and spiritual concerns within health care settings? Are religious and spiritual concerns subsumed within social and psychological constructs and domains that comprise an individual's experience of illness and disease, or are spirituality and religion conceptualized and viewed a priori? This tension is highlighted by recommendations and initiatives that incorporate religion and spirituality in plans to improve care at the end of life. For example, assessment guidelines for palliative care plans developed by the Institute of Medicine embed spiritual assessment within measures of emotional status.[41] However, a report from the Commonwealth-Cummings project lists spiritual and existential beliefs as an independent modifiable dimension of the patient's dying experience.[4]

The inconsistent orientation and lack of conceptual clarity that accompany religion and spirituality raise several secondary questions relative to the operationalization of any guideline or recommendation. Who is responsible for assessing and meeting the spiritual and religious needs of dying patients: physicians, nurses, social workers, psychologists, or clergy and health care chaplains? Some have advocated that physicians or other members of the health care team should address these issues.[42] Yet within the patient-physician relationship, physicians wield a power that is largely positive and salutary, and this power may result in a loss of patient autonomy if left unchecked or unguarded.[43] In the development of treatment goals and care plans, patient autonomy can be threatened when physicians' religious convictions are dissonant with those of patients and family members. For example, studies that measured physician religiousness and PAS support the assumption that physicians' religious belief may influence the patient-physician relationship. In light of these concerns, data from a US national survey suggest that clergy and professional pastoral care providers assume a primary role for religious and spiritual concerns in clinical settings.[44] In this survey, more than 80% of family physicians reported that they refer to these clergy and pastoral care providers in conditions associated with end-of-life care. However, if quality of life is enhanced by the search for personal meaning, should physicians and other health care professionals also incorporate these aspects in care? Would physicians' approaches differ from those of professional pastoral care providers tied to religious or faith traditions? These issues are fertile ground for future research.

Future Directions: Hospice as a Sentinel Model

The hospice movement provides a case study to examine the development of religion and spirituality within end-of-life care. The foundation of the modern hospice movement was grounded in a Western Christian religious tradition.[45] This faith tradition served a primary function for hospice by providing an ethical foundation and a set of core beliefs, initially for a small committed group of people in the United Kingdom in the 1960s. Saunders, who pioneered the hospice movement, provided much of the philosophical framework that still underlies contemporary hospice,[46] and the mission statement for one of the original hospices, St Christopher's, remains rooted within this religious tradition.[45] But as the hospice movement grew and encountered patients and health care professionals who often did not share this tradition, hospice had to accommodate and modify its mission or risk alienating a constituency that it was founded to serve. Today hospice maintains a global approach to patient care with an emphasis on relieving suffering, but the religious basis and foundation for this care are conspicuously absent.

Religious traditions provide a framework for both individual and organizational ethics, and it is uncertain how loosening the ties of hospice to a specific religious tradition may affect the hospice ethos. For example, although the place of euthanasia and PAS is often minimized and discouraged in hospice settings,[46] recent research suggests that these organizational values may not be pervasive. In one survey of US oncologists, approximately 40% of patients were receiving hospice care at the time of euthanasia or PAS,[15] while an additional study found that 32% of patients in Oregon enrolled in a hospice program

requested a prescription for lethal medications.[47] Although these studies do not imply that hospice care has a waning emphasis on religious and spiritual concerns, it is unclear whether these findings represent a limitation of hospice care in individual cases, a compassionate response to the control of pain and suffering in these settings, or the fact that most hospice care is only one, albeit important, component of the patient's life and decision-making contribution.

Hospice considers the religious or spiritual dimension of the person as independent and not subsumed within social or psychological domains. The World Health Organization also holds a similar perspective and defines palliative care as

> the active total care of patients whose disease is not responsive to curative treatment . . .[when] control of pain, of other symptoms, and of psychological, social, and spiritual problems is paramount.[48]

The understanding of spirituality has also evolved. For example, hospice's original religious definition of spirituality as a relationship with God or a Divine Other has been replaced by a definition of spirituality as the personal and psychological search for meaning.[45] This trend is part of a larger cultural movement in the United States in which there is a transition from a traditional membership in a faith community to a spirituality of seeking.[49] The increase in quality-of-life research that includes measures of spirituality and the spiritual resources in hospice care are manifestations of the widespread acceptance of a spirituality that is uprooted from its religious sources. The distancing of religious beliefs from spirituality has facilitated a greater and necessary acceptance of hospice into a multicultural world, one in which hospice workers may move about among many different faith traditions.

Yet religion and faith traditions still occupy a substantial place in end-of-life care. From a social constructionist perspective, social determinants such as social support, education, gender, and religion are primary elements that facilitate the interpretation and understanding of death and dying.[50] In this context, religious and faith traditions may be part of the scaffolding in the construction of meaning as death approaches. Spirituality may be viewed as the actions and interactions of an embodied human actor who is facing death and creating a personally meaningful social world, a constructed world that can be either a resource or an encumbrance.[50] For hospice and palliative care this has several implications: a richer appreciation of the social and demographic determinants of a quality care at the end of life, a greater understanding of the psychological and theological processes involved in "meaning making," and an emphasis on assessment strategies and interventions that are inclusive of these factors.

When viewed from either a constructionist or phenomenological perspective, the ties that bind hospice to palliative care in the assessment and management of spiritual concerns are best understood by examining the locus of care at the end of life. Multiple connotations of hospice exist, yet many associate this term with a physical place of respite and care. In the evolution of end-of-life care and the emergence of the disciplines of palliative care, there has been a shift in the common understanding of hospice from an institution that provides care of the individual.[51] Hospice and palliative care have negotiated much of the difficult terrain that accompanies religion and spirituality and medicine, and they have done so by moving the locus of care out of biomedical institutions back into the community. By offering a health care delivery model that incorporates a community-based approach while emphasizing the uniqueness of the individual, regardless of the importance of religion or spirituality in the individual's life, hospice and palliative care provide a structure for and facilitate the processes that are involved in this most basic of human experiences, that of dying.

Funding/Support: Dr Daaleman is supported by the Robert Wood Johnson Foundation Generalist Faculty Scholars Program and the John A. Hartford Foundation. **Acknowledgment:** We thank Sarah A. Forbes, RN, PhD, for her review of the manuscript.

REFERENCES

1. SUPPORT Principal Investigators. A controlled trial to improve care for seriously ill hospitalized patients: the Study to Understand Prognoses and Preferences for Outcomes and Risks of Treatment (SUPPORT). *JAMA.* 1995;274:1591–1598.

2. Daaleman TP. A cartography of spirituality in end-of-life care. *Bioethics Forum.* 1997;13:49–52.

3. Byock R. *Dying Well: The Prospect for Growth at the End of Life.* New York, NY: Riverhead; 1997.

4. Emanuel EJ, Emanuel LL. The promise of a good death. *Lancet.* 1998;351 (suppl 2):521–529.

5. Cassel CK, Foley KM. *Principles for Care of Patients at the End of Life: An Emerging Consensus Among the Specialties of Medicine.* New York, NY: Millbank Memorial Fund; 1999.

6. Wulff DM. *Psychology of Religion: Classic and Contemporary.* New York, NY: John Wiley & Sons; 1997.

7. O'Connell LJ. Religious dimensions of dying and death. *West J Med.* 1995;163:231–235.

8. Neimeyer RA, ed. *Death Anxiety Handbook, Research, Instrumentation, and Application.* Washington, DC: Taylor & Francis; 1994.

9. National Conference of Catholic Bishops. *Ethical and Religious Directive for Catholic Health Care Services.* Washington, DC: United States Catholic Conference; 1994.

10. General Assembly of Unitarian Universalists. *The Right to Die with Dignity: Proceedings of General Assembly.* Boston, Mass: Unitarian Universalist Association; 1988.

11. Dorff E. A Jewish approach to end-stage medical care. *Conservative Judaism.* 1991;43:3–51.

12. Dubose ER. *Physician Assisted Suicide, Religious and Public Policy Perspectives.* Chicago, Ill: The Park Ridge Center; 1999.

13. Posts SG. Medical futility and the free exercise of religion. *J Law Med Ethics.* 1995;23:20–26.

14. Portenoy RK, Coyle N. Kash KM, et al. Determinants of the willingness to endorse assisted suicide, a survey of physicians, nurses, and social workers. *Psychosomatics.* 1997;38:277–287.

15. Emanuel EJ, Daniels ER, Fairclough DL, Clarridge BR. The practice of euthanasia and physician-assisted suicide in the United States. *JAMA.* 1998;280:507–513.

16. Meier DE, Emmons CA, Wallenstein S. et al. A national survey of physician-assisted suicide and euthanasia in the United States. *N Engl J Med.* 1998;338:967–973.

17. Ganzini L. Johnston WS, McFarland BH, Tolle SW, Lee MA. Attitudes of patients with amyotrophic lateral sclerosis and their care givers toward assisted suicide. *N Engl J Med.* 1998;339:967–973.

18. Seidlitz L. Duberstein PR, Cox C, Conwell Y. Attitudes of older people toward suicide and assisted suicide: an analysis of Gallup Poll findings. *J Am Geriatr Soc.* 1995;l43:993–998.

19. Sullivan M. Ormel J, Kempen GUM, Tymstra T. Beliefs concerning death, dying, and hastening death among older, functionally impaired Dutch adults: a one-year longitudinal study. *J Am Geriatr Soc.* 1998;46:1251–1257.

20. Van Ness PH. *Spirituality and the Secular Quest.* New York, NY: Continuum;1996.

21. Reed PG. Spirituality and well-being in terminally ill hospitalized adults. *Res Nurs Health.* 1987;10:335–344.

22. Larson DB, Swyers JP, McCullough ME, eds. Scientific research on spirituality and health: a consensus report. Rockville, Md: National Institute of Healthcare Research; 1998.

23. Fitchett G, Handzo G. Spiritual assessment, screening, and intervention. In: Holland JC, ed. *Psycho-oncology.* New York, NY: Oxford University Press; 1998:790–808.

24. Coward DD. The lived experience of self-transcendence in women with advanced breast cancer. *Nurs Sci Q.* 1989;3:162–169.

25. Hassey Dow K, Ferrell BR, Leigh S, et al. An evaluation of the QOL among long-term survivors of breast cancer. *Breast Cancer Res Treatment.* 1996;39:261–273.

26. Thompson SC, Janigian AS. Life schemes: a framework for understanding the search for meaning. *J Soc Clin Psychol.* 1988;7:260–280.

27. Lazarus RS, Folkman S. *Stress, Appraisal, and Coping.* New York, NY: Springer;1984.

28. Antonovsky A. *Unraveling the Mystery of Health: How People Manage Stress and Stay Well.* San Francisco, Calif: Jossey-Bass; 1987.

29. Kaczorowski JM. Spiritual well-being and anxiety in adults diagnosed with cancer. *Hospice J.* 1989;5:105–116.

30. Smith ED, Stefanek ME, Joseph MV, et al. Spiritual awareness, personal perspective on death, and psychosocial distress among cancer patients: an initial investigation. *J Psychosoc Oncol.* 1993;11:89–103.

31. Brady MJ, Peterman AH, Fitchett G. Mo M, Cella D. A case for including spirituality in quality of life measurement in oncology. *Psychooncology.* 1999;8:417–428.

32. Testa MA, Simonson DC. Assessment of quality of life outcomes. *N Engl J Med.* 1996;334:835–840.

33. Cohen SR, Mount BM, Tomas J, Mount L. Existential well-being is an important determinant of quality of life: evidence from the McGill Quality of Life Questionnaire. *Cancer.* 1996;77:576–586.

34. Holland JC, Kash KM, Passik S. et al. A brief spiritual beliefs inventory for use in quality of life research in life-threatening illness. *Psychooncology.* 1998;7:460–469.

35. Ellison CG. Religious involvement and subjective well-being. *J Health Soc Behav.* 1991;32:80–99.

36. Spiegel D, Bloom JR, Kraemer HC, Gottheil E. Effects of psychosocial treatment on survival of patients with metastatic breast cancer. *Lancet.* 1989;2:888–891.

37. Cunningham AJ, Edmonds CV, Jenkins GP, et al. A randomized controlled trail of the effects of group psychological therapy on survival in women with metastatic breast cancer. *Psychooncology.* 1998;7:508–517.

38. Krause N, Tan TV. Stress and religious involvement among older blacks. *J Gerontol.* 1989;44:S4–S13.

39. Pargament KI. *The Psychology of Religion and Coping, Theory, Research, and Practice.* New York, NY: Guilford Press; 1997.

40. Jenkins RA, Pargament KI. Cognitive appraisals in cancer patients. *Soc Sci Med.* 1988;26:625–633.

41. Institute of Medicine. *Approaching Death: Improving Care at the End-of-Life.* Washington, DC: National Academy Press; 1997.

42. Lo B, Quill T, Tulsky J, for the ACP-ASIM End-of-Life Care Consensus Panel. Discussing palliative care with patients. *Ann Intern Med.* 1999;130:744–749.

43. Brody H. *The Healer's Power.* New Haven, Conn: Yale University Press; 1992.

44. Daaleman TP, Frey B. Prevalence and patterns of physician referral to clergy and pastoral care providers. *Arch Fam Med.* 1998;7:548–553.

45. Bradshaw A. The spiritual dimension of hospice: the secularization of an ideal. *Soc Sci Med.* 1996;43:409–419.

46. Mathew LM, Scully JH. Hospice care. *Clin Geriatr Med.* 1986;2:617–634.

47. Ganzini L, Nelson HD, Schmidt TA. et al. Physicians experiences with the Oregon Death with Dignity Act. *N Engl J Med.* 2000;342:557–563.

48. World Health Organization. *Cancer Pain Relief and Palliative Care.* Geneva, Switzerland: World Health Organization; 1990. Technical Report Series 804.

49. Wuthnow R. *After Heaven: Spirituality in America Since the 1950's.* Berkeley: University of California Press; 1998.

50. Seale C. *Constructing Death, the Sociology of Dying and Bereavement.* Cambridge, England: Cambridge University Press; 1998.

51. Doyle D, Hanks G, MacDonald N, eds. *Oxford Textbook of Palliative Medicine.* Oxford, England: Oxford University Press; 1999.

Author Affiliations: Departments of Family Medicine and History & Philosophy of Medicine, Center on Aging, University of Kansas Medical Center, Kansas City (Dr Daaleman); and The Healthcare Chaplaincy, New York, NY (Dr Vande-Creek). **Corresponding Author and Reprints:** Timothy P. Daaleman, DO, Department of Family Medicine, University of Kansas Medical Center, 3901 Rainbow Blvd, Kansas City, KS 66160–7370 (e-mail: tdaalema@kumc.edu).

Sometimes Dying Still Stings

"THIS IS HORRIBLE, JUST HORRIBLE." "CAN'T WE DO SOMEthing else for him?" "This sucks."

My mother-in-law, my wife, and her sister were saying these things as we were waiting for my father-in-law Al to die. Their words surprised me because our family, along with Al and his physician, had orchestrated what I considered "a peaceful death" for Al. Our deathbed vigil was not taking place with him on a ventilator in some intensive care unit, surrounded by strangers and high-tech equipment. Al was at home, with his wife, two daughters, and two sons-in-law taking turns providing hands-on care with the assistance of home hospice. Four grandchildren played on the bed with their Pa Al when he felt up to it.

In fact, Al hadn't spent a single night in a hospital since being diagnosed with advanced bronchioloalveolar adenocarcinoma 18 months earlier. After grim consultations at two leading cancer centers, Al had opted for no cancer-specific therapy. He didn't talk to us about his diagnosis or terminal condition. One might even have wondered if Al had been in a state of denial if it weren't for all the activity: straightening out files; reconciling accounts, and labeling everything in the house, including fuse boxes and cabinet drawers, so that his wife would be able to find everything when he was gone. Six weeks before his death, Al traveled from his home in Detroit to Chicago to play a role of honor in our newborn son's *bris*. Al was still ambulatory two weeks before his death. His physician referred him for hospice care only when the dyspnea worsened and Al took to his bed for the last two days of his life. He remained alert until about 48 hours before his death, able to interact with his family and the many friends who came to visit. His symptoms were well controlled with the use of morphine, anxiolytics, and oxygen.

As a geriatrician who does a fair amount of hospice care, I thought Al's care was a textbook case of excellent palliative medicine (if medical texts actually covered end-of-life care adequately). He had had plenty of time to get his affairs in order; he had avoided unwanted and burdensome treatments; his preferences were being followed, including where he wanted to die; his family was around him; and his symptoms were palliated. Al had received the kind of care that I worked hard to deliver to my own parents. Why then were his dying and death so horrible for Al and his family? Why didn't my wife and others appreciate the superb hospice care that he was getting? Where was the spiritual growth, the transcendence described by writers in the medical and popular press?

It didn't take much probing to realize why this excellent end-of-life care still left everyone feeling bad. Al was still dying, he didn't want to die yet, and his family sure didn't want him to die. Al was the cheerful center of the extended family. He was the family peacemaker, the optimist, the one with the corny sense of humor who could turn the most surly waiter or clerk into a pal by the end of an encounter. He was Pa Al, up at the crack of dawn when we visited, to make fresh-squeezed orange juice with our 3-year-old daughter. Although he was approaching 80, and some would say that he had lived a good, long life, there was so much more he wanted to continue doing for and with his family, so much more we wanted him to be a part of. Al was being ripped from our midst and it hurt like hell.

In the months that followed his death, I've thought often about Al's dying and the family's experience. Since Al's death, I have become reluctant to use terms like "the good death," "growth at the end of life," and "spiritual transcendence" when I speak with patients and families. I am fearful of painting too rosy a picture of end-of-life care and of contributing to their setting unrealistic expectations. I do not want families to end up feeling even worse because their experiences fall short of the ideals I may have described previously or that are still portrayed in the media. (I have analogous concerns about my frail, elderly patients and the hype surrounding successful aging, antiaging, and real-aging efforts. Do some of them feel like failures for having aged "unsuccessfully"?) I am more careful with my trainees, as well as patients and families, to acknowledge that because some of the suffering is existential or spiritual, there may be limits to what we can achieve with even superb, multidisciplinary end-of-life medical care. Even with chaplains, social workers, and others attending to spirituality, anticipatory grief, and bereavement, Al's family felt devastated. In my own research, I more clearly recognize that there are some things about dying and death that simply aren't going to be captured and made better by quality improvement score cards or measurements on pain scales.

Observing the dying of a loved family member elicits feelings of fear, awe, pain, and grief and raises questions about the meaning of life. Death means someone is lost to us forever. Maybe, for some families, I can do a better job by acknowledging that while working to make the experience a little less horrible.

Greg A. Sachs, MD
Chicago, Ill

A Piece of My Mind Section Editor: Roxanne K. Young, Associate Editor.

From the *Journal of the American Medical Association*, November 15, 2000, p. 2423. © 2000 by the American Medical Association. Reprinted by permission.

The Patient-Physician Relationship

The Request to Die

Role for a Psychodynamic Perspective on Physician-Assisted Suicide

Philip R. Muskin, MD

Published reports indicate that 2.5% of deaths in the Netherlands are the result of euthanasia or physician-assisted suicide. It is not known how many patients make these requests in the United States, but the issue has gained considerable attention, including that of the Supreme Court. The focus of the writing and discussion regarding the request to die has been on a patient's capacity. There has not been an adequate focus on the possible meanings contained within the request to die. A patient's request to die is a situation that requires the physician to engage in a dialogue to understand what the request means, including whether the request arises from a clinically significant depression or inadequately treated pain. This article outlines some of the thoughts and emotions that could underlie the patient's request to die. Recommendations are made regarding the role of the primary care physician and the role of the psychiatric consultant in the exploration of the meaning of the request.

J.A.M.A. 1998;279:323–328

THE ISSUE to be addressed in this article is not one of ethics or law. The focus is on the variety of potential psychodynamic meanings contained within a patient's request for assistance in bringing about his or her death, and the important role a psychodynamic understanding can play in the physician's response to the patient. Some treatment refusals will result in the death of the patient and, thus, should also be carefully assessed.[1] The principle that every request to die should be subjected to careful scrutiny of its multiple potential meanings has not been part of the standard response to such requests.

Data from a 1995 survey of death certificates in the Netherlands reveals that 2.5% of all deaths result from euthanasia.[2] This is an increase from the 1.7% rate found in the 1990 survey.[2] Whether this increase indicates a "slippery slope" is a matter of controversy.[3] It is not known how many patients in the United States request help in dying. As noted by Hendin, "Strikingly, the overwhelming majority of those who are terminally ill fight for life to the end."[4] Chochinov et al[5] reported that 44% (89 of 200) of terminally ill patients report occasional wishes that death would come soon. Only 9% report a "serious and pervasive wish to die."[5] As in other studies, the desire for death correlates with both physical pain and with poor social support.[5] The most significant correlation is with depression, as 59% of patients who wish to die have a depressive syndrome.[5] Breitbart et al[6] found that 63% of patients infected with the human immunodeficiency virus (HIV) supported policies favoring physician-assisted suicide, and 55% considered physician-assisted suicide as a personal option. This study demonstrated a strong correlation with depression and low social support (patients' rating of fewer visits by family and friends, patients' experiencing less support from family and friends), but not with patients' rating of physical pain.[6] It is possible that the stigma, prejudice, and discrimination that patients with HIV infection experience increases their risk for depression and the wish to die. Some studies demonstrate that uncontrolled pain correlates strongly with suicide in cancer patients[7,8]; others show a negative correlation between patients with pain and a positive attitude toward euthanasia and physician-assisted suicide.[9] The survey of oncology patients by Emanuel et al[9] found that 25% thought about asking their physician for euthanasia or physician-assisted suicide. This study confirmed the association between depression and patients' consideration of death. The patients who were "depressed and psychologically distressed were significantly more likely to seriously discuss euthanasia, hoard drugs, or bought or read Final Exit."[9]

Surveys report a wide range in physicians' reports of requests from patients for assisted death and in physicians' willingness to give a lethal dose of a drug or perform assisted death.[9–18] Seventeen percent of critical care nurses reported receiving requests for death from patients or from the patient's family; 16% reported they aided in a patient's death, and 4% reported that they hastened a patient's death by pretending to provide life-sustaining treatment ordered by the physician.[19]

Fifteen percent of nurses who work with patients with the acquired immunodeficiency syndrome in San Francisco, Calif, have assisted in a patient's suicide.[20] Physicians and other clinicians thus find themselves continuing to struggle with patients' requests to die.

A psychodynamic approach to a patient's communication attempts to understand both the manifest content and also to explore unconscious meanings. Critics of this approach label the search for meaning reductionist, indicating that it entails seeking a different origin or a "true" meaning hidden from that apparent on the surface, without acknowledging the importance of the manifest content. A modern view of psychodynamics is expansionist, ie, seeking to find other important hidden meanings within emotion, thought, and behavior rather than searching for a singularity, a core unity, or a "truth." The premise that follows from this conceptual framework is that every case of a patient requesting to die should be explored in depth by the physician primarily responsible for the care of the patient, mindful of the complex psychodynamics that might be involved. No action should be taken prior to such close scrutiny. Discussions of the psychiatric evaluation of a patient's request to die often focus on whether the patient is "competent," which is too simplistic an approach for so complex a matter. This article is designed to explore some of that complexity using general categories of thoughts and emotion present in patients who express suicidal ideation. This may shed light on the significance to the patient and to the physician of conscious and unconscious meanings in a medically ill patient's request to die.

THE REQUEST TO DIE AS A COMMUNICATION

When a person commits suicide, the note left behind communicates (overtly and symbolically) the reasons for the choice of death. Of greatest importance is the fact that his communication follows the death. There must be a difference between patients who commit suicide, with no communication save the note left behind, and patients who say to their physicians "Would you assist me in my death?" or "Would you kill me?" The very fact that there is a communication while the person is alive suggests the expectation of an interaction with the physician. What could such a request mean to the patient and what does the request signify as a communication to the physician? There are many possibilities, but one that should be considered is that the request to die is an attempt to be given a reason to live[21]; ie, the patient is asking, "Does anyone care enough to talk me out of this request, to want me to be alive, to be willing to share my suffering?" Acting on a patient's wish because he or she is judged to be rational and competent ignores the unspoken or unconscious meaning(s) of the request. Acknowledging this dynamic without stating it overtly, a physician might respond to the patient, "I want to try to do everything I can to work with you and provide you with the best care I can offer. If you die, you will be greatly missed; how can we understand together why you want to die right now?"

CONTROL

"It is always consoling to think of suicide: in that way one gets through many a bad night."[22] Nietzsche's comment suggests that one possibility contained within a patient's request to die may be an effort to take control over life, even if this control is illusory and paradoxical. When a patient has lost control over every aspect of life, the only place control may be established is by asking for death. Many patients find great solace in knowing they can kill themselves at any time by hoarding a lethal dose of medication, even though the medication is never used. Is the person actually seeking death or a magical protection in the form of the pills, a talisman against the agonizing helplessness of having no control? A discussion with the physician could provide the patient with the reassurance that the ability to control his or her destiny is maintained without requesting to die.

A patient awaiting a heart for transplant informed the physician that patients had the "right" to request physician-assisted suicide. A psychiatric consultation was requested to evaluate the patient's "suicidality," and there was great concern on the ward that the patient might remove the battery from the left ventricular assist device (LVAD). When interviewed, the patient was lively and engaging, clearly enjoying the back-and-forth discussion of a patient's right to end his or her life. There were no symptoms of depression, and the patient was hopeful about obtaining a new heart. The patient came from a tradition of argument as a way of interaction with others, and physician-assisted suicide was a topic of personal importance. The discussion made clear the patient's need to feel in control of every aspect of life, control that the idiopathic cardiomyopathy had taken away. In talking about the "right to die," the question of the LVAD arose, especially the fact that this individual could end life at any moment by removing the batteries. The patient responded instantly and passionately that a major concern was that there would not be an adequate supply of batteries to guarantee a charged battery be available every moment of the day, at work, at home, or while traveling. The patient looked directly at the interviewer and said, "Do you think I am crazy, if I did that I would die! We're not talking about death here, we're talking about my rights."

SPLIT IN THE EXPERIENCE OF THE SELF

A cognition found in suicide and in some medically ill patients' request to die is the wish that the bad, ie, medically sick, part of the self be killed, leaving the healthy self to survive. This fantasized split may be unconscious; however, some patients may have a conscious experience of another, "sick self," who feels like an alien within the patient. Such patients make comments such as "I don't know the person I've become" or "This isn't how I usually act." Patients may complain that they feel "taken over" by their physical, medical, or emotional needs to the exclusion of their "normal" personality. Conscious or not, the wish to kill off a part of the self in order to survive or to be willing to die along with the sick self with the fantasy that the healthy self will be reborn may be a motivation contained within the request to die. In such a situation a psychological intervention could enable the individual to resolve this split so that there is no longer a healthy and sick self but one self who is suffering and ill. The physician might make a comment such as "It may feel at times as if you don't recognize yourself, particularly when you have many complaints or when you have a great deal of physical discomfort. But the 'real' you still comes through. It's okay to complain and okay to have needs." Such patients, after an initial discussion with their physician, should be referred for psychological treatment if the split in self-experience persists.

RAGE AND REVENGE

Patients who are desperately ill may feel some degree of rage: rage at themselves, rage at their doctors, rage at the world, rage at God for their illness and for their suffering. Rage, caused by physical suffering, psychological suffering, or both, may induce wishes to kill. The impact of hopelessness, the experience of being helpless, the agony of experiencing oneself as out of control, the terror of the unknown, and the physical suffering from inadequately treated pain may cause the patient to seek revenge by demanding death. To kill whom? Along with the emotion of rage comes the wish for revenge. A psychodynamic understanding of some suicidal patients indicates they are seeking revenge by murdering what is an unconscious image of an important person who is simultaneously loved and hated. Atonement for the murder is achieved by the person's death via suicide. This mental mechanism is presumed to be unconscious, though patients with severe character disorder are often aware of the wish to seek revenge on others via their own death. These are patients for whom a psychiatric consultation is necessary. Patients can have fantasies of harming the doctor or of harming significant others by dying. A successful psychotherapeutic intervention could lead to the realization on the part of the patient that there is no actual revenge that will accrue from his or her death. The patient arrives at an understanding that the focus of this love and hatred is a psychological creation. Suicide will end his or her life and potentially have an emotional impact on people who care about the person, but not the impact the patient desires.

HOPELESSNESS AND SUFFERING

Beck et al[23] note that the seriousness of suicidal intent correlates better with the degree of hopelessness about the future than with any other indicator of depressive severity. When a patient is hopeless, the physician should investigate whether the patient is depressed. Hopelessness, desperation, and despair are also emotions that accompany suffering. Suffering poses a great challenge to patient and physician. Is it the prospect of death some days, weeks, months, or years in the future that causes the patient to feel despair, hopelessness, and desperation and request death now? Or is it the patient's prospect of suffering unremitting physical pain that prompts the request for death (see below)? Patients' experience of hopelessness or hopefulness is associated with what they have been told by their physician. Informing patients about their illness and treatment necessitates that the physician strike a balance between giving too little or too much information. Inadequate information fosters a situation of hopelessness because patients have no facts with which they can make decisions. Patients can usually sense when information is withheld or is slanted. This creates distrust of the physician and seriously damages the potential effectiveness of the patient-physician relationship. At the other end of the communication spectrum is "truth dumping," which takes away all hope by telling patients morbid statistical "facts" without balancing the seriousness of the illness with a basis for hope. The physician's evaluation of the patient's hopelessness relies on his or her understanding of what information has been provided to the patient, and how that information has been communicated. The physician of a patient with diabetes, hypertension, and renal disease received a call when the patient regained consciousness after an unsuccessful suicide attempt. The patient requested that the physician assist in suicide because the diabetes and renal dysfunction were experienced as intolerable. The physician arranged for the patient to be taken to an emergency room of another hospital, where the patient was admitted in mild diabetic ketoacidosis and uncontrolled hypertension. The patient described a state of despair and felt physician-assisted suicide was a reasonable plan given the hopelessness of the renal disease. The ketoacidosis and hypertension were quickly stabilized. The family was contacted, and the patient's mother flew from out of state to bring her adult child home. History from a friend and the mother and some from the patient revealed the onset of juvenile onset diabetes 20 years previously. The patient had recently sent all personal effects to the parents' home, simultaneously refusing to talk with them or with friends. This occurred after the physician had informed the patient of the need for dialysis (and likelihood of a kidney transplant) within the next year at the rate the renal function was declining. It was also revealed that the physician had presented the "facts" that there was little long-term hope for a successful transplant 2 days before the suicide attempt and the request for physician-assisted suicide. The patient's mother, having contacted a group investigating renal and pancreatic transplants, came ready to take the patient home for such an evaluation. The despair disappeared when this news was received. The patient spoke about the "important things left to do with life" and was "glad" that the suicide attempt had been unsuccessful.

PAIN

Pain is a physical experience that also creates emotional suffering. Inadequate pain control may cause rage, sadness, and hopelessness or contribute to the development of an affective illness. Some patients suffer from ineffective treatment of physical pain as a result of insufficient analgesia, the product of inadequate physician education and moralistic views regarding narcotics.[24,25] The situation has not been remedied by journal articles, textbooks, newspaper articles, or guidelines.[26–29] In the Netherlands the request for "hastened death" is withdrawn in 85% of patients when their symptoms are better controlled.[30] The availability of reliable and effective palliative care may reduce dramatically the requests for physician-assisted suicide.[31] Without optimal treatment, we cannot be sure that the request for death does not derive from an attempt to escape from physical pain. No more powerful statement can be made to a patient who is in pain than that of the physician who says, "I will do everything that can be done to alleviate your pain, and I guarantee that nothing will be withheld from you unless you tell me to do otherwise."

SADNESS AND DEPRESSION

Distinction must be made between depression, a treatable medical illness, and the experience of sadness. "Periods of sadness are inherent aspects of the human experience. These periods should not be diagnosed as a Major Depressive Disorder."[32] Arriving at a diagnosis of depression in physically ill patients may be complicated by the somatic symptoms that accompany illness and medical or surgical therapies.[33–35] Nonpsychiatric physicians frequently miss the diagnosis of depression,[36–38] particularly where "depression" is presumed to be a normal response to the situation. This "pseudoempathy" prevents physicians from distinguishing sadness from depression.[1] Physicians are not convinced that they could recognize depression in terminally ill patients.[10] As the patient's request for death may arise from a depression, the evaluation should be performed by physicians skilled in making the diagnosis. The judge who ruled that the Oregon physician-assisted suicide law was unconstitutional commented, "The very lives of terminally ill persons depend on their own rational assessment of the value of their existence, and yet there is no requirement that they be evaluated by a mental health specialist."[39] The physician should ask for a psychiatric consultation in every case where he or she is unsure whether the patient's request for death arises from a depression.

That does not mean that every patient who is depressed is suicidal or that the depression is the source of every patient's request to die. Ganzini et al[40] note, "When depression influences decision making, this influence is evident to a trained observer on clinical interview." While it may be difficult for physicians always to be sure of the diagnosis of depression, Chochinov et al[41] recently demonstrated that the easiest and best method for quickly assessing depression in terminally ill patients is to ask the question, "Are you depressed?" A 90-year-old woman was admitted to the hospital after a fall. Though she did not sustain a fracture, she was found to be in congestive heart failure, with pitting edema of her legs. She was anemic and had heme-positive stools. She had been widowed several years and complained that all of her friends had passed away. All of her family lived out of state except for a grandchild attending a local college. It was expected that she would fully recover with medical treatment. From the beginning of her admission she asked if she could die, and she was uncooperative with the medical evaluation. Ambulation had become increasingly difficult for her, and she stated strongly that she was "old and had lived long enough." A piece of history casually revealed during the psychiatric consultation was that she was once a professional dancer with a famous dance troupe. The many losses in her life, including the recent loss of the use of her legs, suggested a clinically significant depression, and a psychostimulant was prescribed. She was dis-

appointed in the doctor's decision not to end her life but reluctantly complied with the continuation of the medical evaluation and with taking medication. After a week of treatment, realizing that she would regain the ability to walk, she began to press for more aggressive physical therapy. When a nursing home placement was obtained, she refused the transfer because she believed the physical therapy offered in the hospital was superior to the nursing home, and she was anxious to regain full use of her legs and return home.

GUILT, SELF-PUNISHMENT, AND ATONEMENT

Guilt is a potentially destructive emotion that may occur in both patient and physician. Patients may attribute their cancer to unacceptable emotions and bad deeds.[42] Some patients may conclude, "If I was not bad, I would not have gotten this terrible illness. I don't love people who are bad; thus, nobody could love me. Now I have been a bad patient because I have not recovered from my illness. My failure has made my doctor fail and my doctor must hate me. If I die, it will make amends for being a bad person." Self-punishment and the desire to atone can thus become a motivation for the request to die. In patients for whom illness is equated with a personal failure, death is equated with deserved punishment. Such thoughts may seem logical to patients influenced by the regressive pull of physical illness, by pain, by the threat of loss of body parts or functions, by the chaos of the hospital, and by the intrusive nature of being a patient.[43]

Patients' feelings of guilt may be stimulated or exacerbated by interactions within the patient-physician relationship. Physicians are imbued with omnipotent powers by patients, derived from the child's experience of the parent as omnipotent.[44,45] One has only to witness or participate in the "kissing of a boo-boo" to perceive the power of the child's belief in the parent's omnipotence to heal. Powerful fantasies about the physician, deriving from the patient's childhood experiences, often remain unknown. The patient may perceive that his or her physical and emotional suffering causes the physician to suffer, accompanied by the patient's perception of the physician's wish to end his or her own emotional suffering. This wish may be interpreted by the patient as the physician's wish that the patient be dead. The patient's request to die can therefore be an attempt to accede to what the patient believes is the "doctor's wish."

When the physician cannot accept that some patients do not respond to treatment, he or she may experience guilt for having failed. Some physicians blame the patient for having the illness or for the poor treatment response. The patient's guilt influences the physician's response to the patient's request to die.[46] The patient's experience of the physician's guilt and the physician's unchallenged acquiescence to the patient's request to die confirm the patient's guilty experience of being bad and unworthy of the physician's healing power. Where there is no avenue for a discussion that will uncover these complex dynamics, action may replace affects and words. The patient's death thus replaces the opportunity for understanding and life. Miles[47] has stated, "Openness to my distress at a patient's suffering improves therapeutic insight into a patient's pain, demoralization, and depression." There are times that the physician might benefit from a discussion with a psychiatric colleague about thoughts and feelings encountered in the relationship with a particular patient.

THE LIVING DEAD

Some patients who request to die seem to experience themselves as already dead. This may occur more readily in individuals rendered vulnerable by a childhood devoid of a warm, nurturing parent. This self-experience may also occur as the result of physical suffering, emotional suffering, or both, the fear of unremitting agony, the loss of social support that accompanies catastrophic illness for some patients, and the impact of significant depressive and/or anxiety disorders. While not a diagnosis in the *Diagnostic and Statistical Manual of Mental Disorders, Fourth Edition,* this self-experience takes the form of a condition that might be called "the living dead," and it robs the person of all hope for recovery or for a more comfortable existence. The person "knows" that he or she is going to die, which leads to the decision to attempt to get it over with quickly. It is extremely challenging for the physician to work with such a patient, as the physician too may have the experience that the person, though alive, feels already deceased. The physician's confrontation of the patient's self-experience requires skill, tact, and the belief that there remains life worth living for this patient. Therapeutics for pain, insomnia, anxiety, and depression, as well as recommending and instituting psychological treatments, can effectively treat this condition. The patient is restored to the living, able to acknowledge the seriousness of the illness, without feeling overwhelmed. An emergency consultation was requested for a woman in her mid-40s who decided she was unable to continue with chemotherapy. She complained of severe pain, nausea, and fear of the pain associated with each treatment. Aware that she had a rare cancer that carried a poor prognosis, she questioned continuation of the treatment that had just begun. During the consultation, which lasted 3 hours, she cried continuously, referring frequently to the fact she would never see her garden bloom again, though spring was only a few months away. "I have no reason to go on with this," she stated, simultaneously listing all of the things and people that were important to her, especially her impending graduation from professional school, while repeatedly emphasizing the pain of not seeing her garden again. The comment was made to her that she acted as if she were already dead, in spite of the fact that the indications were that she had many months to live, and live comfortably, even if the therapy was ultimately unsuccessful. Her response was dramatic and instantaneous, her tears dried up, she looked at the consultant and took his hand, "You mean I have something to live for?" she asked; "I will see my garden bloom again, won't I." This was not asked as a question. She never again, through her difficult course and her death a year later, stopped being alive, often reminding the consultant and herself of the importance of "not being dead until your time comes."

THE ROLE OF THE PSYCHIATRIST

Psychiatrists bring the potential for expert exploration and understanding of the issues involved in a patient's request to die. In the evaluation of the patient's request, psychiatrists help identify both the psychodynamic issues and psychiatric disorders, particularly depression, that would benefit from treatment.[1] These evaluations should not be limited to the determination of a patient's capacity to make decisions.[48] Nor should the evaluation be a single diagnostic visit. Only a small number of psychiatrists surveyed in the Oregon study felt confident that they could determine whether a psychiatric disorder impairs a patient's judgment in a single visit.[49] There is an additional significant role for the psychiatrist, who, through the psychotherapeutic process, can offer relief from psychological suffering in a terminally ill patient.[50,51] This is not the tendering of foolish optimism or naive hope, but offers an expectation of self-understanding that can lead to a reduction of the individual's suffering. It is a coming to terms with oneself and with the significant people in one's life, both those who are living and those who are dead but with whom the patient continues an active relationship. In concert with the physician responsible for the person's medical care, psychiatrists can assist in assuring the patient that his or her suffering will be reduced to a minimum with appropriate treatment. This includes a frank discussion of the possibility that the person's consciousness might be compromised by maximal analgesic treatment.

There may be times that the psychiatrist's role in the process requires that he or she tell a colleague "You are overinvolved, it is time to let this patient die" or "You are not adequately treating this patient's pain" or "You have given the patient information in such a way as to rob him or her of hope." In each of these and other communications, the psychiatrist must make it clear that these observations do not reflect on the colleague's competence or ideals, but rather that the psychiatrist's focus is on different needs of the patient that may have gone unrecognized.

In speaking with patients, I (and psychiatrists who have described their experiences to me) have encountered the criticism from patients and families that, under the guise of investigating the meaning of a patient's communication, we are violating the patient's basic human rights, ie, "the right to die." I contend that not discussing a patient's motivation is the real violation of his or her rights, as there exists the possibility that the role of psychological factors has been underestimated.[52] Some of the skills in communication required for this exploration are those that every physician should possess[53–55]; however, some of the skills required for the in-depth exploration are not those of the primary care physician, the oncologist, or the surgeon. These are the skills of the psychiatrist who has the training and skills in both psychodynamic exploration and interaction with medically ill patients. Not all psychiatrists are comfortable in this arena, nor do all psychiatrists have clinical experience with medically ill and dying patients. The psychiatrist in these cases should have the training and experience to provide patient and physician with a meaningful consultation. There are some psychologists and social workers who have clinical expertise from their work with patients who have medical illness. Such consultants would also be appropriate to conduct this type of psychological exploration.

POLICY, PHYSICIAN-ASSISTED SUICIDE, AND THE ROLE OF THE PHYSICIAN

In every situation where a patient makes the request for his or her physician to end the person's life, the physician's answer should not be a simple yes or no. Answering yes without exploring the meaning of the request, while seemingly giving the patient what he or she asks for, in actuality may abolish the opportunity for patient and physician to more fully understand and know one another. Answering no leaves the patient in a situation of helplessness to control his or her destiny and closes off further communication. Inquiring about the patients' emotional state, validating the patient's experience, and helping the patient identify the motivations for the request to die allow the physician to engage in a truly meaningful communication at a crucial time in the patient's life. An initial response might be, "That is a serious request. Before we can know what would be the best way to proceed, let's talk about why you are asking me to help you die now." Not every request for physician-assisted suicide indicates complex unspoken psychodynamics, but that cannot be known until the physician and the patient talk. A psychiatric consultation is necessary in cases where there is complexity regarding the psychological motivations, cases where the physician feels there is a psychiatric disorder, cases where there is a suggestion that the patient is clinically depressed, and cases where the physician has intense emotions regarding the patient (particularly feelings of guilt, anger, or inadequacy). The request for suicide may be found to be "rational" but not until there has been an adequate exploration of its meaning.[56] The willingness of a physician to enter into such a dialogue with patients is not without an emotional impact on the physician, but it is what is required if physicians are to appropriately respond to such requests.[47]

The US Supreme Court decision on physician-assisted suicide has not ended the debate. Decriminalizing physician-assisted suicide is insufficient as there is no requirement to explore the patient's request. It is our professional responsibility to make provision for an exploration of the motivation in patients who make such a request. Regardless of the outcome of the societal and legal debate regarding physician-assisted suicide, physicians should recognize that patients who make a request to die deserve a compassionate and comprehensive evaluation.

I am indebted to Donald Kornfeld, MD, and Karen Antman, MD, for their encouragement and invaluable assistance in the preparation of this article.

References

1. Sullivan MD, Youngner SJ. Depression, competence and the right to refuse lifesaving medical treatment. *Am J Psychiatry.* 1993;151:971–978.
2. van der Maas PJ, van der Wal G, Haverkate I, et al. Euthanasia, physician-assisted suicide, and other medical practices involving the end of life in the Netherlands, 1990–1995. *N Engl J Med.* 1996;335:1699–1705.
3. Hendin H, Rutenfrans C, Zyliez Z: Physician-assisted suicide and euthanasia in the Netherlands: lessons from the Dutch. *JAMA.* 1997;277:1720–1722.
4. Hendin H. *Seduced by Death: Doctors, Patients and the Dutch Cure.* New York, NY: WW Norton & Co; 1997.
5. Chochinov HM, Wilson KG, Enns M, et al. Desire for death in the terminally ill. *Am J Psychiatry.* 1995;152:1185–1191.
6. Breitbart W, Rosenfeld BD, Passik SD. Interest in physician-assisted suicide among ambulatory HIV-infected patients. *Am J Psychiatry.* 1996;153:238–242.
7. Breitbart W. Cancer pain and suicide. *Adv Pain Res Ther.* 1990;16:399–412.
8. Helig S. The San Francisco Medical Society euthanasia survey: results and analysis. *San Francisco Med.* 1988;61:24–34.
9. Emanuel EJ, Fairclough DL, Daniels ER, Clarridge BR. Euthanasia and physician-assisted suicide: attitudes and experiences among oncology patients, oncologists, and the general public. *Lancet.* 1996;347:1805–1810.
10. Lee MA, Nelson HD, Tilden VP, et al. Legalizing assisted suicide: views of physicians in Oregon. *N Engl J Med.* 1996;334:310–315.
11. Kuhse H, Singer P. Doctors practices and attitudes regarding voluntary euthanasia. *Med J Aust.* 1998;148:623–627.
12. Caralis PV, Hammond JS. Attitudes of medical students, housestaff, and faculty physicians toward euthanasia and termination of life-sustaining treatment. *Crit Care Med.* 1992;20:683–690.
13. Shapiro RS, Derse AR, Gootlieb M, et al. Willingness to perform euthanasia: a survey of physician attitudes. *Arch Intern Med.* 1994;154:575–584.
14. Back AL, Wallace JI, Starks HE, Pearlman RA. Physician-assisted suicide and euthanasia in Washington State: patient requests and physician responses. *JAMA.* 1996;275:919–925.
15. Bachman JG, Alcser KH, Doukas DJ, et al. Attitudes of Michigan physicians and the public toward legalizing physician-assisted suicide and voluntary euthanasia. *N Engl J Med.* 1996;334:303–309.
16. Cohen JS, Fihn SD, Boyko EJ, Jonsen AR, Wood RW. Attitudes toward assisted suicide and euthanasia among physicians in Washington State. *N Engl J Med.* 1994;331:89–94.
17. Ward BJ, Tate PA. Attitudes among NHS doctors to requests for euthanasia. *BMJ* 1994;308:1332–1335.
18. Roberts LW, Muskin PR, Warner TD, et al. Attitudes of consultation-liaison psychiatrists toward physician-assisted death practices. *Psychosomatics.* 1997;38:459–471.
19. Asch DA. The role of critical care nurses in euthanasia and assisted suicide. *N Engl J Med.* 1996;334:1374–1379.
20. Leiser RJ, Mitchell TF, Hahn JA, Abrams DI. The role of critical care nurses in euthanasia and assisted suicide. *N Engl J Med.* 1996;335:972–973.
21. Block SD, Billings JA. Patient requests for euthanasia and assisted suicide in terminal illness: the role of the psychiatrist. *Psychosomatics.* 1995;36:445–457.
22. Nietzsche F. *Beyond Good and Evil* (1886). Quoted in: *The Columbia Dictionary of Quotations.* New York: NY: Columbia University Press; 1993.
23. Beck AT, Steer RA, Kovacs M, Garrison G. Hopelessness and eventual suicide: a 10-year prospective study of patients hospitalized with suicidal ideation. *Am J Psychiatry.* 1985;142:559–563.
24. Marks RM, Sachar ES. Undertreatment of medical inpatients with narcotic analgesics. *Ann Intern Med.* 1973;78:173–181.
25. Foley KM. The relationship of pain and symptom management to patient requests for physician-assisted suicide. *J Pain Symptom Manage.* 1991;6:289–297.
26. Cleeland C. Barriers to the management of cancer pain. *Oncology.* 1987;1(April suppl):19–26.
27. Massie MJ, Holland JC. The cancer patient with pain: psychiatric complications and their management. *Med Clin North Am.* 1987;71:243–258.
28. Max MB. Improving outcomes of analgesic treatment: is education enough? *Ann Intern Med.* 1990;113:885–889.
29. Jacox A, Carr DB, Payne R, et al. *Management of Cancer Pain: Clinical Practice Guideline No. 9.* Rockville, Md: Agency for Health Care Policy Research, US Dept of Health and Human Services; March 1994. AHCPR publication 94-0592.
30. Admiraal p. Personal communication. Cited in: Lo B. Euthanasia: the continuing debate. *West J Med.* 1988;49:211–212.
31. McKeogh M. Physician-assisted suicide and patients with HIV disease. *N Engl J Med.* 1997;337:56.
32. American Psychiatric Association. *Diagnostic and Statistical Manual of Mental Disorders, Fourth Edition.* Washington, DC: American Psychiatric Association; 1994:326.

33. Cavanaugh S. The diagnosis and treatment of depression in the medically ill. In: Guggenheim F, Weiner MF, eds. *Manual of Psychiatric Consultation and Emergency Care.* New York, NY: Jason Aronson; 1984:211–222.

34. Ormel J, Van Den Brink W, Koeter MWJ, et al. Recognition, management and outcome of psychological disorders in primary care: a naturalistic follow-up study. *Psychol Med.* 1990;20:909–923.

35. Sherbourne CD, Wells KB, Hays RD, et al. Subthreshold depression and depressive disorder: clinical characteristics of general medical and mental health specialty outpatients. *Am J Psychiatry.* 1994;151:1777–1784.

36. Schulberg HC, Saul M, McCelland M, et al. Assessing depression in primary medical and psychiatric practices. *Arch Gen Psychiatry.* 1985;42:1164–1170.

37. Eisenberg L. Treating depression and anxiety in primary care: closing the gap between knowledge and practice. *N Engl J Med.* 1992;326:1080–1084.

38. Badger LW, deGruy FV, Hartman J, et al. Patient presentation, interview content, and the detection of depression by primary care physicians. *Psychosomat Med.* 1994;56:128–135.

39. *Lee v State of Oregon,* 891 F Supp 1429, WL 471792 (D Or 1995).

40. Ganzini L, Lee MA, Heintz RT, et al. The effect of depression treatment on elderly patients' preferences for life-sustaining medical therapy. *Am J Psychiatry.* 1994;151:1631–1636.

41. Chochinov HM, Wilson KG, Enns M, Lander S. 'Are you depressed?' screening for depression in the terminally ill. *Am J Psychiatry.* 1997;154:674–676.

42. Sontag S. *Illness as Metaphor.* New York, NY: Farrar Straus & Giroux: 1978.

43. Muskin PR. The medical hospital. In: Schwartz HJ, Bleiberg E, Weissman SH, eds. *Psychodynamic Concepts in General Psychiatry.* Washington, DC: American Psychiatric Press; 1995:69–88.

44. Kohut H. *The Analysis of the Self.* New York, NY: International Universities Press; 1971.

45. Kohut H. *The Restoration of the Self.* New York, NY: International Universities Press; 1977.

46. Goldstein WN. Clarification of projective identification. *Am J Psychiatry.* 1991;148:153–161.

47. Miles SH. Physicians and their patients' suicides. *JAMA.* 1994;271:1786–1788.

48. Huyse FJ, van Tilburg W. Euthanasia policy in the Netherlands: the role of consultation-liaison psychiatrists. *Hosp Community Psychiatry.* 1993;44:733–738.

49. Ganzini L, Fenn DS, Lee MA, Heintz RT, Bloom JD. Attitudes of Oregon psychiatrists toward physician-assisted suicide. *Am J Psychiatry.* 1996;153:1469–1475.

50. Eissler KR. *The Psychiatrist and the Dying Patient.* New York, NY: International Universities Press; 1955.

51. Druss RG. *The Psychology of Illness.* Washington, DC: American Psychiatric Press; 1995.

52. Ganzini L, Lee MA. Psychiatry and assisted suicide in the United States. *N Engl J Med.* 1997;336:1824–1826.

53. Cohen-Cole SA. *The Medical Interview: The Three-Function Approach.* St Louis, Mo: Mosby-Year Book Inc; 1991.

54. Roter DL, Hall JA. *Doctors Talking With Patients/Patients Talking With Doctors.* Westport, Conn: Auburn House; 1992.

55. Roter DL, Hall JA. Strategies for enhancing patient adherence to medical recommendations. *JAMA.* 1994;271:80.

56. Battin MP. Rational suicide: how can we respond to a request for help? *Crisis.* 1991;12:73–80.

From the Department of Psychiatry, Columbia-Presbyterian Medical Center, Columbia University, College of Physicians and Surgeons, and Columbia University Psychoanalytic Center for Training and Research, New York, NY.

Presented at the American Academy of Psychoanalysis, New York, NY, May 3, 1996.

Reprints: Philip R. Muskin, MD, Columbia-Presbyterian Medical Center, 622 W 168th St, Mailbox 427, New York, NY 10032-3784.

The Patient-Physician Relationship section editor: Richard M. Glass, MD, Deputy Editor, *JAMA.*

Quality End-of-Life Care

Patients' Perspectives

Peter A. Singer, MD, MPH, FRCPC

Douglas K. Martin, PhD

Merrijoy Kelner, PhD

BECAUSE EVERYONE DIES, END-of-life care is among the most prevalent issues in health care. Both health care professionals and patients see room for improvement.[1] Encouragingly, major initiatives, such as the American Medical Association's Education for Physicians on End-of-Life Care project, Open Society Institute's Project on Death in America, and Robert Wood Johnson Foundation's Last Rites Campaign, are under way to improve the quality of end-of-life care.

A necessary scientific step to focus these efforts is the development of a taxonomy or conceptual framework for quality end-of-life care.[2] However, what end-of-life care means and how to measure it is still a matter of debate and ongoing research. Three expert groups have recently published frameworks for quality end-of-life care (TABLE 1).[3-5] These taxonomies derive from the medical expert perspective rather than the perspective of patients and families.[6] We are unaware of any descriptions of quality end-of-life care from the patient perspective, from which quality end-of-life care is arguably most appropriately viewed. This is the perspective that clinicians and health care organizations will need to understand to improve the quality of care they deliver to dying patients. Therefore, the purpose of this study was to identify and describe elements of quality end-of-life care as identified by those most affected: patients.

METHODS

Design

This study used a qualitative research method called *content analysis*, in which "standardized measurements are applied to metrically defined units [of text] and these are used to characterise and compare documents."[7]

Context Quality end-of-life care is increasingly recognized as an ethical obligation of health care providers, both clinicians and organizations. However, this concept has not been examined from the perspective of patients.

Objective To identify and describe elements of quality end-of-life care from the patient's perspective.

Design Qualitative study using in-depth, open-ended, face-to-face interviews and content analysis.

Setting Toronto, Ontario.

Participants A total of 126 participants from 3 patient groups: dialysis patients (n = 48), people with human immunodeficiency virus infection (n = 40), and residents of a long-term care facility (n = 38).

Outcome Measures Participants' views on end-of-life issues.

Results Participants identified 5 domains of quality end-of-life care: receiving adequate pain and symptom management, avoiding inappropriate prolongation of dying, achieving a sense of control, relieving burden, and strengthening relationships with loved ones.

Conclusion These domains, which characterize patients' perspectives on end-of-life care, can serve as focal points for improving the quality of end-of-life care.

JAMA. 1999;281:163–168

www.jama.com

Participants

We analyzed data from interviews with patients who participated in 3 recent studies.[8-10] Participants from the 3 studies were dialysis patients, persons infected with the human immunodeficiency virus (HIV), and residents of a long-term care facility. In this study, we examined all participant interviews from the dialysis (n = 48) and long-term care (n = 38) studies, and a random selection of 40 participant interviews (from a total of 140 participants) from the HIV study.

Dialysis patients were a sample of individuals receiving hemodialysis at all 6 units serving adults in metropolitan Toronto, Ontario. They were originally enrolled in a study examining the acceptability of generic vs. dialysis-specific advance directive (AD) forms[11] and interviewed 6 months later.[8] Participants were excluded if they were younger than 18 years, were unable to understand written English, were incapable of completing an AD form, would experience undue emotional distress from completing an AD form, had received dialysis for less than 3 months, or refused to participate in the research. Of 532 patients receiving hemodialysis, 310 were excluded, 81 refused, 43 withdrew, 7 died, 43 were not approached, and 48 completed the study.

Participants with HIV were a sample of persons who responded to the study advertisements or posters distributed by the AIDS Committee of Toronto and placed in the waiting rooms of the Toronto Hospital Immunodeficiency Clinic. They were originally enrolled in a previous study that examined the preference for either an HIV-specific or generic AD form[12] and interviewed 6 months later.[9] Participants were excluded if they were younger than 16 years, were not fluent in English, could not read, were incapable of completing an AD form (as measured by a Standardized Mini-Mental State Examination test score <23), would experience undue emotional distress from completing an AD form, resided outside metropolitan Toronto, or refused to participate in the research. Of 587 possible participants, 200 were not approached for the study, 85 were excluded, 52 refused, 93 withdrew, 17 died, and 140 were interviewed (of whom 40 were randomly selected for this analysis).

Long-term care residents were a sample of persons from a 398-bed hospital in Toronto that provides both rehabilitative and long-term care for adults who are chronically ill and disabled by neurological problems, respiratory conditions, amputations, and age-related disorders.[10] The purpose of the original study was to examine residents' views about control at the end of life. Three criteria were established for selecting participants: patients had to be 65 years or older, capable of understanding and answering questions in English, and healthy enough, both physically and mentally, to take part in a short interview. Nurse managers recruited participants in each unit of the hospital in which appropriate patients could be identified. No patients refused. The 38 participants represent the total population of eligible patients during the data collection period.

Data Collection

Data were gathered by in-depth, open-ended, face-to-face interviews. The interviewer asked open-ended questions, followed up participants' responses, pursued themes as they arose, and sought clarification or elaboration as required. In the dialysis and HIV studies, the interviews were audiotaped and transcribed; in the long-term care study, the interviewer wrote down the participants' comments. Opportunities were consistently made available for participants to express unsolicited opinions and recount their clinical experiences and life histories. As the interviews proceeded and ideas were suggested by patients' reflections and clarifications, new questions were added and others were refined. The interview guide was modified to follow up issues emerging from the data as the interviews and analysis progressed.

The initial interview guide for dialysis patients covered 3 themes: (1) had the participant completed an AD form? (2) if not, why not? and (3) if so, what was the process and was it acceptable?

In the HIV study, participants were asked about their reasons for engaging in advance care planning (ACP), the process and content of their ACP discussions, their perspective on the importance of ACP, and their evaluation of the ACP process.

Long-term care residents were asked the following questions about patient control at the end of life: (1) had they previously thought about it? (2) what were their general views on control over decision making at the end of life? (3) what would be their personal preference "when the time comes"? (4) did they see any potential obstacles to having their wishes honored? and (5) what were their personal views about withdrawal or termination of treatment, as well as euthanasia and physician-assisted suicide?

Data Analysis

The data were read and participants' views regarding quality end-of-life care were identified. These units of text were underlined and descriptive notes were written in the margins of the transcripts, a process referred to as *coding*. Coded units were then labeled as specific end-of-life care issues. Many issues were not mutually exclusive, but issues that were conceptually different were given different descriptive labels. Labeled issues were then compared within and between interviews. Similar issues were grouped together under 1 overarching domain label and the data were recoded by domain. The prevalence of each domain was recorded and descriptive statements about each were developed using the patients' words. Quotes that were selected for presentation in the article were good illustrations of the domain and provide data from the various patient populations. This process was conducted by 1 analyst (D.K.M.), who frequently consulted with a second analyst (P.A.S.) regarding excerpts of the primary transcript data and the clustering of the data into domains.

Several steps were taken to verify the results, a concept in qualitative research analogous to reliability and validity in quantitative research.[13,14] These included (1) use of 3 separate data sets to verify the conceptual domains, (2) general familiarity with the data sets by investigators (P.A.S. and M.K.) other than the primary analyst, (3) systematic checking of the developing conceptual domains against supporting quotations by a second analyst (P.A.S.), (4) review of the manuscript by an independent scholar studying quality end-of-life care (James Tulsky, MD), and (5) explicit comparison of our taxonomy with 3 other taxonomies derived from a different methodological perspective.[3–5]

Sample Size

Sample size was not formally calculated. Instead, participants were enrolled until no new concepts arose during analysis of the successive interviews, a concept called *saturation* by qualitative researchers.

Research Ethics

All 3 studies were approved by the University of Toronto Committee on Research With Human Subjects, and written informed consent was obtained from all subjects.

RESULTS

Demographic characteristics of the 126 patients from the 3 data sets are shown in TABLE 2. As shown in TABLE 3, the analysis identified 5 domains of quality end-of-life care: receiving adequate pain and symptom

Table 1. Domains of Quality End-of-Life Care

Journal of the American Geriatrics Society Statement[3]	Institute of Medicine Committee[4]	Emanuel and Emanuel[5*]	Patient Perspectives†
• Physical and emotional symptoms	• Overall quality of life	• Physical symptoms	• Receiving adequate pain and symptom management
• Support of function and autonomy	• Physical well-being and functioning	• Psychological and cognitive symptoms	• Avoiding inappropriate prolongation of dying
• Advance care planning	• Psychosocial well-being and functioning	• Social relationships and support	• Achieving a sense of control
• Aggressive care near death	• Spiritual well-being	• Economic demands and caregiving needs	• Relieving burden
• Patient and family satisfaction	• Patient perception of care	• Hopes and expectations	• Strengthening relationships
• Global quality of life	• Family well-being and perceptions	• Spiritual and existential beliefs	
• Family burden			
• Survival time			
• Provider continuity and skill			
• Bereavement			

*"Modifiable dimensions of patient's experience" from Emanuel and Emanuel.[5]
†Patient perspectives are from the current study.

management, avoiding inappropriate prolongation of dying, achieving a sense of control, relieving burden, and strengthening of relationships with loved ones. The next most prevalent theme was mentioned by less than 5% of participants. We present a description of these domains with verbatim quotes from participants.

Receiving Adequate Pain and Symptom Management

Pain was a concern for many respondents. A few participants mentioned other symptoms such as vomiting, breathlessness, and diarrhea.

I've been adamant that I wanted treatment in sort of end stage to be minimal—pain reduction, but not life sustaining. I don't—if anyone could say they did—like being in pain and I don't find the idea of being incontinent or bowel-dysfunctional, not to mention mentally incompetent, remotely interesting.

I wouldn't want a lot of pain; it's one of the worst ways to go.

If I'm in pain, severe pain, and the doctors can do nothing, the pain persists and there's nothing to take the pain away, I don't think it's fair to let me suffer like that, or anybody. We don't let the animals suffer; why should we?

Avoiding Inappropriate Prolongation of Dying

Participants were afraid of "lingering" and "being kept alive" after they no longer could enjoy their lives. Quality-of-life concerns seemed to fuel this fear; many were terrified of becoming a "vegetable" or living in a coma. These participants adamantly denounced "being kept alive by a machine." They wanted to be "allowed to die naturally" or "in peace."

I didn't want to be kept alive artificially forever just to die later on and suffer, you know, without need for an extra year. Let me go anyways. Get it done with the first time.

I wouldn't want life supports if I'm going to die anyway. There's no dignity in it. It's just a guinea pig thing.

I've always told my mother ... if it ever comes down to being put on a life-support system, I wouldn't go for it unless there's a chance that I would come around and be normal again. But if there is chance of me being put on a life-support system and becoming a vegetable, I said forget it.

Achieving a Sense of Control

Participants were adamant that they wanted to retain control of their end-of-life care decisions while they were capable of doing so, and that they wanted the proxy of their choice to retain control if they became incapable.

I have very definite ideas of what I would want done and what I wouldn't want done, especially after watching various friends go through their deaths.

I want control, but it shouldn't be disruptive. It can be productive if it's thoughtful and if others are consulted.

That's my life. Nobody has any right to tell me that. I can't let a stranger talk me out of anything. That's what I want. They don't know

how I live. It's very, very important to me now that I can make choices for myself.

Relieving Burden

The participants were greatly concerned about the burden that their dying would impose on loved ones. They identified 3 specific burdens: provision of physical care, witnessing their death, and substitute decision making for life-sustaining treatment.

I don't want them making the decisions for me without knowing how I would decide the same thing. It just makes life easier for everybody. They don't have to say, 'Well, what would he do in this situation?' if it's already written down. I know if I was incapacitated, it would be a stressful time for the people I've chosen as my proxy. It would be tough

Table 2. Participant Characteristics

	Participants		
Characteristics	Dialysis (n = 48)	HIV* (n = 40)	Long-term Care (n = 38)
Sex, No.			
Male	30	35	13
Female	18	5	25
Race/ethnicity, No.			
White	30	37	35
African American	8	0	0
Hispanic	2	1	0
Asian	3	0	0
Other	5	2	3
Education, No.			
No high school	2	0	6
Some high school	4	3	12
High school graduate	13	3	9
Some college	7	17	3
College graduate	22	17	8
Age, mean (range), y	48.3 (20-80)	39.6 (25-54)	76.3 (65-≥85)†

*HIV indicates human immunodeficiency virus.
†In long-term care study, data were gathered by strata. Therefore, mean age was derived using an estimated and weighted calculation.

Table 3. Domains of End-of-Life Care From Patients' Perspectives*

	Participants			
	Dialysis (n = 48)	HIV/AIDS (n = 40)	Long-term Care (n = 38)	Total (N = 126)
Receiving adequate pain and symptom management	3 (6.2)	10 (25.0)	15 (39.5)	28 (22.2)
Avoiding inappropriate prolongation of dying	23 (47.9)	29 (72.5)	25 (65.8)	77 (61.1)
Achieving a sense of control	9 (18.8)	21 (52.5)	18 (47.4)	48 (38.1)
Relieving burden	14 (29.2)	21 (52.5)	13 (34.2)	48 (38.1)
Strengthening relationships with loved ones	16 (33.3)	21 (52.5)	12 (31.6)	49 (38.9)

*Data are number (percentage). HIV indicates human immunodeficiency virus; AIDS, acquired immunodeficiency syndrome.

in some situations to make those decisions. So by doing it in advance I save them the bother. . . . I chose not to designate my parents as proxies. I felt that would probably be a little bit hard on them. I mean, I'm sure they'd be willing to do so, but I think from the standpoint of just saving their feelings as much as possible, I'd rather not have them make those decisions, if the time came that it was necessary.

I'd want to die here, not at home. I wouldn't want to put that burden on my family.

I hope to stop myself from becoming a burden to them [children]. Looking after somebody either takes a lot of money, in which case you may get somebody to baby-sit for you, or you have to do it yourself, and I do not wish my children to be in the position of having to do that. Therefore, I would rather die faster than later.

Strengthening Relationships With Loved Ones

A majority of participants felt that considerations with respect to loved ones were integral to their dying experience. For the dying experience to be meaningful, participants desired the full involvement of loved ones in communication about their dying. At times, this meant overcoming resistance, their own and others', to engage with uncomfortable subject matter. But even so, participants felt that the need for communication with loved ones was of overwhelming importance. When this intimacy was achieved, participants found their relationships strengthened.

I've never told anyone in my family that I was HIV-positive. And so, in order to complete my living will, I had to tell him [brother] I was HIV-positive, which was really quite a challenge for me. And I did tell him, and everything has just worked out fine. He's a hundred percent supportive and it couldn't be better. Our relationship is even closer now; we were close before—we've always been a close family. But now we're really close.

It was one of the decisions we discussed and she [wife] says when I am in this situation she is capable to make decisions for me. She didn't want to leave it to me because I cannot make decisions when I, you know. It was nice because she was showing me this kind of love and this kind of sympathy; when I am in that situation, she will be able to

continue assisting me. So I was very happy about that, really. She always tells me she is going to be there for me when I cannot make a decision.

It helped me get closer to my family, to get an idea how they feel about me. There were so many times I wanted to get their opinion on certain things, and when I discussed that with them they showed me that they are going to be there for me every time.

COMMENT

From these patients' perspectives, quality end-of-life care includes 5 domains: receiving adequate pain and symptom management, avoiding inappropriate prolongation of dying, achieving a sense of control, relieving burden on loved ones, and strengthening relationships with loved ones.

Comparison With Expert Models

Table 1 compares the patients' perspectives on quality end-of-life care with 3 models derived from an expert perspective. The similarities among the models support the validity of the conceptual domains with respect to all the models.

There are also important differences between patient- and expert-derived models. First, compared with taxonomies from an expert perspective, the patient-derived description of quality end-of-life care is simpler and more straightforward. For instance, it has the fewest domains of the 4 models. Second, the patient-derived taxonomy is more specific. For example, rather than using general labels such as "psychological," the patient perspective speaks of "achieving a sense of control"; rather than "social," it speaks of "relieving burden" and "strengthening relationships." Third, the patient-derived taxonomy is less bound by established concepts for which measurement scales are available (such as quality of life). This raises the question of whether the measurable has been driving out the important in the development of expert-derived taxonomies of quality end-of-life care. Fourth, the patient-derived model omits general and possibly vague concepts such as "global quality of life," "overall quality of life," and "patient perception of care." Fifth, the patient-derived taxonomy is more homogeneously focused on outcomes rather than processes of care (such as ACP or "provider continuity and skill") or periods of care (such as "bereavement"). Finally, the description is derived from the perspective of patients, giving it inherent authenticity. The patient's (and family's) concerns rightfully belong in the center of our focus because they are at the center of the dying experience. The following comments explore the individual domains from

the patient's perspective with reference to existing knowledge.

Receiving Adequate Pain and Symptom Management

Although the issue of treating pain and other symptoms has been championed by the palliative care movement, it is still a problem for many dying patients. For instance, Lynn et al[15] found that 4 in 10 dying patients had severe pain most of the time. Greater attention to the attitudes and skills of health care workers with respect to pain and symptom control may be warranted. Clearer guidelines separating appropriate pain control from euthanasia may also help alleviate clinicians' fears with respect to pain management.

Avoiding Inappropriate Prolongation of Dying

Ahronheim et al[16] found that 47% of incurably ill patients with advanced dementia and metastatic cancer received nonpalliative treatments. Solomon et al[17] found that 78% of health care professionals surveyed reported that they sometimes felt the treatments they offered patients were overly burdensome. Hanson et al[18] found that a frequent recommendation of bereaved family members was to improve end-of-life care, emphasizing better communication. Based on their own observations and data from Tulsky et al,[19] which highlighted inadequacies in end-of-life communication, Hanson et al speculated that "discussions that focus on specific treatment decisions may not satisfy the real needs of dying patients and their families."[18] This is also the sense that one gets when reading the data from our study. The current approach of asking for consent to specific treatments may not meet the needs of dying patients and their families. Dying patients sometimes overestimate their survival probabilities, and these estimates may influence their treatment choices.[20] Specific treatment discussions may not adequately support the patient's hope and discourage false hope. Indeed, emphasizing consent for specific procedures may often be a way to avoid confronting the larger issue of death and discussing the patient's dying. Physicians may use informed consent discussions as a proxy for the more important communications about values and dying. Although such consent is legally required and, therefore, necessary, it is not sufficient. The primary focus of discussions about the use of life-sustaining treatment should be on the realistic and achievable goals of care.[21,22]

Achieving a Sense of Control

When participants said they wanted to achieve a sense of control, they seemed to have in mind a psychosocial outcome rather than a precise specification of what treatments would be received. Although the SUPPORT study[23] showed that incorporating patients' wishes into care may not affect the rate of use of life-sustaining treatments, this may not be the outcome patients have in mind, based on our data. Patients want a voice in their end-of-life care rather than specific control over each life-sustaining treatment decision. This finding further supports the notion discussed herein that our current approach to end-of-life communication, which focuses on the use of individual treatments, may be too specific to address patients' psychosocial needs in the face of death.

Relieving Burden and Strengthening Relationships With Loved Ones

Participants emphasized their desire to relieve burdens and strengthen relationships with their loved ones. These psychosocial outcomes were achieved through involving loved ones in decisions about end-of-life treatments. When dying patients had discussions with their loved ones, they seemed to feel less isolated in the face of death. The discussions also relieved their loved ones of the burden of having to make treatment decisions alone. These social and family considerations are not well captured in the current approach to end-of-life decision making in bioethics, which focuses on the patient's rights individually and not in his or her social and family context. Traditional approaches to bioethics may underestimate the importance of social and family ties.[24–27] As noted by Byock, [28] dying offers important opportunities for growth, intimacy, reconciliation, and closure in relationships. Although most commentators focus on end-of-life communication between physicians and patients,[29,30] these results suggest that communication between dying people and their loved ones is crucial.

Implications for Research and Practice

This taxonomy has implications for research and practice. Researchers are beginning to improve end-of-life care in "breakthrough" collaboratives of health care organizations. If the focus of these initiatives is primarily (or exclusively) on medical expert-derived domains of quality end-of-life care, it is likely that they will miss issues of concern to patients and families. This study underscores the importance of a patient perspective in these important quality improvement initiatives.

The domains of quality end-of-life care described here can be easily used by clinicians at the bedside to review the quality of care of dying patients, and to teach students principles of quality end-of-life care.[31] One of us (P.A.S.) has used this framework at the bedside of dying patients and found that it can clarify the goals of treatment for the health care team and provide a helpful conceptual framework for teaching the care of dying patients to medical students and residents. The domains we have identified from the patient perspective can be used by clinicians as a checklist for the adequacy of the end-of-life care they provide. Some questions clinicians can ask themselves are: Am I adequately treating pain and other symptoms? Am I appropriately prolonging dying? Am I helping patients achieve a sense of control, relieve burdens on their families, and strengthen relationships with loved ones?

Strengths and Limitations

Generalizability is both a strength and a limitation of this study. The patient perspective on quality end-of-life care was derived from 3 diverse populations: dialysis, HIV, and long-term care. Moreover, this study includes patients not traditionally studied; most of what we know about palliative care comes from studies of patients with cancer. However, the data should be generalized with caution beyond the specific patient populations studied. Also, our participants were predominantly white; culture and ethnicity influence perceptions of end-of-life care.

The main limitation of this study is that it represents a secondary analysis of data. The original purpose of the studies was to examine ACP (for the dialysis and HIV studies) and control at the end of life (for the long-term care studies). Thus, the data may overemphasize issues related to ACP and underemphasize other issues in end-of-life care. Three of the issues identified in this study (achieving a sense of control, relieving burden, and strengthening relationships with loved ones) were identified in the previous studies on ACP.[8,9] However, 2 other issues (avoiding inappropriate prolongation of dying and receiving adequate pain and symptom control) were identified in this study alone. There may be other domains, such as spirituality or economic issues (identified in some of the expert taxonomies), that were overlooked. Moreover, this limitation may also have distorted the relative importance of the issues we identified to patients; we make no claim that the frequency with which these issues were mentioned indicates their priority to patients.

CONCLUSIONS

From a patient's perspective, quality end-of-life care includes 5 domains: receiving adequate pain and symptom management, avoiding inappropriate prolongation of dying, achieving a sense of control, relieving burden, and strengthening relationships with loved ones. These domains could form the conceptual foundation for research and practice with respect to quality end-of-life care.

Funding/Support: Dr Singer was supported by the National Health Research and Development Program, Ottawa, Ontario, through a National Health Research Scholar Award and is currently supported by a Scientist Award from the Medical Research Council of Canada, Ottawa. Dr Singer is Sun Life Chair in Bioethics at the University of Toronto, Toronto, Ontario. The work was also supported by the Physicians' Services Incorporated Foundation of Ontario.
Disclaimer: The views expressed herein are those of the authors and do not necessarily reflect those of the supporting groups.
Acknowledgment: We thank Edward E. Etchells, MD, Laura Purdy, PhD, James Tulsky, MD, Leigh Turner, PhD, and James G. Wright, MD, for reviewing an early version of the manuscript; Elaine C. Thiel, for serving as research coordinator of the dialysis and HIV studies; and reviewers for helpful comments.

References

1. Council on Scientific Affairs, American Medical Association. Good care of the dying. JAMA. 1996;275:474–478.

2. Feinstein AR. Clinical Judgment. Baltimore, Md: Williams & Wilkins; 1967.

3. Measuring quality of care at the end of life: a statement of principles. J Am Geriatr Soc. 1997;45:526–527.

4. Field MJ, Cassel CK, eds, for the Institute of Medicine. Approaching Death: Improving Care at the End of Life. Washington, DC: National Academy Press; 1997.

5. Emanuel EJ, Emanuel LL. The promise of a good death. Lancet. 1998;351(suppl 2):21–29.

6. Cleary PD, Edgeman-Levitan S. Health care quality: incorporating consumer perspectives. JAMA. 1997;278:608–612.

7. Manning PK, Cullum-Swan B. Narrative, content, and semiotic analysis. In: Denzin NK, Lincoln YS, eds. Handbook of Qualitative Research. Thousand Oaks, Calif: Sage Publications Inc; 1994:463–477.

8. Singer PA, Martin DK, Lavery JV, Thiel EC, Kelner M. Mendelssohn DC. Reconceptualizing advance care planning from the patient's perspective. Arch Intern Med. 1998;158:879–884.

9. Martin DK, Thiel EC, Singer PA. A new model of advance care planning: observations from people with HIV. Arch Intern Med. In press.

10. Kelner MJ. Activists and delegates: elderly patients' preferences about control at the end of life. Soc Sci Med. 1995;4:537–545.

11. Singer PA, Thiel EC, Naylor CD et al. Treatment preferences of dialysis patients: implications for advance directives. J Am Soc Nephrol. 1995;6:1410–1417.

12. Singer PA, Thiel EC, Salit I, Flanagan W, Naylor CD. The HIV-specific advance directive. J Gen Intern Med. 1997;12:729–735.

13. Strauss A, Corbin J. Grounded theory methodology: an overview. In: Denzin NK, Lincoln YS, eds. *Handbook of Qualitative Research*. Thousand Oaks, Calif: Sage Publications Inc; 1994:273–285.

14. Strauss A, Corbin J. *Basics of Qualitative Research: Grounded Theory Procedures and Techniques*. Thousand Oaks, Calif: Sage Publications Inc; 1990.

15. Lynn J, Teno JM, Phillips RS, et al. Perceptions by family members of the dying experience of older and seriously ill patients. *Ann Intern Med*. 1997;126:97–106.

16. Ahronheim JC, Morrison S, Baskin SA, Morris J, Meier DE. Treatment of the dying in the acute care hospital. *Arch Intern Med*. 1996;-156:2094–2100.

17. Solomon MZ, O'Donnell L, Jennings B, et al. Decisions near the end of life: professional views on life-sustaining treatments. *Am J Public Health*. 1993;83:14–23.

18. Hanson LC, Danis M, Garrett J. What is wrong with end-of-life care? opinions of bereaved family members. J Am Geriatr Soc. 1997;45:1339–1344.

19. Tulsky JA, Chesney MA, Lo B. How do medical residents discuss resuscitation with patients? J Gen Intern Med. 1995;10:436–442.

20. Weeks JC, Cook F, O'Day SJ, et al. Relationship between cancer patients' predictions of prognosis and their treatment preferences. *JAMA*. 1998;279:1709–1714.

21. Fischer GS, Alpert HR, Stoeckle JD, Emanuel LL. Can goals of care be used to predict intervention preferences in an advance directive? *Arch Intern Med*. 1997;157:801–807.

22. Pearlman RA, Cain KC, Patrick DL, et al. Insights pertaining to patient assessments of states worse than death: *J Clin Ethics*. 1993;4:33–41.

23. The SUPPORT Principal Investigators. A controlled trial to improve care for seriously ill hospitalized patients: the Study to Understand Prognoses and Preferences for Outcomes and Risks of Treatments (SUPPORT).*JAMA*. 1995:274: 1591–1598.

24. Lindemann Nelson H, Lindemann Nelson J. *The Patient in the Family*. New York, NY: Routledge; 1995.

25. Hardwig J. What about the family? *Hastings Cent Rep*. March/April 1990:5–10.

26. Blustein J. The family in medical decision making. *Hastings Cent Rep*. May/June 1993:6–13.

27. High DM. Families' roles in advance directives. *Hastings Cent Rep*. November/December 1994 (suppl):S16–S18.

28. Byock I. *Dying Well: Peace and Possibilities at the End of Life*. New York, NY: Riverhead Books; 1997.

29. Emanuel LL, Danis M, Pearlman RA, Singer PA. Advance care planning as a process: structuring the discussions in practice. *J Am Geriatr Soc*. 1995;43:440–446.

30. Virmani J, Schneiderman LJ, Kaplan RM. Relationship of advance directives to physician-patient communication. Arch Intern Med. 1994; 154:909–913.

31. Singer PA, MacDonald N. Bioethics for clinicians, 15: quality end of life care. *CMAJ*. 1998;159:159–162.

Author Affiliations: *Toronto Hospital and the Department of Medicine (Dr Singer), Joint Centre for Bioethics (Drs Singer and Martin), and the Institute of Human Development, Life Course, and Aging (Dr Kelner), University of Toronto, Toronto, Ontario.*
Corresponding Author and Reprints: *Peter A. Singer, MD, MPH, FRCPC, University of Toronto Joint Centre for Bioethics, 88 College St, Toronto, Ontario, Canada M5G 1L4 (e-mail: peter.singer@utoronto.ca).*

Partnership for Good Dying. (A Piece of My Mind)

Ms Fahnestock, who worked as a counselor for Vietnam veterans in Tucson, has spent time during her final months speaking to nursing and medical personnel about dying as a natural and passionate experience. The editors thank Deborah's friend and physician, Russell H. Greenfield, MD, for bringing her thoughts and insights to our attention.

Deborah I. Fahnestock

WHEN CURING IS NO LONGER VIABLE AND THIS MESsage is communicated to or intuited by the patient, a pregnant moment for healing arises for both physician and patient. The focus and fight for life can give way to a new alliance based on sharing the inevitabilities of the human contract. Because in our society we project limitless power onto physicians and other health care professionals, their fantasized power can be used to help dying patients. The smallest, most humble act of a physician's reaching out can have exponential benefit to the patient's subjective sense of well-being.

I am a 52-year-old woman, treated with surgery, chemotherapy, and radiation after a diagnosis of metastatic adenocarcinoma of the lung in April 1997. I have broadened my conventional treatment at the Arizona Cancer Center of the University of Arizona Medical Center with a complementary health regimen through the Integrative Medicine Program. After a significant recurrence at the invasion site, I decided not to go further with conventional treatment because the odds of its being successful were slim and because I hold dying to be a natural part of living. I felt that if I tried to "beat cancer and live" and it didn't work, I might be too cure-focused or too sick and tired to actively prepare for dying in an artful, fulfilling way. The staff at Integrative Medicine proposed an alternative treatment option, but in keeping with their tradition of partnering with patients, they accepted my decision.

Having watched both mainstream and alternative complementary doctors rise to the occasion of my dying with commitment to my care as a human being, I have some observations to make. I am aware of how little literature exists on the subject of care-responses to the dying, and how they may be fundamentally different from care-responses to ill patients.

Medical Impotence and the Use of the Self as Medical Intervention

Confronted with a patient facing death, physicians may feel a sense of medical impotence and failure. Years of training and zeal to heal have focused on doing anything and everything to save the patient. Death is treated as the enemy. One might ask, What use can I be if I cannot fix? One may be tempted to withdraw. There may be no meaningful closure with a patient other than referral to home care or hospice.

Feelings evoked by a patient's dying are also antithetical to the original "call" to medicine—the desire to make a difference in people's lives and the alleviation of pain and suffering. Over time these inner directives may have been obscured by the rigors of a pressured practice, not to mention the climate of malpractice litigation. This threat necessitates obsessive attention to the details of intervention options, possibly at the cost of considering the needs of the whole person at hand.

So the moment when death raises its specter is a crossroads. Herein lies the opportunity for physicians to go beyond their conventional model of relating to patients. This is when the conventional therapeutic tools can be set aside in favor of the most powerful contribution of all: the physician's caring itself. The only requirement is a willingness to extend conscious listening and basic humanity to the dying patient. The simple act of visitation, of presence, of taking the trouble to witness the patient's process can be in itself a potent healing affirmation—

From the *Journal of the American Medical Association,* August 18, 1999, p. 615. © 1999 by the American Medical Association. Reprinted by permission.

a sacramental gesture received by the dying person who may be feeling helpless, diminished, and fearful that they have little to offer others. The patient may also fear that he or she has failed.

How meaningful it is to be told by my physicians that they are learning from me! I feel honored and joined by my physicians as we participate in these human, vulnerable, and mysterious moments at the end of my life. I and many dying persons would agree that beyond pain control, the three elements we most need are feeling cared about, being respected, and enjoying a sense of continuity, be it in relationships or in terms of spiritual awareness.

Conscious Listening

Being with the dying patient requires some ability to tolerate vulnerability and decline, which are so different from the active "doings" of medical practice. Here is a chance to embody the mandate "Physician, heal thyself" by looking within to contemplate one's own mission and one's own death. Death is the ultimate mystery: out of beholding the unknown comes the openness that the act of dying requires.

Conscious listening does not require formulations, interpretations, prescriptions, or agendas. This can be a challenge for the "doer" part of the physician's habitual role. Conscious listening is an impartial witnessing where people feel free to ramble in a nonlinear way. Or they may simply be silent. Restraint from guilt and defensiveness is necessary if patients voice disappointment or anger about not being cured. Remember, dying is a natural part of the life cycle, but the human tendency is to hold on rather than to let go. In the process of following mixed feelings, denial, contradictions, and paradox, nonjudgmental acceptance helps the patient embrace with grace the unacceptable. Encourage the patient to express all of these feelings: they are normal. Much letting go is the order of the day. There may be no answers. As Rainer Maria Rilke said in Letters to a Young Poet, "Be patient toward all that is unsolved in your heart and learn to love the questions themselves."

Listening in this way brings relief from distress and isolation and fosters deep pride in the dying person. And the physician may take satisfaction in fulfilling the ultimate mandate for continuity of care.

Just as there is no "right" way for a person to die, there is no right way to be with the dying. The willingness to extend to the patient with freshness, innocence, and sincere concern far outweighs any technique or expertise in the art of listening. Practice and exposure hone these skills and deepen one's personal awareness, which in itself is the fertile soil for end-of-life completion work for both parties.

Secular Blessing

In ancient times the physician and the priest were the same person: the doctor of the body and the doctor of the soul. In the face of death, the physician may still embody in the unconscious the archetype of "guardian of life-and-death mysteries." This awesome power can be worked with. Psychoanalytic theory would call it "using the transference." Conferring of blessing on a patient will not only affect his or her inner life but also impact physical attributes such as breathing, muscle tension, and pain levels. Balancing emotional components brings about increased levels of confidence, relaxation, and peace.

The time, effort, and care the physician takes to be present will be experienced as a blessing in itself. "Blessing" need not be a "religious" word or gesture. It can be a genuine, heartfelt well-wishing for the patient's equanimity. Blessing statements can be as elementary as "I wish you well," "May you find peace," and "Blessings on your way." Accompanying a blessing statement with a touch to the arm hand, or head potentiates the effectiveness and meaning of this simple but sacramental act.

Final Comments

In attending the dying, physicians need not give up the medical model. It is simply a matter of taking up a more priestly and simultaneously human mantle in extending care. This can be a threshold experience for both in partnering together (1) the unfolding of death as a natural cycle, (2) the potential of release from holding on, (3) the possibility for unconditional positive evolution even in the latest stage of life, and (4) the satisfaction of continuity and meaning in the patient-physician relationship.

Access to Palliative Care and Hospice in Nursing Homes

Nursing homes are the site of death for many elderly patients with incurable chronic illness, yet dying nursing home residents have limited access to palliative care and hospice. The probability that a nursing home will be the site of death increased from 18.7% in 1986 to 20.0% by 1993. Dying residents experience high rates of untreated pain and other symptoms. They and their family members are isolated from social and spiritual support. Hospice improves end-of-life care for dying nursing home residents by improving pain control, reducing hospitalization, and reducing use of tube feeding, but it is rarely used. For example, in 1997 only 13% of hospice enrollees were in nursing homes while 87% were in private homes, and 70% of nursing homes had no hospice patients. Hospice use varies by region, and rates of use are associated with nursing home administrators' attitudes toward hospice and contractual obligations. Current health policy discourages use of palliative care and hospice for dying nursing home residents. Quality standards and reimbursement rules provide incentives for restorative care and technologically intensive treatments rather than labor-intensive palliative care. Reimbursement incentives, contractual requirements, and concerns about health care fraud also limit its use. Changes in health policy, quality standards, and reimbursement incentives are essential to improve access to palliative care and hospice for dying nursing home residents.

JAMA. 2000;284:2489–2494   *www.jama.com*

Judy Zerzan, MD
Sally Stearns, PhD
Laura Hanson, MD, MPH

NURSING HOMES ARE COMMON SITES OF TERMINAL care. The United States has an aging population, and by the year 2030, 23% of the population will be aged 65 years and older.[1]

Nearly half of Americans who live to 65 years of age will enter a nursing home before they die.[2] Two thirds of persons who consider a nursing home their usual place of residence will remain in the nursing home until death.[3] In the 2 most recent years of the National Mortality Follow-back Survey, the probability that a nursing home will be the site of death increased from 18.7% in 1986 to 20.0% in 1993.[3-5] Current health care trends, including aging of the population and pressures to decrease hospital and home health costs, are likely to promote the use of nursing homes as a site for terminal care.

Most nursing home residents have incurable chronic diseases, and more than half have been diagnosed with a progressive dementia.[6] Patients in the final stages of chronic physical illnesses or dementia often prefer treatment that

From the *Journal of the American Medical Association*, November 15, 2000, pp. 2489-2494. © 2000 by the American Medical Association. Reprinted by permission.

emphasizes pain management and supportive care for themselves and their families, while limiting use of life-prolonging therapies.[7,8] Palliative care is comprehensive interdisciplinary care designed to promote quality of life for patients and families living with a terminal or incurable illness.[9] It includes expert pain and symptom management, emotional and spiritual care, and bereavement support for survivors. These services are typically, though not exclusively, delivered by hospice providers. Palliative care may be offered at any point during the course of illness, but reimbursement for hospice services is usually limited to the final 6 months of life expectancy.

Hospice care in the United States was originally conceived as a home-based service to support family caregivers, but in 1989 the rules for the Medicare hospice benefit were clarified to include residents of long-term care institutions. The nursing home hospice population expanded from 7.7% of all Medicare hospice beneficiaries in 1989 to 17% in 1995.[10]

Despite this rapid growth, hospice care reaches very few dying nursing home residents. Only 1% of the nursing home population enrolls in hospice care.[11] Similar numbers of Medicare beneficiaries die in nursing homes and in private homes, yet those who die at home are more likely to receive hospice care. For example, in 1997 in North Carolina, 19% of deaths occurred in nursing homes and 22% in private homes. During the same year only 13% of hospice enrollees were in nursing homes, while 87% were in private homes.[12] Furthermore, access to hospice care in nursing homes varies markedly by region, and 70% of nursing homes have no hospice patients.[11] Nursing home residents are unlikely to receive hospice care prior to death, and access to care may be more influenced by the facility or county in which they live than by their preference for treatment.

Surviving family members report greater dissatisfaction with nursing homes than with any other component of terminal care.[13] Residents increasingly forgo life-sustaining treatment and hospitalization, but these decisions are not linked to effective plans for palliative care.[14,15] Usual nursing home care results in high rates of untreated severe pain[16–19] and provides little or no support for bereaved family members.[20] Onsite palliative care programs in nursing homes are rare but may improve pain management or reduce costs.[21–24] Two studies provide evidence that hospice services improve quality of care in nursing homes. The first study asked families of nursing home hospice enrollees to compare quality of care before and after enrollment in hospice. The addition of hospice care increased favorable ratings of symptom management from 64% to 90%. Family respondents identified unique hospice services, and 53% believed hospice care reduced the need for hospitalization.[25] The second study used the Minimum Data Set to compare clinical outcomes for dying nursing home residents with and without hospice care. Decedents with hospice care had improved pain management, decreased hospitalization, and decreased use of feeding tubes.[26]

Although nursing home residents benefit from palliative care, few facilities have staff with this expertise and their use of hospice care is limited. Several aspects of current health policy limit nursing home residents' access to palliative care and hospice, including emphasis on restorative care and reimbursement mechanisms.

EMPHASIS ON RESTORATIVE CARE IN NURSING HOMES

Nursing homes provide housing, nursing care, and rehabilitative services for people with physical, cognitive, or behavioral impairments. Residents typically require help with 3 or more activities of daily living and often seek care in nursing homes because they lack a family caregiver or access to home-based services to meet their dependency needs.[1]

Federal policy emphasizes rehabilitation and restoration of function as the goals of nursing home care. Following an Institute of Medicine report documenting uneven and often seriously neglectful care in nursing homes,[27,28] the US Congress passed landmark legislation aimed at improving the quality of care and quality of life for residents. Nursing home reforms codified in the Omnibus Budget Reconciliation Act of 1987 define the primary goal of care to be "to attain or maintain the highest practicable physical, mental, and psychosocial well-being of each resident."[29]

To improve the quality of care, subsequent regulations require the use of a comprehensive, uniform assessment system for all nursing home residents focused on "identifying treatable, reversible causes of functional limitations and on restoring and maintaining function."[30] The Resident Assessment Instrument (RAI) was developed as a consequence of this mandate. The RAI consists of the Minimum Data Set, a 9-page form documenting residents' status on a wide range of indicators, and a separate set of in-depth Resident Assessment Protocols. These in-depth assessments are triggered by the presence of specific health conditions thought to be indicators of inadequate treatment. Some of the expected signs and symptoms of terminal illness—functional decline, weight loss, and dehydration—are used as indicators of potentially treatable illness. Assessment protocols assume that care plans will include treatment to reverse these conditions. The RAI does not include protocols for palliative care outcomes such as symptom control. Use of the RAI has corresponded to temporal improvements in the prevalence of the target conditions but has not led to improvements in other important outcomes such as pain control.[31]

The restorative focus of the RAI assessment system is reinforced by surveys of all nursing homes based on the same data. Since 1999, surveyors receive periodic summary reports that compare 24 quality indicators within a specific facility with average rates. Surveyors use these data to plan their investigations. If they determine that conditions such as functional decline or weight loss were medically avoidable, they then recommend penalties. While this process has promoted improved care for reversible or preventable conditions, it does not include quality standards specific to the needs of residents suffering or actively dying from progressive incurable illness. Clinical experts have proposed adding standards for palliative care in nursing homes, such as documentation of advance directives and pain management plans, but these quality indicators are not emphasized in the current survey process.[32–36]

REIMBURSEMENT INCENTIVES FOR RESTORATIVE CARE

Reimbursement policy also encourages nursing homes to focus on restorative care. While Medicaid covers a larger portion of nursing home costs, Medicare provides higher reimbursement for restorative care following hospitalization. The Medicare skilled nursing benefit covers skilled nursing and therapy, and many facilities attempt to maximize the number of resident-days with this coverage. Beginning in 1999, Medicare reimbursement rules require that a new resident be prospectively categorized in 1 of 44 Resource Utilization Groups (RUGs). Each RUG has a different reimbursement rate, but the highest rates are for intensive rehabilitation or procedural nursing skills such as intravenous medications or tube feedings. Reimbursement rates are lower for intensive personal care services, symptom management, and emotional and spiritual care needed in terminal illness. For example, per diem payments are more than $300 to treat a resident with a hip fracture who requires intensive rehabilitation and intravenous feedings. A nursing home would receive about half this rate to care for an equally dependent resident with metastatic cancer and a pathologic hip fracture who needs intensive pain management, assisted feeding, and treatment for depression. As with the RAI-based quality standards, Medicare reimbursement rules assume that rehabilitative care and medical technology are more costly to provide, and that restoration of function is the rationale for economic valuation of services. The RUG categories do not acknowledge the many hours of nursing and social work needed for skilled pain and symptom management, personal care, and emotional support during dying. Therefore, this payment structure may fail to cover the cost of palliative care or create financial incentives to promote restorative care or use of medical technology.

REIMBURSEMENT FOR HOSPICE CARE IN NURSING HOMES

Medicare covers the majority of hospice care (65%), with smaller proportions of funding from private insurance (12%) and Medicaid (8%).[37] Medicare and most other insurers pay a per diem amount to the hospice providing services to a nursing home resident.[38,39] With this payment the hospice program covers a range of services related to the terminal illness including nursing care, medical equipment, outpatient drugs, short-term inpatient care, aide services, social services, spiritual support, and counseling. Hospice programs must also provide 1 year of bereavement support to family and to nursing home staff as part of the overall benefit. Usual nursing home services, room and board, and other illnesses are not included in the Medicare hospice benefit and must be paid using other sources. Reimbursement for hospice care in the nursing home is therefore a result of a contractual arrangement between the nursing home and a hospice agency that varies based on the nursing home resident's insurance coverage.

Residents Insured by Medicare Alone

Nursing home residents with Medicare as their only insurance may elect coverage under the skilled nursing care benefit following an acute hospital stay or may elect coverage under the hospice benefit if they are terminally ill with a life expectancy of 6 months or less. A terminally ill Medicare recipient admitted to the nursing home from the hospital could choose the skilled nursing benefit or the hospice benefit, but the choice is not financially neutral.[40,41] Compared wit hospice, the Medicare skilled nursing benefit provides a higher reimbursement rate to the nursing home and covers room and board costs otherwise billed to the resident. The skilled nursing benefit is therefore financially advantageous to both the nursing home and the resident. For example, a newly admitted Medicare resident with cancer and failure to thrive could elect either the skilled nursing benefit or hospice care. However, if the resident elects hospice care, the nursing home will receive less and the resident will have to pay for room and board. Many nursing homes simply do not offer hospice care to residents who are eligible for the Medicare skilled nursing benefit. Recent actions will partially address this problem: the graduated Medicare payments implemented in 1999 have lessened the magnitude of the financial incentive to use skilled nursing care. While residents with Medicare hospice will still be responsible for their room and board costs, nursing homes may now find it more financially reasonable to offer hospice care as an option.

Residents Dually Eligible for Medicare and Medicaid

Most nursing home residents who receive hospice care are dually eligible for Medicare and Medicaid. After 1 year in nursing home care, approximately 90% of elderly residents receiving Medicare also become eligible for Medicaid as they spend their savings down to Medicaid poverty levels.[6] Dual coverage provides Medicaid payment for room and board and Medicare payment for hospice care.[40,41] With Medicare and Medicaid, a terminally ill patient admitted from the hospital may choose the skilled nursing benefit or hospice care. However, in contrast to a resident with Medicare alone, Medicaid coverage of room and board costs makes this choice financially neutral.

Both Medicare and Medicaid payments are initially directed to the hospice provider, and the hospice passes on the room and board amount to the nursing home. State Medicaid programs must pay hospice providers at least 95% of the usual rate for room and board. Room and board services are not uniformly defined, but this payment is generally assumed to cover personal care services, assistance with activities of daily living, activities, medication administration, cleaning, and use of durable medical equipment and prescribed therapies unrelated to the terminal diagnosis.[30] The incentive for nursing homes to participate in a hospice program may vary with the perceived adequacy of this room and board "pass-through" payment. Some hospice-nursing home contracts have given nursing homes more money for room and board services than the state Medicaid payment. However, this practice is likely to decrease, as federal investigations have interpreted increased room and board payments as potential health care fraud.[42,43]

Residents Insured by Medicaid Alone

Since 70% of deaths occur after 65 years of age,[3] most dying patients in the United States have Medicare coverage for hospice services. However, nursing homes also house some impoverished younger patients with chronic diseases, particularly human immunodeficiency virus disease and progressive neuromuscular disorders such as amyotrophic lateral sclerosis or muscular dystrophy. Medicaid covers nursing home care in all states, and it covers hospice care in 43 states.[40] Although Medicaid is the single largest insurer for overall nursing home costs, only 0.1% of total Medicaid dollars are spent on hospice care.[44,45] The Medicaid hospice benefits are state-specific but typically cover the same services and reimburse at rates similar to the Medicare hospice benefit with the addition of coverage for room and board.[39,40] Enrollment in hospice care is financially neutral for residents covered by Medicaid, and it adds services at no financial disincentive for the nursing home.

SIX-MONTH PROGNOSTIC CRITERION FOR HOSPICE CARE IN NURSING HOMES

Anyone may refer a patient to hospice care—the patient, a family member, nursing home staff, or a physician.[46] To use the Medicare hospice benefit or other insurance coverage, a physician must certify that a patient has 6 months or less to live if the disease follows its usual and expected course. In 1996, 58% of all hospice patients had a primary cancer diagnosis, in part due to physicians' ability to identify the final phase of illness in cancer.[47] This level of prognostic certainty is more difficult in causes of death other than cancer.[48]

Compared with people who die at home or in hospitals, nursing home residents more often die of heart disease and stroke and are less likely to die of cancer.[4,5] Thus, the 6-month prognosis requirement for hospice services may limit access to hospice care even when the resident prefers a palliative approach to care. To address the difficulty of predicting a 6-month life expectancy, the National Hospice Organization published specific guidelines to document prognosis in some noncancer diagnoses.[49] However, even these guidelines cannot identify patients with dementia who will die within 6 months. As a consequence, physicians may be reluctant to refer nursing home residents with end-stage dementia or cardiopulmonary diseases to hospice care.[48,50,51] Strict reliance on disease-specific guidelines will result in the exclusion of many dying nursing home residents who prefer palliative care or need expert symptom management. In response to this difficulty, some hospice advocates have suggested cost-effectiveness studies of alternatives such as hospice or palliative consultation services, extended eligibility periods, or complete lifting of the 6-month criterion.

HOSPICE AND NURSING HOME CONTRACTUAL OBLIGATIONS

For a nursing home resident to enroll in hospice care, the nursing home must first contract with a hospice agency to define a shared plan of care and payment arrangement. The hospice and nursing home must create a coordinated care plan with specific roles. Under Medicare regulations, the hospice agency assumes overall responsibility for management and implementation of the care plan related to the terminal illness.[41] The nursing home is required to continue the same level of service and personal care as if the patient had not been in hospice care, while hospice staff provided added palliative care. Services unique to hospice include expert pain and symptom assessment and management, emotional and spiritual care, and bereavement services for nursing home staff as well as family.

Collaboration between nursing home and hospice staff members is dependent on good communication and coordination of care, and many providers may be unwilling or unable to enter into contracts. Nursing home staff may see the hospice as interfering with or duplicating their work or as another source of criticism and oversight.[52] The nursing home continues to provide most direct care to hospice enrollees, and nursing home staff members remain responsible for the quality of care under the survey process. Hospices must acquire specialized clinical and administrative skills to contract with and provide care in nursing homes, and many smaller agencies may be less willing to assume the care of nursing home residents.

Nursing home administrators decide whether they will accept hospice contracts, and some evidence suggests that organizational characteristics account for regional variation in access to the hospice care in the nursing home. One survey study has examined the relationship between the use of hospice services and administrators' attitudes toward hospice care.[53] In 23 facilities owned by a single company, rates of hospice use ranged from 2% to 39% of dying residents. Investigators found that the rate of hospice use was correlated with administrators' attitudes toward hospice care generally and toward the potential burdens imposed by contractual obligations. In another national cross-sectional study of nursing home hospice use, Petrisek and Mor[11] found that 70% of nursing homes do not have any residents enrolled in hospice care. Organizational characteristics of both the hospice and the nursing home were correlated with rates of use of the hospice benefit. Thus, some nursing home residents may not be able to access their hospice benefit under Medicare because of local barriers to contractual agreements.

FEDERAL INVESTIGATION OF HEALTH CARE FRAUD

In 1995, the Office of the Inspector General (OIG) within the US Department of Health and Human Services undertook an investigation of waste, fraud, and abuse practices in services funded by the Health Care Financing Administration. The investigation, called Operation Restore Trust, was designed to identify programs' vulnerabilities to fraud and abuse. In its first 2 years, Operation Restore Trust identified more than $187.5 million in unjustified Medicare and Medicaid payments potentially due to fraud and abuse.[54] In hospice, OIG investigators focused on providers with longer lengths of stay, higher rates of noncancer diagnoses, and large numbers of nursing home enrollees. The investigators cited numerous examples of abuse within the hospice nursing home system, and at one point recommended eliminating the nursing home hospice Medicare benefit.[43]

Critics of the OIG report argued that the investigation used flawed methods to define enrollees who met the 6-month prognostic criterion. Prognosis, especially in noncancer diagnoses, is of necessity imprecise.[48,50,55] Clinically, a 6-month prognosis may mean an average life expectancy or a maximum life expectancy of 6 months.[55] The OIG used the more conservative definition and scrutinized hospices with higher than average numbers of patients who lived longer than 6 months.

Investigators from the OIG also found fault with the methods used to pass along room and board payments from hospices to nursing homes for residents receiving both Medicare and Medicaid coverage. When pass-through payments exceeded 95% of Medicaid room and board reimbursement, inspectors interpreted the excess payments as potentially fraudulent incentives for hospice referrals.[42,43] Hospices and nursing homes, in turn, have argued that the definition of room and board varies, and payments should be varied by contractual divisions of responsibility for services between the 2 care providers. Investigations performed by the OIG found and penalized some fraud and abuse in hospice care, but their investigations have acted as a broader deterrent on further expansion of hospice care in nursing homes.

IMPROVING ACCESS TO PALLIATIVE CARE IN NURSING HOMES

In nursing homes, as in home or hospice care, the preferences of patients and families tempered by the judgment of physicians should be the primary determinant of the decision to use palliative care or enroll in hospice care. These clinical considerations do not change in the nursing home setting, yet residents have less access to palliative care services. Federal nursing home quality assessments and reimbursement incentives both emphasize restorative care while failing to reward high-quality palliative care. Administrative and contractual barriers, as well as suspicions of fraudulent use, limit access to hospice care in nursing homes. Since nursing homes are an increasingly important site for terminal care, it is reasonable to anticipate growing demand for palliative care and hospice in this setting.

Changes in current incentives and policies could be used to promote the appropriate use of palliative care for people who live the final phase of their lives in a nursing home. The following strategies could enhance access to palliative care services in nursing homes:

1. Add assessment of pain management and advance directives to the RAI as quality standards for care of residents near the end of their lives.
2. Train state surveyors to identify quality of care deficiencies in nursing homes deaths, including failure to offer treatment options or respect advance directives, and failure to provide adequate pain and symptom management prior to death.
3. Fund demonstration projects to test the cost-effectiveness of hospice as a palliative care consultation service in nursing homes. Hospice care could then be available to residents with severe pain or other palliative care needs who do not meet the 6-month prognostic criterion.
4. Create financially neutral reimbursement for nursing home hospice under Medicare, so Medicare beneficiaries may elect hospice care without penalty to the nursing home or themselves.
5. Modify the Medicare RUG system of reimbursement to cover the costs of intensive personal care services and skilled symptom management in terminal illness.
6. Replace the Medicaid "pass-through" with a direct payment for room and board for residents on the Medicare hospice benefit and clarify the services covered by this payment.
7. Include a palliative care or hospice benefits in all state Medicaid programs that now fail to cover hospice care.
8. Create incentives for health care training programs to include palliative care content in nursing home education for physicians, nurses, social workers, nursing aides, and others who will provide long-term care.

As the population ages, increasing numbers of persons with serious chronic illness will spend the final phase of their lives in a nursing home. Training for nursing home staff and physicians must be coupled with changes in health policy and reimbursement to meet the palliative care needs of residents in long-term care settings. Increasing access to nursing home hospice care can expand the capacity for palliative care, but the model of hospice care may need to be modified to match service delivery in nursing homes. Changes in nursing home hospice contractual rules may also decrease geographic variation and permit access to services in the nursing homes that do not currently enroll residents. For many nursing home residents, palliative care may be the preferred approach to care in their final months—or even years—of life. Quality standards, reimbursement policy, and clinical practice will need to change in synchrony to make this care possible.

Funding/Support: This work was funded by a Soros Foundation Project on Death in America award to Dr Hanson.

REFERENCES

1. Weiner J. Financing long-term care. *JAMA*. 1994;271:1525–1529.

2. Kemper P, Murtaugh CM. Lifetime use of nursing home care. *N Engl J Med.* 1991;324:595–600.

3. Hanson LC, Henderson M. Rodgman E. Where will we die? a national study of nursing home death. *J Gen Intern Med.* 1999;14:101.

4. McMillan A. Mentech RM, Lubitz J, McBean AM, Russell D. Trends and patterns in place of death for Medicare enrollees. *Health Care Financing Rev.* 1990;12:1–7.

5. Sager MA, Easterling DV, Kindig DA, Anderson OW. Changes in the location of death after passage of Medicare's prospective payment system. *N Engl J Med.* 1989;320:433–439.

6. Collopy B, Boyle P. Jennings B. New directions in nursing home ethics. *Hastings Cent Rep.* 1991;21(2):1–15.

7. Singer PA, Martin DK, Kelner M. Quality end-of-life care: patients' perspectives. *JAMA.* 1999;281:163–168.

8. O'Brien LA, Grisso JA, Maislin G, et al. Nursing home residents' preferences for life-sustaining treatments. *JAMA.* 1995;274:1775–1779.

9. Billings JA. What is palliative care? *J Palliat Med.* 1998;1:73–81.

10. Miller SC, Mor V, Coppola K, Teno J, Laliberte L, Petrisek AC. The Medicare hospice benefit's influence on dying in nursing homes. *J Palliat Med.* 1998;1:367–376.

11. Petrisek AC, Mor V. Hospice in nursing homes: a facility-level analysis of the distribution of hospice beneficiaries. *Gerontologist.* 1999;39:279–290.

12. North Carolina Division of Facility Services. *Annual Hospice Licensure Data Supplement, 1997.* Chapel Hill: North Carolina Division of Facility Services; 1997.

13. Hanson LC, Danis M, Garrett J. What is wrong with end of life care? opinions of bereaved family members. *J Am Geriatr Soc.* 1997;45:1339–1344.

14. Mor V, Intrator O, Fries BE, et al, Changes in hospitalization associated with introducing the Resident Assessment Instrument. *J Am Geriatr Soc.* 1997;45:1002–1010.

15. Holtzman J, Pheley AM, Lurie N. Changes in orders limiting care and the use of less aggressive care in a nursing home population. *J Am Geriatr Soc.* 1994;42:275–279.

16. Bernabei R, Gambassi G, Lapane K, et al. Management of pain in elderly patients with cancer. *JAMA.* 1998;279:1877–1882.

17. Won A, Lapane K, Gambassi G, et al. Correlates and management of nonmalignant pain in the nursing home. *J Am Geriatr Soc.* 1999;47:936–942.

18. Ferrell BA. Pain evaluation and management in the nursing home. *Ann Intern Med.* 1995;123:681–687.

19. Sengstaken EA, King SA. The problems of pain and its detection among geriatric nursing home residents. *J Am Geriatr Soc.* 1993;41:541–544.

20. Murphy K, Hanrahan P. Luchins D. A Survey of grief and bereavement in nursing homes: the importance of hospice grief and bereavement for the end-stage Alzheimer's disease patient and family. *J Am Geriatr Soc.* 1997;45:1104–1107.

21. Linn MW, Linn BS, Stein S, Stein EM. Effect of nursing home staff training on quality of patient survival. *Int J Aging Hum Dev.* 1998;28:305–315.

22. Volicer L. Collard A, Hurley A, Bishop C, Kern D, Karon S. Impact of special care unit for patients with advanced Alzheimer's disease on patients' discomfort and costs. *J Am Geriatr Soc.* 1994;42:597–603.

23. Wilson SA, Kovach CR, Stearns SA. Hospice concepts in the care for end-stage dementia. *Geriatr Nurs.* 1996;17:6–10.

24. Weissman D, Dahl JL. Update on the cancer pain role model education program. *J Pain Symptom Manage.* 1995;10:292–297.

25. Baer Wm, Hanson LC. Families' perceptions of the added value of hospice in the nursing home. *J Am Geriatr Soc.* 2000;48:879–882.

26. Miller SC, Gozalo P, Mor V. Outcomes and utilization for hospice and non-hospice nursing facility decedents. Contract No.

100–97–0010, US Dept of Health and Human Services, Office of Disability, Aging and Long-Term Care Policy and the Urban Institute. Available at: www.aspe.hhs.gov/daltcp/reports/oututil.htm. Accessed September 11, 2000.

27. Vladeck BC. The past, present, and future of nursing home quality [From the Health Care Financing Administration]. *JAMA.* 1996;275:425.

28. Institute of Medicine. *Improving the Quality of Care in Nursing Homes.* Washington, DC: National Academy Press; 1986.

29. Omnibus Budget Reconciliation Act of 1987 (OBRA-87), *56 Federal Register* 187:48865–49921.

30. Phillips CD, Morris JN, Hawes C, et al. Association of the Resident Assessment Instrument (RAI) with changes in function, cognition, and psychosocial status. *J Am Geriatr Soc.* 1997;45:986–993.

31. Fries BE, Hawes C, Morris JN, et al. Effect of the National Resident Assessment Instrument on selected health conditions and problems. *J Am Geriatr Soc.* 1997;45:994–1001.

32. Keay TJ, Fredman L, Taler GA, Datta S, Levenson SA. Indicators of quality medical care for the terminally ill in nursing homes. *J Am Geriatr Soc.* 1994;42:853–860.

33. Hayley DC, Cassel CK, Snyder L, Rudberg MA. Ethical and legal issues in nursing home care. *Arch Intern Med.* 1996;156:249–256.

34. Degner LF, Gow CM, Thompson LA. Critical nursing behaviors in care for the dying. *Cancer Nurs.* 1991;14:246–253.

35. Broder M. Ethical decision making in long term care. In: Monagle JF, Thomasma DC, eds. *Medical Ethics: Policies, Protocols, Guidelines and Programs.* Gaithersburg, Md: Aspen Publishers; 1996.

36. Won A, Morris JN, Nonemaker S, Lipsitz LA. A foundation for excellence in long-term care: the Minimum Data Set. *Ann Long-Term Care.* 1999;7:92–97.

37. Hospice Fact Sheet. National Hospice Organization. Available at: http://www.nho.org. Accessed March 23, 1999.

38. Kidder D. The effects of hospice coverage on Medicare expenditures. *Health Serv Res.* 1992;27:195–217.

39. Health Care Financing Administration. *Medicare Program Manual and State Medicaid Manual and Statistics.* Washington, DC: Health Care Financing Administration; 1997.

40. Leland J. The nursing home Medicare hospice benefit. *Nurs Home Econ.* 1996;3:8–13.

41. Keay TJ, Schonwetter RS, Hospice care in the nursing home. *Am Fam Physician.* 1998;57:491–494.

42. Office of Inspector General, US Department of Health and Human Services. *Hospice and Nursing Home Contractual Relationships.* Washington, DC: Office of Inspector General, US Dept of Health and Human Services; November 1997. Document OEL-05-95-00251.

43. Office of Inspector General, US Department of Health and Human Services. *Hospice Patients in Nursing Homes.* Washington, DC: Office of Inspector General, US Dept of Health and Human Services; September 1997. Document OEL-05-95-00250.

44. US General Accounting Office. *Salary Guidelines for Therapy Services.* Washington, DC: US General Accounting Office; August 1996. Document GAO/HEHS-96-145.

45. Office of Inspector General, US Department of Health and Human Services. *Summary of OIG Activities on Medicaid.* Washington, DC: Office of Inspector General, US Dept of Health and Human Services; June 1993. Document OEL-12-92-00550.

46. Watt K. Hospice and the elderly: a changing perspective. *Am J Hosp Palliat Care.* 1996;13:47–48.

47. Haupt BJ. Characteristics of hospice care users: data from the 1996 National Home and Hospice Care Survey. *Adv Data.* Aug 28, 1998;299:1–16.

48. Fox E, Landrum-McNiff K, Zhong Z, Dawson NV, Wu AW, Lynn J, for the SUPPORT Investigators. Evaluation of prognostic criteria for determining hospice eligibility in patients with

advanced lung, heart, or liver disease. *JAMA.* 1999;282:1638–1645.

49. National Hospice Organization Medical Guidelines Task Force. *Medical Guidelines for Determining Prognosis in Selected Noncancer Diseases.* Arlington, Va: National Hospice Organization; 1996.

50. Luchins DJ, Hanrahan P, Murphy K. Criteria for enrolling dementia patients in hospice. *J Am Geriatr Soc.* 1997;45:1054–1059.

51. Christakis NA, Escarce JJ. Survival of Medicare patients after enrollment in hospice programs. *N Engl J Med.* 1996;335:172–178.

52. Watt CK. Hospices within nursing homes: should a long-term care facility wear both hats? *Am J Hosp Palliat Care.* 1997;14:63–65.

53. Jones B. Nackerud L, Boyle D. Differential utilization of hospice services in nursing homes: *Hosp Palliat Care.* 1997;12:41–57.

54. Mangano MF. Testimony from the DHHS Office of Inspector General, March 3, 1998. Available at: http://www.hhs.gov. Accessed November 30, 1998.

55. Von Gunten CF, Neely KJ, Martinez J. Hospice and palliative care: program needs and academic issues. *Oncology.* 1996;10:1070–1074.

Author Affiliations: Department of Medicine, Oregon Health Sciences University, Portland (Dr Zerzan); Department of Health Policy and Administration, School of Public Health (Dr Stearns), and Department of Medicine and Center for Health Ethics and Policy (Dr Hanson), University of North Carolina at Chapel Hill.

Corresponding Author and Reprints: Laura C. Hanson, MD, MPH, Division of General Medicine, CB 7110, 5035 Old Clinic Bldg, University of North Carolina, Chapel Hill, NC 27599–7110 (e-mail: Laura_Hanson@med.unc. edu).

Unit 4

Unit Selections

19. **Doctor, I Want to Die. Will You Help Me?** Timothy E. Quill
20. **The Supreme Court and Physician-Assisted Suicide: The Ultimate Right,** Marcia Angell
21. **Competent Care for the Dying Instead of Physician-Assisted Suicide,** Kathleen M. Foley
22. **A Conversation With My Mother,** David M. Eddy
23. **Euthanasia: To Cease Upon the Midnight,** *The Economist*
24. **Attitudes Toward Suicidal Behavior: A Review of the Literature,** Ellen Ingram and Jon B. Ellis
25. **Elisabeth Kübler-Ross's Final Passage,** Leslie Bennetts

Key Points to Consider

❖ The question, "What is a good death?" has been asked for centuries. What would constitute a good death in this time of high-tech medical care? Does the concept of a good death include the taking of a life? Defend your answer.

❖ Does the role of the health care provider include taking life or providing the means for others to do so? Why or why not?

❖ Are constraints required to prevent the killing of persons we do not consider worthwhile contributors to our society? Explain.

❖ Should limits be placed on the length of life as we consider the expenses involved in the care of the elderly and the infirm?

❖ For some individuals, suicide may seem to be the best solution to their situation. How might our society help such individuals "solve" their problems?

❖ Is the concept of "rational suicide" rational? Why or why not?

❖ Do you believe that high-risk-taking persons—such as heavy smokers, race-car drivers, overeating or undereating individuals, or persons mixing alcohol and drugs—are suicidal? Explain.

 **Links**   **www.dushkin.com/online/**

22. **Articles on Euthanasia: Ethics**
http://www.acusd.edu/ethics/euthanasia.html
23. **Kearl's Guide to the Sociology of Death: Moral Debates**
http://WWW.Trinity.Edu/~mkearl/death-5.html#eu
24. **The Kevorkian File**
http://www.rights.org/deathnet/KevorkianFile.html
25. **The Living Will and Values History Project**
http://www.euthanasia.org/lwvh.html
26. **Living Wills (Advance Directive)**
http://www.mindspring.com/~scottr/will.html
27. **Not Dead Yet**
http://acils.com/NotDeadYet/
28. **Suicide Awareness: Voices of Education**
http://www.save.org
29. **Suicide Prevention Advocacy Network**
http://www.spanusa.org
30. **UNOS: United Network for Organ Sharing**
http://www.unos.org/frame_default.asp
31. **Youth Suicide League**
http://www.unicef.org/pon96/insuicid.htm

These sites are annotated on pages 4 and 5.

One of the concerns about dying and death pressing hard upon our consciences is the question of helping the dying to die sooner with the assistance of the physician. Public awareness of the horrors that can be visited upon us by artificial means of ventilation and other support measures in a high-tech hospital setting has produced a literature that debates the issue of euthanasia—a "good death." As individuals think through their plans for care when dying, there is a steady increase in the demand for control of that care.

Another controversial issue is physician-assisted suicide. Is it the function of the doctor to assist patients in their dying—to actually kill them at their request? The highly publicized suicides in Michigan, along with the jury decisions that found Dr. Kevorkian innocent of murder, as well as the popularity of the book *Final Exit*, make these issues prominent national and international concerns. Legislative action has been taken in some states to permit this, and the issue is pending in a number of others. We are in a time of intense consideration by the courts, by the legislatures, and by the medical and nursing professions of the legality and the morality of providing the means by which a person can be given the means to die. Is this the role of health care providers? The pro and contra positions are presented in several of the unit's articles. Although the issue is difficult and personally challenging, as a nation we are in the position of being required to make difficult choices. There are no "right" answers; the questions pose dilemmas that require choice based upon moral, spiritual, and legal foundations.

The word *suicide,* meaning "self" and "to kill," was first used in English in 1651. Early societies sometimes forced certain members into committing suicide for ritual purposes and occasionally expected such of widows and slaves. There is also a strong inheritance from Hellenic and Roman times of rational suicide when disease, dishonor, or failure were considered unbearable. Attitudes toward suicide changed when St. Augustine laid down rules against it that became basic Christian doctrine for centuries.

In recent years, suicide has attracted increasing interest and scrutiny by sociologists, psychologists, and others in efforts to reduce its incidence. Suicide is a major concern in the United States today, and understanding suicide is important so that warning signs in others can be recognized. Various suicide types, cross-cultural rates, and a history of suicide are presented in the article "Attitudes Toward Suicidal Behavior: A Review of the Literature."

Just what constitutes suicide is not clear today. Risky behavior that leads to death may or may not be classified as suicide. We have differing attitudes toward suicide. Suicide rates are high in adolescents, the elderly, and males. A person with high vulnerability is an alcoholic, depressed male between the ages of 75 and 84. Suicidal persons often talk about the attempt prior to the act and display observable signs of potential suicide. Males are more likely to complete suicide than females because they use more lethal weapons. For suicidal persons, the act is an easy solution to their problems—a permanent answer to an often temporary set of problems.

Doctor, I Want to Die. Will You Help Me?

Timothy E. Quill, MD

IT HAD been 18 months since a 67-year-old retired man whose main joy in life was his two grandchildren was diagnosed with inoperable lung cancer. An arduous course of chemotherapy helped him experience a relatively good year where he was able to remain independent, babysitting regularly for his grandchildren.

Recent tests revealed multiple new bony metastases. An additional round of chemotherapy and radiation provided little relief. By summer, pain and fatigue became unrelenting. He was no longer able to tolerate, much less care for, his grandchildren. His wife of 45 years devoted herself to his care and support. Nonetheless, his days felt empty and his nights were dominated by despair about the future. Though he was treated with modern pain control methods, his severe bone pain required daily choices between pain and sedation. Death was becoming less frightening than life itself.

A particularly severe thigh pain led to the roentgenogram that showed circumferential destruction of his femur. Attempting to preserve his ability to walk, he consented to the placement of a metal plate. Unfortunately, the bone was too brittle to support the plate. He would never walk again.

One evening in the hospital after his wife had just left, his physician sat down to talk. The pain was "about the same," and the new sleep medication "helped a little." He seemed quiet and distracted. When asked what was on his mind, he looked directly at his doctor and said, "Doctor, I want to die. Will you help me?"

Such requests are dreaded by physicians. There is a desperate directness that makes sidestepping the question very difficult, if not impossible. Often,

See also Box "Compassion Needs Reason Too"

we successfully avoid hearing about the inner turmoil faced by our terminally ill patients—what is happening to the person who has the disease. Yet, sometimes requests for help in dying still surface from patients with strong wills, or out of desperation when there is nowhere else to turn. Though comfort care (ie, medical care using a hospice philosophy) provides a humane alternative to traditional medical care of the dying,[1-7] it does not always provide guidance for how to approach those rare patients who continue to suffer terribly in spite of our best efforts.

This article explores what dying patients might be experiencing when they make such requests and offers potential physician responses. Such discussions are by no means easy for clinicians, for they may become exposed to forms and depths of suffering with which they are unfamiliar and to which they do not know how to respond. They may also fear being asked to violate their own moral standards or having to turn down someone in desperate need. Open exploration of requests for physician-assisted death can be fundamental to the humane care of a dying person, because no matter how terrifying and unresolvable their suffering appears, at least they are no longer alone with it. It also frequently opens avenues of "help" that were not anticipated and that do not involve active assistance in dying.

"Doctor, I want to die" and "Will you help me?" constitute both a statement and a query that must each be independently understood and explored. The initial response, rather than a yes or no based on assumptions about the patient's intent and meaning, might be something like: "Of course, I will try to help you, but first I need to understand your wish and your suffering, and then we can explore how I can help." Rather than shying away from the depths of suffering, follow-up questions might include, "What is the worst part?" or "What is your biggest fear?"

THE WISH TO DIE

Transient yearnings for death as an escape from suffering are extremely common among patients with incurable, relentlessly progressive medical illnesses.[8-10] They are not necessarily signs of a major psychiatric disorder, nor are they likely to be fully consid-

From *Journal of the American Medical Association,* Vol. 270, August 18, 1993, pp. 870–875. © 1993 by the American Medical Association. Reprinted by permission.

ered requests for a physician-assisted death. Let us explore some of their potential meanings through a series of case vignettes.

Tired of Acute Medical Treatment

A 55-year-old woman with very aggressive breast cancer found her tumor to be repeatedly recurring over the last 6 months. The latest instance signaled another failure of chemotherapy. When her doctor was proposing a new round of experimental therapy, she said, "I wish I were dead." By exploring her statement, the physician learned that the patient felt strongly she was not going to get better and that she could not fathom the prospect of more chemotherapy with its attendant side effects. She wanted to spend what time she had left at home. He also learned that she did not want to die at that moment. A discussion about changing the goals of treatment from cure to comfort ensued, and a treatment plan was developed that exchanged chemotherapy for symptom-relieving treatments. The patient was relieved by this change in focus, and she was able to spend her last month at home with her family on a hospice program.

Comfort care can guide a caring and humane approach to the last phase of life by directing its energy to relieving the patients' suffering with the same intensity and creativity that traditional medical care usually devotes to treating the underlying disease.[1–7] When comprehensively applied, in either a hospice program or any other setting, comfort care can help ensure a dignified, individualized death for most patients.

Unrecognized or Undertreated Physical Symptoms

A stoical 85-year-old farmer with widely metastatic prostate cancer was cared for in his home with the help of a hospice program. Everyone marveled at his dry wit and engaging nature as he courageously faced death. He was taking very little medication and always said he was "fine." Everyone loved to visit with him, and his stories about life on the farm were legendary. As he became more withdrawn and caustic, people became concerned, but when he said he wished he were dead, there was a panic. All the guns on the farm were hidden and plans for a psychiatric hospitalization were entertained. When his "wish for death" was fully explored, it turned out that he was liv-

ing with excruciating pain, but not telling anyone because he feared becoming "addicted" to narcotics. After a long discussion about pain-relieving principles, the patient agreed to try a regular, around-the-clock dosage of a long-acting narcotic with "as needed" doses as requested. In a short time, his pain was under better control, he again began to engage his family and visitors, and he no longer wanted to die. For the remainder of his life, the physical symptoms that developed were addressed in a timely way, and he died a relatively peaceful death surrounded by his family.

Though not all physical symptoms can be relieved by the creative application of comfort care, most can be improved or at least made tolerable. New palliative techniques have been developed that can ameliorate most types of physical pain, provided they are applied without unnecessary restraint. One must be sure that unrelieved symptoms are not the result of ignorance about or inadequate trials of available medical treatments, or the result of exaggerated patient or physician fears about addiction or about indirectly hastening death. Experts who can provide formal or informal consultation in pain control and in palliative care are available in most major cities and extensive literature is available.[11–14]

Emergent Psychosocial Problems

A 70-year-old retired woman with chronic leukemia that had become acute and had not responded to treatment was sent home on a home hospice program. She was prepared to die, and all of her physicians felt that she would "not last more than a few weeks." She had lived alone in the past, but her daughter took a leave of absence from work to care for her mother for her last few days or weeks. Ironically (though not necessarily surprisingly), the mother stabilized at home. Two months later, outwardly comfortable and symptom-free under the supportive watch of her daughter, she began to focus on wanting to die. When asked to elaborate, she initially discussed her fatigue and her lack of a meaningful future. She then confided that she hated being a burden on her daughter—that her daughter had children who needed her and a job that was beginning to cause serious strain. The daughter had done her best to protect her mother from these problems, but she became aware of them anyway. A family meeting where the problems were openly discussed resulted in a compromise where

the mother was admitted to a nursing facility where comfort care was offered, and the daughter visited every other weekend. Though the mother ideally would have liked to stay at home, she accepted this solution and was transferred to an inpatient unit where she lived for 2 more months before dying with her daughter at her side.

Requests for help in dying can emanate from unrecognized or evolving psychosocial problems.[15] Sometimes these problems can be alleviated by having a family meeting, by arranging a temporary "respite" admission to a health care facility, or by consulting a social worker for some advice about finances and available services. Other psychosocial problems may be more intractable, for example, in a family that was not functioning well prior to the patient's illness or when a dominating family member tries to influence care in a direction that appears contrary to the patient's wishes or best interest. Many patients have no family and no financial resources. The current paucity of inpatient hospices and nursing facilities capable of providing comfort care and the inadequate access to health care in general in the United States often mean that dying patients who need the most help and support are forced to fend for themselves and often die by themselves. The health care reimbursement system is primarily geared toward acute medical care, but not terminal care, so the physician may be the only potential advocate and support that some dying patients have.

Spiritual Crisis

A 42-year-old woman who was living at home with advanced acquired immunodeficiency syndrome (AIDS) began saying that she wished she were dead. She was a fundamentalist Christian who at the time of her diagnosis wondered, "Why would God do this to me?" She eventually found meaning in the possibility that God was testing her strength, and that this was her "cross to bear." Though she continued to regularly participate in church activities over the 5 years after her initial diagnosis, she never confided in her minister or church friends about her diagnosis. Her statements about wishing she were dead frightened her family, and they forced her to visit her doctor. When asked to elaborate on her wish, she raged against her church, her preacher, and her God, stating she found her disease humiliating and did not want to be seen in the end stages of AIDS where everyone would know.

She had felt more and more alone with these feelings, until they burst open. Once the feelings were acknowledged and understood, it was clear that they defied simple solution. She was clearly and legitimately angry, but not depressed. She had no real interest in taking her own life. She was eventually able to find a fundamentalist minister from a different church with an open mind about AIDS who helped her find some spiritual consolation.

The importance of the physician's role as witness and support cannot be overemphasized. Sharing feelings of spiritual betrayal and uncertainty with an empathetic listener can be the first step toward healing. At least isolation is taken out of the doubt and despair. The physician must listen and try to fully understand the problem before making any attempt to help the patient achieve spiritual resolution. Medically experienced clergy are available in many communities who can explore spiritual issues with dying patients of many faiths so that isolation can be further lessened and potential for reconnection with one's religious roots enhanced.

Clinical Depression

A 60-year-old man with a recently diagnosed recurrence of his non-Hodgkin's lymphoma became preoccupied with wanting to die. Though he had a long remission after his first course of chemotherapy, he had recently gone through a divorce and felt he could not face more treatment. In exploring his wishes, it was evident he was preoccupied with the death of his father, who experienced an agonizing death filled with severe pain and agitation. He had a strong premonition that the same thing would happen to him, and he was not sleeping because of this preoccupation. He appeared withdrawn and was not able to fully understand and integrate his options and the odds of treatment directed at his lymphoma, the likelihood that comfort care would prevent a death like his father's, or his doctor's promise to work with him to find acceptable solutions. Though he was thinking seriously of suicide, he did not have a plan and therefore was treated intensively as an outpatient by his internist and a psychotherapist. He accepted the idea that he was depressed, but also wanted assurances that all possibilities could be explored after a legitimate trial of treatment for depression. He responded well to a combination of psychotherapy and medication. He eventually underwent acute treatment

directed at his lymphoma that unfortunately did not work. He then requested hospice care and seemed comfortable and engaged in his last months. As death was imminent, his symptoms remained relatively well controlled, and he was not overtly depressed. He died alone while his family was out of the house. Since his recently filled prescription bottles were all empty, it may have been a drug overdose (presumably to avoid an end like his father's), though no note or discussion accompanied the act.

Whenever a severely ill person begins to talk about wanting to die and begins to seriously consider taking his or her own life, the question of clinical depression appropriately arises.[16] This can be a complex and delicate determination because most patients who are near death with unrelenting suffering are very sad, if not clinically depressed. The epidemiologic literature associating terminal illness and suicide assumes that all such acts arise from unrecognized and/or untreated psychiatric disorders,[17-19] yet there is a growing clinical literature suggesting that some of these suicides may be rational.[2,16,20-25]

Two fundamental questions must be answered before suicide can be considered rational in such settings: (1) Is the patient able to fully understand his or her disease, prognosis, and treatment alternatives (ie, is the decision rational), and (2) is the patient's depression reversible, given the limitations imposed by his illness, in a way that would substantially alter the circumstances? It is vital not to overnormalize (eg, "anyone would be depressed under such circumstances") or to reflexively define the request as a sign of psychopathology. Each patient's dilemma must be fully explored. Consultation with an experienced psychiatrist can be helpful when there is doubt, as can a trial of grief counseling, crisis intervention, or antidepressant medications if a potentially reversible depression is present and the patient has time and strength to participate.

Unrelenting, Intolerable Suffering

The man with widely metastatic lung cancer described in the introduction felt that his life had become a living hell with no acceptable options. His doctors agreed that all effective medical options to treat his cancer had been exhausted. Physical activity and pride in his body had always been a central part of who he was. Now, with a pathologic fracture in his femur that could not be

repaired, he would not even be able to walk independently. He also had to make daily trade-offs between pain, sedation, and other side effects. At the insistence of his doctor, he had several visits with a psychiatrist who found his judgment to be fully rational. Death did not appear imminent, and his condition could only get worse. Even on a hospice program, with experts doing their best to help address his medical, social, personal, and spiritual concerns, he felt trapped, yearning for death. He saw his life savings from 45 years of work rapidly depleting. His family offered additional personal and financial resources. They wanted him to live, but having witnessed the last months of progressive disability, loss, and pain, with no relief in sight other than death, they respected his wishes and slowly began to advocate on his behalf. "We appreciate your efforts to keep him comfortable, but for him this is not comfortable and it is not living. Will you help him?"

Physicians who have made a commitment to shepherd their patients through the dying process find themselves in a predicament. They can acknowledge that comfort care is sometimes far less than ideal, but it is the best that they can offer, or they can consider making an exception to the prohibition against physician-assisted death, with its inherent personal and professional risks. Compassionate physicians differ widely on their approach to this dilemma,[20-24, 26-29] though most would likely agree with an open discussion with a patient who raises the issue and an extensive search for alternatives.

Clinical criteria have been proposed to guide physicians who find assisted suicide a morally acceptable avenue of last resort[25]: (1) the patient must, of his or her own free will and at his or her own initiative, clearly and repeatedly request to die rather than continue suffering; (2) the patient's judgment must not be distorted; (3) the patient must have a condition that is incurable and associated with severe, unrelenting, intolerable suffering; (4) the physician must ensure that the patient's suffering and the request are not the result of inadequate comfort care; (5) physician-assisted suicide should only be carried out in the context of a meaningful doctor-patient relationship[22]; (6) consultation with another physician who is experienced in comfort care is required; and (7) clear documentation to support each condition above should be required (if and when such a process becomes openly sanctioned). It is not the purpose of this article to review the policy implications of formally accepting these criteria or of maintaining current prohibitions.[20–29] Instead, it is to encourage and guide clinicians on both sides of the issue to openly explore the potential meanings of a patient's request for help in dying and to search as broadly as possible for acceptable responses that are tailored to the individual patient.

THE REQUEST FOR HELP IN DYING

Dying patients need more than prescriptions for narcotics or referrals to hospice programs from their physicians. They need a personal guide and counselor through the dying process—someone who will unflinchingly help them face both the medical and the personal aspects of dying, whether it goes smoothly or it takes the physician into unfamiliar, untested ground. Dying patients do not have the luxury of choosing not to undertake the journey, or of separating their person from their disease. Physicians' commitment not to abandon their patients is of paramount importance.

Requests for assistance in dying only rarely evolve into fully considered requests for physician-assisted suicide or euthanasia. As illustrated in the case vignettes, a thorough exploration and understanding of the patient's experience and the reason the request is occurring at a given moment in time often yield avenues of "help" that are acceptable to almost all physicians and ethicists. These clinical summaries have been oversimplified to illustrate distinct levels of meaning. More often, multiple levels exist simultaneously, yielding several avenues for potential intervention. Rather than making any assumptions about what kind of help is being requested, the physician may ask the patient to help clarify by asking, "How were you hoping I could help?" Exploring a patient's request or wish does not imply an obligation to accede, but rather to seriously listen and to consider with an open mind. Even if the physician cannot directly respond to a rational request for a physician-assisted death because of personal, moral, or legal constraints, exploring, understanding, and expressing empathy can often be therapeutic.[30,31] In addition, the physician and the patient may be able to find some creative middle ground that is acceptable to both.[32,33] Finding common ground that can enhance the patient's comfort, dignity, and personal choice at death without compromising the physician's

personal and professional values can be creative, challenging, and satisfying work for physicians.

WHAT DO DYING PERSONS WANT MOST FROM THEIR PHYSICIANS?

Most patients clearly do not want to die, but if they must, they would like to do so while maintaining their physical and personal integrity.[34] When faced with a patient expressing a wish for death, and a request for help, physicians (and others) should consider the following.

Listen and Learn From the Patient Before Responding

Learning as much as possible about the patient's unique suffering and about exactly what is being requested is a vital first step. Physicians tend to be action oriented, yet these problems only infrequently yield simple resolutions. This is not to say they are insoluble, but the patient is the initial guide to defining the problem and the range of acceptable interventions.

Be Compassionate, Caring, and Creative

Comfort care is a far cry from "not doing anything." It is completely analogous to intensive medical care, only in this circumstance the care is directed toward the person and his or her suffering, not the disease. Dying patients need our commitment to creatively problem-solve and support them no matter where their illness may go. The rules and methods are not simple when applied to real persons, but the satisfaction and meaning of helping someone find his or her own path to a dignified death can be immeasurable.

Promise to Be There Until the End

Many people have personally witnessed or in some way encountered "bad deaths," though what this might mean to a specific patient is varied and unpredictable. Patients need our assurance that, if things get horrible, undignified, or intolerable, we will not abandon them, and we will continue to work with them to find acceptable solutions. Usually those solutions do not involve directly assisting death, but they may often involve the aggressive

use of symptom-relieving measures that might indirectly hasten death.[3,35] We should be able to reassure all our patients that they will not die racked by physical pain, for it is now accepted practice to give increasing amounts of analgesic medicine until the pain is relieved even if it inadvertently shortens life. Many patients find this promise reassuring, for it both alleviates the fear of pain, and also makes concrete the physician's willingness to find creative, aggressive solutions.

If Asked, Be Honest About Your Openness to the Possibility of Assisted Suicide

Patients who want to explore the physician's willingness to provide a potentially lethal prescription often fear being out of control, physically dependent, or mentally incapacitated, rather than simply fearing physical pain.[36] For many, the possibility of a controlled death if things become intolerable is often more important than the reality. Those who secretly hold lethal prescriptions or who have a physician who will entertain the possibility of such treatment feel a sense of control and possibility that, if things became intolerable, there will be a potential escape. Other patients will be adequately reassured to know that we can acknowledge the problem, talk about death, and actively search for acceptable alternatives, even if we cannot directly assist them.

Try to Approach Intolerable End-of-Life Suffering With an Open Heart and an Open Mind

Though acceptable solutions can almost always be found through the aggressive application of comfort care principles, this is not a time for denial of the problem or for superficial solutions. If there are no good alternatives, what should the patient do? There is often a moment of truth for health care providers and families faced with a patient whom they care about who has no acceptable options. Physicians must not turn their backs, but continue to problem-solve, to be present, to help their patients find dignity in death.

Do Not Forget Your Own Support

Working intensively with dying patients can be both enriching and draining. It forces us to face our own mortality, our abilities, and our limita-

Commentary

COMPASSION NEEDS REASON TOO

A growing number of physicians today believe that it is morally permissible, perhaps even required, to assist certain of their patients in the act of suicide.[1-4] They take their inspiration from Quill's account of the way he assisted his young patient, Diane, to kill herself.[5] They are impressed by Quill's compassion and respect for his patient. Like him, they would limit the physician's participation in suicide to extreme cases in which suffering is unrelenting, unrelievable, and unbearable. Like him, they follow a flawed line of moral reasoning in which a compassionate response to a request for assisted suicide is deemed sufficient in itself to justify an ethically indefensible act.

In his article[6] in this issue of THE JOURNAL, Quill provides a more formal and systematic outline of what he believes the appropriate response of physicians should be to a request for suicide. He emphasizes that the reasons for the request must be identified and ameliorated (ie, pain and depression should be properly treated and psychosocial and spiritual crises resolved). To do these things properly, physicians themselves must listen and learn; accept their own mortality; be compassionate, honest, and "present" to their patients; and remain "open" to assisted suicide. If this approach fails to relieve suffering, Quill deems the case extreme enough to justify transgressing the ethical proscription against assisted suicide.

Most of Quill's recommendations are consistent with a physician's responsibility to provide comprehensive palliative care.[7] They would be equally binding on those opposed to assisted suicide. What is not acceptable is the faulty line of reasoning that underlies Quill's seemingly reasonable and moderate approach. That reasoning is marred by three ethical assumptions: (1) that compassion in decision making confers moral validity on the act of assisted suicide; (2) that Quill's decision-making process is, itself, morally sound; and (3) that, by itself, close analysis of cases is sufficient to establish the right and good thing to do in "extreme" cases.

To begin with, Quill begs the most important ethical question, namely, whether in certain cases assisted suicide can be ethically justified. This is the heart of a debate that is far from settled.[8] It cannot be settled here. Elsewhere,[9] I have tried to show that, like active euthanasia, assisted suicide is never morally permissible: both are acts of intentional killing; they are violent remedies in the name of beneficence; they seriously distort the healing purposes of medicine; they are based on erroneous notions of compassion, beneficence, and autonomy; and they divert attention from comprehensive palliative care.[10-12] Moreover, euthanasia and assisted suicide are socially disastrous. They are not containable by placing legal limits on their practice. Arguments to the contrary, the "slippery slope" is an inescapable logical, psychological, historical and empirical reality.

Quill's first implicit assumption is that assisted suicide can sometimes be justified, ie, a morally wrong act can be made morally right if the process used in deciding to perform it and the way it is performed are compassionate and beneficently motivated. The moral psychology of an act has a certain weight in assessing an agent's guilt, but not in changing the nature of the act itself.[10] Even a person's consent is insufficient to make suicide

morally right. Nor is it justified by a gentle or genteel "approach" to the act. This, for example, is the stance of those who reject Jack Kevorkian's unseemly and preemptory use of his death machine, but commend Quill's modulated approach.[3] To be sure, Kevorkian shows a shocking disregard for the most elementary responsibilities of a physician to a patient who becomes desperate enough to ask for assisted death.[18] But regardless of whether patients use Kevorkian's machine or Quill's compassionate prescription for sedatives, they are dead by premeditated intention. In either case, physicians, who are the necessary instruments of the patient's death, are as much a moral accomplice as if they had administered the dose themselves.

Even if we grant Quill's first assumption, we are left questioning the moral validity of Quill's recommended decision-making process. On the surface, Quill seems to place the initiative in the patient's hands and suggests that the physician merely be "open" to assisted suicide under the right circumstances. But, ultimately, the determination of the right circumstances is in the physician's hands. The physician controls the availability and timing of the means whereby the patient kills himself. Physicians also judge whether the patients are clinically depressed, their suffering really unbearable, and their psychological and spiritual crises resolvable. Finally, the physician's assessment determines whether the patient is in the "extreme" category that, per se, justifies suicide assistance.

The opportunities for conscious or unconscious abuse of this power are easy to obscure, even for the best-intentioned physician. Physicians' valuation of life and its meaning, the value or nonvalue of suffering, the kind of life they would find bearable, and the point at which life becomes unbearable cannot fail to influence their decisions. These values will vary widely even among those who take assisted suicide to be morally licit. The physician might follow all of Quill's recommendations (eg, be honest and compassionate and listen to the patient), but find it virtually impossible to separate personal values from interaction with the patient.

Moreover, physicians must face their own frustrations, fatigue, and secret hopes for a way out of the burdens of caring for a suffering, terminally ill patient. The kind of intense emotional involvement Quill describes in Diane's case can induce emotional burnout in which the physician moves imperceptibly from awaiting the patient's decision and readiness, to subtle elicitation of a request for death. "Getting it over with" may not be only the patient's desire, but that of the physician, other health professionals, and family and friends.[14] Each will have his or her own reason for being open to assisting in suicide. Each reason is capable of being imputed to a vulnerable, exhausted, guilty, and alienated patient. When assisted suicide is legitimated, it places the patient at immense risk from the "compassion" of others. Misdirected compassion in the face of human suffering can be as dangerous as indifference.

Wesley's[15] astute analysis of Quill's treatment of his patient Diane[5] suggests that Quill himself was not totally immune to some of these psychodynamic dangers. The decision to respond to a request for assistance in suicide

(Box Continued)

can be as much a danger to, as a safeguard of, the patient's right to self-determination. If it is known to be a viable option at the outset, it cannot fail to influence the patient, the physician, and everyone else involved in the patient's care. If it is not known at the outset, the patient is deprived of the clues needed to interpret her physician's actions. No matter how we examine it, Quill's "approach" is as morally dubious as the act to which it leads.

Finally, Quill's article implies that with an ever greater knowledge of the patient's circumstances, thoughts, and values and a sincere effort to understand them, we can reliably arrive at a point at which we move from the morally unacceptable to the morally acceptable. This is the "line of cases" approach that relies for its moral validity on the recently revived method of casuistry.[15] Casuistry is a useful method of case analysis rooted in legal procedure, but it is a dubious way to establish a moral norm.

Brody[1] recently used the casuistic method in a logically fallacious attempt to wipe out the distinction between killing and letting die. The problem with relying solely on the casuistic method of paradigm cases is that there must be something beyond the case by which to judge the case. This would be true even if we could encompass all the details of any case. We must still explicate why this case is a paradigm case that can be used in locating other cases along a moral spectrum. When we do, we discover that a normative principle has been at work. Behind every paradigm case, there is a moral system. Different moral systems judge paradigm cases differently. In the end, we must decide among moral systems, not cases.

It is important, therefore, to read through Quill's metaphorically elegant and compassionate story of Diane's death to the reasons underlying his actions. Clearly for Quill, the undeniably important affect of compassion takes on the status of an overriding moral principle. But compassion is a virtue, not a principle. Morally weighty as it is, compassion can become maleficent unless it is constrained by principle. In the world's history, too many injustices have been committed in the name of someone's judgment about what was compassionate for his neighbor. Compassion, too, must be subject to moral analysis, must have its reasons, and those reasons must also be cogent.

Edmund D. Pellegrino, MD

1. Brody H. Causing, intending and assisting death, *J Clin Ethics*. 1993; 4: 112–113.
2. Wanzer SH, Dyders DD, Edelstein SJ, et al. The physician's responsibility toward hopelessly ill patients, *N Engl J Med*. 1989; 320: 844–849.
3. Cassel CK, Meir DE. Morals and moralism in the debate over euthanasia and assisted suicide. *N Engl J Med*. 1990; 923: 750–752.
4. Ubel PA. Assisted suicide and the case of Dr Quill and Diane. *Issues Law Med*. 1993; 8: 487–502.
5. Quill TE. Death and dignity: a case of individualized decision making. *N Engl J Med*. 1991; 324: 691–694.
6. Quill TE. Doctor, I want to die, will you help me? *J.A.M.A.* 1993; 270: 870–873.
7. Lynn J. The health care professional's role when active euthanasia is sought. *J Palliat Care*. 1988; 4: 100–102.
8. Kass L. Neither for love nor money; why doctors must not kill. *Public Interest*. 1989; 94: 25–46.
9. Pellegrino ED. Doctors must not kill. *J Clin Ethics*. 1992; 8: 95–102.
10. Kamisar Y. Are laws against assisted suicide unconstitutional? *Hastings Cent Rep*. 1993; 23: 32–41.
11. Arkes H, Berke M, Doctor M, et al. Always to care, never to kill; a declaration on euthanasia. *First Things*. 1992; 20: 46.
12. Council on Ethical and Judicial Affairs, American Medical Association. Decisions near the end of life. *J.A.M.A.* 1991; 267: 2229–2233.
13. Kevorkian J. *Prescription Medicine; The Goodness of Planned Death*. Buffalo, NY: Prometheus Books; 1991.
14. It's over, Debbie. *J.A.M.A.* 1986; 259: 272. A Piece of My Mind.
15. Wesley P. Dying safety issues. *J Law Med*. 1993; 8: 467–485.
16. Jonsen AR. Casuistry as a methodology in clinical ethics. *Thsor Med*. 1991; 12: 295–307.

From the Georgetown University Medical Center, Washington, DC. Reprints not available.

tions. It is vital to have a place where we can openly share our own grief, doubts, and uncertainties, as well as take joy in our small victories.[37] For us to deepen our understanding of the human condition and to help humanize the dying process for our patients and ourselves, we must learn to give voice to and share our own private experience of working closely with dying patients.

The patients with whom we engage at this level often become indelibly imprinted on our identities as professionals. Much like the death of a family member, the process that they go through and our willingness and ability to be there and to be helpful are often replayed and rethought. The intensity of these relationships and our ability to make a difference are often

without parallel. Because the road is traveled by us all, but the map is poorly described, it is often an adventure with extraordinary richness and unclear boundaries.

In memory of Arthur Schmale, MD, who taught me how to listen, learn, and take direction from the personal stories of dying patients.

References

1. Wanzer SH, Adelstein SJ, Cranford RE, et al. The physician's responsibility toward hopelessly ill patients. *N Engl J Med*. 1984; 310: 955–959.

2. Wanzer, SH, Federman, DO, Adelstein SJ, et al. The physician's responsibility toward hopelessly ill patients: a second look. *N Engl J Med*. 1989; 320: 844–849.

3. Council on Ethical and Judicial Affairs, American Medical Association. Decisions near the end of life. *JAMA*. 1992; 267: 2229–2233.

4. Rhymes J. Hospice care in America. *JAMA*. 1990; 264: 369–372.

5. Hastings Center Report. *Guidelines on the Termination of Life-Sustaining Treatment and the Care of the Dying*. New York, NY: The Hastings Center; 1987.

6. Zimmerman JM. *Hospice: Complete Care for the Terminally Ill*. Baltimore, Md: Urban & Schwarzenberg; 1981.

7. Quill T. *Death and Dignity: Making Choices and Taking Charge*. New York, NY: WW Norton & Co; 1993.

8. Aries P. *The Hour of Our Death*. New York, NY: Vintage Books; 1982.

9. Kubler-Ross E. *On Death and Dying*. New York, NY: Macmillan Publishing Co Inc; 1969.

10. Richman J. A rational approach to rational suicide. *Suicide Life Threat Behav.* 1992; 22: 130–141.

11. Foley KM. The treatment of cancer pain. *N Engl J Med.* 1989; 313: 84–95.

12. Kane RL, Bernstein L, Wales J, Rothenberg R. Hospice effectiveness in controlling pain. *JAMA.* 1985; 253: 2683–2686.

13. Twyeross RG, Lack SA. *Symptom Control in Far Advanced Cancer: Pain Relief*. London, England; Pitman Books Ltd; 1984.

14. Kerr IG, Some M, DeAngelis C, et al. Continuous narcotic infusion with patient-controlled analgesia for chronic cancer outpatients. *Ann Intern Med.* 1988; 108: 554–557.

15. Garfield C. *Psychosocial Care of the Dying Patient*. New York, NY: McGraw-Hill International Book Co; 1978.

16. Conwell Y, Caine ED. Rational suicide and the right to die: reality and myth. *N Engl J Med.* 1991; 325: 1100–1103.

17. Allenbeck P, Bolund C, Ringback G. Increased suicide rate in cancer patients. *J Clin Epidemiol.* 1989; 42: 611–616.

18. Breitbart W. Suicide in cancer patients. *Oncology.* 1989; 49–55.

19. MacKenzie TB, Popkin MK. Suicide in the medical patient. *Int J Psychiatry Med.* 1987; 17: 3–22.

20. Cassel CK, Meier DE. Morals and moralism in the debates on euthanasia and assisted suicide. *N Engl J Med.* 1990; 323: 750–752.

21. Quill TE. Death and dignity: a case of individualized decision making. *N Engl J Med.* 1991; 324: 691–694.

22. Jecker NS. Giving death a hand: when the dying and the doctor stand in a special relationship. *J Am Geriatr Soc.* 1991; 39: 831–835.

23. Angell M. Euthanasia. *N Engl J Med.* 1988; 319: 1348–1350.

24. Brody H. Assisted death: a compassionate response to a medical failure. *N Engl J Med.* 1992; 327: 1384–1388.

25. Quill TE, Cassel CK, Meier DE. Care of the hopelessly ill: potential clinical criteria for physician-assisted suicide. *N Engl J Med.* 1992; 327: 1380–1384.

26. Singer PA, Siegler, M. Euthanasia: a critique. *N Engl J Med.* 1990; 322: 1881–1883.

27. Orentlicher D. Physician participation in assisted suicide. *JAMA.* 1989; 262: 1844–1845.

28. Gaylin WL, Kass R, Pellegrino ED, Siegler M. Doctors must not kill. *JAMA.* 1988; 259: 2139–2140.

29. Gomez CF. *Regulating Death: Euthanasia and the Case of the Netherlands*. New York, NY: Free Press; 1991.

30. Novack DH. Therapeutic aspects of the clinical encounter. *J Gen Intern Med.* 1987; 2: 346–355.

31. Suchman AL, Matthews DA. What makes the doctor-patient relationship therapeutic: exploring the connexional dimension of medical care. *Ann Intern Med.* 1988; 108: 125–130.

32. Quill TE. Partnerships in patient care: a contractual approach. *Ann Intern Med.* 1983; 98: 228–234.

33. Fisher R, Ury W. *Getting to Yes: Negotiating Agreement Without Giving In*. Boston, Mass: Houghton Mifflin Co; 1981.

34. Cassel EJ. The nature of suffering and the goals of medicine. *N Engl J Med.* 1982; 306: 639–645.

35. Meier DE, Cassel CK. Euthanasia in old age: a case study and ethical analysis. *J Am Geriatr Soc.* 1983; 31: 294–298.

36. van der Maas PJ, van Delden JJM, Pijnenborg L, Looman CWN. Euthanasia and other medical decisions concerning the end of life. *Lancet.* 1991; 338: 669–674.

37. Quill TE, Williams PR. Healthy approaches to physician stress. *Arch Intern Med.* 1990; 150: 1857–1861.

From the Program for Biopsychosocial Studies, School of Medicine, University of Rochester, and the Department of Medicine, The Genesee Hospital, Rochester, NY.

The views expressed in this article are those of the author and do not necessarily represent those of the University of Rochester or the Department of Medicine.

Reprint requests to the Department of Medicine, The Genesee Hospital, Rochester, NY 14607 (Dr Quill).

THE SUPREME COURT AND PHYSICIAN-ASSISTED SUICIDE —THE ULTIMATE RIGHT

Editorials

The important and contentious issue of physician-assisted suicide, now being argued before the U.S. Supreme Court, is the subject of the following two editorials. Writing in favor of permitting assisted suicide under certain circumstances is the Journal's *executive editor, Dr. Marcia Angell. Arguing against it is Dr. Kathleen Foley [see next article] co-chief of the Pain and Palliative Care Service of Memorial Sloan-Kettering Cancer Center in New York. We hope these two editorials, which have in common the authors' view that care of the dying is too often inadequate, will help our readers in making their own judgments.*

JEROME P. KASSIRER, M.D.

THE U.S. Supreme Court will decide later this year whether to let stand decisions by two appeals courts permitting doctors to help terminally ill patients commit suicide.[1] The Ninth and Second Circuit Courts of Appeals last spring held that state laws in Washington and New York that ban assistance in suicide were unconstitutional as applied to doctors and their dying patients.[2,3] If the Supreme Court lets the decisions stand, physicians in 12 states, which include about half the population of the United States, would be allowed to provide the means for terminally ill patients to take their own lives, and the remaining states would rapidly follow suit. Not since *Roe v. Wade* has a Supreme Court decision been so fateful.

The decision will culminate several years of intense national debate, fueled by a number of highly publicized events. Perhaps most important among them is Dr. Jack Kevorkian's defiant assistance in some 44 suicides since 1990, to the dismay of many in the medical and legal establishments, but with substantial public support, as evidenced by the fact that three juries refused to convict him even in the face of a Michigan statute enacted for that purpose. Also since 1990, voters in three states have considered ballot initiatives that would legalize some form of physician-assisted dying, and in 1994 Oregon became the first state to approve such a measure.[4] (The Oregon law was stayed pending a court challenge.) Several surveys indicate that roughly two thirds of the American public now support physician-assisted suicide,[5,6] as do more than half the doctors in the United States,[6,7] despite the fact that influential physicians' organizations are opposed. It seems clear that many Americans are now so concerned about the possibility of a lingering, high-technology death that they are receptive to the idea of doctors' being allowed to help them die.

In this editorial I will explain why I believe the appeals courts were right and why I hope the Supreme Court will uphold their decisions. I am aware that this is a highly contentious issue, with good people and strong arguments on both sides. The American Medical Association (AMA) filed an amicus brief opposing the legalization of physician-assisted suicide,[8] and the Massachusetts Medical Society, which owns the Journal, was a signatory to it. But here I speak for myself, not the Journal or the Massachusetts Medical Society. The legal aspects of the case have been well discussed elsewhere, to me most compellingly in Ronald Dworkin's essay in the New York Review of Books.[9] I will focus primarily on the medical and ethical aspects.

I begin with the generally accepted premise that one of the most important ethical principles in medicine is respect for each patient's autonomy, and that when this principle conflicts with others, it should almost always take precedence. This premise is incorporated into our laws governing medical practice and research, including the requirement of informed consent to any treatment. In medicine, patients exercise their self-determination most dramatically when they ask that life-sustaining treatment be withdrawn. Although others may sometimes consider the request ill-founded, we are bound to honor it if the patient is mentally competent—that is, if the patient can understand the nature of the decision and its consequences.

A second starting point is the recognition that death is not fair and is often cruel. Some people die quickly, and others die slowly but peacefully. Some find personal or religious meaning in the process, as well as an opportunity for a final reconciliation with loved ones. But others, especially those with cancer, AIDS, or progressive neurologic disorders, may die by inches and in great anguish, despite every effort of their doctors and nurses. Although nearly all pain can be relieved, some cannot, and other symptoms, such as dyspnea, nausea, and weakness, are even more difficult to control. In addition, dying sometimes holds great indignities and existential suffering. Patients who happen to require some treatment to sustain their lives, such as assisted ventilation or dialysis, can hasten death by having the life-sustaining treatment withdrawn, but those who are not receiving life-sustaining treatment may desperately need help they cannot now get.

If the decisions of the appeals courts are upheld, states will not be able to prohibit doctors from helping such patients to die by prescribing a lethal dose of a drug and advising them on its use for suicide. State laws barring euthanasia (the administration of a lethal drug by a doctor) and assisted suicide for patients who are not terminally ill would not be affected. Furthermore, doctors would not be *required* to assist in suicide; they would simply have that option. Both appeals courts based their decisions on constitutional questions. This is important, because it shifted the focus of the debate from what the majority would approve through the political process, as exemplified by the Oregon initiative, to a matter of fundamental rights, which are largely immune from the political process. Indeed, the Ninth Circuit Court drew an explicit analogy between suicide and abortion, saying that both were personal choices protected by the Constitution and that forbidding doctors to assist would in effect nullify these rights. Although states could regulate assisted suicide, as they do abortion, they would not be permitted to regulate it out of existence.

It is hard to quarrel with the desire of a greatly suffering, dying patient for a quicker, more humane death or to disagree that it may be merciful to help bring that about. In those circumstances, loved ones are often relieved when death finally comes, as are the attending doctors and nurses. As the Second Circuit Court said, the state has no interest in prolonging such a life. Why, then, do so many people oppose legalizing physician-assisted suicide in these cases? There are a number of arguments against it, some stronger than others, but I believe none of them can offset the overriding duties of doctors to relieve suffering and to respect their patients' autonomy. Below I list several of the more important arguments against physician-assisted suicide and discuss why I believe they are in the last analysis unpersuasive.

Assisted suicide is a form of killing, which is always wrong. In contrast, withdrawing life-sustaining treatment simply allows the disease to take its course. There are three methods of hastening the death of a dying patient: withdrawing life-sustaining treatment, assisting suicide, and euthanasia. The right to stop treatment has been recognized repeatedly since the 1976 case of Karen Ann Quinlan[10] and was affirmed by the U.S. Supreme Court in the 1990 *Cruzan* decision[11] and the U.S. Congress in its 1990 Patient Self-Determination Act.[12] Although the legal underpinning is the right to be free of unwanted bodily invasion, the purpose of hastening death was explicitly acknowledged. In contrast, assisted suicide and euthanasia have not been accepted; euthanasia is illegal in all states, and assisted suicide is illegal in most of them.

Why the distinctions? Most would say they turn on the doctor's role: whether it is passive or active. When life-sustaining treatment is withdrawn, the doctor's role is considered passive and the cause of death is the underlying disease, despite the fact that switching off the ventilator of a patient dependent on it looks anything but passive and would be considered homicide if done without the consent of the patient or a proxy. In contrast, euthanasia by the injection of a lethal drug is active and directly causes the patient's death. Assisting suicide by supplying the necessary drugs is considered somewhere in between, more active than switching off a ventilator but less active than injecting drugs, hence morally and legally more ambiguous.

I believe, however, that these distinctions are too doctor-centered and not sufficiently patient-centered. We should ask ourselves not so much whether the doctor's role is passive or active but whether the *patient's* role is passive or active. From that perspective, the three methods of hastening death line up quite differently. When life-sustaining treatment is withdrawn from an incompetent patient at the request of a proxy or when euthanasia is performed, the patient may be utterly passive. Indeed, either act can be performed even if the patient is unaware of the decision. In sharp contrast, assisted suicide, by definition, cannot occur without the patient's knowledge and participation. Therefore, it must be active—that is to say, voluntary. That is a crucial distinction, because it provides an inherent safeguard against abuse that is not present with the other two methods of hastening death. If the loaded term "kill" is to be used, it is not the doctor who kills, but the patient. Primarily because euthanasia can be performed without the patient's participation, I oppose its legalization in this country.

Assisted suicide is not necessary. All suffering can be relieved if care givers are sufficiently skillful and compassionate, as illustrated by the hospice movement. I have no doubt that if expert palliative care were available to everyone who needed it, there would be few requests for assisted suicide. Even under the best of circumstances, however, there will always be a few patients whose suffering simply cannot be adequately alleviated. And there will be some who would prefer suicide to any other measures available, including the withdrawal of life-sustaining treatment or the use of heavy sedation. Surely, every effort should be made to improve palliative care, as I argued 15 years ago,[13] but when those efforts are unavailing and suffering patients desperately long to end their lives, physician-assisted suicide should be allowed. The argument that permitting it would divert us from redoubling our commitment to comfort care asks these patients to pay the penalty for our failings. It is also illogical. Good comfort care and the availability of physician-assisted suicide are no more mutually exclusive than good cardiologic care and the availability of heart transplantation.

Permitting assisted suicide would put us on a moral "slippery slope." Although in itself assisted suicide might be acceptable, it would lead inexorably to involuntary euthanasia. It is impossible to avoid slippery slopes in medicine (or in any aspect of life). The issue is how and where to find a purchase. For example, we accept the right of proxies to terminate life-sustaining treatment, despite the obvious potential for abuse, because the reasons for doing so outweigh the risks. We hope our procedures will safeguard patients. In the case of assisted suicide, its voluntary nature is the best protection against sliding down a slippery slope, but we also need to ensure that the request is thoughtful and freely made. Although it is possible that we may someday decide to legalize voluntary euthanasia under certain circumstances or assisted suicide for patients who are not terminally ill, legalizing assisted suicide for the dying does not in itself make these other decisions inevitable. Interestingly, recent reports from the Netherlands, where both euthanasia and physician-assisted suicide are permitted, indicate that fears about a slippery slope there have not been borne out.[14–16]

Assisted suicide would be a threat to the economically and socially vulnerable. The poor, disabled, and elderly might be coerced to request it. Admittedly, overburdened families or cost-conscious doctors might pressure vulnerable patients to request suicide, but similar wrongdoing is at least as likely in the case of withdrawing life-sustaining treatment, since that decision can be made by proxy. Yet, there is no evidence of widespread abuse. The Ninth Circuit Court recalled that it was feared *Roe v. Wade* would lead to coercion of poor and uneducated women to request abortions, but that did not happen. The concern that coercion is more likely in this era of managed care, although understandable, would hold suffering patients hostage to the deficiencies of our health care system. Unfortunately, no human endeavor is immune to abuses. The question is not whether a perfect system can be devised, but whether abuses are likely to be sufficiently rare to be offset by the benefits to patients who otherwise would be condemned to face the end of their lives in protracted agony.

Depressed patients would seek physician-assisted suicide rather than help for their depression. Even in the terminally ill, a request for assisted suicide might signify treatable depression, not irreversible suffering. Patients suffering greatly at the end of life may also be depressed, but the depression does not necessarily explain their decision to commit suicide or make it irrational. Nor is it simple to diagnose depression in terminally ill patients. Sadness is to be expected, and some of the vegetative symptoms of depression are similar to the symptoms of terminal illness. The success of antidepressant treatment in these circumstances is also not ensured. Although there are anecdotes about patients who changed their minds about suicide after treatment,[17] we do not have good studies of how often that happens or the relation to antidepressant treatment. Dying patients who request assisted suicide and seem depressed should certainly be strongly encouraged to accept psychiatric treatment, but I do not believe that competent patients should be *required* to accept it as a condition of receiving assistance with suicide. On the other hand, doctors would not be required to comply with all requests; they would be expected to use their judgment, just as they do in so many other types of life-and-death decisions in medical practice.

Doctors should never participate in taking life. If there is to be assisted suicide, doctors must not be involved. Although most doctors favor permitting assisted suicide under certain circumstances, many who favor it believe that doctors should not provide the assistance.[6,7] To them, doctors should be unambiguously committed to life (although most doctors who hold this view would readily honor a patient's decision to have life-sustaining treatment withdrawn). The AMA, too, seems to object to physician-assisted suicide primarily because it violates the profession's mission. Like others, I find that position too abstract.[18] The highest ethical imperative of doctors should be to provide care in whatever way best serves patients' interests, in accord with each patient's wishes, not with a theoretical commitment to preserve life no matter what the cost in suffering.[19] If a patient requests help with suicide and the doctor believes the request is appropriate, requiring someone else to provide the assistance would be a form of abandonment. Doctors who are opposed in principle need not assist, but they should make their patients aware of their position early in the relationship so that a patient who chooses to select another doctor can do so. The greatest harm we can do is to consign a desperate patient to unbearable suffering—or force the patient to seek out a stranger like Dr. Kevorkian. Contrary to the frequent assertion that permitting physician-assisted suicide would lead patients to distrust their doctors, I believe distrust is more likely to arise from uncertainty about whether a doctor will honor a patient's wishes.

Physician-assisted suicide may occasionally be warranted, but it should remain illegal. If doctors risk prosecution, they will think twice before assisting with suicide. This argument wrongly shifts the focus from the patient to the doctor. Instead of reflecting the condition and wishes of patients, assisted suicide would reflect the courage and compassion of their doctors. Thus, patients with doctors like Timothy Quill, who described in a 1991 *Journal* article how he helped a patient take her life,[20] would get the help they need and want, but similar patients with less steadfast doctors would not. That makes no sense.

People do not need assistance to commit suicide. With enough determination, they can do it themselves. This is perhaps the cruelest of the arguments against physician-assisted suicide. Many patients at the end of life are, in fact, physically unable to commit suicide on their own. Others lack the resources to do so. It has sometimes been suggested that they can simply stop eating and drinking and kill themselves that way. Although this method has been described as peaceful under certain conditions,[21] no one should count on that. The fact is that this argument leaves most patients to their suffering. Some, usually men, manage to commit suicide using violent methods. Percy Bridgman, a Nobel laureate in physics who in 1961 shot himself rather than die of metastatic cancer, said in his suicide note, "It is not decent for Society to make a man do this to himself."[22]

My father, who knew nothing of Percy Bridgman, committed suicide under similar circumstances. He was 81 and had metastatic prostate cancer. The night before he was scheduled to be admitted to the hospital, he shot himself. Like Bridgman, he thought it might be his last chance. At the time, he was not in extreme pain, nor was he close to death (his life expectancy was probably longer than six months). But he was suffering nonetheless—from nausea and the side effects of antiemetic agents, weakness, incontinence, and hopelessness. Was he depressed? He would probably have freely admitted that he was, but he would have thought it beside the point. In any case, he was an intensely private man who would have refused psychiatric care. Was he overly concerned with maintaining control of the circumstances of his life and death? Many people would say so, but that was the way he was. It is the job of medicine to deal with patients as they are, not as we would like them to be.

I tell my father's story here because it makes an abstract issue very concrete. If physician-assisted suicide had been available, I have no doubt my father would have chosen it. He was protective of his family, and if he had felt he had the choice, he would have spared my mother the shock of finding his body. He did not tell her what he planned to do, because he knew she would stop him. I also believe my father would have waited if physician-assisted suicide had been available. If patients have access to drugs they can take when they choose, they will not feel they must commit suicide early, while they are still able to do it on their own. They would probably live longer and certainly more peacefully, and they might not even use the drugs.

Long before my father's death, I believed that physician-assisted suicide ought to be permissible under some circumstances, but his death strengthened my conviction that it is simply a part of good medical care—something to be done reluctantly and sadly, as a last resort, but done nonetheless. There should be safeguards to ensure that the decision is well considered and consistent, but they should not be so daunting or violative of privacy that they become obstacles instead of protections. In particular, they should be directed not toward reviewing the reasons for an autonomous decision, but only toward ensuring that the decision is indeed autonomous. If the Supreme Court upholds the decisions of the appeals courts, assisted suicide will not be forced on either patients or doctors, but it will be a choice for those patients who need it and those doctors willing to help. If, on the other hand, the Supreme Court overturns the lower courts' decisions, the issue will continue to be grappled with state by state, through the political process. But sooner or later, given the need and the widespread public support, physician-assisted suicide will be demanded of a compassionate profession.

MARCIA ANGELL, M.D.

REFERENCES

1. Greenhouse L. High court to say if the dying have a right to suicide help. New York Times. October 2, 1996:A1.

2. Compassion in Dying v. Washington, 79 F.3d 790 (9th Cir. 1996).

3. Quill v. Vacco, 80 F.3d 716 (2d Cir. 1996).

4. Annas GJ. Death by prescription—the Oregon initiative. N Engl J Med 1994;331:1240–3.

5. Blendon RJ, Szalay US, Knox RA. Should physicians aid their patients in dying? The public perspective. JAMA 1992;267:2658–62.

6. Bachman JG, Alcser KH, Doukas DJ, Lichtenstein RL, Corning AD, Brody H. Attitudes of Michigan physicians and the public toward legalizing physician-assisted suicide and voluntary euthanasia. N Engl J Med 1996;334:303–9.

7. Lee MA, Nelson ND, Tilden VP, Ganzini L, Schmidt TA, Tolle SW. Legalizing assisted suicide—views of physicians in Oregon. N Engl J Med 1996;334:310–5.

8. Gianelli DM. AMA to court: no suicide aid. American Medical News. November 25, 1996:1, 27, 28.

9. Dworkin R. Sex, death, and the courts. New York Review of Books. August 8, 1996.

10. In re: Quinlan, 70 N.J. 10, 355 A.2d 647 (1976).

11. Cruzan v. Director Missouri Department of Health, 497 U.S. 261, 110 S.Ct. 2841 (1990).

12. Omnibus Budget Reconciliation Act of 1990, P.L. 101-508, sec. 4206 and 4751, 104 Stat. 1388, 1388-115, and 1388-204 (classified respectively at 42 U.S.C. 1395cc(f) (Medicare) and 1396a(w) (Medicaid) (1994)).

13. Angell M. The quality of mercy. N Engl J Med 1982;306:98-9.

14. van der Maas PJ, van der Wal G, Haverkate I, et al. Euthanasia, physician-assisted suicide, and other medical practices involving the end of life in the Netherlands, 1990–1995. N Engl J Med 1996;335:1699–705.

15. van der Wal G, van der Maas PJ, Bosma JM, et al. Evaluation of the notification procedure for physician-assisted death in the Netherlands. N Engl J Med 1996;335:1706–11.

16. Angell M. Euthanasia in the Netherlands—good news or bad? N Engl J Med 1996;335:1676–8.

17. Chochinov UM, Wilson KG, Enns M, et al. Desire for death in the terminally ill. Am J Psychiatry 1995;152:1185–91.

18. Cassel CK, Meier DE. Morals and moralism in the debate over euthanasia and assisted suicide. N Engl J Med 1990;323:750–2.

19. Angell M. Doctors and assisted suicide. Ann R Coll Physicians Surg Can 1991;24:493–4.

20. Quill TE. Death and dignity—a case of individualized decision making. N Engl J Med 1991;324:691–4.

21. Lynn J, Childress JF. Must patients always be given food and water? Hastings Cent Rep 1983;13(5):17–21.

22. Nuland SB. How we die. New York: Alfred A. Knopf, 1994:152.

COMPETENT CARE FOR THE DYING INSTEAD OF PHYSICIAN-ASSISTED SUICIDE

Editorials

The important and contentious issue of physician-assisted suicide, now being argued before the U.S. Supreme Court, is the subject of . . . two editorials. Writing in favor of permitting assisted suicide under certain circumstances is the Journal *'s executive editor, Dr. Marcia Angell [see previous article]. Arguing against it is Dr. Kathleen Foley, co-chief of the Pain and Palliative Care Service of Memorial Sloan-Kettering Cancer Center in New York. We hope these two editorials, which have in common the authors' view that care of the dying is often too inadequate, will help our readers in making their own judgments.*

JEROME P. KASSIRER, M.D.

WHILE the Supreme Court is reviewing the decisions by the Second and Ninth Circuit Courts of Appeals to reverse state bans on assisted suicide, there is a unique opportunity to engage the public, health care professionals, and the government in a national discussion of how American medicine and society should address the needs of dying patients and their families. Such a discussion is critical if we are to understand the process of dying from the point of view of patients and their families and to identify existing barriers to appropriate, humane, compassionate care at the end of life. Rational discourse must replace the polarized debate over physician-assisted suicide and euthanasia. Facts, not anecdotes, are necessary to establish a common ground and frame a system of health care for the terminally ill that provides the best possible quality of living while dying.

The biased language of the appeals courts evinces little respect for the vulnerability and dependency of the dying. Judge Stephen Reinhardt, writing for the Ninth Circuit Court, applied the liberty-interest clause of the Fourteenth Amendment, advocating a constitutional right to assisted suicide. He stated, "The competent terminally ill adult, having lived nearly the full measure of his life, has a strong interest in choosing a dignified and humane death, rather than being reduced to a state of helplessness, diapered, sedated, incompetent."[1] Judge Roger J. Miner, writing for the Second Circuit Court of Appeals, applied the equal-rights clause of the Fourteenth Amendment and went on to emphasize that the state "has no interest in prolonging a life that is ending."[2] This statement is more than legal jargon. It serves as a chilling reminder of the low priority given to the dying when it comes to state resources and protection.

The appeals courts' assertion of a constitutional right to assisted suicide is narrowly restricted to the terminally ill. The courts have decided that it is the patient's condition that justifies killing and that the terminally ill are special—so special that they deserve assistance in dying. This group alone can receive such assistance. The courts' response to the New York and Washington cases they reviewed is the dangerous form of affirmative action in the name of compassion. It runs the risk of further devaluing the lives of terminally ill patients and may provide the excuse for society to abrogate its responsibility for their care.

Both circuit courts went even further in asserting that physicians are already assisting in

From *The New England Journal of Medicine,* January 2, 1997, pp. 54–58. © 1997 by the Massachusetts Medical Society. All rights reserved. Reprinted by permission.

patients' deaths when they withdraw life-sustaining treatments such as respirators or administer high doses of pain medication that hasten death. The appeals courts argued that providing a lethal prescription to allow a terminally ill patient to commit suicide is essentially the same as withdrawing life-sustaining treatment or aggressively treating pain. Judicial reasoning that eliminates the distinction between letting a person die and killing runs counter to physicians' standards of palliative care.[3] The courts' purported goal in blurring these distinctions was to bring society's legal rules more closely in line with the moral value it places on the relief of suffering.[4]

In the real world in which physicians care for dying patients, withdrawing treatment and aggressively treating pain are acts that respect patients' autonomous decisions not to be battered by medical technology and to be relieved of their suffering. The physician's intent is to provide care, not death. Physicians do struggle with doubts about their own intentions.[5] The courts' arguments fuel their ambivalence about withdrawing life-sustaining treatments or using opioid or sedative infusions to treat intractable symptoms in dying patients. Physicians are trained and socialized to preserve life. Yet saying that physicians struggle with doubts about their intentions in performing these acts is not the same as saying that their intention is to kill. In palliative care, the goal is to relieve suffering, and the quality of life, not the quantity, is of utmost importance.

Whatever the courts say, specialists in palliative care do not think that they practice physician-assisted suicide or euthanasia.[6] Palliative medicine has developed guidelines for aggressive pharmacologic management of intractable symptoms in dying patients, including sedation for those near death.[3,7,8] The World Health Organization has endorsed palliative care as an integral component of a national health care policy and has strongly recommended to its member countries that they not consider legalizing physician-assisted suicide and euthanasia until they have addressed the needs of their citizens for pain relief and palliative care.[9] The courts have disregarded this formidable recommendation and, in fact, are indirectly suggesting that the World Health Organization supports assisted suicide.

Yet the courts' support of assisted suicide reflects the requests of the physicians who initiated the suits and parallels the numerous surveys demonstrating that a large proportion of physicians support the legalization of physician-assisted suicide.[10–15] A smaller proportion of physicians are willing to provide such assistance, and an even smaller proportion are willing to inject a lethal dose of medication with the intent of killing a patient (active voluntary euthanasia). These survey data reveal a gap between the attitudes and behavior of physicians; 20 to 70 percent of physicians favor the legalization of physician-assisted suicide, but only 2 to 4 percent favor active voluntary euthanasia, and only approximately 2 to 13 percent have actually aided patients in dying, by either providing a prescription or administering a lethal injection. The limitations of these surveys, which are legion, include inconsistent definitions of physician-assisted suicide and euthanasia, lack of information about nonrespondents, and provisions for maintaining confidentiality that have led to inaccurate reporting.[13,16] Since physicians' attitudes toward alternatives to assisted suicide have not been studied, there is a void in our knowledge about the priority that physicians place on physician-assisted suicide.

The willingness of physicians to assist patients in dying appears to be determined by numerous complex factors, including religious beliefs, personal values, medical specialty, age, practice setting, and perspective on the use of financial resources.[13,16–19] Studies of patients' preferences for care at the end of life demonstrate that physicians' preferences strongly influence those of their patients.[13] Making physician-assisted suicide a medical treatment when it is so strongly dependent on these physician-related variables would result in a regulatory impossibility.[19] Physicians would have to disclose their values and attitudes to patients to avoid potential conflict.[13] A survey by Ganzini et al. demonstrated that psychiatrists' responses to requests to evaluate patients were highly determined by their attitudes.[13] In a study by Emanuel et al., depressed patients with cancer said they would view positively those physicians who acknowledged their willingness to assist in suicide. In contrast, patients with cancer who were suffering from pain would be suspicious of such physicians.[11]

In this controversy, physicians fall into one of three groups. Those who support physician-assisted suicide see it as a compassionate response to a medical need, a symbol of non-abandonment, and a means to reestablish patients' trust in doctors who have used technology excessively.[20] They argue that regulation of physician-assisted suicide is possible and, in fact, necessary to control the actions of physicians who are currently providing assistance surreptitiously.[21] The two remaining groups of physicians oppose legalization.[19,22–24] One group is morally opposed to physician-assisted suicide and emphasizes the need to preserve the professionalism of medicine and the commitment to "do no harm." These physicians view aiding a patient in dying as a form of abandonment, because a physician needs to walk the last mile with the patient, as a witness, not as an executioner. Legalization would endorse justified killing, according to these physicians, and guidelines would not be followed, even if they could be developed. Furthermore, these physicians are concerned that the conflation of assisted suicide with the withdrawal of life support or adequate treatment of pain would make it even harder for dying patients, because there would be a backlash against existing policies. The other group is not ethically opposed to physician-assisted suicide and, in fact, sees it as acceptable in exceptional cases, but these physicians believe that one cannot regulate the unregulatable.[19] On this basis, the New York State Task Force on Life and the Law, a 24-member committee with broad public and professional representation, voted unanimously against the legalization of physician-assisted suicide.[24] All three groups of physicians agree that a national effort is needed to improve the care of the dying. Yet it does seem that those in favor of legalizing physician-assisted suicide are disingenuous in their use of this issue as a wedge. If this form of assistance with dying is legalized, the courts will be forced to broaden the assistance to include active voluntary euthanasia and, eventually, assistance in response to requests from proxies.

One cannot easily categorize the patients who request physician-assisted suicide or euthanasia. Some surveys of physicians have attempted to determine retrospectively the prevalence and nature of these requests.[10] Pain, AIDS, and neurodegenerative disorders are the most common conditions in patients requesting assistance in dying. There is a wide range in the age of such patients, but many are younger persons with AIDS.[10] From the limited data available, the factors most commonly involved in requests for assistance are concern about future loss of control, being or becoming a burden to others, or being unable to care for oneself and fear of severe pain.[10] A small number of recent studies have directly asked terminally ill patients with cancer or AIDS about their desire for death.[25–27] All these studies show that the desire for death is closely associated with depression and that pain and lack of social support are contributing factors.

Do we know enough, on the basis of several legal cases, to develop a public policy that will profoundly change medicine's role in society?[1,2] Approximately 2.4 million Americans die each year. We have almost no information on how they die and only general information on where they die. Sixty-one percent die in hospitals, 17 percent in nursing homes, and the remainder at home, with approximately 10 to 14 percent of those at home receiving hospice care.

The available data suggest that physicians are inadequately trained to assess and manage the multifactorial symptoms commonly associated with patients' requests for physician-assisted suicide. According to the American Medical Association's report on medical education, only 5 of 126 medical schools in the United States require a separate course in the care of the dying.[28] Of 7048 residency programs, only 26 percent offer a course on the medical and legal aspects of care at the end of life as a regular part of the curriculum. According to a survey of 1068 accredited residency programs in family medicine, internal medicine, and pediatrics and fellowship programs in geriatrics, each resident or fellow coordinates the care of 10 or fewer dying patients annually.[28] Almost 15 percent of the programs offer no formal training in terminal care. Despite the availability of hospice programs, only 17 percent of the training programs offer a hospice rotation, and the rotation is required in only half of those programs; 9 percent of the programs have residents or fellows serving as members of hospice teams. In a recent survey of 55 residency programs and over 1400 residents, conducted by the American Board of Internal Medicine, the residents were asked to rate their perception of adequate training in care at the end of life. Seventy-two percent reported that they had received adequate training in managing pain and other symptoms; 62 percent, that they had received adequate training in telling patients that they are dying; 38 percent, in describing what the process will be like; and 32 percent, in talking to patients who request assistance in dying or a hastened death (Blank L: personal communication).

The lack of training in the care of the dying is evident in practice. Several studies have concluded that poor communication between physicians and patients, physicians' lack of knowledge about national guidelines for such care, and their lack of knowledge about the control of symptoms are barriers to the provision of good care at the end of life.[23,29,30]

Yet there is now a large body of data on the components of suffering in patients with advanced terminal disease, and these data provide the basis for treatment algorithms.[3] There are three major factors in suffering: pain and other physical symptoms, psychological distress, and existential distress (described as the experience of life without meaning). It is not only the patients who suffer but also their families and the health care professionals attending them. These experiences of suffering are often closely and inextricably related. Perceived distress in any one of the three groups amplifies distress in the others.[31,32]

Pain is the most common symptom in dying patients, and according to recent data from U.S. studies, 56 percent of outpatients with cancer, 82 percent of outpatients with AIDS, 50 percent of hospitalized patients with various diagnoses, and 36 percent of nursing home residents have inadequate management of pain during the course of their terminal illness.[33–36] Members of minority groups and women, both those with cancer and those with AIDS, as well as the elderly, receive less pain treatment than other groups of patients. In a survey of 1177 physicians who had treated a total of more than 70,000 patients with cancer in the previous six months, 76 percent of the respondents cited lack of knowledge as a barrier to their ability to control pain.[37] Severe pain that is not adequately controlled interferes with the quality of life, including the activities of daily living, sleep, and social interactions.[36,38]

Other physical symptoms are also prevalent among the dying. Studies of patients with advanced cancer and of the elderly in the year before death show that they have numerous symptoms that worsen the quality of life, such as fatigue, dyspnea, delirium, nausea, and vomiting.[36,38]

Along with these physical symptoms, dying patients have a variety of well-described psychological symptoms, with a high prevalence of anxiety and depression in patients with cancer or AIDS and the elderly.[27,39] For example, more than 60 percent of patients with advanced cancer have psychiatric problems, with adjustment disorders, depression, anxiety, and delirium reported most frequently. Various factors that contribute to the prevalence and severity of psychological distress in the terminally ill have been identified.[39] The diagnosis of depression is difficult to make in medically ill patients[3,26,40]; 94 percent of the Oregon psychiatrists surveyed by Ganzini et al. were not confident that they could determine, in a single evaluation, whether a psychiatric disorder was impairing the judgment of a patient who requested assistance with suicide.[13]

Attention has recently been focused on the interaction between uncontrolled symptoms and vulnerability to suicide in patients with cancer or AIDS.[41] Data from studies of both groups of patients suggest that uncontrolled pain contributes to depression and that persistent pain interferes with patients' ability to receive support from their families and others. Patients with AIDS have a high risk of suicide that is independent of physical symptoms. Among New York City residents with AIDS, the relative risk of suicide in men between the ages of 20 and 59 years was 36 times higher than the risk among men without AIDS in the same age group and 66 times higher than the risk in the general population.[41] Patients with AIDS who committed suicide generally did so within nine months after receiving the diagnosis; 25 percent had made a previous suicide attempt, 50 percent had reported severe depression, and 40 percent had seen a psychiatrist within four days before committing suicide. As previously noted, the desire to die is most closely associated with the diagnosis of depression.[26,27] Suicide is the eighth leading cause of death in the United States, and the incidence of suicide is higher in patients with cancer or AIDS and in elderly men than in the general population. Conwell and Caine reported that depression was under-diagnosed by primary care physicians in a cohort of elderly patients who subsequently committed suicide; 75 percent of the patients had seen a primary care physician during the last month of life but had not received a diagnosis of depression.[22]

The relation between depression and the desire to hasten death may vary among subgroups of dying patients. We have no data, except for studies of a small number of patients with cancer or AIDS. The effect of treatment for depression on the desire to hasten death and on requests for assistance in doing so has not been examined in the medically ill population, except for a small study in which four of six patients who initially wished to hasten death changed their minds within two weeks.[26]

There is also the concern that certain patients, particularly members of minority groups that are estranged from the health care system, may be reluctant to receive treatment for their physical or psychological symptoms because of the fear that their physicians will, in fact, hasten death. There is now some evidence that the legalization of assisted suicide in the Northern Territory of Australia has undermined the Aborigines' trust in the medical care system[42]; this experience may serve as an example for the United States, with its multicultural population.

The multiple physical and psychological symptoms in the terminally ill and elderly are compounded by a substantial degree of existential distress. Reporting on their interviews with Washington State physicians whose patients had requested assistance in dying, Back et al. noted the physicians' lack of sophistication in assessing such nonphysical suffering.[10]

In summary, there are fundamental physician-related barriers to appropriate, humane, and compassionate care for the dying. These range from attitudinal and behavioral barriers to educational and economic barriers. Physicians do not know enough about their patients, themselves, or suffering to provide assistance with dying as a medical treatment for the relief of suffering. Physicians need to explore their own perspectives on the meaning of suffering in order to develop their own approaches to the care of the dying. They need insight into how the nature of the doctor-patient relationship influences their own decision making. If legalized, physician-assisted suicide will be a substitute for rational therapeutic, psychological, and social interventions that might otherwise enhance the quality of life for patients who are dying. The medical profession needs to take the lead in developing guidelines for good care of dying patients. Identifying the factors related to physicians, patients, and the health care system that pose barriers to appropriate care at the end of life should be the first step in a national dialogue to educate health care professionals and the public on the topic of death and dying. Death is an issue that society as a whole faces, and it requires a compassionate response. But we should not confuse compassion with competence in the care of terminally ill patients.

KATHLEEN M. FOLEY, M.D.
Memorial Sloan-Kettering Cancer Center
New York, NY 10021

REFERENCES

1. Reinhardt, Compassion in Dying v. State of Washington, 79 F. 3d 790 9th Cir. 1996.

2. Miner, Quill v. Vacco 80 F. 3d 716 2nd Cir. 1996.

3. Doyle D, Hanks, GWC, MacDonald N. The Oxford textbook of palliative medicine. New York: Oxford University Press, 1993.

4. Orentlicher D. The legalization of physician-assisted suicide. N Engl J Med 1996; 335: 663–7.

5. Wilson WC, Smedira NG, Fink C, McDowell JA, Luce JM. Ordering and administration of sedatives and analgesics during the withholding and withdrawal of life support from critically ill patients. JAMA 1992; 267: 949–53.

6. Foley KM. The relationship of pain and symptom management to patient requests for physician-assisted suicide. J Pain Symptom Manage 1991; 6: 289–97.

7. Cherny NI, Coyle N, Foley KM. Guidelines in the care of the dying patient. Hematol Oncol Clin North Am 1996; 10: 261–86.

8. Cherny NI, Portenoy RK. Sedation in the management of refractory symptoms: guidelines for evaluation and treatment. J Palliat Care 1994; 10(2): 31–8.

9. Cancer pain relief and palliative care. Geneva: World Health Organization, 1989.

10. Back AL, Wallace JI, Starks HE, Pearlman RA. Physician-assisted suicide and euthanasia in Washington State: patient requests and physician responses. JAMA 1996; 275: 919–25.

11. Emanuel EJ, Fairclough DL, Daniels ER, Clarridge BR. Euthanasia and physician-assisted suicide: attitudes and experiences of oncology patients, oncologists, and the public. Lancet 1996; 347: 1805–10.

12. Lee MA, Nelson HD, Tilden VP, Ganzini L, Schmidt TA, Tolle SW. Legalizing assisted suicide—views of physicians in Oregon. N Engl J Med 1996; 334: 310–15.

13. Ganzini L, Fenn DS, Lee MA, Heintz RT, Bloom JD. Attitudes of Oregon psychiatrists toward physician-assisted suicide. Am J Psychiatry 1996; 153: 1469–75.

14. Cohen JS, Fihn SD, Boyko EJ, Jonsen AR, Wood RW. Attitudes toward assisted suicide and euthanasia among physicians in Washington State. N Engl J Med 1994; 331: 89–94.

15. Doukas DJ, Waterhouse D, Gorenflo DW, Seid J. Attitudes and behaviors on physician-assisted death: a study of Michigan oncologists. J Clin Oncol 1995; 13: 1055–61.

16. Morrison S, Meier D. Physician-assisted dying: fashioning public policy with an absence of data. Generations. Winter 1994: 48–53.

17. Portenoy RK, Coyle N, Kash K, et al. Determinants of the willingness to endorse assisted suicide: a survey of physicians, nurses, and social workers. Psychosomatics (in press).

18. Fins J. Physician-assisted suicide and the right to care. Cancer Control 1996; 3: 272–8.

19. Callahan D, White M. The legalization of physician-assisted suicide: creating a regulatory Potemkin Village. U Richmond Law Rev 1996; 30: 1–83.

20. Quill TE. Death and dignity—a case of individualized decision making. N Engl J Med 1991; 324: 691–4.

21. Quill TE, Cassel CK, Meier DE. Care of the hopelessly ill—proposed clinical criteria for physician-assisted suicide. N Engl J Med 1992; 327: 1380–4.

22. Conwell Y, Caine ED. Rational suicide and the right to die—reality and myth. N Engl J Med 1991; 325: 1100–3.

23. Foley KM. Pain, physician assisted suicide and euthanasia. Pain Forum 1995; 4: 163–78.

24. When death is sought: assisted suicide and euthanasia in the medical context. New York: New York State Task Force on Life and the Law, May 1994.

25. Brown JH, Henteleff P, Barakat S, Rowe CJ. Is it normal for terminally ill patients to desire death? Am J Psychiatry 1986; 143: 208–11.

26. Chochinov HM, Wilson KG, Enns M, et al. Desire for death in the terminally ill. Am J Psychiatry 1995; 152: 1185–91.

27. Breitbart W, Rosenfeld BD, Passik SD. Interest in physician-assisted suicide among ambulatory HIV-infected patients. Am J Psychiatry 1996; 153: 238–42.

28. Hill TP. Treating the dying patient: the challenge for medical education. Arch Intern Med 1995; 155: 1265–9.

29. Callahan D. Once again reality: now where do we go. Hastings Cent Rep 1995; 25 (6): Suppl: S33–S36.

30. Solomon MZ, O'Donnell L, Jennings B, et al. Decisions near the end of life: professional views on life-sustaining treatments. Am J Public Health 1993; 83: 14–23.

31. Cherny NI, Coyle N, Foley KM. Suffering in the advanced cancer patient: definition and taxonomy. J. Palliat Care 1994; 10 (2): 57–70.

32. Cassel EJ. The nature of suffering and the goals of medicine. N Engl J Med 1982; 306: 639–45.

33. Cleeland CS, Gonin R, Hatfield AK, et al. Pain and its treatment in outpatients with metastatic cancer. N Engl J Med 1994; 330: 592–6.

34. Breitbart W, Rosenfeld BD, Passik SD, McDonald MV, Thaler H, Portenoy RK. The undertreatment of pain in ambulatory AIDS patients. Pain 1996; 65: 243–9.

35. The SUPPORT Principal Investigators. A controlled trial to improve care for seriously ill hospitalized patients. JAMA 1995; 274: 1591–8.

36. Seale C, Cartwright A. The year before death. Hants, England: Avebury, 1994.

37. Von Roenn JH, Cleeland CS, Gonin R, Hatfield AK, Pandya KJ. Physician attitudes and practice in cancer pain management: a survey from the Eastern Cooperative Oncology Group. Ann Intern Med 1993; 119: 121–6.

38. Portenoy RK. Pain and quality of life: clinical issues and implications for research. Oncology 1990; 4: 172–8.

39. Breitbart W. Suicide risk and pain in cancer and AIDS patients. In: Chapman CR, Foley KM, eds. Current and emerging issues in cancer pain. New York: Raven Press, 1993.

40. Chochinov H, Wilson KG, Enns M, Lander S. Prevalence of depression in the terminally ill: effects of diagnostic criteria and symptom threshold judgments. Am J Psychiatry 1994; 151: 537–40.

41. Passik S, McDonald M, Rosenfeld B, Breitbart W. End of life issues in patients with AIDS: clinical and research considerations. J Pharm Care Pain Symptom Control 1995; 3: 91–111.

42. NT "success" in easing rural fear of euthanasia. The Age. August 31, 1996: A7.

Article 22

A Piece of My Mind

A Conversation With My Mother

You have already met my father.[1] Now meet my mother. She died a few weeks ago. She wanted me to tell you how.

Her name was Virginia. Up until about 6 months ago, at age 84, she was the proverbial "little old lady in sneakers." After my father died of colon cancer several years ago, she lived by herself in one of those grand old Greek revival houses you see on postcards of small New England towns. Hers was in Middlebury, Vermont.

My mother was very independent, very self-sufficient, and very content. My brother and his family lived next door. Although she was quite close to them, she tried hard not to interfere in their lives. She spent most of her time reading large-print books, working word puzzles, and watching the news and professional sports on TV. She liked the house kept full of light. Every day she would take two outings, one in the morning to the small country store across the street to pick up the *Boston Globe,* and one in the afternoon to the Grand Union across town, to pick up some item she purposefully omitted from the previous day's shopping list. She did this in all but the worst weather. On icy days, she would wear golf shoes to keep from slipping and attach spikes to the tip of her cane. I think she was about 5 feet 2 and 120 pounds, but I am not certain. I know she started out at about 5 feet 4, but she seemed to shrink a little bit each year, getting cuter with time as many old people do. Her wrinkles matched her age, emphasizing a permanent thin-lipped smile that extended all the way to her little Kris Kringle eyes. The only thing that embarrassed her was her thinning gray hair, but she covered that up with a rather dashing tweed fedora that matched her Talbots outfits. She loved to tease people by wearing outrageous necklaces. The one made from the front teeth of camels was her favorite.

To be sure, she had had her share of problems in the past: diverticulitis and endometriosis when she was younger, more recently a broken hip, a bout with depression, some hearing loss, and cataracts. But she was a walking tribute to the best things in American medicine. Coming from a family of four generations of physicians, she was fond of bragging that, but for lens implants, hearing aids, hip surgery, and Elavil, she would be blind, deaf, bedridden, and depressed. At age 84, her only problems were a slight rectal prolapse, which she could reduce fairly easily, some urinary incontinence, and a fear that if her eyesight got much worse she would lose her main pleasures. But those things were easy to deal with and she was, to use her New England expression, "happy as a clam."

"David, I can't tell you how content I am. Except for missing your father, these are the best years of my life."

Yes, all was well with my mother, until about six months ago. That was when she developed acute cholelithiasis. From that point on, her health began to unravel with amazing speed. She recovered from the cholecystectomy on schedule and within a few weeks of leaving the hospital was resuming her walks downtown. But about six weeks after the surgery she was suddenly hit with a case of severe diarrhea, so severe that it extended her rectal prolapse to about 8 inches and dehydrated her to the point that she had to be readmitted. As soon as her physician got her rehydrated, other complications quickly set in. She developed oral thrush, apparently due to the antibiotic treatment for her diarrhea, and her antidepressants got out of balance. For some reason that was never fully determined, she also became anemic, which was treated with iron, which made her nauseated. She could not eat, she got weak, her skin itched, and her body ached. Oh yes, they also found a lump in her breast, the diagnosis of which was postponed, and atrial fibrillation. Needless to say, she was quite depressed.

Her depression was accentuated by the need to deal with her rectal prolapse. On the one hand, she really disliked the thought of more surgery. She especially hated the nasogastric tube and the intense postoperative fatigue. On the other hand, the prolapse was very painful. The least cough or strain would send it out to rub against the sheets, and she could not push it back the way she used to. She knew that she could not possibly walk to the Grand Union again unless it was fixed.

It was at that time that she first began to talk to me about how she could end her life gracefully. As a physician's wife, she was used to thinking about life and death and prided herself on being able to deal maturely with the idea of death. She had signed every living will and advance directive she could find, and carried a card that donated her organs. Even though she knew they would not do anyone much good (*"Can they recycle my artificial hip and lenses?"*), she liked the way the card announced her acceptance of the fact that all things must someday end. She dreaded the thought of being in a nursing home, unable to take care of herself, her body, mind, and interests progressively declining until she was little more than a blank stare, waiting for death to mercifully take her away.

"I know they can keep me alive a long time, but what's the point? If the pleasure is gone and the direction is steadily down, why should I have to draw it out until I'm 'rescued' by cancer, a heart attack, or a stroke? That could take years. I understand that some people want to hang on until all the possible treatments have been tried to squeeze out the last drops of life. That's fine for them. But not for me."

My own philosophy, undoubtedly influenced heavily by my parents, is that choosing the best way to end your life should be the ultimate individual right—a right to be exercised between oneself and one's beliefs, without intrusions from governments or the beliefs of others. On the other hand, I also believe that such decisions should be made only with an accurate understanding of one's prognosis and should never be made in the middle of a correctable depression or a temporary trough. So my brother, sister, and I coaxed her to see a rectal surgeon about having her prolapse repaired and to put off thoughts of suicide until her health problems were stabilized and her antidepressants were back in balance.

With the surgeon's help, we explored the possible outcomes of the available procedures for her prolapse. My mother did not mind the higher mortality rates of the more extensive operations—in fact, she wanted them. Her main concern was to avoid rectal incontinence, which she knew would dampen any hopes of returning to her former lifestyle.

Unfortunately, that was the outcome she got. By the time she had recovered from the rectal surgery, she was totally incontinent "at both ends," to use her words. She was bedridden, anemic, exhausted, nauseated, achy, and itchy. Furthermore, over the period of this illness her eyesight had begun to fail to the point she could no longer read. Because she was too sick to live at home, even with my brother's help, but not sick enough to be hospitalized, we had to move her to an intermediate care facility.

On the positive side, her antidepressants were working again and she had regained her clarity of mind, her spirit, and her humor. But she was very unhappy. She knew instinctively, and her physician confirmed, that after all the insults of the past few months it was very unlikely she would ever be able to take care of herself alone or walk to the Grand Union. That was when she began to press me harder about suicide.

"Let me put this in terms you should understand, David. My 'quality of life'—isn't that what you call it?—has dropped below zero. I know there is nothing fatally wrong with me and that I could live on for many more years. With a colostomy and some luck I might even be able to recover a bit of my former lifestyle, for a while. But do we have to do that just because it's possible? Is the meaning of life defined by its duration? Or does life have a purpose so large that it doesn't have to be prolonged at any cost to preserve its meaning?

"I've lived a wonderful life, but it has to end sometime and this is the right time for me. My decision is not about whether I'm going to die—we will all die sooner or later. My decision is about when and how. I don't want to spoil the wonder of my life by dragging it out in years of decay. I want to go now, while the good memories are still fresh. I have always known that eventually the right time would come, and now I know that this is it. Help me find a way."

I discussed her request with my brother and sister and with her nurses and physician. Although we all had different feelings about her request, we agreed that she satisfied our criteria of being well-informed, stable, and not depressed. For selfish reasons we wanted her to live as long as possible, but we realized that it was not our desires that mattered. What mattered to us were her wishes. She was totally rational about her conviction that this was "her time." Now she was asking for our help, and it struck us as the height of paternalism (or filialism?) to impose our desires over hers.

I bought *Final Exit*[2] for her, and we read it together. If she were to end her life, she would obviously have to do it with pills. But as anyone who has thought about this knows, accomplishing that is not easy. Patients can rarely get the pills themselves, especially in a controlled setting like a hospital or nursing home. Anyone who provides the pills knowing they will be used for suicide could be arrested. Even if those problems are solved and the pills are available, they can be difficult to take, especially by the frail. Most likely, my mother would fall asleep before she could swallow the full dose. A way around this would be for her to put a bag over her head with a rubber band at her neck to ensure that she would suffocate if she fell asleep before taking all the pills. But my mother did not like that idea because of the depressing picture it would present to those who found her body. She contemplated drawing a happy smile on the bag, but did not think that would give the correct impression either. The picture my mother wanted to leave to the world was that her death was a happy moment, like the end of a wonderful movie, a time for good memories and a peaceful acceptance of whatever the future might hold. She did not like the image of being a quasi-criminal sneaking illegal medicines. The way she really wanted to die was to be given a morphine drip that she could control, to have her family around her holding her hands, and for her to turn up the drip.

As wonderful as that might sound, it is illegal. One problem was that my mother did not have a terminal condition or agonizing pain that might justify a morphine drip. Far from it. Her heart was strong enough to keep her alive for 10 more years, albeit as a frail, bedridden, partially blind, partially deaf, incontinent, and possibly stroked-out woman. But beyond that, no physician would dare give a patient access to a lethal medicine in a way that could be accused of assisting suicide. Legally, physicians can provide lots of comfort care, even if it might hasten a patient's death, but the primary purpose of the medicine must be to relieve suffering, not to cause death. Every now and then my mother would vent her frustration with the law and the arrogance of others who insist that everyone must accept their philosophy of death, but she knew that railing at what she considered to be misguided laws would not undo them. She needed to focus on finding a solution to her problem. She decided that the only realistic way out was for me to get her some drugs and for her to do her best to swallow them. Although I was very nervous at the thought of being turned in by someone who discovered our plan and felt it was their duty to stop it, I was willing to do my part. I respected her decision, and I knew she would do the same for me.

I had no difficulty finding a friend who could write a prescription for restricted drugs and who was willing to help us from a distance. In fact, I have yet to find anybody who agrees with the current laws. (*"So why do they exist?"*) But before I actually had to resolve any lingering conflicts and obtain the drugs, my mother's course took an unexpected and strangely welcomed twist. I received a call that she had developed pneumonia and had to be readmitted to the hospital. By the time I made contact with her, she had already reminded her attendants that she did not want to be resuscitated if she should have a heart attack or stroke.

"Is there anything more I can do?"

Pneumonia, the old folks' friend, I thought to myself. I told her that although advance directives usually apply to refusing treatments for emergencies such as heart attacks, it was always legal for her to refuse any treatment. In particular, she could refuse the antibiotics for the pneumonia. Her physician and nurses would undoubtedly advise her against it, but if she signed enough papers they would have to honor her request.

"What's it like to die of pneumonia? Will they keep me comfortable?"

I knew that without any medicine for comfort, pneumonia was not a pleasant way to die. But I was also confident that her physician was compassionate and would keep her comfortable. So she asked that the antibiotics be stopped. Given the deep gurgling in her throat every time she breathed, we all expected the infection to spread rapidly. She took a perverse pleasure in that week's cover story of *Newsweek*, which described the spread of resistant strains.

"Bring all the resistant strains in this hospital to me. That will be my present to the other patients."

But that did not happen. Against the odds, her pneumonia regressed. This discouraged her greatly—to see the solution so close, just to watch it slip away.

"What else can I do? Can I stop eating?"

I told her she could, but that that approach could take a long time. I then told her that if she was really intent on dying, she could stop drinking. Without water, no one, even the healthiest, can live more than a few days.

"Can they keep me comfortable?"

I talked with her physician. Although it ran against his instincts, he respected the clarity and firmness of my mother's decision and agreed that her quality of life had sunk below what she was willing to bear. He also knew that what she was asking from him was legal. He took out the IV and wrote orders that she should receive adequate medications to control discomfort.

My mother was elated. The next day happened to be her 85th birthday, which we celebrated with a party, balloons and all. She was beaming from ear to ear. She had done it. She had found the way. She relished her last piece of chocolate, and then stopped eating and drinking.

Over the next four days, my mother greeted her visitors with the first smiles she had shown for months. She energetically reminisced about the great times she had had and about things she was proud of. (She especially hoped I would tell you about her traveling alone across Africa at the age of 70, and surviving a capsized raft on Wyoming's Snake River at 82.) She also found a calming self-acceptance in describing things of which she was not proud. She slept between visits but woke up brightly whenever we touched her to share more memories and say a few more things she wanted us to know. On the fifth day it was more difficult to wake her. When we would take her hand she would open her eyes and smile, but she was too drowsy and weak to talk very much. On the sixth day, we could not wake her. Her face was relaxed in her natural smile, she was breathing unevenly, but peacefully. We held her hands for another two hours, until she died.

I had always imagined that when I finally stood in the middle of my parents' empty house, surrounded by the old smells, by hundreds of objects that represent a time forever lost, and by the terminal silence, I would be overwhelmingly saddened. But I wasn't. This death was not a sad death; it was a happy death. It did not come after years of decline, lost vitality, and loneliness; it came at the right time. My mother was not clinging desperately to what no one can have. She knew that death was not a tragedy to be postponed at any cost, but that death is a part of life, to be embraced at the proper time. She had done just what she wanted to do, just the way she wanted to do it. Without hoarding pills, without making me a criminal, without putting a bag over her head, and without huddling in a van with a carbon monoxide machine, she had found a way to bring her life gracefully to a close. Of course we cried. But although we will miss her greatly, her ability to achieve her death at her "right time" and in her "right way" transformed for us what could have been a desolate and crushing loss into a time for joy. Because she was happy, we were happy.

"Write about this, David. Tell others how well this worked for me. I'd like this to be my gift. Whether they are terminally ill, in intractable pain, or, like me, just know that the right time has come for them, more people might want to know that this way exists. And maybe more physicians will help them find it."

Maybe they will. Rest in peace, Mom.

David M. Eddy, MD, PhD
Jackson, Wyo

My mother wants to thank Dr Timothy Cope of Middlebury, Vermont, for his present on her 85th birthday.

1. Eddy DM. Cost-effectiveness analysis: a conversation with my father. *JAMA*. 1992;267:1669–1672, 1674–1675.

2. Humphry D. *Final Exit*. Secaucus, NJ: Carol Publishing Group; 1991.

Edited by Roxanne K. Young, Associate Editor.

EUTHANASIA

To cease upon the midnight

The putative right of an individual to determine the manner of his own death conflicts with the supreme value that most societies place on the preservation of life. Recently, the individual has been gaining ground

CRIPPLED in a swimming accident in 1968, Ramon Sanpedro can move only his head. He wants someone to help him commit suicide. So far, two Spanish courts have refused their consent.

Tony Bland, a British football fan, suffered terrible brain injuries in a crowd pileup at a sports stadium in April 1989, and was left in a persistent vegetative state with no hope of recovery. In March 1993 the House of Lords, Britain's highest judicial authority, gave permission for Bland's feeding tubes to be disconnected. He died 20 days later.

Sue Rodriguez, a Canadian, was suffering from amyotrophic lateral sclerosis, an incurable disease which attacks the brain and spinal cord and impairs functions such as walking, speaking and breathing, when she asked in 1992 for someone to be allowed, legally, to help her die. Canada's Supreme Court found against her by five votes to four. She died in February 1994 with the help of an anonymous doctor.

Jack Kevorkian—"Dr Death"—is an American former pathologist whose eccentricities include creating ghoulish paintings using his own blood. He has "assisted" 20 suicides in the state of Michigan; juries have refused to convict him.

Such are the cases that are driving forward a public and legal debate in the West about the right to die and the right to medical assistance in doing so—a debate mainly for the rich West because in poor countries the artificial prolongation of life is at best a rare luxury; in Japan patients are often not told when they are terminally ill. The

debate has been intensifying with the development of medical technologies capable of supporting life, in a narrowly defined form, almost indefinitely; and it has been influenced by a growing sense in many western societies that more responsibility for, and control over, medical treatment should be transferred from doctors to patients. Last year, the Dutch parliament voted to permit doctors to kill severely ill patients under certain conditions (see box, The Dutch Way of Dying). This week, Germany's constitutional court ruled that doctors could allow a terminally ill patient to die. Previously, German doctors had been allowed only to withdraw life-support from patients who were actually dying.

In America, many of the terms of the euthanasia debate in its present form were defined in 1976 by the tragedy of a young woman called Karen Ann Quinlan, who was being kept alive by machines while in a coma that doctors judged to be irreversible. When her parents asked that the machines be disconnected, the hospital refused; the Quinlans won a court judgment establishing the right of a patient or his surrogate to refuse treatment. The right to pull the plug, sometimes referred to as "passive euthanasia", is now well established.

Doctors in most countries now honour the wish of a terminally ill or very old patient not to be revived should he suffer cardiac or respiratory arrest in hospital. The policy of the American Medical Association is that a doctor "has an ethical obligation to honour the resuscitation preferences expressed by the patient." In Britain, the Royal College of Nursing, and the doc-

tors' professional body, the British Medical Association (BMA), have come to a similar conclusion. They recommend that hospitals try to determine the wishes of such patients.

More recently, ethicists and the medical establishment have reached a consensus on the treatment of pain in the terminally ill. The principle used to be that pain-relievers should not be administered in such a way as to expose a patient to risk of addiction. The absurdity of worrying about addiction in someone with a short time left to live is now acknowledged. Pain relief is recognised as an overriding priority; and it is considered ethical to provide as much pain relief as necessary even if a doctor believes that doing so may hasten death. Even so, according to Mildred Solomon, co-founder of a Massachusetts organisation called Decisions Near the End of Life, which provides training to carers for the terminally ill, four out of five doctors surveyed in 1993 said that under-treatment of pain among the dying was a more serious problem than over-treatment.

Agreement is more elusive on the issue of what constitutes "appropriate care" of the terminally ill and dying. Some ethicists, for example, see significance in the means needed to nourish a patient, arguing that the surgical insertion of feeding tubes may amount to over-treatment. Other authorities, such as the Royal College of Nursing, see feeding a patient as a basic duty just like keeping him clean, and as difficult to disregard. When the House of Lords agreed that Tony Bland's feeding tubes could be disconnected, it said the decision should not be taken as a

The Dutch way of dying

HOLLAND has the most liberal regime for voluntary euthanasia of any western country. As a case study, its lessons are much disputed. Admirers cite the care with which the Dutch debated the issue until consensus was reached, and the safeguards that they built into their system. Critics say the safeguards are ineffective and that Holland is skidding down a slippery slope towards licensed killing.

The Dutch parliament decided last year to authorise euthanasia under certain conditions—thus recognising officially a practice common there for at least 20 years. No legal right to euthanasia was created, and doctors could still face prosecution if they failed to follow strict guidelines. These were that a patient must be in a state of unbearable suffering; the desire to die must be "lasting"; the decision to die must be given freely; and the patient must have a clear understanding of his condition.

Few would quarrel with such propositions taken in isolation. But there is a worrying drift in the Dutch experience. An official report found that, in addition to 2,300 reported cases of euthanasia in Holland in 1990, a further 1,040 people had had their deaths hastened without making a formal request for intervention. That figure gives pause for thought; so does the case of a physically healthy but severely depressed Dutch woman who in 1991 asked her psychiatrist to help her die. After consulting with seven colleagues the psychiatrist agreed to the request and gave the patient sleeping pills and a toxic potion; she took them and died. In June the Dutch Supreme Court ruled out prosecution. It thus appears that not all of the notional safeguards may be enforced by the courts.

Johan Legemaate, legal counsel of the Royal Dutch Medical Association, defends the way euthanasia is practised in Holland. He notes that in more than two-thirds of the cases where patients request euthanasia, it is denied, and that in most cases where patients had not formally requested euthanasia and yet received it, there had been previous discussion of the subject. (In most such cases in 1990, according to the report cited above, life was shortened only by a few hours or days. All cases went through an extensive process of review and consultation.) "We feel we have succeeded in creating a large amount of openness and accountability," Mr Legemaate says.

Critics counter, however, that the result is a climate of indifference in which most cases of euthanasia go unreported and patients' rights are being eroded. Euthanasia, they say, so far from giving more freedom to patients, is giving more power over them to doctors.

cancer. She did not want to undergo another series of painful and debilitating treatments with only a 25% chance of surviving. She preferred to choose the time of her death, and asked Dr Quill for barbiturates. He gave them to her and advised her of the amount needed to commit suicide—which she later did. Legally, American doctors can provide patients with drugs that might kill them provided that the drug has a legitimate medical purpose other than suicide. To provide drugs knowing that their likely application will be in suicide is frowned on.

Dr Quill was among the first American doctors to declare openly his role in assisting a death, albeit indirectly. The reaction was muted. Not everyone agreed with his conduct, but there was no rush to condemn it. Giving death a gentle push at a patient's behest does not happen often because the urge to live is usually so strong; but most doctors with long experience of critical care know of cases where it has occurred. A grand jury refused to indict Dr Quill, and in 1992 he and two other doctors published an essay suggesting guidelines for doctor-assisted suicide. The medical establishment remained opposed to the practice, but the taboo of talking about it was at last breached by someone who did not carry the baggage of Mr Kevorkian.

A right to choose

A still more difficult question is whether society should approve, tacitly or otherwise, the next step in the logical sequence, namely the practice of active euthanasia—ie, a doctor administering a substance for no reason other than to cause death. Those who favour legalisation of active euthanasia point to anecdotal evidence from surveys of doctors showing that it already happens. Better to have the decisions made after open discussion with some sort of institutional safeguards, it is argued, than to leave them to the conscience of individual doctors.

Campaigners for voluntary euthanasia argue that some ethical distinctions between what is and is not taboo are already untenable. Withdrawing life-support, for example, is considered a form of passive euthanasia. But it is not really passive. To unplug a machine is a deliberate action.

In the case of Tony Bland, the British football fan, almost three weeks elapsed after the disconnecting of his feeding tubes during which he was left to waste away. It is hard to see why

general mandate and that each such case should go before a court.

Dr Death comes calling

An even more contentious area is "doctor-assisted suicide", in which a doctor helps a patient to take his own life. This has been Mr Kevorkian's speciality. In each of the 20 deaths he facilitated, the patient took the final step in the process—by connecting a hose, say, or pushing a button. Most western countries, and 44 American states, have laws against assisting suicide; in those that do not, such as Switzerland, medical tradition is against it. That record, however, suggests a unanimity absent in practice.

The *Medical Journal of Australia* reported a survey of 354 doctors who had been asked by patients to hasten death* (for footnotes, see final page). Only 107 had done so, but twice as many thought the law should be changed to allow such a thing in certain circumstances. A more recent poll of British doctors, reported in the *British Medical Journal,* found a similar pattern†. Of 273 respondents, 124 had been asked to hasten actively a patient's death; of those, about a third had done so; but almost half of the total sample said they might do so if the practice was legal (see tables).

In America, a widely remarked article in the *New England Journal of Medicine‡* in 1991 created something of a turning-point in attitudes. Timothy Quill, a former hospice director, told the story of "Diane", who had been diagnosed as having leukaemia. Diane had previously recovered from vaginal that was more compassionate "treatment" than a lethal injection that would have given him, and his family, an equally sure release from their agony.

Nor is it easy to draw a clear line between injecting a dose of pain-killer that is likely to cause death (as some doctors do), and injecting a drug that is certain to kill (which is a crime in most places). In 1992 a British rheumatologist, Nigel Cox, was convicted of attempted murder for giving a lethal injection of potassium cyanide to a pain-wracked patient who had begged him to end her suffering. If Dr Cox had given her a huge dose of pain-killers he would never have been put in the dock.

The case for euthanasia is gaining a more sympathetic hearing as modern medicine and institutional care make dying a more prolonged, impersonal and often agonising business. To see a loved one shrivelled in pain for weeks or months can be a devastating experience for friends and family; but it is one that may become more common-place as quick and relatively easy cardiac deaths decline as a percentage of deaths in rich countries, and proportionately more people die of cancer and AIDS. Nor may all hospitals be equal to the task of maintaining some measure of decency and comfort for the dying.

Some arguments for euthanasia insist on parallels with abortion, which the American Supreme Court declared to be a legal right on the grounds that the decision to bear a child was a matter of private choice. An American district court made explicit use of this rationale in May when it overturned a statute prohibiting assisted suicide; now under appeal, the case may reach the Supreme Court. This line of argument sees a decision to end one's life as the ultimate act of self-determination. In doing so, it raises legal and philosophical questions about the state of mind of any person taking such a decision; and it probably invites the question of whether such a right, were it to exist, should be restricted to certain classes of person. Could the young, or the healthy, or the clinically depressed, be denied a "right to die" that was conceded to the old or the desperately sick?

A further problem arises in applying this logic of self-determination to cases where the practical issue is not the right to commit suicide, or to be left to die, but to be helped to die by a doctor. A patient does not have a right to demand, say, a voodoo cure

Last rights		%
"In the course of your medical practice, has a patient ever asked you to hasten his or her death?"		
	GPs	Consultants
Had been asked to hasten death	64	52
Had been asked for:		
Passive euthanasia only	13	16
Active euthanasia only	25	11
Passive and active euthanasia	27	25
Total who had been asked for active euthanasia	51	36
Not asked to hasten death	36	48
"Have you ever taken active steps to bring about the death of patient who asked you to do so?"		
	GPs	Consultants
Yes	30	36
No	70	64
"Sometimes I would be prepared to withdraw or withhold a course of treatment from a terminally ill patient, knowing the treatment might prolong the patient's life."		
	GPs	Consultants
Strongly agree	34	45
Agree	54	50
Undecided	5	2
Disagree	5	2
Strongly disagree	1	1
"If a terminally ill patient asked me to bring an end to his or her life, I would consider doing so if it were legal."		
	GPs	Consultants
Strongly agree	10	10
Agree	41	30
Undecided	21	21
Disagree	19	26
Strongly disagree	9	12

Source: *British Medical Journal* May 21st 1994
Totals may not equal 100 because of rounding

from a doctor; it is not obvious that he should have a right to demand death.

The danger of duty

Organised opposition to the cause of voluntary euthanasia comes chiefly from the handicapped, medical associations and some religious groups, including the Roman Catholic church and orthodox Jews. Interest groups for the handicapped are uncomfortable with any form of euthanasia because they fear its use would inevitably be extended to those with long-term disabilities. The underlying fear is that the right to die will become a duty to die, and that society, the principle of euthanasia once established, might tend to categorise some people as expendable. The old, senile, mentally ill and physically helpless could become tempting targets for cost-cutting.

For doctors and nurses, euthanasia is troubling because they are trained to heal and to save life. Doing the opposite, even with the noblest of intentions, runs counter to their oath. Practitioners in hospices that care for

the terminally ill have been at the forefront of medical opposition to euthanasia, arguing that techniques for controlling pain are now so far advanced that fewer people need die in agony. They fear that the availability of euthanasia as an easy option would diminish the incentive to provide compassionate care for those who preferred to let death take its course. Doctors are also worried that practising euthanasia openly would lead some patients to regard them as bringers of death. The BMA thinks it "contrary to the doctor's role deliberately to kill patients, even at their request".

Most medical associations would agree with that as a general statement. In practice, however, things are less clear-cut. On August 16th the Canadian Medical Association voted not to allow doctors any role in active euthanasia or assisted suicide—but by a fairly narrow majority of 93 to 74. In Britain, though Dr Cox was convicted by a criminal court, he was allowed by a regulatory body, the General Medical Council, to retain his practitioner's licence, a sign that his peers did not consider his action monstrous.

For the Christian churches, the issue is equally fraught. Even in western countries where people have lost the habit of going to church on Sundays, Christian values are still influential. One of the central Christian beliefs is that life is a gift from God which individuals guard but do not own; another is that suffering is a wellspring of redemption and, as such, has value in itself.

This idea has proved a source of strength to many sufferers for centuries. But it is possible to respect that belief and yet still to wonder if at some point suffering can become pointless. Must every single possible moment of suffering be extracted as payment for redemption? And should those not attached to this system of belief be subject to its consequences?

The moral muddle

Most people would say no, albeit often hesitantly. But merely coming to that conclusion is not enough to bring societies any closer to defining a new conceptual framework for regulating death and dying. Opinion polls in many western countries have found majority support for allowing assisted suicide and active euthanasia in certain circumstances, but legislators have not judged the trend a sufficiently compelling one for them to make significant changes to existing laws. In the United States, four state legislatures have rejected bills to allow assisted suicide; referendums in California and Washington have found majorities against change. Initiatives in the British and European parliaments have failed. The Canadian parliament, which has defeated four bills on the issue in the past, has formed a Senate committee on euthanasia and assisted suicide to collect opinion.

The result, in many places, is to leave justice in a muddle. Perhaps that is appropriate. Inadvertently, a sensible mean may have been struck. Laws against assisted suicide, it maybe said, are there to express society's unease. At the same time, it is very rare for a practising doctor to be charged with helping a terminally ill patient to die.

"The current law is just about right," says George Annas, an ethicist at the Boston University School of Medicine. "Physicians should understand they are at some risk and so should assist suicide only in very extreme circumstances." He points out the difficulty of creating a better law, particularly one that would be proof against malpractice lawyers: "How do you define the circumstances? What kind of procedural mechanisms would there have to be? It would be such a nightmare."

It is, in fact, not surprising that commissions and parliaments and the public at large should have such difficulty delineating the boundaries of death. To do so means coming to grips not only with the mystery of dying, but also with the meaning of life, and with the relationship between the free will of the individual and the interests of society. To decide not to decide, how-ever, is irresponsible. One of the strongest arguments for more liberal (and more honest) legislation on euthanasia is that it would lighten the burden on doctors who must at present make such terribly difficult decisions alone and without knowing what consequences they may face. In the words of Ian Kennedy, professor of medical law and ethics at King's College, London: "It cannot be fair to doctors to present them with a situation in which they have to guess whether people will subsequently endorse what they have done or whether, if they guess wrong, the law will be applied in all its rigour and they will face a charge of murder."

---

* MJA 1988; 148: 623-627; † BMJ 1994; 308: 1332–1334; ‡NEJM 1991; 324: 691–694

ATTITUDES TOWARD SUICIDAL BEHAVIOR: A REVIEW OF THE LITERATURE

Ellen Ingram and Jon B. Ellis

The attitudes people in any given culture [hold] regarding death and suicidal behavior may be viewed as a reflection of that culture's values toward life. This article reviews the literature in the area of societal attitudes toward suicidal behavior. Attitudes include not only how society feels about those who kill themselves but the family members who are left behind as well. Although surveys have shown that many Americans see suicidal people as psychologically disturbed, some groups argue that suicide can be seen as a rational behavior. The idea is postulated that the answer to whether suicide is a rational or irrational act may not be as simple as yes or no.

The opinions that members of a society hold regarding suicidal behavior is a reflection of their values toward human life. These values influence how members of a society are taught to think and behave. Societal attitudes regarding the appropriateness of suicide remain confused and contradictory. Death by suicide affects not only the victim but the victim's family, friends, members of the community, and our entire society. Surviving relatives are thought to be more grief stricken because their loved one willfully took his or her own life, and that they must also deal with more severe and negative attitudes of the people in the community when suicide is the

cause of death (Cain & Fast, 1972; Calhoun, Selby, & Selby, 1982; McGinnis, 1987; Range, McDonald, & Anderson, 1987; Range & Thompson, 1986). Suicidal behavior is now viewed as an illness, but it may be a symptom of many illnesses because it is an overt expression of emotions such as rage, guilt, loneliness, shame, sorrow, agony, fear, and hopelessness (McGinnis, 1987).

Douglas (1967) conjectured that suicide was widely condemned in our society and could be understood only by a study of the meaning the self-destructive individual attached to the behavior. The meaning in turn should be studied within the context of the values of a particular society attaches to suicide. Singh, Williams, and Ryther (1986) asserted that the situation itself largely defines the extent to which suicide will be approved as an acceptable alternative to living. Society evaluates the appropriateness in terms of the individual involved and the specific circumstances surrounding the suicide. Community attitudes may even influence suicide rates (de Catanzaro, 1981; Douglas, 1967; Dublin, 1963). Some clinicians suggested that a hardening of attitudes toward suicidal behavior may result in lessening of such behavior (Koller & Slaghuis, 1978). Alternatively, a growing influence that is promoting the acceptance of suicide is the right-to-die movement, which advocates an individ-

ual's right to commit suicide particularly when a terminal illness is involved (Klagsburn, 1981).

HISTORICAL OVERVIEW

Some cultures encouraged suicide among certain members of their society, usually for religious purposes, believing in life after death (Siegel, 1988). In the Fiji Islands, suicide was expected of the wives of a chief when he died. The women rushed to kill themselves believing the first to die would become the chief's favorite wife in the spirit world. In India, widows practiced suttee. They threw themselves on their husband's funeral pyre believing they could atone for their husband's sins.

The Chinese regarded suicide as acceptable and honorable, particularly for defeated generals or deposed rulers. The Japanese ritualized suicide in the form of hara-kiri, a long drawn out process of disembowelment. A samurai warrior or a member of the military was bestowed much honor if he died in such a way. Ancient Greek and Roman cities differed greatly in their views of suicide. In Thebes, suicide was strongly condemned, but in other Greek communities tribunals existed to hear the arguments of people who wanted to commit suicide.

During the Middle Ages into the 19th century in Western cultures, society

From *Death Studies,* Volume 16, 1992, pp. 31–43. © 1992 by Taylor & Francis, Inc., 625 Chestnut Street, 8th Floor, Philadelphia, PA, 19106. All rights reserved. Reprinted by permission.

placed negative social sanctions on people who attempted or committed suicide. The sanctions included assigning disgrace to the reputation of the deceased, mutilation of the corpse, hanging the corpse from public gallows, denial of Christian burial, confiscation of the deceased's estate, and excommunication of the deceased from the church.

INFLUENCES ON CURRENT ATTITUDES

The general attitude of the public toward [suicide] remains confused and often contradictory (Kluge, 1975). Today there are two extreme views, amid more moderate views, on suicide. The extreme views range from total acceptance to total rejection of the right of an individual to commit suicide. At the center of the debate is the question of whether people should be allowed the right to die without interference. In its narrowest sense, the question relates to people who are terminally ill or in great pain. In its broadest sense, it extends to any person who wants to die (Klagsburn, 1981). Others regard the right to die as a right to refuse life-sustaining treatment (Weber, 1988). A small number of individuals insist that all persons have the right to control their own bodies even in matters of suicide. Any interference with this right is a violation of fundamental liberties. Szasz (1974) was among the most vocal advocates for the individual's right to commit suicide. He stated, "While suicide is not necessarily morally desirable, it is nonetheless a fundamental inalienable right" (p. 67). Maris (1986) disagreed with Szasz's radical individual autonomy. He pointed out that Szasz has no appreciation for loving the unlovable in our society. He foresaw this view as even contributing to self-destructive behavior.

Most right-to-die advocates make a distinction between a healthy or terminally ill person committing suicide. Advocates argue that medical science has now been able to prolong life artificially to the point that life becomes meaningless. Once the assumption is accepted that there are conditions under which it may be preferable not to sustain life, suicide may be viewed as a reasonable option (Klagsburn, 1981).

Suicide as a Rational Act

Several organizations have been established to promote wider acceptance of the right-to-die movement. Humphry (1987) described the Hemlock Society's position on suicide. Suicide is separated into two types. The first is emotional suicide or irrational self-murder. Their thinking on this type of suicide is to prevent it whenever possible. The second type is justifiable suicide described as rational and planned self-deliverance. They advocate what they call autoeuthanasia. They ethically justify suicide only under certain circumstances. One involves a case of an advanced terminal illness that is causing unbearable suffering to the individual. Another involves a grave physical handicap that is so restrictive that the individual cannot, after due consideration and training, tolerate such a limited existence. This group believes that suicide is ethical only when the person is a mature adult and has made a considered decision. A considered decision is one that was not made at the first knowledge of a life-threatening illness and for which the treating physician's response has been taken into account. Also the person has made plans that do not involve others in criminal liability, and he or she leaves a note stating exactly why he or she is committing suicide. Humphry believed that for many people just knowing how to kill themselves is in itself a great comfort and often extends their lives. They will often renegotiate with themselves the conditions of their dying.

Another group, Concern for the Dying (Sachs, 1987), has furnished thousands of copies of the Living Will document. The Living Will document expresses the desire of an individual to cease medical intervention under certain conditions. The Society for the Right to Die lobbies state legislatures in an effort to protect the right to refuse extraordinary life-preserving measures. Other groups propose schemes for regulating suicidal acts. Collectively, these groups advocate what is called rational suicide. Rational suicide is characterized by a possession of a realistic assessment of the situation by the individual who is faced with the decision to commit suicide. The individual's mental processes are not impaired by psychological illness or distress, and the person's motivation for the decision would be understandable if presented to objective

bystanders (Siegel, 1988). The goals of these groups are for the most part humane, advocating the "right to die with dignity" (Quinnett, 1987).

Opposition to Suicide

Among the opponents, some argue that a person does not have the right to commit suicide regardless of the circumstances. Others believe certain circumstances may be so unbearable that it is understandable why a person commits suicide, but this should be an individual act, and society or the legal system should not encourage this type of behavior. Opponents who hold extreme views argue that life should be preserved regardless of circumstances even in the case of a terminal illness. They believe no one has a right to decide at what point life becomes expendable. They believe condoning any kind of suicide condones them all (Klagsburn, 1981). They argue that there is medical and social justification to intervene and prevent someone from taking his or her life. Suicide is seen as an ambivalent act: Every person who wants to die also wants to live. This view postulates that a person is suicidal only for a short period of time, and if intervention is instigated, the suicidal crisis often passes and the person changes his or her mind.

ACCEPTABILITY OF SUICIDAL BEHAVIOR

Feherman (1989) chaired a 12-member committee that made recommendations to physicians about their responsibility toward terminally ill patients. The committee members agreed that it was not immoral for a physician to assist a terminally ill patient in committing suicide by prescribing sleeping pills and advising the patient of the amount of a lethal dose. Five years before this, the committee had recommended that physicians listen to the final wishes of their dying patients including removal of a feeding tube. Since then, many recommendations of the committee have been adopted by physicians and the court system.

Forty states and the District of Columbia have living will laws that allow people to specify in advance what treatments they would find acceptable in their final days. A New York State Supreme Court Justice ruled in January 1990 that a family did not have to pay

2 years worth of fees ($100,000) to a nursing home for tending a comatose patient after the family had asked to have the feeding tube removed. Less than 6 months later, in June 1990, the U.S. Supreme Court made a ruling by which family members can be barred from ending the lives of long-term comatose relatives who have not made their wishes known conclusively. In the absence of conclusive evidence that a patient does not wish to be sustained by artificial life-saving devices, the states were given broad power to keep such patients on life-saving systems. The court interprets the [C]onstitution that a competent person, as opposed to someone in a coma, is guaranteed the right to refuse medical treatment.

A poll conducted for *Time Magazine*/CNN television network in 1990 found that 80% of those surveyed thought decisions about ending lives of the terminally ill, who cannot decide for themselves, should be made by the patient's family and physician rather than lawmakers. Of the respondents, 81% believed that a physician with an unconscious patient who has left a living will should be allowed to withdraw life-sustaining treatment, and 57% believed physicians should go even further in such cases and [administer] lethal injections or provide a lethal amount of pills (Gibbs, 1990). Public acceptance of the right of an individual with a terminal illness to commit suicide has been growing, and between 1977 and 1983 the percentage of adults in the United States who believe a terminally ill person has a right to commit suicide increased from 39% to almost 50% (Siegel, 1988). Wellman and Wellman (1986) conducted two surveys assessing attitudes toward suicide. In the first surveys, over one half of both men and women believed that no one should be allowed to commit suicide. In the second survey, 70% of both sexes believed no one should be allowed to commit suicide.

Singh (1979) reported that suicide was considered a rational alternative for those who were suffering from an incurable disease by approximately 40% of the respondents in a national survey. Singh et al. (1986) compared four national surveys conducted between 1977 and 1983. The study examined public opinion on suicide in four situations: incurable disease, bankruptcy, family dishonor, and being tired of living. The highest approval rate for suicide was in the situation in which a person had an incurable disease. In each year an increasing percentage approved of suicide in this situation, from approximately 39% in 1977 to nearly 50% in 1983. There was very little support for a person to commit suicide after having dishonored his or her family or after having gone bankrupt. A person who approved of suicide in the incurable-disease situation would most likely be a college-educated white male under the age of 35 who infrequently attended church services and had a high degree of support for freedom of expression. The approval of suicide was highest in the Pacific region and lowest in the southern regions of the United States. Ginsburg (1971) found a generally punitive and rejecting attitude toward suicidal behavior with little sympathy for those who attempted or completed suicide. Of the respondents, 42% of those who had known someone who had committed suicide felt a person had the right to take his or her own life. Kalish, Reynolds, and Farberow (1974) concluded that respondents to their survey found the victim's situation as well as the victim equally responsible. Johnson, Fitch, Alston, and McIntosh (1980) found that public acceptance of both suicide and euthanasia was highly conditional and limited to certain segments of the population. They found that blacks are less likely to approve of suicide when an individual has an incurable disease than are whites. However, both whites and blacks are equally likely to disapprove of suicide when an individual has dishonored his or her family or because of bankruptcy. Euthanasia is more acceptable to the general white public than is suicide. Men and women are likely to approve of euthanasia with increased education.

Ramsey and Bagley's (1985) findings suggest a more accepting attitude toward suicide than reported in previous studies. Of the respondents, 90% understood the loneliness and depression associated with suicidal behavior.

REACTIONS TO SURVIVORS OF SUICIDE

Survivors who are bereaved because of the death of a loved one by suicide must deal with their personal grief and at the same time deal with community reactions, which have been found to be more severe and negative than when death is by any other cause (Cain & Fast, 1972; Calhoun et al., 1982). Negative community reactions bring about reduced emotional support (Haim, 1970; Hatton & Valente, 1981; Whitis, 1972) and, at the same time, blame toward the family for the death (Calhoun, Selby, & Faulstich, 1980; Gordon, Range, & Edwards, 1987; Rudestam & Imbroll, 1983). People are more curious about the nature of a suicidal death than a natural death (Rudestam & Imbroll, 1983; Range & Calhoun, in press). Survivors are more likely to experience guilt and have a lengthy psychological resolution of the grief experience (Parks & Weiss, 1983; Rudestam, 1977). Calhoun et al. (1982) found that bereaved survivors of suicide victims reported feeling socially isolated, rejected, and stigmatized. Shneidman (1972) observed that, from all the varied modes of death, suicide brings the greatest stigma on the survivors and produces greater expectations of discomfort in those who must interact with family members (Shepherd & Barraclough, 1974). This reflects what has been termed *ambivalent avoidance* (Whitis, 1972). The most entrenched attitude taken toward suicide is to ignore it (Haim, 1970). Danto (1977) and Danto and Fast (1966) found that the absence of emotional support often reflects the stigma attached to the act of committing suicide (Cain & Fast, 1966). Calhoun, Selby, and Abernathy (1984) investigated reactions of persons who had experienced suicidal bereavement versus bereavement of death resulting from an accident or natural causes. Potential comforters thought that suicide was a more difficult life experience than other modes of death and that they would have difficulty expressing sympathy and would be more uncomfortable at the funeral. These findings were not as pronounced if the comforter was a close friend to the bereaved person. Thus, in this situation, the cause of death may play a lesser role in determining reactions to the survivors.

Calhoun et al. (1986) examined the social rules that govern interactions with bereaved persons. Rules are beliefs by members of a group about whether a specific behavior should or should not be performed in particular situations (Argyle, Furnham, & Graham, 1981). The pattern of the results suggests that the rules for suicide are more constraining. Judgments about the existence of social rules tend to be more inclusive and extreme in a "should not" direction when death is by suicide. They suggested that although individuals may feel greater compassion for the survivors of suicide (Calhoun, Selby, & Steelman, 1983), they may still avoid the situation for fear of violating one of the rules.

Range and Thompson (1986) found that students viewed people in the community as providing mixed messages or unhelpful messages to those who were bereaved as a result of suicide or homicide but as providing helpful messages to those bereaved as a result of other modes of death. Students viewed themselves as being equally helpful regardless of the cause of death. Students viewed those people who were bereaved as a result of homicide as having a more severe reaction than from any other cause of death. Students viewed those who were bereaved as a result of suicide as reacting about the same as those bereaved because of natural or accidental causes. These differences are contrary to the reports of those who have actually been bereaved as a result of suicide (Range & Calhoun, 1985). It was suggested that the students may have overestimated their own helpfulness.

Several researchers found that a child depicted in a scenario as having committed suicide is perceived as having been psychologically unhealthier than if death had occurred in a different way (Calhoun et al., 1980; Ginn, Range, & Hailey, 1988; Kalish, Reynolds, & Farberow, 1974). This [has] also been found to be true of adolescents (Gordon et al., 1987; Range, Goggin, & Cantrell, in press). Range, Bright, and Ginn (1985) found that people in the community thought that suicidal adolescents were more psychologically disturbed than suicidal children. Community members blamed parents of suicidal adolescents less than they blamed parents of suicidal children and expected to like parents of suicidal adolescents more than parents of suicidal children. It seems people react differently depending on the age of the victim. Ginn et al. (1988) reported that subjects did not attribute psychological disturbance to the parents of a child who committed suicide, but Gordon et al. (1987) found that the mother was also viewed as more psychologically disturbed than if the child had died of natural causes. Also more people are opposed to publishing the cause of death in the newspaper when the cause is suicide (Calhoun et al., 1980; Ginn et al., 1988). Gordon et al. (1987) surveyed parents and their children and found that the parents perceived a youth who died of suicide as more psychologically disturbed than did their adolescent children, but parents expected to experience less tension and have less difficulty in expressing sympathy when visiting the survivors than did their adolescent children. It was found that parents may be more supportive to the bereaved than are adolescents.

Bell (1977) found that college students viewed suicidal peers as cowardly, sick, unpleasant, and disreputable and were much more negative in their attitudes toward peers who attempted suicide and lived than toward those who completed suicide. Linehan (1973) reported that college students ascribed traditional male and female qualities to completed suicide as opposed to attempted suicide. College students perceived completed suicide to be more active and potent, and which may explain why Bell (1977) found that students judged peers who attempted suicide and lived more harshly than those who died.

Wellman and Wellman (1986) conducted two surveys with college students to assess gender differences in attitudes toward suicide. Most men and women recognized that people could be suicidal, did not judge them harshly, and were receptive to and supportive of suicidal people. However, men, more so than women, were likely to have harsher attitudes toward suicidal people and were less likely to discuss the subject with them because of the belief that discussing it would precipitate suicide. Men were more likely to deny that suicidal people showed warning signs, believing it was more an impulsive act, and men were more likely to deny the increase in adolescent suicide, believing the media was exaggerating the incidence. The authors emphasized that most men do not have negative attitudes toward suicide, but men are more likely to have negative attitudes than women.

SUMMARY

Attitudes toward suicide have varied throughout time and across cultures. As this review points out, such widespread assumptions as "life is sacred" are open to interpretation. Even the idea that life should be saved at all costs has been questioned. The issues that are confronted by researchers who investigate society's attitudes toward not only the person who kills her or himself but the parents, family, and friends of that person call for a serious examination. The idea that suicide is a rational or irrational act has been argued. Like most societal problems, suicide is probably not as simple as that. Should the suicide of an individual who is suffering from a terminal illness and whose prognosis calls for a short life with intense pain be labeled a rational, well-thought-out act or the behavior of a psychologically disturbed person?

Opponents of rational suicide equate suicide with psychological disturbance. Thus, they argue that suicide is irrational. Anecdotal clinical evidence, as well as research, examined the demographics and characteristics of suicidal individuals and suggested that suicide is often a well-thought-out plan of action that may not be a result of severe psychological disturbance (Fox & Weissman, 1975; Patsiokas, Clum, & Luscomb, 1979).

Thus, society's view of suicidal behavior appears to be mixed. Current attitudes include maintaining life. However, growing movements that have stressed an individual's right to die in certain situations served to move societal attitudes away from a simplistic dichotomy of good or bad.

REFERENCES

Argyle, M., Furnham, A., & Graham, J. (1981). *Social situations.* Cambridge, England: Cambridge University Press.

Bell, D. (1977). Sex and chronicity as variables affecting attitudes of undergraduates toward peers with suicidal behaviors. *Dissertation Abstracts International, 38,* 3380B.

Cain, A., & Fast, I. (1966). The legacy of suicide: Observations on the pathogenic impact of suicide upon marital partners. *Psychiatry, 29,* 406–441.

Cain, A., & Fast, I. (1972). The legacy of suicide: Observations on the pathogenic impact of suicide upon marital partners. In A. C. Cain (Ed.), *Survivors of suicide.* Springfield, IL: Charles C. Thomas.

Calhoun, L., Abernathy, C., & Selby, J. (1986). The rules of bereavement: Are suicidal deaths different? *Journal of Community Psychology, 14,* 213–218.

Calhoun, L., Selby, J. & Abernathy, C. (1984). Suicidal death: Social reactions to bereaved survivors. *Journal of Psychology, 116,* 225–261.

Calhoun, L., Selby, J., & Faulstich, M. (1980). Reactions to the parents of the child's suicide: A study of social impressions. *Journal of Consulting and Clinical Psychology, 48*, 535–536.

Calhoun, L., Selby, J., & Selby, L. (1982). The psychological aftermath of suicide: An analysis of current evidence. *Clinical Psychological Review, 2*, 409–420.

Calhoun, L., Selby, J., & Steelman, J. (1983). *Individual and social elements in acute grief. A collection of funeral directors' impressions of suicidal deaths.* Unpublished manuscript, University of North Carolina, Charlotte.

Danto, B. (1977). Family survivors of suicide. In B. L. Danto & A. H. Kutscher (Eds.) *Suicide and bereavement* (pp. 11–20). New York: MSS Information Corp.

de Catanzaro, D. (1981). *Suicide and self-damaging behavior: A sociobiological perspective.* New York: Academic Press.

Douglas, J. (1967). *The social meaning of suicide.* Princeton: NJ: Princeton University Press.

Dublin L. (1963). *Suicide: A social and statistical study.* New York: Ronald Press.

Feherman, (1989). Ethical recommendations. *New England Journal of Medicine.*

Fox, K., & Weissman, H. (1975). Suicide attempts and drugs: Contradiction between method and intent. *Social Psychiatry, 10*, 31–38.

Gibbs, N. (1990, March 19). Love and let die. *Time*, pp. 62–71.

Ginn, P., Range, L., & Hailey, B. (1988). Community attitudes toward childhood suicide and attempted suicide. *Journal of Community Psychology, 16*, 144–151.

Ginsburg, G. (1971). Public perceptions and attitudes about suicide. *Journal of Health and Social Behavior, 12*, 200–207.

Gordon, R., Range, L., & Edwards, R. (1987). Generational differences in reactions to adolescent suicide. *Journal of Community Psychology, 15*, 268–273.

Haim, A. (1970). *Adolescent suicide.* (A. M. S. Smith, Trans.). New York: International University Press.

Hatton, C. C., & Valente, S. M. (1981). Bereavement group for parents who suffered a suicidal loss of a child. *Suicide and Life-Threatening Behavior, 11*, 141–150.

Humphry, D. (1987). The case for rational suicide [Letter to the editor] *Suicide and Life-Threatening Behavior, 17*, 335–338.

Johnson, D., Fitch, S., Alston, J., & McIntosh, W. (1980). Acceptance of conditional suicide and euthanasia among adult Americans. *Suicide and Life-Threatening Behavior, 10*, 157–166.

Kalish, R., Reynolds, D., & Farberow, N. (1974). Community attitudes toward suicide. *Community Mental Health Journal, 10*, 301–308.

Klagsburn, F. (1981). *Too young to die—youth and suicide.* New York: Houghton Mifflin.

Kluge, E. (1975). *The practice and death.* New Haven, CT: Yale University Press.

Koller, K., & Slaghuis, W. (1978). Suicide attempts 1973–1977 in urban Hobbart: A further five year follow up reporting a decline. *Australian and New Zealand Journal of Psychiatry, 12*, 169–173.

Lampke, R. (1989). AIDS and the allied health care worker: Fears, fantasies, and facts. *Advances in Thanatology, 7*, 92–103.

Linehan, M. (1973). Suicide and attempted suicide: Study of perceived sex differences. *Perceptual and Motor Skills, 37*, 31–34.

Maris, R. (1986). Basic issues in suicide prevention: Resolutions of liberty and love (the Dublin lecture). *Suicide and Life-Threatening Behavior, 16*, 326–334.

McGinnis, J. (1987). Suicide in America—moving up the public agenda. *Suicide and Life-Threatening Behavior, 18*, 18–32.

Parkes, C., & Weiss, R. (1983). *Physical and psychological responses to suicide in the family—recovery from bereavement.* New York: Basic Books.

Patsiokas, A., Blum, G., Luscomb, R. (1983). Cognitive characteristics of suicide attempters. *Journal of Consulting and Clinical Psychology, 47*, 478–484.

Quinnett, P. (1987). *Suicide the forever decision.* New York: Continuum Publishing.

Ramsay, T., & Bagley, C. (1985). The prevalence of suicidal behaviors, attitudes and associated social experiences in an urban population. *Suicide and Life-Threatening Behavior, 15*, 151–167.

Range, L., Bright, P., & Ginn, P. (1985). Public reactions to child suicide: Effects of age and method used. *Journal of Community Psychology, 113*, 288–294.

Range, L., & Calhoun, L. (1985, March). The impact of type of death on the bereavement experience. In L. G. Calhoun (Chair), *Bereavement: Clinical and social aspects.* Symposium conducted at the annual meeting of the Southeastern Psychological Association.

Range, L., Goggin, W., & Cantrell, P. (in press). The false consensus bias as applied to psychologically disturbed adolescents. *Adolescence.*

Range, L., McDonald, D., & Anderson, H. (1987). Factor structure of Calhoun's youth suicide

scale. *Journal of Personality Assessment, 51*, 262–266.

Range, L., & Thompson, K. (1986). Community responses following suicide, homicide and other deaths: The perspective of potential comforters. *Journal of Psychology, 121*, 193–198.

Rudestam, K. (1977). Physical and psychological responses to suicide in the family. *Journal of Consulting and Clinical Psychology, 45*, 162–170.

Rudestam, K., & Imbroll, D. (1983). Societal reactions to a child's death by suicide. *Journal of Consulting and Clinical Psychology, 51*, 461–462.

Sachs, A. (1990, November 28). To my family, my physician, my lawyer and all others whom it may concern. *Time*, p. 70.

Shepherd, T., & Barraclough, B. (1974). The aftermath of suicide. *British Medical Journal, 2*, 600–603.

Schneidman, E. S. (1972). Forward. In A. C. Cain (Ed.), *Survivors of suicide* (pp. ix–xi). Springfield, IL: Charles C. Thomas.

Siegel, K. (1988). Rational suicide. In S. Lesse (Ed.), *What we know about suicidal behavior and how to treat it* (pp. 85–102). Northvale, NJ: Jason Anderson.

Singh, B. (1979). Correlates of attitudes toward euthanasia. *Social Biology, 26*, 247–254.

Singh, B., Williams, J., & Ryther, B. (1986). Public approval of suicide: A situational analysis. *Suicide and Life-Threatening Behavior, 16*, 409–418.

Szasz, T. (1974). *The second sin.* London: Routledge and Kegan Paul.

Weber, W. (1988). What right to die? [Letter to the editor]. *Suicide and Life-Threatening Behavior, 18*, 181–188.

Wellman, M., & Wellman, R. J. (1986). Sex differences in peer responsiveness to suicide ideation. *Suicide and Life-Threatening Behavior, 16*, 360–378.

Whitis, P. (1972). The legacy of a child's suicide. In A. C. Cain (Ed.), *Survivors of suicide* (pp. 155–166). Springfield, IL: Charles C. Thomas.

Ellen Ingram, M.A., is a licensed psychological examiner. Jon Ellis, Ph.D., is a licensed clinical psychologist and assistant professor at East Tennessee State University.

ELISABETH KÜBLER-ROSS'S FINAL PASSAGE

Internationally renowned author of the groundbreaking 1969 book *On Death and Dying* Elisabeth Kübler-Ross transformed American attitudes toward death. Now the increasingly controversial guru, whose autobiography appears this month, wants nothing more than her own

BY LESLIE BENNETTS

The rutted roads meandering off into the Arizona desert are unmarked, but it's not hard to find Elisabeth Kübler-Ross's house: it's the one with the towering burlap tepee and the carved wooden totem pole in its scorched front yard. Overhead the sky is vast and cloudless: the sun is so bright that you are momentarily blinded by the sudden Stygian gloom as you step inside.

"Over here." The voice is weak, but it bristles with rage. It emanates from the darkest corner of an enormous, cluttered room, where the blinds are drawn and the only light is cast by a television flickering mutely. Crumpled in a reclining chair, buttoned up in a sweater despite the midday heat, Kübler-Ross regards her visitor with a baleful glare. How is she? "In constant pain," she snaps. How does she like Scottsdale? "I commute from here to the potty," she says, gesturing at the commode next to her chair. "For an active person like me to sit here 15 hours a day like a dummy—that's no pleasure. It's a useless existence. The only part of my body that functions is my brain." She has had several strokes in the last couples of years, and by now the 70-year-old Kübler-Ross is thoroughly fed up with her infirmities.

She fumbles for her Dunhills and lights a cigarette. "I tried to smoke myself to death, but it doesn't work," she says, scowling at me as if it were my fault.

I venture a question about why she sounds so mad. "Mad? That's not the word!" she exclaims. "I can't use a word that's strong enough. 'Frustrated' is too polite a word. 'Pissed' is a much better word. I'm *pissed!*"

A housekeeper offers me a cup of tea. "Just don't say to my health." Kübler-Ross warns. "To my quick transition—that's all I want."

Transition" is Kübler-Ross-speak for death, that final passage she has spent her entire professional life studying. For 30 years she has been internationally renowned as a pioneer in the field, the author of the groundbreaking 1969 book *On Death and Dying* and a slew of books that followed, the controversial guru who revolutionized the care of the terminally ill, who helped transform the medical profession's attitudes toward a once taboo subject, and who helped launch the hospice movement in America. She has shepherded thousands of patients through their transitions. But all she wants now is her own.

She knows exactly how it will be: the radiant light, the overwhelming feeling of peace and love, the spirit guides who will usher her into the next world, the transcendent knowledge. "I've been on the other side, and it's better than anything you can imagine," she says. "I don't have a shadow of a doubt."

With all that ahead of her, she is furious that she is being forced to wait. The primary objects of her wrath are her spirit guides, or "my spooks," as she calls them—those mysterious entities who guided her for so long. She won't even talk to them anymore.

"I'm on strike," she snarls. "They let me down. They're supposed to help you, and they don't help me. You're not supposed to know the time of your death; they keep it a top secret. I've asked about a thousand times, but they just don't answer it. All the languages I used to speak. I collected all the worst curse words, and I call them those names. Anybody who knows a language I don't know, I ask them for the strongest curse words. But it doesn't help. I don't know what they have up their sleeve."

From *Vanity Fair,* June 1997, pp. 70, 75-77, 80, 82, 89. Copyright © 1997 with permission of the author, Leslie Bennetts.

It's unwise to propose a more peaceful acceptance of her situation. "I'm not a person for resignation," she says ferociously. " 'Surrender' and 'resignation' don't exist in my vocabulary. Not me! Like the saints–they make me *sick!*" She spits out the word as if it were a scorpion. "All this meek surrender—to me that's nauseating!"

Nor is suicide an option, since she believes in reincarnation. "The thought crossed my mind so many times, but if you end your life before the right time, you have to come back and learn all the lessons

> ## " 'Surrender' and 'resignation' don't exist in my vocabulary. Like the saints— they make me *sick!*"

you didn't learn," she explains grumpily. "I'm not going to ruin my chance to be able to stay there. I don't have another life. I'm not coming back. That's it! I've asked my spooks many times. They said that I'm done with my work."

She stares into space, as if gazing at something I cannot see. Dark and unblinking, her eyes blaze fiercely in her leathery old face, fathomless as those of an ancient sea turtle. Is she really so unafraid of death?

"I'm looking forward to it," she says, her brusque tone softening. "Every night I think: Maybe tonight."

She tilts her face upward, as if to receive a blessing, or a caress. And for the briefest of moments, she smiles. She is not smiling at me.

It was the spooks that really did it. A tiny Swiss-born firebrand, Kübler-Ross had always been controversial; way back in the 1960s, when she started lecturing the medical profession about all the things it was doing wrong, the combination of her abrasive personality and her unwelcome message—that doctors and nurses were routinely failing their terminally ill patients by not helping them come to terms with death—meant that Kübler-Ross was not going to win any popularity contests.

But her work quickly earned her a worldwide reputation. Her books have sold millions of copies and have been translated into 20 languages, from Catalan to Serbo-Croatian; her most influential ideas have helped transform medicine. Kübler-Ross's description of the so-called stages of dy-

ing—the progression of a patient's coping mechanisms from denial and isolation through anger, bargaining with God, depression, and finally acceptance of the inevitable–provided a framework for treatment that endures to this day. Some researchers have questioned Kübler-Ross's model, troubled by how schematic and absolute it seems amid the messy human realities of living and dying, when emotions rarely conform so neatly to discrete categories. But until Kübler-Ross, no one was even talking about such issues, and even her critics acknowledge that her contribution in beginning the debate was invaluable.

Her personal style offended many. For her admirers, her certainty was inspirational and her charisma indisputable. "The room was packed, and within five minutes, this diminutive, tired-looking woman, with a heavy Germanic accent and a first appearance of extreme toughness, had transfixed the audience," reported a *Playboy* interviewer who heard Kübler-Ross speak 17 years ago. "What shone through her and hypnotized more than 500 people was her compassion, her deep vulnerability and her love of human beings. There was not a dry eye in the house, and my friend and I agreed that Elisabeth was the most powerful speaker we had ever heard."

But to her detractors, Kübler-Ross seemed arrogant if not downright insufferable. She didn't care; she was a woman with a mission, and she has never let anything— from philosophical opposition to actual attempts on her life—stand in her way.

For a long time Kübler-Ross—a physician, after all, an experienced psychiatrist with Establishment credentials—was accepted by the scientific community. Then she went public with her belief in the spirit world, and by the late 1970s she had started talking about her own spooks—the muscular, stoic-looking Indian who confirmed that she had lived a previous life as a Native American in the Southwest; "Salem," the tall figure in a turban and a flowing robe who took her back to the time of Jesus, when, he claimed, Kübler-Ross was a respected teacher named Isabel; "Pedro" and "Willie" and "Mario" and a host of others she described with great enthusiasm in her books and lectures.

> ## The primary objects of her wrath are her spirit guides, or "my spooks," as she calls them.

Such startling assertions polarized opinion for good. The more conservative elements in the medical establishment dismissed her as a kook, while at the opposite end of the spectrum many New Age aficionados came to regard Kübler-Ross as a visionary. Go to any bookstore and check out the death-and-dying section; it will be full of books that invoke her name and credit her with inspiring a whole genre.

The debate is likely to resurface this month with the publication of Kübler-Ross's autobiography, *The Wheel of Life,* which is being billed as her final statement. To her acolytes, the story of her life is already familiar; key anecdotes have been repeated again and again. Until she was incapacitated, Kübler-Ross traveled more than 250,000 miles a year, leading workshops and speaking; her lectures drew 15,000 people a week, and she received a quarter of a million letters a year. But even her most faithful devotees will find some surprises: the book reveals a few juicy details Kübler-Ross kept private until now— such as the exact nature of the message her beloved ex-husband, a Jew who didn't believe in an afterlife, allegedly sent her from the spirit world after he died.

To Kübler-Ross, these events are a matter of course; when others question her claims, they receive only a dismissive shrug. "My mother has no doubt," says her son, Ken Ross, a photographer who lives in Phoenix. "That's what makes her a leader in her field."

She may be small, but she has always been formidable. Back in her native Switzerland, her very birth was cause for consternation. Her parents had been expecting a child, of course, but when the unprepossessing Elisabeth appeared, weighing scarcely two pounds, she was the firstborn of triplets. No one thought she would survive, let alone rebel.

I was supposed to have been a nice, churchgoing Swiss housewife," she remarks dryly at the beginning of her autobiography. But she dreamed of becoming a physician—a goal her tyrannical father, a bureaucrat at a Zurich office-supply company, refused to support. When she was in the sixth grade, he decreed her fate: "You will work in my office. I need an efficient and intelligent secretary."

Horrified, Elisabeth commenced her lifelong pattern of bucking authority whenever it got in the way of her plans. When she finished school and wouldn't go to work for her father, he threw her out of the house. She spent years working as a laboratory assistant before managing to get through medical school.

In the meantime, she had already begun her career as a humanitarian; when World War II ended, she took repeated leaves of absence from various jobs to do volunteer work throughout war-ravaged Europe. While working in Poland, she traveled to Maidanek, a Nazi concentration camp where hundreds of thousands of people had been murdered. In the barracks, prisoners had carved their names and drawings with their fingernails. Kübler saw one symbol repeated over and over: there were butterflies everywhere. It would be a quarter of a century before she understood why.

After she became a physician and married Emanuel Ross, an American neuropathologist, they moved to New York. Following two miscarriages, Elisabeth had her son, two more miscarriages, and then her daughter, Barbara. At the hospital where she worked, Kübler-Ross found herself increasingly appalled by the standard treatment of dying patients. "They were shunned and abused," she writes in her book. "Nobody was honest with them." Unlike her colleagues, she made it a point to sit with terminal patients, listening as they poured out their hearts to her.

At the University of Colorado, Kübler-Ross began giving lectures featuring dying patients who talked about what they were going through—thereby forcing other physicians and students to hear them. By the time the Rosses moved to Chicago, Elisabeth's lectures were attracting standing-room-only audiences. Many of the other doctors were furious, particularly after *On Death and Dying* made Kübler-Ross an international celebrity, but her determination never faltered. "My goal was to break through the layer of professional denial that prohibited the patients from airing their innermost concerns," she writes.

Kübler-Ross came to believe that people often clung to life long after they were "supposed" to die because they had unfinished business. When given the opportunity to make amends, to say the necessary good-byes, to make appropriate arrangements for survivors, they were able to relax and die a peaceful death, even a joyful one. While Kübler-Ross's prescriptions seem simple—listen to your patients, learn what their concerns are and help to address them—their impact was revolutionary. To her grateful patients and their families, she was revered as a virtual saint.

Having sat by the bedsides of thousands of dying men, women, and children, Kübler-Ross was also struck by how many of them saw visions of spirits who appeared to them in their final moments. Usually these were perceived as the spirits of departed loved ones who had come to help guide the dying person out of earthly life. These visions brought great peace to the dying, and some consolation to family members. Pondering the peculiar serenity of the dying, Kübler-Ross suddenly realized the meaning of the butterflies she had seen scratched into the walls at Maidanek so many years earlier. "Those prisoners were like my dying patients and aware of what was going to happen," she explains in *The Wheel of Life*. "Once dead, they would be out of that hellish place. . . . Soon they would leave their bodies like a butterfly leaves its cocoon. And I realized that was the message they wanted to leave for future generations. It also provided the imagery that I would use for the rest of my career to explain the process of death and dying."

Among Kübler-Ross's patients was a terminally ill woman named Mrs. Schwartz. She had been pronounced dead, but hours later, a nurse found that Mrs. Schwartz not only had come back to life but was able to repeat conversations and a joke one doctor had told while she was clinically dead. After Mrs. Schwartz spoke about this at a lecture, the students insisted the whole thing must have been a hallucination. Kübler-Ross wasn't so sure. "If I blew a dog whistle right now, none of us would hear it," she pointed out. "But every dog would. Does that mean it doesn't exist?"

Kübler-Ross began to interview patients who had been revived after the cessation of their vital signs. She also decided she was going to stop giving death-and-dying seminars, and to quit her job at the hospital where she was then working. As she prepared to resign, Mrs. Schwartz, who had finally died 10 months earlier, materialized to tell Kübler-Ross "not to give up your work on death and dying. . . . Do you hear me? Your work has just begun. We will help you." Even the unflappable Kübler-Ross was disconcerted, although she did manage to ask Mrs. Schwartz to scribble a note with earthly pen on paper before she vanished.

Kübler-Ross and her associates went on to interview 20,000 people about their near-death experiences. From Muslims to Eskimos, 2 years old to 99, they all seemed to report virtually the same thing. "Up till then I had absolutely no belief in an afterlife, but the data convinced me that these were not coincidences or hallucinations," Kübler-Ross reports in her book. "These remarkable findings led to an even more remarkable scientific conclusion that death did not exist—not in its traditional definition. I felt any new definition had to go beyond the death of the physical body."

Over the years, she too had several out-of-body experiences, including two near-death events (one because of a bowel obstruction and another due to cardiac fibrillation). "They were all good; they were all different," she tells me. "They have the same common denominator: the light, the peace, the love—more than anything you ever experienced in this lifetime. A totally different kind of love. What we call love is for the birds. 'I love you if you buy me a mink coat.' Pfffft." She waves her hand with eloquent contempt.

At least one of her otherworldly experiences was also terrifying. During one endless night of agony, she felt she was reliving the deaths of all her patients—but after re-experiencing their pain and fear, she emerged into what she calls cosmic consciousness, a state of grace that was temporary but life-altering. Such incidents persuaded her to reconsider her own attitude toward paranormal phenomena. "As I have learned since then, if you are not ready for mystical experiences, you will never believe them," she writes in her book. "But if you are open, then you not only have them, and believe in them; people can hang you by your thumbnails and you will know that they are absolutely real."

Unfortunately, Kübler-Ross's growing openness soon led her into the most ignominious chapter of her life. According to her book, in early 1976 she was contacted by a San Diego couple who promised to introduce her to spiritual entities. A high-school dropout and former sharecropper who had recently founded his own "Church of the Facet of Divinity," Jay Barham had developed a following based on his alleged ability to channel spirits. To Kübler-Ross's delight, he proceeded to do so for her; during her very first session, a spirit guide led her back a couple of thousand years, and she spent a most enjoyable afternoon sitting on a hillside, listening to Jesus preach to a group of people.

Kübler-Ross's husband was appalled. "How can you believe that garbage?" Ross demanded. "Barham is taking advantage of you!"

A spirit guide led Kübler-Ross back a couple of thousand years and she listened to Jesus preach.

When Ross abruptly asked for a divorce, on Father's Day, his wife was dumbfounded. They had been married 21 years, and she never got over his departure. But then Salem asked her to come out to San Diego and establish her own healing center on a mountain-top. Soon she was leading weeklong death-and-transition workshops at which Barham was the featured attraction. When visitors grew suspicious and challenged his ability to conjure up spirits, Barham issued a stern warning: If anyone turned on the lights while he was channeling, that person risked harming the spirits as well as Barham himself. (One woman, a friend of Kubler-Ross's, did so anyway—and there stood Barham, stark naked, wearing a turban.)

Ignoring a growing chorus of rumors about strange sexual goings-on, Kubler-Ross continued to describe Barham as "the greatest healer the world has ever known." Even after the San Diego district attorney's office launched an investigation of the alleged sexual abuse of a 10-year-old child by a "spirit entity" who may or may not have been Barham in disguise, setting off a firestorm of negative publicity, Kubler-Ross maintained her belief in his integrity. (No formal charges were ever filed.) Two years later, in a 1981 *Playboy* interview, she was still insisting that she had never witnessed any sexual activity and that the naysayers were trying to destroy Barham.

Kubler-Ross also vowed that if she were ever to discover that Barham was a phony she would have to commit suicide. The realization was apparently slow in dawning, and it failed to inspire such drastic action, but there is no question today that Kubler-Ross has reluctantly accepted the idea that she was deceived and exploited. She hates talking about Barham: "I don't want to give him any publicity!" But on the second day of my visit, she launches into a tirade about his alleged transgressions. "He was a dangerous man," she says grimly.

Barham moved to Honolulu in 1986, and he describes himself as retired. "I just play on the beach and enjoy the lovely bikinis," he tells me when I reach him by telephone. His wife is working as a marriage and family therapist, he adds. When I ask him about Kubler-Ross, Barham chuckles. "She's a great woman," he says. "Isabel—that's what I called her when I worked with her—she's real neat. She is a genius, and I enjoyed the five years I worked with her very much." As for Kubler-Ross's various accusations, he adds, "I have no need to defend myself. I have done nothing in my life that I regret, or that has ever harmed anybody—physically, verbally, or emotionally."

Then his tone changes. He is not going to continue our conversation unless I give him a "whole lot of money," he says. "You get on a plane and bring $40,000 in cash,

and we'll talk all you want." When I tell him that *Vanity Fair* doesn't pay for news or interviews, he says it's been nice talking with me. "You take care of yourself, now," he adds, a distinct note of menace in his voice. Then he hangs up. The next day he calls back, threatening to sue if *Vanity Fair* prints Kubler-Ross's charges against him.

When Kubler-Ross's San Diego house burned to the ground, investigators suspected arson; although no charges were ever filed. Kubler-Ross broke with Barham and has not been in touch with him since. Next, Kubler-Ross bought a 300-acre farm in the Shenandoah Valley, where she moved in 1984, hoping to set up a center for AIDS babies. Her plan set off a hysterical wave of local opposition that included not only protests, petitions, and town meetings to denounce Kubler-Ross but an escalating pattern of harassment, including burglaries and vandalism. Although she continued to live in Virginia for years, celebrating the official grand opening of the Elisabeth Kubler-Ross Center in 1990, eventually that chapter of her life ended in an eerie recapitulation of her experience in California. One night in 1994, as she was preparing to adopt 20 babies with AIDS, Kubler-Ross returned to Virginia from a trip to Baltimore and found her house in flames. All her possessions were destroyed, from family pictures and her father's diaries to hundreds of thousands of pages of research notes and documentation. Even her pet llama had been shot. Once again, arson was suspected, but no charges were ever filed—even though a local man was rumored to have bragged publicly

> **A patient not only had come back to life but was able to repeat a joke one doctor had told while she was clinically dead.**

about having incinerated Kubler-Ross's house. "My county would never have put him in jail," she says. "They were happy somebody did it."

At this point Kubler-Ross's son whisked her off to Arizona. "He was afraid they were going to shoot me next," she says. Safely ensconced in Scottsdale, she promptly had a massive stroke.

Kubler-Ross has achieved a bizarre equanimity about her horrendous losses. She

has been betrayed; she shrugs. "Things always work out the way they have to." Two houses burned to the ground, everything she owned lost forever: no matter. "It was a blessing," she says. "I never even had to pack."

Many leaders are controversial, but only a few arouse passions violent enough to provoke attempted murder. Some people appear to thrive on conflict, even to relish it: but with Kubler-Ross it seems more an incidental by-product of her single-mindedness. When she wants to accomplish something, she simply has no interest in other people's objections.

When I ask if even her mistakes had meaning, she gives me a withering look. "Naturally," she says with contempt, as if I were a moron even to ask. "You have to be true to yourself, and that's one thing I have been all my life."

Even the Barham episode has been assimilated. "If I had it to do over again, I would still do it, because I learned a lot." Kubler-Ross says (although she later makes it clear to me that this enlightenment came through the spirits, not Barham).

Nowadays she spends most of her time alone, fending for herself; her housekeeper comes only three days a week. Although Ken lives in Phoenix, he travels constantly, and Barbara, a psychologist, lives in Seattle. But Kubler-Ross isn't quite as isolated as she seems: as her guest book attests. Shirley MacLaine had visited two days before I arrived, inscribing her entry in the book "To darling Elisabeth . . ." Kubler-Ross numbers a vast assortment of other notables among her acquaintances. When she dies, she wants to have 1,000 balloons with the image of E. T. imprinted on them released into the sky, to celebrate, (Why E. T.? "Because I loved him," she says.) When she was told she couldn't do that, because of copyright issues, she called up Steven Spielberg, she says, and got his permission. She spends her days surrounded by photographs of her family, a large picture of herself with Mother Teresa, and images of E. T. and angels and Jesus and the Virgin Mary; she seems to be on intimate speaking terms with all of them.

She wastes no time worrying about what history will make of her. The verdict is likely to be quite mixed. On one hand, Kubler-Ross is full of apocalyptic predictions, including one about an imminent natural cataclysm that will wipe out California and New York, among other places, and be followed by a period of enlightened earthly consciousness. On the other hand, even Kubler-Ross's harshest critics acknowledge her extraordinary legacy. A couple of years ago Dr. Samuel Klagsbrun, a clinical professor of psychiatry at Albert Einstein College of Medicine and one of the three physicians who brought a suit against New York State to decriminalize physician-assisted suicide, raised eyebrows by telling *The New York Times* that Kübler-Ross was destroying her life's work with her more outlandish proclamations. But he certainly doesn't deny her contribution.

"She is an enormously important pioneer in this area; I can't overemphasize how important," Klagsbrun tells me. "She put the subject on the map. . . . She identified the stages of dying in a way that made it less scary and more manageable. And she targeted the medical profession as having to change its approach and attitudes. Death became something you could talk about, anticipate, and deal with."

Kübler-Ross also played a crucial role in establishing alternatives to hospitals. "She had a tremendous influence on the hospice movement," says Florence Wald, a founding member of the Connecticut Hospice and former dean of the Yale University School of Nursing. "Doctors and nurses had been simply avoiding the problem of death, and focusing on patients who could get better. We have this tendency in medicine to be very academic, and to look at things as a scientist would. Elisabeth just took another path, which relied very much on her ability to capture an audience. She's almost a preacher."

To the less scientifically inclined, Kübler-Ross is practically a goddess. "She is a heroine of mine," says Betty Eadie, who credits Kübler-Ross with moving her to write her own best-selling account of a near-death experience, *Embraced by the Light,* as well as her subsequent best-seller, *The Awakening Heart.*

"She gave me the strength to do what I knew I had to do. She's one of the leaders who were sent here on Earth to make a difference, who were developed by God for a purpose," Eadie explains.

While Kübler-Ross's more mystically oriented admirers see her as a courageous voyager into the beyond, other observers offer psychiatric explanations for her long drift toward the supernatural. Klagsbrun sees it as a result of the years Kübler-Ross spent at the bedsides of the dying, particularly those of thousands of doomed children. "It's not unknown for people who delve into this area to find themselves needing to soothe their losses by moving more and more toward a spiritual way of life," he observes. "Her psychological need to deny what she was experiencing, which was repeated losses, may have led her to escape those losses by turning to a denial of the losses. It's a way to undo the pain. She's an extreme example of burnout. I think that's sad. There are real

consequences to not dealing with loss: you don't grow."

Dr. Sherwin Nuland, the surgeon whose best-seller, *How We Die,* won the 1994 National Book Award for nonfiction, views Kübler-Ross's philosophical evolution in terms of her own denial of death. "Like all the rest of us, she is having difficulty with the concept of the end of her consciousness," he suggests. "That's the rea-

> **During one endless night of agony, Kübler-Ross felt she was reliving the deaths of all her patients. She emerged into what she calls cosmic consciousness, a state of grace.**

son we have invented the afterlife. We all clothe our thinking in philosophical terminology, but inside we're scared as hell and quaking in our shoes. She is no longer using the objectivity and rational thinking of a lifetime; she is creating a scenario that reassures her. I think she is guilty of magical thinking. I believe it's an extreme form of narcissistic self-absorption, where she finds it necessary to think she will be preserved. What she has done is create a belief system that defuses the terror of death."

When you ask doctors like Klagsbrun and Nuland how they explain near-death experiences, they talk about physiological factors like oxygen deprivation to the brain. But those who have actually done clinical research claim that that explanation doesn't hold up. "A lot of medical professionals speak glibly, but don't really know what's in the literature," says Dr. Melvin Morse, a Seattle pediatrician whose own work prompted him to write the best-seller *Closer to the Light.* "There are dozens of studies of lack of oxygen to the brain that don't cause these kinds of experiences. People who are skeptical of near-death experiences are invariably people who are not keeping up. They don't know what's been published in the last 10 years."

Although Kübler-Ross's detractors often cite her own failure to publish her findings in scientific journals, Morse shrugs off such

technicalities. "It's true that Kübler-Ross hasn't published a lot of rigorous scientific studies; she's just reached her own conclusions through thousands of interviews," he acknowledges. "But she's a giant in the field of near-death research. I might have been a little more scientific and systematic about it, but there's very little in my own research that she didn't anticipate. Fifty years from now, no one will know who her critics were, and Elisabeth Kübler-Ross will be a brighter light than ever."

Of course, from a purely objective standpoint, Kübler-Ross's belief in spirit guides is no more fantastical than a Hindu's belief in reincarnation, or a Christian's belief that Jesus was the son of God and was resurrected after his physical demise. At base, every belief system is predicated on faith, as is the scientific rationalist's conviction that there is no afterlife; since no one really knows for sure, even the nonbeliever is ultimately making a choice based on belief rather than verifiable empirical evidence. And as Kübler-Ross's friends point out, humankind has been grappling with such issues for millennia. "The real question at issue here is the mind-body problem," notes Dr. Raymond Moody, author of *Life After Life,* a pioneering study of near-death experiences. "After 2,500 years, Western civilization hasn't gotten any closer to the question of how consciousness is related to material substance. This is a chronically unresolvable controversy."

Kübler-Ross is well aware that her detractors think she's out of her mind; that's their problem. Puffing on her cigarette, she gives me a sly glance. "They'll know soon enough," she says calmly.

On my final visit to Kübler-Ross, I notice as I drive out into the desert that all the place names along the way are upbeat: from Paradise Road and Happy Valley to the Carefree Cactus Garden, they constitute a powerful testimonial to the relentless retirement-community optimism of Arizona. But farther out, the street signs dwindle, and when I come to Kübler-Ross's road, it is marked simply "No Outlet."

Her low adobe house is set in a broad, flat desert plain surrounded by barren mountains heaped with jumbles of bleached rock. From an airplane, the desiccated land looks monochromatic and cracked, driven everywhere with deep fissures. As I share another cup of tea with Kübler-Ross, I realize how much the landscape resembles her own sand-colored face: ravaged by time, carved into creases and canyons like the wrinkles of the earth's own skin, itself a silent testimonial to eons of upheaval.

Outside, in the gathering twilight, coyotes prowl through the underbrush, their eyes hungry and wolfish. The sun is setting, and the wind chimes stir, sending a faint tinkling music through the air, like cowbells from a faraway Alpine meadow.

> When Kübler-Ross dies, she wants to have a thousand balloons with the image of E. T. imprinted on them released into the sky.

Once in a while a mountain lion materializes in the dusty driveway. This parched land seems a strange place for a Swiss girl to end her days, so far from the verdant valleys and flower-strewn mountain passes of her childhood. No matter; she will see them again soon enough. In her dreams her "transition" looks just like Switzerland.

She has all sorts of plans. She wants to chat with Jung, and Gandhi; it would be nice to visit with her childhood idol, Marie Curie, as well. And despite all her years of traveling around the world, she never made it to Nepal, Guatemala, or Peru. "I'll have to go after I make my transition," she says, as if this were merely a matter of speaking to her travel agent.

There may be other planets that need help, as well. "I think I had my share of Earth," she says with a distinct note of sourness.

And then there is Manny. She still considers him her husband: "I'm a one-man woman," she says, shrugging, as if his 10-year marriage to his second wife (whom Kübler-Ross refers to as "that lulu"), with whom he had a child, were an unfortunate momentary error. "I think once you get married, it's forever."

When Manny's heart began to fail, Kübler-Ross rented a condominium for him in Scottsdale; leaving his wife and child in Chicago, he moved to Arizona, where Ken and Elisabeth took care of him. The last time she saw him, Elisabeth made him promise that if she was right about life after death, he would send her some kind of signal from the beyond.

Manny died that afternoon. At the funeral in Chicago, it was snowing heavily, and Elisabeth noticed dozens of roses strewn in the snow around the grave site. She gathered them up and gave one to Barbara, who started to laugh—and then made a confession. When she was 10 years old, her father and mother had been arguing about Elisabeth's views on the afterlife, and Manny had promised Barbara that when he died, there would be red roses blooming in the snow if Elisabeth turned out to be right.

The night Manny died, Barbara had come home to find a dozen longstemmed roses on her doorstep. It had been snowing in Seattle for hours, and the roses were buried up to their buds in snow. Barbara knew instantly that her father was dead, but she didn't tell her mother about their agreement until the signal reappeared at the funeral in Chicago.

Elisabeth, of course, was ecstatic. Now she knows for sure that he is waiting for her. "I told Manny already: he better get ready for dancing in the galaxies. I'm going to drag him along," she reports, smiling as if she could already hear the music.

"I'm going to dance in all the galaxies," she says dreamily. "Just dance."

Unit 5

Key Points to Consider

❖ Describe how the funeralization process can assist in coping with grief and facilitate the bereavement process. Distinguish between grief, bereavement, and funeralization.

❖ Discuss the psychological, sociological, and theological/philosophical aspects of the funeralization process. How do each of these aspects facilitate the resolution of grief?

❖ Describe and compare each of the following processes: burial, cremation, cryonics, and body donation for medical research. What would be your choice for final disposition of your body? Why would you choose this method, and what effects might this choice have upon your survivors (if any)? Would you have the same or different preferences for a close loved one such as a spouse, child, or parent? Why or why not?

 **Links** **www.dushkin.com/online/**

These sites are annotated on pages 4 and 5.

Decisions relating to the disposition of the body after death often involve feelings of ambivalence—on one hand, attachments to the deceased might cause one to be reluctant to dispose of the body, on the other hand, practical considerations make the disposal of the body necessary. Funerals or memorial services provide methods for disposing of a dead body, remembering the deceased, and helping survivors accept the reality of death. They are also public rites of passage that assist the bereaved in returning to routine patterns of social interaction. In contemporary America, 79 percent of deaths involve earth burial and 21 percent involve cremation. These public behaviors, along with the private process of grieving, comprise the two components of the bereavement process.

This unit on the contemporary American funeral begins with a general article on the nature and functions of public bereavement behavior by Michael Leming and George Dickinson. Leming and Dickinson provide an overview of the present practice of funeralization in American society, including traditional and alternative funeral

arrangements. They also discuss the functions of funerals relative to the sociological, psychological, and theological needs of adults and children.

In the next article, "Psychocultural Influences on African-American Attitudes Towards Death, Dying and Funeral Rites," Ronald Barrett puts death and dying rituals within a pluralistic and multicultural perspective. Then, "How Different Religions Pay Their Final Respects," by William Whalen, discusses commonalities and differences among many religious traditions.

"Cemeteries of the Rich and Famous" suggests that touring cemeteries can make for an interesting experience and introduces the reader to a few famous American cemeteries. The next article, Linda Goldman's "We Can Help Children to Grieve: A Child-Oriented Model or Memorializing," discusses two methods for aiding children in expressing their grief and assisting them in the process of memorializing.

The remaining two articles by Cynthia Fox ("A Do-It-Yourself Funeral") and Pat Andrus ("A Time to Mourn") conclude this unit by discussing new trends in funeral rituals and services for the bereaved.

Funerals and Burial Rites

The Contemporary American Funeral

Michael R. Leming
St. Olaf College

George E. Dickinson
College of Charleston

Most people use the words *death, grief,* and *bereavement* imprecisely, which can lead to difficulty in communication. The words are closely interrelated, but each has a specific content or meaning. As discussed in chapter 1, death is that point in time when life ceases to exist. *Death* is an event. It can be attached to a certain day, hour, and minute. *Grief* is an emotion, a very powerful emotion. It is triggered or stimulated by death. Although one can have anticipatory grief prior to the death of a significant other, grief is an emotional response to death. *Bereavement* is the state of having lost a significant other to death. Alternative processes—such as denial, avoidance, and defiance—have been shown by psychologists and psychiatrists to be only aberrations of the grief process and, as such, are not viable means of grief resolution.

The decisions about ultimate method of final **disposition** of the body should be determined by the persons in bereavement. Those charged with these decisions will be guided by their personal values and by the norms of the culture in which they live.

With over three fourths of American deaths occurring in hospitals or other institutions for the care of the sick and infirm, the contemporary process of body disposition begins at the time of death when the body is removed from the institutional setting. Most frequently the body is taken to a funeral home. There, the body is bathed, embalmed, and dressed. It is then placed into a casket selected by the family. Typically, arrangements are made for the ceremony, assuming that a ceremony is to follow. The funeral director, in consultation with the family, will determine the type, time, place and day of the ceremony. In most instances, the ceremony will have a religious content (Pine, 1971). The procedure just described is followed in approximately 75 percent of funerals. Alternatives to this procedure will be examined later in this chapter.

Following this ceremony, final disposition of the body is made by either earth burial (79 percent) or cremation (21 percent). (These percentages are approximate national averages and will vary by region.) The bereavement process will then be followed by a period of post-funeral adjustment for the family.

HOW THE FUNERAL MEETS THE NEEDS OF THE BEREAVED

Paul Irion (1956) has described the following needs of the bereaved: reality, expression of grief, social support, and meaningful context for the death. For Irion, the funeral is an experience of significant personal value insofar as it meets the religious, social, and psychological needs of the mourners. Each of these must be met for bereaved individuals to return to everyday living and, in the process, resolve their grief.

The *psychological* focus of the funeral is based on the fact that grief is an emotion. Edgar Jackson (1963) has indicated that grief is the other side of the coin of love. He contends that if a person has never loved the deceased—never had an emotional investment of some type and degree—he or she will not grieve upon death. Evidence of this can easily be demonstrated by the number of deaths that we hear, see, or read about daily that do not have an impact on us unless we have some kind of emotional involvement with those deceased persons. We can read of 78 deaths in a plane crash and not grieve over any of them unless we personally knew the individuals killed. Exceptions to the preceding might include the death of a celebrity or other public figure, when people experience a sense of grief even though there has never been any personal contact.

In his original work on the symptomatology of grief, Erich Lindemann (1944) stressed this concept of grief and its importance as a step in the resolution of grief. He defines how the emotion of grief must support the reality and finality of death. As long as the finality of death is avoided, Lindemann believes, grief resolution is impeded. For this reason, he strongly recommends that the bereaved persons view the dead. When the living confront the dead, all of the intellectualization and avoidance techniques break down. When we can say, "He or she is dead, I am alone, and from this day forward my life will be forever different," we have broken through the devices of denial and avoidance and have accepted the reality of death. It is only at this point that we can begin to withdraw the emotional capital that we have invested in the deceased and seek to create new relationships with the living.

On the other hand, viewing the corpse can be very traumatic for some. Most people are not accustomed to seeing a cold body and a significant other stretched out with eyes closed. Indeed, for some this scene may remain in their memories for a life-time. Thus, they remember the cold corpse, not the warm, responsive person. Whether or not to view the body is not a cut-and-dried decision. Many factors should be taken into account when this decision is made.

Grief resolution is especially important for family members, but others are affected also—the neighbors, the business community in some instances, the religious community in most instances, the health care community, and the circle of friends and associates (many of whom may be unknown to the family). All of these groups will grieve to some extent the death of their relationship with the deceased. Thus, many people are affected by the death. These affected persons will seek not only a means of expressing their grief over the death, but also a network of support to help cope with their grief.

Sociologically, the funeral is a social event that brings the chief mourners and the members of society into a confrontation with death. The funeral becomes a vehicle to bring persons of all walks of life and degrees of relationship to the deceased together for expression and support. It is for this reason that in our contemporary culture the funeral becomes an occasion to which no one is invited but to which all may come. This was not always the case, and some cultures make the funeral ceremony an "invitation only" experience. It is perhaps for this reason that private funerals (restricted to the family or a special list of persons) have all but disappeared in our culture. (The possible exception to this statement is a funeral for a celebrity—where participation by the public is limited to media coverage.)

At a time when emotions are strong, it is important that human interaction and social support become high priorities. A funeral can provide this atmosphere. To grieve alone can be devastating because it becomes necessary for that lone person to absorb all of the feelings into himself or herself. It has often been said that "joy shared is joy increased"; surely grief shared is grief diminished. People need each other at times when they have intense emotional experiences.

A funeral is in essence a onetime kind of "support group" to undergird and support those grieving persons. A funeral provides a conducive social environment for mourning. We may go to the funeral home either to visit with the bereaved or to work through our own grief.

Most of us have had the experience of finding it difficult to discuss a death with a member of the family. We seek the proper atmosphere, time, and place. It is during the funeral, the wake, the shivah, or the visitation with the bereaved that we are provided with the opportunity to express our condolences and sympathy comfortably.

Anger and guilt are often deeply felt at the time of death and will surface in words and actions. They are permitted within the funeral atmosphere as honest and candid expressions of grief, whereas at other times they might bring criticism and reprimand. The funeral atmosphere says in essence, "You are okay, I am okay; we have some strong feelings, and now is the time to express and share them for the benefit of all." Silence, talking, feeling, touching, and all means of sharing can be expressed without the fear of their being inappropriate.

Another function of the funeral is to provide a *theological* or *philosophical* perspective to facilitate grieving and to provide a context of meaning in which to place one of life's most significant experiences. For the majority of Americans, the funeral is a religious rite or ceremony (Pine, 1971). Those grievers who do not possess a religious creed or orientation will define or express death in the context of the values that the deceased and the grievers find important. Theologically or philosophically, the funeral functions as an attempt to bring meaning to the death and life of the deceased individual. For the religiously oriented person, the belief system will perhaps bring an understanding of the afterlife. Others may see only the end of biological life and the beginning of symbolic immortality created by the effects of one's life on the lives of others. The funeral should be planned to give meaning to whichever value context is significant for the bereaved.

"Why?" is one of the most often asked questions upon the moment of death or upon being told that someone we know has died. Though the funeral cannot provide the final answer to this question, it can place death within a context of meaning that is significant to those who mourn. If it is religious in context, the theology, creed, and articles of faith confessed by the mourners will give them comfort and assurance as to the meaning of death. Others who have developed a personally meaningful philosophy of life and death will seek to place the death in that philosophical context.

Cultural expectations typically require that we dispose of the dead with ceremony and dignity. The funeral can also ascribe importance to the remains of the dead.

THE NEEDS OF CHILDREN AND THEIR ATTENDANCE AT FUNERALS

For children, as well as for their elders, the funeral ceremony can be an experience of value and significance. At a very early age, children are interested in any type of family reunion, party, or celebration. To be excluded from the funeral may create questions and doubts in the minds of children as to why they are not permitted to be a part of an important family activity.

Another question to be considered when denying the child an opportunity to participate in postdeath activities is what goes through the child's mind when such participation is denied. Children deal with other difficult situations in life, and when denied this opportunity, many will fantasize. Research suggests that these fantasies may be negative, destructive, and at times more traumatic than the situation from which the children are excluded.

Children also should not be excluded from activities prior to the funeral service. They should be permitted to attend the visitation, wake, or shivah. (In some situations it would be wise to permit children to confront the deceased prior to the public visitation.) It is obvious that children should not be forced into this type of confrontation, but, by the same token, children who are curious and desire to be involved should not be denied the opportunity.

Children will react at their own emotional levels, and the questions that they ask will usually be asked at their level of comprehension. Two important rules to follow: Never lie to the child, and do not overanswer the child's question.

At the time of the funeral, parents have two concerns about their child's behavior at funerals. The first concern is that the child will have difficulty observing the grief of others—particularly if the child has never seen an adult loved one cry. The second concern is that parents themselves become confused when the child's emotional reactions may be different than their own. If the child is told of a death and responds by saying, "Oh, can I go out and play?" the parents may interpret this as denial or as a suppressed negative reaction to the death. Such a reaction can increase emotional concern by the parents. However, if the child's response is viewed as only a first reaction, and if the child is provided with loving, caring, and supportive attention, the child will ordinarily progress into an emotional resolution of the death.

The final reasons for involving children in postdeath activities are related to the strength and support that children give other grievers. They often provide positive evidence of the fact that life goes on. In other instances, because they have been an important part of the life of the deceased, their presence is symbolic testimony to the immortality of the deceased. Furthermore, it is not at all unusual for children to change the atmosphere surrounding bereavement from one of depression and sadness to one of laughter, verbalization, and celebration. Many times children do this by their normal behavior, without any understanding of the kind of contribution being made.

Psychocultural Influences on African-American Attitudes towards Death, Dying and Funeral Rites

Ronald K. Barrett

• • •

THE AMERICAN FUNERAL RITES

An historical and retrospective look at the American funeralization process over a four-hundred-year period reveals a number of changes and evolving traditions, demonstrating causality and coincidence in the evolution of the contemporary American funeral industry [24]. In the early years of our country the abundance of lumber and land allowed people to build large homes to shelter often large, extended families. Many of their ceremonial occasions were held in the home. The 1880s characterized the undertaker as a tradesman and merchant who supplied materials and funeral paraphernalia (i.e., caskets, carriages, door badges and scarfs, special clothing, memorial cards, chairs, candles, and other ornaments). By the end of the 19th century the undertakers began to assume a much larger role—assisting more with the deposition of the dead. After the Civil War, embalming became increasingly a conventional American custom, and most states required funeral directors and embalmers to be certified by state licensing. In the 1880s the National Funeral Directors Association began to regulate the profession and established minimum standards of service. With the advent of smaller houses and increasing urbanization, the funeral "parlour" became the place for the preparation of the dead, replacing the family parlor. Although the one-room funeral parlor became the substitute ceremonial room as people no longer used their homes, the custom of survivors sitting up in a vigil with the dead until burial, called the "wake," was often held in the family parlor [15].

The contemporary funeralization process is initialized by the authorization of the funeral home, which removes the body from the place of death. Frequently, upon removing the body, the funeral home begins to prepare the body via bathing, embalming, and dressing. Afterwards it is placed in a casket selected by the family. The traditional wake is an opportunity for members of the community to "pay their respects" and visit with the family prior to the formal funeral service. The preference for viewing or having the body present is optional. Similarly, arrangements for the ceremony and the details of the funeral ritual (i.e., time, place, type of service, etc.) vary and often depend upon family preferences, religion, and ethnicity. In most contemporary American funerals a public rite or ceremony with a religious content is typical in 75 percent of funerals [24]. Following the funeral ceremony, the final disposition of the body is made. The survivors must choose between either burial (85%), cremation (10%), or entombment (5%) [9].1

THE AFRICAN PERSPECTIVE ON DEATH AND FUNERAL RITES

The African cultural heritage provides enormous resources for understanding of life and death. According to Opuku [25], these resources are the product of many centuries of experienced and mature reflection and represent Africa's own insights into the meaning and significance of life and death.

According to Chief Musamasli Nangol, the traditional African belief is that in the beginning God intended man to live forever [26]. African scholar and writer John B. Mbiti supports this view [27]. According to Mbiti, there

From *Personal Care in an Impersonal World: A Multidimensional Look at Bereavement*, edited by John D. Morgan, 1993, pp. 216–230. © 1993 by Baywood Publishing Company, Inc. Reprinted by permission.

are hundreds of myths in Africa concerning ideas about the origin of death—some documented and researched, others are unrecorded and undocumented. According to traditional African beliefs, God gave the first men one or more of the three gifts of immortality, resurrection, and the ability to become young again. But all three gifts were somehow lost and death came into the world. There are many different explanations as to how the loss took place and how death came about [28].

The variation in myths reflects a general belief that death came about by mistake, but has since remained due to some blame laid upon people themselves (especially women), animals, and, in some cases, evil spirits or monsters. Death therefore spoiled the original paradise of men, separating God from men and bringing many associated sorrows and agonies to men. While there are many variations in beliefs about the origin of death there are no myths in Africa about how death might one day be overcome or removed from the world [27].

Death was accepted as one of the rhythms of life, firmly integrated into the totality of life as an unalterable sequence. Life without death was viewed as clearly contrary to our nature as human beings [25]. A traditional Asante myth illustrates this traditional African view. The Asante believe that when the early human beings started experiencing death, they pleaded with God to put a stop to death. Their request was granted and for three years no one died; however, strangely enough, no one gave birth to a child during this time. The people found this situation unbearable and again pleaded with God, this time to grant them the ability to have children even if it meant accepting death also. Consequently, among the Asante, death and birth are complementary—death taking away members from the society, while birth compensates for the losses death inflicts on the community [25].

Therefore, the traditional African attitude towards death is positive and accepting and comprehensively integrated into the totality of life. Life in the African cultural tradition is so whole that death does not destroy its wholeness. Death becomes, therefore, a prolongation of life. And, instead of a break between life and death, there is continuity between the two [29, p. 138]. Accord-

ing to Mbiti, death is regarded as a journey to man's original place as home, and not as an end or an annihilation [30, p. 157]. The deceased goes to join the ancestors, to live in the land of the spirits ("living dead").

This means that the relationship between the living and the "living dead," as Mbiti describes them, remains unbroken and that the community of the living and the community of the "living dead" experience a reciprocal permeability characterized by a constant interaction between the two communities. This wholeness of life expresses itself in the fact that the African family as community is made up of the living as well as the dead. Therefore, the belief in a supernatural or extra-human dimension of the family and community is an extension of the traditional African belief system and world view of life and death [25].

The traditional African funeral rites and ritual reflect a view of death as sorrowful and important. Even though death is accepted as part of life, it is regarded as impolite to state bluntly that someone is dead. It reflects good breeding and courteous comportment to refer to the death of someone in euphemistic terms (i.e., "has gone home," "has joined the ancestors," etc.). Throughout the mourning period, which may last up to three moons, the close relatives of the deceased may not do any work. These tasks are eagerly performed by distant relatives and community friends. Women tend to wail, while men sing and dance, often in praise of the departed one. According to African customs, men are not to cry in front of women because they would appear weak before the very group they are to protect. It is therefore reasonable to assume the traditional funeral masks worn by men may have served as a cover of facial affect as well as a funeral ritual ornament. The body of the deceased is displayed either inside the house or outside on a veranda for public view. The body is displayed until all the relatives have gathered and paid their respects. Any relative who fails to show up for the funeral is often accused or suspected of having bewitched the deceased. A failure to acknowledge the dead is a social offense which is punishable in some communities. Traditional African customs require that gifts of money be

Cultural Groups	Orientation		Life View		Ritual Priority		Funeral Social Sig.		Investment		Funeral Disposition
	Avoid	Accept	Life-Death	Death-Birth	Primary	Secondary	Low	High	Low	High	
AFRICAN		✓		✓	✓			✓		✓	GROUND BURIAL
AFRICAN-AMERICAN		✓		✓	✓			✓		✓	GROUND BURIAL

Figure 1. Comparative and descriptive model of traditional African and African-American Funeral Rites.

given to the family of the deceased to help defray funeral expenses [25].

The African funeral rites vary according to the social status and importance of the deceased. The funeral for children and unmarried people is usually simple and often attended by only close relatives, whereas the funeral for a chief or a king could take on the significance of a national affair requiring much preparation, pomp, and expense [27]. African customs vary considerably in terms of the extent and methods used to prepare the body—sometimes ritually and other times without formality. Generally, the disposal of the body takes place the same day or the next day due to the effects of the tropical heat that accelerate decomposition. In most parts of Africa the traditional ground burial is most commonly favored, although there are vast variations in terms of place of burial, position of the grave, the position of the body in the grave, and grave markings [25–27].

Often after the initial shock of a death and the customary funeral rites, the atmosphere of sadness is soon replaced by laughter and the sharing of funny stories about the dead. When the deceased is a person of note, such as a chief or king, the burial often assumes a carnival atmosphere accompanied with music from drums, dancing, and food for the assembled mourners. Often, the funeral festivities may go on for some time until the community agrees that the important person has been properly acknowledged and properly escorted to the next world. According to custom and tradition, a child of the same sex as the deceased will be born into the family and, according to African custom and tradition, given the name of the deceased—honoring the deceased and symbolizing the wholeness of life [25, 26, 31].

THE AFRICAN-AMERICAN PERSPECTIVE ON DEATH AND FUNERAL RITES

The African-American contemporary response to death is intimately connected and deeply rooted in the traditional African tradition, yet tempered by the American sociocultural experience [32]. Much has been written about the traditional African response to death, yet very few people have acknowledged the African-American response. The African-American funeralization practices and customs have evolved over centuries, reflecting a characteristic disposition and tradition rich in cultural symbolism and customs deeply rooted in and resembling the African experience (see Figure 1).

The earliest, most authoritative work on African-American attitudes towards death and dying is contained in a classic cross-cultural study by Kalish and Reynolds [3]. In this largest study of its type, the researchers examine 100 or more persons in four ethnic groups (African-American, Japanese-American, Mexican-

American, and Anglo). Inevitably, a number of ethnic differences were found.

To be an African-American in America is to be part of a history told in terms of contact with death and coping with death. For the Black race in the era of slavery, death or other forms of personal loss could come at any time, at any age, randomly, and often at the whim of someone else [3]. According to Chapman, African-American artists reflect this history in artistic expression in music, spirituals, poetry, novels, drama, and visual arts [34]. Kalish and Reynolds' survey data indicate that contemporary Black Americans also have significantly more contact with homicide, accidents, and war-time deaths than any other group.

The American sociocultural attitudes and behavior in response to death have been termed "death-avoiding" [1] and "death denying" [18, 20]. However, African-Americans tend to be more accepting and less fearful of death than the three other ethnic groups studied [3]. In a study by Myers, Wass, and Murphey, elderly African-Americans showed a higher level of fear towards death than elderly whites [34]. However, researchers [2, 3] argue that devout and true believers can cope with death more effectively than those with vague or ambivalent views. Kalish and Reynolds report findings that African-Americans perceive themselves as more religious than Anglos and tend to rely on their belief systems more in times of crisis and need [3]. This observation lends more support to the perception of Blacks as less fearful of death than Anglos [35].

The various art forms (i.e., music, literature, theatre, and visual arts, etc.) mirror the attitudes of African-Americans towards death [36]. A consistent theme of death is reflected and often connected to a sense of solace in a theology and belief in the afterlife and promise of a better life [33]. Similarly, another study conducted in

CULTURAL GROUPS	ORIENTATION	
	AVOIDANCE	ACCEPTANCE
AFRICAN		Opuku (1989) Nangol (1986) Mbiti (1975) Parinder (1976)
AFRICAN-AMERICAN	Myers, Wass & Murphy (1980)	Kalish and Reynolds (1981) Martin & Wrightsman (1965) Lewis (1971) Nichols (1989) Fenn (1989) Connor (1989)
AMERICAN	Rando (1984) Kübler-Ross (1969) Leming and Dickinson (1985) Kavanaugh (1972) Feifel (1959) Feifel (1971) Mitford (1963) Kastenbaum and Aisenberg (1972)	

Figure 2. Cultural influences on attitudes towards death.

Detroit showed that African-Americans, substantially more than Anglos, believed that people should live as long as they can, and that helplessness, but not pain and suffering, would justify dying [37]. Kalish and Reynolds report findings that African-Americans are more likely than Anglos to disapprove of allowing people who want to die to do so [3]. The basic premise appears to hold true: whether it is their religiousness or their survival ordeal, African-Americans express a high acceptance of life and death [3].

Elaine Nichols' *The Last Miles of the Way* is the most comprehensive and authoritative documented anthropological study of African-American cultural traditions and funeral rituals in the southeastern United States (i.e. the South Carolina low-lands) [32]. Nichols' work supports and carefully documents the African cultural origin of many African-American beliefs, traditions, and practices in funeral rites. Nichols' efforts also illustrate and detail the intricate symbolism of burials and grave markings. Fenn also supports Nichols' thesis of African cultural roots in grave markings as Fenn documents methods and symbolism rooted in African Kongo traditions [38]. An anthropological analysis of African-American mortuary practices by Conner [39], also supports Elaine Nichols' classic and insightful scholarly work.[2] While a number of aspects of Nichols' findings may be unique to the southeastern region of the United States (i.e., South Carolina), striking similarities in the African-American experience in other regions lend support to the generalizability of similar cultural influences and behaviors in the subculture of the African-American experience.

The available research [3, 39, 40] provides documented support of the thesis that many of the attitudes, beliefs, and traditions regarding funeral rites, death and dying are deeply rooted in African cultural traditions. The African-American attitudes, beliefs, and funeral rites are also significantly influenced by American attitudes, beliefs, and cultural traditions regarding death, dying, and funeral rites. These studies make a significant contribution to our knowledge and understanding of the African-American experience; however, more research and study is needed to understand better death-related behaviors and also provide needed documentation of a very important and regarded sacred psychocultural complex tradition.

African-American attitudes toward funeral rites have remained for too long largely undocumented and lacking in systematic study and observation. Halloween Lewis' [41] analysis of the role of the church and religion in the life of southern Blacks suggests that the religious connection took on special meaning in funeral customs. Lewis notes variations occurring according to the community reputation of the deceased, family wishes, and local church practices. As is common among Protestants, most African-American Protestant churches have no formally prescribed funeral ritual dictated by church hierarchy. Local church custom is followed [42]. According

CULTURAL GROUPS	LIFE VIEW	
	LIFE-DEATH	DEATH-BIRTH
AFRICAN		Opuku (1989) Mbiti (1969) Methuh (1982) Mulago (1969)
AFRICAN-AMERICAN		Lomax (1970) Chapman (1968) Nichols (1989) Fenn (1989) Conner (1989)
AMERICAN	Rando (1984) Leming and Dickinson (1985) Kastenbaum and Aisenberg (1972) Kearl (1989) Ranum (1974)	

Figure 3. Cultural influences on attitudes towards death.

CULTURAL GROUPS	RITUAL PRIORITY		FUNERAL SOCIAL SIG.	
	PRIMARY	SECONDARY	LOW	HIGH
AMERICAN	Opuku (1969) Mbiti (1969) Nangol (1969)			Opuku (1989) Mbiti (1969) Nangol (1969)
AFRICAN-AMERICAN	Kalish and Reynolds (1981) Chapman (1968) Nelson (1971) Carter (1971) Nichols (1989) Fielding (1989) Fenn (1989) Conner (1989)			Kalish and Reynolds (1981) Chapman (1968) Nelson (1971) Carter (1971) Nichols (1989) Fielding (1989) Fenn (1989) Conner (1989)
AMERICAN	Mitford (1963)	Reather (1971) Kübler-Ross Gorer (1955)	Reather (1971) Gorer (1955) Harmer (1971)	Mitford (1963) Fulton (1965)

Figure 4. Cultural influences on attitudes towards death.

CULTURAL GROUPS	INVESTMENT		FUNERAL DISPOSITION
	LOW	HIGH	
AFRICAN		Opuku (1989) Nangol (1986) Mbiti (1975)	Ground Burial Opuku (1989) Nangol (1986) Mbiti (1975) Fenn (1989) Nichols (1989)
AFRICAN-AMERICAN		Kalish and Reynolds (1981) Nichols (1989) Fenn (1989) Conner (1989) Fielding (1989)	Ground Burial Kalish and Reynolds (1981) Nichols (1989) Fenn (1989) Conner (1989) Fielding (1989)
AMERICAN		Mitford (1963) Raether (1971) De Spelder and Strickland (1987) Tegg (1876)	Ground Burial Cremation (10%) Emtombment (5%) Leming and Dickinson (1985)

Figure 5. Cultural influences on attitudes towards death.

to the denominational procedure outlined in Habenstein and Lamers [8], the only generalizations that can really be made are: 1) that family members can select the equipment, music, participants, and place of service without dogmatic restriction, and 2) that the minister leads the procession from church to the funeral coach and from the coach to grave site, positioning himself at the head of the grave. This leaves room for considerable variation [3].

While regional and denominational backgrounds influencing the African-American funeral rites vary, there are some striking similarities linked to traditional African-American beliefs and traditions. In a social context where people are treated like objects and with minimal respect, and the channels by which respect can be achieved are blocked, it is understandable for victims to desperately seek a way to affirm themselves and confirm some sense of self-worth and positive self-identity [3]. African-American funerals in the African-American subculture represent a posthumous attempt for dignity and esteem denied and limited by the dominant culture [32, 40]. Funerals in the African-American experience historically are "primary rituals" of symbolic importance. Kalish and Reynolds'[3] survey reveals that African-Americans were more likely to have taken out life and burial insurance than any other group surveyed [3]. It appears that funeral pre-arrangements, wills, and insurance represent psychological readiness, as these are the most practical arrangements that people can make for death. As expected, Kalish and Reynolds report that older African-Americans are more likely to have made death arrangements than middle-aged or younger adults [3].

The African-American mourners, like the African mourners, were more likely to depend upon the church and the community (extended family) for support during bereavement and mourning [40]. Unlike the other ethnic groups surveyed, African-Americans were more likely to rely on friends, church members, neighbors, and non-relatives for practical assistance consistent with the finding that devout believers had less death anxiety, those active in churches had more traditional sources of spiritual and social support [3].

The social support of family and friends is important to those in mourning. Since a death is a significant event and the funeral is an important social occasion, social expectations require participation and some expression of condolence. It is a standard custom that if one cannot attend the funeral, flowers or other expressions of condolences should be sent. The African-American funeral is indeed a primary ritual and a focal occasion with a big social gathering after the funeral and the closest thing to a family union that might ever take place [32, 40, 43].

Kalish and Reynolds [3] report that the great majority of African-American respondents expressed opposition to elaborate funerals; did not expect friends to participate in covering funeral costs; preferred a funeral with only close friends and relatives; desired African-American clergymen and funeral directors; did not want a wake; wanted the funeral in the church; did not oppose an autopsy; and wanted to be buried. Overall, the African-American funeral is an important event characterized by a programmed atmosphere that is official, ritualistic, serious, and dignified.

ACKNOWLEDGMENTS

The author wishes to acknowledge Luvenia Morant Addison; Dorothy Addison Barrett; Deborah Freathy, Graduate Research Assistant, Loyola Marymount University; Elaine Nichols, Curator, South Carolina State Museum; Harri Close, President, National Funeral Directors & Morticians Association, Inc.; John Hill, III, Chief Administrator, Angelus Funeral Home; Chief Medical Examiner and Staff, Los Angeles County Coroners Office.

NOTES

1. The percentages are based on national averages and may vary by geographic region.
2. Elaine Nichols' unprecedented anthropological work involved the procurement and analysis of physical evidence and cultural artifacts obtained from both library research and private individual collectors that are a part of a special exhibit in the South Carolina State Museum scheduled for a national tour.
3. The term "primary ritual" is used in this context to refer to an event of primary, major importance in that social context. (Contrastingly, a "secondary ritual" is an event of lesser social priority or significance—informal gatherings, family meetings, local holidays, etc.)

REFERENCES

1. R. Kastenbaum and B. R. Aisenberg, The Psychology of Death, Springer, New York, 1972.
2. E. Kübler-Ross, On Death and Dying, Macmillan, New York, 1969.
3. R. Kalish and D. Reynolds, Death and Ethnicity: A Psychocultural Study, Baywood, Amityville, New York, 1981.
4. J. Choron, Death and Western Thought, The Macmillan Company, New York, 1963.
5. R. Huntington and P. Metcalf, Celebration of Death: The Anthropology of Mortuary Ritual, Cambridge, Cambridge, 1979.
6. D. C. Rosenblatt, Grief in Cross-Cultural and Historical Perspective, in Death and Dying, P. F. Pegg and E. Metza (eds.), Pitman Press, London, 1981.
7. M. McGoldrick, P. Hines, E. Lee, and G. H. Preto, Mourning Rituals: How Culture Shapes the Experience of Loss, Networker, 1986.
8. W. R. Habenstein and M. W. Lamers, Funeral Customs the World Over, Bulfin, Milwaukee, 1963.
9. R. M. Leming and E. G. Dickinson, Understanding Dying, Death, and Bereavement, Holt, Rinehart and Winston, New York, 1985.
10. R. P. Cuzzort and W. E. King, Twentieth Century Social Thought, Holt, Rinehart and Winston, New York, 1980.
11. J. R. Averill, Grief: Its Nature and Significance, Psychological Bulletin, 70:61, 1968.
12. E. Durkheim, The Elementary Forms of Religious Life, Macmillan, New York, 1915.
13. M. C. Kearl, Endings—A Sociology of Death and Dying, Oxford, New York, 1989.
14. C. Geerty, The Interpretations of Cultures: Selected Essays, Basic Books, New York, 1973.
15. L. A. DeSpelder and L. A. Strickland, The Last Dance: Encountering Death and Dying, Mayfield, Mountain View, California, 1987.

16. A. M. Hocart, Death Customs, in *Encyclopedia of the Social Sciences 5*, E. R. A. Seligman and A. Johnson (eds.), Macmillan, New York, 1937.

17. P. G. Mandelbaum, Social Issues of Funeral Rites, in *The Meaning of Death*, H. Feifel (ed.), McGraw-Hill, New York, 1959.

18. T. A. Rando, *Grief, Dying and Death*, Research Press Co., Champaign, Illinois, 1984.

19. R. E. Kavanaugh, *Facing Death*, Penguin, Baltimore, Maryland, 1971.

20. H. Feiffel, The Meaning of Death in American Society: Implications for Education, 1971.

21. G. Gorer, *Death, Grief & Mourning*, Crescent Press, London, 1965.

22. H. Feifel, *The Meaning of Death*, McGraw-Hill, New York, 1959.

23. J. Mitford, *The American Way of Death*, Simon and Schuster, New York, 1963.

24. H. C. Raether, The Place of the Funeral: The Role of the Funeral Director in Contemporary America, *Omega*, 2, pp. 136–149, 1971.

25. K. A. Opuku, African Perspectives on Death and Dying, in *Perspectives on Death and Dying*, A. Berger, P. Badham, J. Berger, V. Cerry, and J. Beloff (eds.) The Charles Press, Philadelphia, 1989.

26. C. M. Nangoli, *No More Lies About Africa*, African Heritage, East Orange, New Jersey, 1988.

27. J. S. Mbiti, *Introduction to African Religion*, Heinemann, London, 1975.

28. E. G. Parinder, *African Mythology*, Paul Hamlyn, London, 1967.

29. V. Mulago, Vital Participation: The Cohesive Principle of the Bantu Community, in *Biblical Revelation and African Beliefs*, K. Dickson and P. Ellingworth (eds.), Butterworth, London, 1979.

30. J. S. Mbiti, *African Religions and Philosophy*, Heinemann, London, 1969.

31. I. E. Metuh, *God and Man in African Religion: A Case of the Igbo of Nigeria*, G. Chapman, London, 1982.

32. E. Nichols (ed.), *The Last Miles of the Way: African American Homegoing Traditions 1890–Present*, Dependable, Columbia, South Carolina, 1989.

33. A. Chapman (ed.), *Black Voices: An Anthology of Afro-American Literature*, New American Library, New York, 1968.

34. J. E. Myers, H. Wass, and M. Murphey, Ethnic Differences in Death Anxiety among the Elderly, *Death Education*, 4, pp. 237–244, 1980.

35. D. S. Martin and L. Wrightsman, The Relationship between Religious Behaviour and Concern about Death, *Journal of Social Psychology*, 65, pp. 317–323, 1965.

36. A. Lomax, The Homogeneity of African-Afro-American Musical Style, in *Afro-American Anthropology*, N. E. Whitten and J. F. Szwed (eds.), Free Press, New York, 1970.

37. R. Koenig, N. S. Goldner, R. Kresojevich, and G. Lockwood, Ideas About Illness of Elderly Black and White in an Urban Hospital, *Aging and Human Development*, 2, pp. 217–225, 1971.

38. E. A. Fenn, Honouring the Ancestors: Kongo-American Graves in the American South, in *The Last Miles of the Way*, E. Nichols (ed.), Dependable, Columbia, South Carolina, 1989.

39. C. Connor, Archaeological Analysis of African-American Mortuary Behaviour, in *The Last Miles of the Way*, Dependable, Columbia, South Carolina, 1989.

40. H. U. Fielding, Mourning and Burying the Dead: Experiences of a Lowcountry Funeral Director, in *The Last Miles of the Way*, Dependable, Columbia, South Carolina, 1989.

41. H. Lewis, Blackways of Kent: Religion and Salvation, in *The Black Church in America*, H. M. Nelson, et al. (eds.), Basic Books, New York, 1971.

42. H. M. Nelson, et al. (eds.), *The Black Church in America*, Basic Books, New York, 1971.

43. W. B. Carter, Suicide, Death, and Ghetto Life, *Life-Threatening Behaviour*, L. 1971.

BIBLIOGRAPHY

Abrahamson, H., *The Origin of Death: Studies in African Mythology*, Almgvist, Uppsala, 1951.

Balandier, G. and Maguet, J. *Dictionary of Black African Civilization*, Leon Amiel, New York, 1974.

Boulby, J., Process of Mourning, *International Journal of Psycho-Analysis*, 43, pp. 314–340, Grune and Statton, New York. Reprinted in G. E. Daniels (ed.), 1965, *New Perspectives in Psychoanalysis*, 1961.

Feifel, H., The Taboo on Death, *The American Behavioral Scientist*, 6, 1963.

Fulton, R., The Sacred and the Secular: Attitudes of the American Public toward Death, Funerals, and Funeral Directors, in *Death and Identity*, R. Fulton (ed.), Wiley, New York, 1965.

Goody, J., *Death, Property, and the Ancestors: A Study of the Mortuary Customs of the LoDagaa of West Africa*, Stock, London, 1962.

Harmer, R., Funerals, Fantasy, and Flight, *Omega*, 2, pp. 127–135, 1971.

Idowu, E. B., *African Traditional Religion*, SCM Press, London, 1973.

Jackson, M., The Black Experience with Death: A Brief Analysis through Black Writings, *Omega*, 3, pp. 203–209, 1972.

Kopytoff, E., Ancestors as Elders in Africa, *Africa*, 41, 1971.

Kutscher, A. H., *Death and Bereavement*, Charles C. Thomas, Springfield, Illinois, 1969.

Lindemann, E., Symptomatology and Management of Acute Grief, *American Journal of Psychiatry*, 101. Reprinted in R. Fulton (ed.) (1965) *Death and Identity*, Wiley, New York, 1944.

Lend, F. H., Why Do We Weep? *Journal of Social Psychology*, 1, 1930.

Opuku, K. A., Death and Immortality in the African Religious Heritage, in *Death and Immortality in the Religions of the World*, P. Badham and L. Badham (eds.), Paragon, New York, 1987.

Parinder, E. G., *African Traditional Religion*, SPCK, London, 1962.

Pinkney, A., *Black Americans*, Prentice Hall, Englewood Cliffs, New Jersey, 1969.

Ranum, P. M., *Western Attitudes toward Death: From the Middle Ages to the Present*, Johns Hopkins University Press, Baltimore, 1974.

Tegg, W., *The Last Act Being the Funeral Rites of Nations and Individuals*, William Tegg & Co., London, 1876.

Thomas, L. R., Litany of Home—Going—Going Forth: The African Concept of Time, Eternity and Social Ontology, in *The Last Miles of the Way*, E. Nichols, Dependable, Columbia, South Carolina, 1989.

Zahan, D., The *Religion, Spirituality, and Thought of Traditional Africa*, E. Martin and L. M. Martin (trans.), University of Chicago, Chicago, 1979.

How different religions pay their final respects

From mummies to cremation to drive-up wakes, funeral rituals reflect religious traditions going back thousands of years as well as up-to-the-minute fads.

William J. Whalen

Most people in the United States identify themselves as Protestants; thus, most funerals follow a similar form. Family and friends gather at the funeral home to console one another and pay their last respects. The next day a minister conducts the funeral service at the church or mortuary; typically the service includes hymns, prayers, a eulogy, and readings from the Bible. In 85 percent of the cases today, the body is buried after a short grave-side ceremony. Otherwise the body is cremated or donated to a medical school.

But what could be called the standard U.S. funeral turns out to be the funeral of choice for only a minority of the rest of the human race. Other people, even other Christians, bury their dead with more elaborate and, to outsiders, even exotic rites.

How your survivors will dispose of your body will in all likelihood be determined by the religious faith you practiced during your life because funeral customs reflect the theological beliefs of a particular faith community.

For example, the Parsi people of India neither bury nor cremate their dead. Parsis, most of whom live in or near Bombay, follow the ancient religion of Zoroastrianism. Outside Bombay, Parsis erected seven Towers of Silence in which they perform their burial rites. When someone dies, six bearers dressed in white bring the corpse to one of the towers. The Towers of Silence have no roofs; within an hour, waiting vultures pick the body clean. A few days later the bearers return and cast the remaining bones into a pit. Parsis believe that their method of disposal avoids contaminating the soil, the water, and the air.

Out of the ashes

The Parsis' millions of Hindu neighbors choose cremation as their usual burial practice. Hindus believe that as long as the physical body exists, the essence of the person will remain nearby; cremation allows the essence, or soul, of the person to continue its journey into another incarnation.

Hindus wash the body of the deceased and clothe it in a shroud decorated with flowers. They carry the body to a funeral pyre, where the nearest male relative lights the fire and walks around the burning body three times while reciting verses from Hindu sacred writings. Three days later someone collects and temporarily buries the ashes.

On the tenth day after the cremation, relatives deposit the ashes in the Ganges or some other sacred river. The funeral ceremony, called the *Shraddha,* is then held within 31 days of the cremation. Usually the deceased's son recites the prayers and the invocation of ancestors; that is one reason why every Hindu wants at least one son.

Prior to British rule in India, the practice of suttee was also common.

Suttee is the act of a Hindu widow willingly being cremated on her husband's funeral pyre. Suttee was outlawed by the British in 1829, but occasionally widows still throw themselves into the flames.

Like the Hindus, the world's Buddhists, who live primarily in China, Japan, Sri Lanka, Myanmar, Vietnam, and Cambodia, usually choose cremation for disposing a corpse. They believe cremation was favored by Buddha. A religious teacher may pray or recite mantras at the bedside of the dying person. These actions are believed to exert a wholesome effect on the next rebirth. Buddhists generally believe that the essence of a person remains in an intermediate state for no more than 49 days between death and rebirth.

While Hindus and Buddhists prescribe cremation, the world's 900 million Muslims forbid cremation. According to the Qu'ran, Muhammad taught that only Allah will use fire to punish the wicked.

If a Muslim is near death, someone is called in to read verses from the Qu'ran. After death, the body is ceremonially washed, clothed in three pieces of white cloth, and placed in a simple wooden coffin. Unless required by law, Muslims will not allow embalming. The body must be buried as soon as possible after death—usually within 24 hours. After a funeral service at a mosque or at the grave side, the body is removed from the coffin and buried with the head of the deceased turned toward Mecca. In some Muslim countries the women engage in loud wailing and lamentations during the burial.

Some Islamic grave sites are quite elaborate. The Mogul emperor Shah Jahan built the world-famous Taj Mahal as a mausoleum for his wife and himself. The Taj Mahal, which is one of the finest examples of Islamic architecture, was finished in 1654. It took 20,000 workers about 22 years to complete the project.

The Baha'i faith, which originated in Persia in the nineteenth century as an outgrowth of the Shi'ite branch of Islam, also forbids cremation and embalming and requires that the body not be transported more than an hour's journey from the place of death. Because Bahaism has no ordained clergy, the funeral may be conducted by any member of the family or the local assembly. All present at the funeral must stand during the recitation of the Prayer for the Dead composed by Baha'u'llah. Several million Baha'is live in Iran, India, the Middle East, and Africa; and an estimated 100,000 Baha'is live in the United States.

In Judaism, the faith of some 18 million people, the Old Testament only hints at belief in an afterlife; but later Jewish thought embraced beliefs in heaven, hell, resurrection, and final judgment. In general, Orthodox Jews accept the concept of a resurrection of the soul and the body while Conservative and Reform Jews prefer to speak only of the immortality of the soul.

Orthodox Judaism prescribes some of the most detailed funeral rites of any religion. As death approaches, family and friends must attend the dying person at all times. When death finally arrives, a son or the nearest relative closes the eyes and mouth of the deceased and binds the lower jaw before rigor mortis sets in. Relatives place the body on the floor and cover it with a sheet; they place a lighted candle near the head.

Judaism in its traditional form forbids embalming except where required by law. After a ritual washing, the body is covered with a white shroud and placed in a wooden coffin. At the funeral, mourners symbolize their grief by tearing a portion of an outer garment or wearing a torn black ribbon. The Orthodox discourage flowers and ostentation at the funeral.

The Jewish funeral service includes a reading of prayers and psalms, a eulogy, and the recitation of the Kaddish prayer for the dead in an Aramaic dialect. Like other Semitic people, Jews forbid cremation. Orthodox Jews observe a primary mourning period of seven days; Reform Jews reduce this period to three days. During the secondary yearlong mourning period, the Kaddish prayer is recited at every service in the synagogue.

Dearly beloved

Christianity, the world's largest religion, carries over Judaism's respect for the body and firmly acknowledges resurrection, judgment, and eternal reward or punishment.

These Christian beliefs permeate the liturgy of a Catholic funeral. Older Catholics remember the typical funeral of the 1940s and '50s: the recitation of the rosary at the wake, the black vestments, the Latin prayers. They probably recall the *"Dies Irae,"* a thirteenth-century dirge and standard musical piece at Catholic funerals prior to the liturgical changes of the Second Vatican Council in the 1960s.

Nowadays, those attending a Catholic wake may still say the rosary, but often there is a scripture service instead. The priest's vestments are likely to be white or violet rather than black. Prayers tend to emphasize the hope of resurrection rather than the terrors of the final judgment.

As death approaches, the dying person or the family may request the sacrament of the Anointing of the Sick. Once called Last Rites or Extreme Unction, this sacrament is no longer restricted to those in imminent danger of death; it is regularly administered to the sick and the elderly as an instrument of healing as well as a preparation for death.

Sacred remains

The Catholic Church raises no objections to embalming, flowers, or an open casket at a wake. At one time Catholics who wished to have a church funeral could not request cremation. In 1886 the Holy Office in Rome declared that "to introduce the practice (of cremation) into Christian society was un-Christian and Masonic in motivation." Today Catholics may choose the option of cremation over burial "unless," according to canon law, "it has been chosen for reasons that are contrary to Christian teaching."

The church used to deny an ecclesiastical burial to suicides, those killed in duels, Freemasons, and members of the ladies' auxiliaries of Masonic lodges. Today the church refuses burial only to "notorious apostates, heretics, and schismatics" and to "sinners whose funerals in church would scandalize the faithful." Catholics who join Masonic lodges no longer incur excommunication, although they still may not receive Communion.

The church has also softened its position on denying funeral rites to suicides. Modern pastoral practice is based on the understanding that anyone finding life so unbearable as to end it voluntarily probably was acting with a greatly diminished free will.

For Roman Catholics, the Mass is the principal celebration of the Christian funeral; and mourners are invited to receive the Eucharist. Most Protestant denominations, except for some Lutherans and Episcopalians, do not incorporate a communion service into their funeral liturgies. The Catholic ritual employs candles, holy water, and incense but does not allow non-Christian symbols, such as national flags or lodge emblems, to rest on or near the coffin during the funeral. In many parishes the pastor encourages the family members to participate where appropriate as eucharistic ministers, lectors, and singers. In the absence of a priest, a deacon can conduct the funeral service but cannot preside at a Mass of Christian burial.

The revised funeral liturgy of the Catholic Church is meant to stress God's faithfulness to people rather than God's wrath toward sinners. The Catholic Church declares that certain men and women who have lived lives of such heroic virtue that they are indeed in heaven are to be known as saints. The church also teaches that hell is a reality but has never declared that anyone, even Judas, has actually been condemned to eternal punishment.

Unlike Protestant churches, Catholicism also teaches the existence of a temporary state of purification, known as purgatory, for those destined for heaven but not yet totally free from the effects of sin and selfishness. At one time some theologians suggested that unbaptized babies spent eternity in a place of natural happiness known as limbo, but this was never church doctrine and is taught by few theologians today.

At the committal service at the grave site, the priest blesses the grave and leads the mourners in the Our Father and other prayers for the repose of the soul of the departed and the comfort of the survivors. Catholics are usually buried in Catholic cemeteries or in separate sections of other cemeteries.

Dressed for the occasion

The funeral rite in the Church of Jesus Christ of Latter-day Saints, which is the fastest growing church in the United States, resembles the standard Protestant funeral in some ways; but one significant difference is in the attire of the deceased. Devout Mormons receive the garments of the holy priesthood during their endowment ceremonies when they are teens. These sacred undergarments are to be worn day and night throughout a Mormon's life. When a Mormon dies, his or her body is then attired in these garments in the casket. At one time Mormon sacred garments resembled long johns, but they now have short sleeves and are cut off at the knees. The garments are embroidered with symbols on the right and left breasts, the navel, and the right knee, which remind the wearer of the oaths taken in the secret temple rites.

Mormons who reached their endowments are also clothed in their temple garb at death. For the men, this includes white pants, white shirt, tie, belt, socks, slippers, and an apron. Just before the casket is closed for the last time, a fellow Mormon puts a white temple cap on the corpse. If the deceased is a woman, a high priest puts a temple veil over her face; Mormons believe the veil will remain there until her husband calls her from the grave to resurrection. Mormons forbid cremation.

Freemasons conduct their own funeral rites for a deceased brother, and they insist that their ceremony be the last one before burial or cremation. Thus, a separate religious ceremony often precedes the Masonic rites. Lodge members will bury a fellow Mason only if he is a member in good standing and he or his family has requested the service.

All the pallbearers at the Masonic services must be Masons, and each wears a white apron, white gloves, a black band around his left arm, and a sprig of evergreen or acacia in his left lapel. The corpse is clothed in a white apron and other lodge regalia.

Masonry accepts the idea of the immortality of the soul but makes no reference to the Christian understanding of the resurrection of the soul and the body. The Masonic service speaks of the soul's translation from this life to that "perfect, glorious, and celestial lodge above" presided over by the Grand Architect of the Universe.

In memorium

Other small religious groups have much less elaborate and formalized funeral services. Christian Scientists, for example, have no set funeral rite because their founder, Mary Baker Eddy, denied the reality of death. The family of a deceased Christian Scientist often invites a Christian Science reader to present a brief service at the funeral home.

Unitarian-Universalists enroll many members who would identify themselves as agnostics or atheists. Therefore, in a typical Unitarian Universalist funeral service, the minister and loved ones say little about any afterlife but extol the virtues and good works of the deceased.

Salvation Army officers are buried in their military uniforms, and a Salvationist blows taps at the grave side. In contrast, the Church of Christ, which allows no instrumental music during Sunday worship, allows no organs, pianos, or other musical instruments at its funerals.

The great variety of funeral customs through the ages and around the world would be hard to catalog. The Egyptians mummified the bodies of royalty and erected pyramids as colossal monuments. Viking kings were set adrift on blazing boats. The Soviets mummified the body of Lenin, and his tomb and corpse have become major icons in the U.S.S.R.

In a funeral home in California, a drive-up window is provided for mourners so that they can view the remains and sign the book without leaving their cars. In Japan, where land is scarce, one enterprising cemetery owner offers a time-share plan whereby corpses are displaced after brief burial to make room for the next occupant. Complying with the wishes of the deceased, one U.S. undertaker once dressed a corpse in pajamas and positioned it under the blankets in a bedroom for viewing.

The reverence and rituals surrounding the disposal of the body reflect religious traditions going back thousands of years as well as up-to-the-minute fads. All of the elements of the burial—the preparation of the body, the garments or shroud, the prayers, the method of disposal, the place and time of burial—become sacred acts by which a particular community of believers bids at least a temporary farewell to one of its own.

CEMETERIES OF THE RICH AND FAMOUS

A lively look at some grave attractions

by Patricia Brooks

It may seem ghoulish, but a cemetery visit can often enliven (oops) a trip. Think of all the tourists who make their way to Père Lachaise in Paris to view the graves of Oscar Wilde, Marcel Proust, and Jim Morrison, or to the Jewish Cemetery in Prague where Franz Kafka is buried. Then, too, some of the most famous sights in the world are tombs: the Pyramids and the Taj Mahal, among them.

Closer to home, there are many memorable but less well-known cemeteries. Here are my favorites, along with some of their most famous and infamous occupants.

Bellefontaine Cemetery in St. Louis is the burial site of so many illustrious names that a five-page single-spaced list, along with a map, is provided at the gate. After all, in the 19th century St. Louis was the Gateway to the West, so anybody who was anybody passed through (and sometimes passed on). Today, one drives along Bellefontaine's winding roadways past Victorian cenotaphs, winged angels, Gothic sepulchres, Greek temples, and majestic marble mausoleums.

Noted permanent residents include Thomas Hart Benton, who was Missouri's first U.S. senator; poet Sara Teasdale; and Charlotte Dickson Wainwright, wife of a millionaire brewer, whose limestone mausoleum, with its bronze grilles and stone carvings, was designed by architect Louis Sullivan as a modern-day Taj Mahal. The equally striking mausoleum of Adolphus Busch, patriarch of the Anheuser-Busch beer empire, bears the words VENI, VIDI, VICI above a bronze gate, visible through a Gothic arch. The grave of General William Clark, of Lewis and Clark expedition fame, who ended his days as superintendent of Indian affairs for the Missouri Territory, is topped by an obelisk that rises from a granite platform; his accomplishments are carved on all four sides, and there's a bronze bust of him in front.

Buried on the shaded grounds of **Calvary**, a Roman Catholic cemetery next door to Bellefontaine, are Dred Scott, the runaway slave whose precedent-setting trial was held in the city's Old Courthouse, and novelist Kate Chopin, who dropped dead after a long day's tour of the 1904 St. Louis World's Fair. Two surprises are the graves of General William Tecumseh Sherman and Tennessee Williams. Sherman, who worked for the railroad in St. Louis after retiring from the U.S. Army, has an imposing granite memorial with a large cross; it is surrounded by smaller headstones marking the graves of his wife, daughter, and two sons. Tennessee Williams' large, upright, pink marble slab (near his mother's plainer, gray granite stone) is inscribed with a quotation from his play *Camino Real:* "The violets in the mountains have broken the rocks."

Tomb Tours

Samuel Clemens (a.k.a. Mark Twain) rests in a secluded grove of oak trees at **Woodlawn Cemetery** in Elmira, New York, hometown of his wife. His monument—a tall granite column at the end of a shaded walkway—is topped by a bronze medallion bearing his profile; just below it, on the same column, is a similar profile of his son-in-law, a concert pianist, who shares the column (and the glory) because he was Clara Clemens' husband and *she* erected the memorial.

Graceland Cemetery, near Wrigley Field on Chicago's north side, is a veritable Who Was Who, with the tombs of retailer Marshall Field, inventor Cyrus McCormick, detective Allan Pinkerton, railroad pioneer George Pullman, and boxing champion Jack Johnson. So imposing are the tombs and sculptures, many designed by Daniel Chester French, Lorado Taft (whose *Eternal Silence* hooded bronze figure is a Graceland landmark), and Louis Sullivan, that the Chicago Architecture Foundation offers two-hour walking tours.

Notable graves: Real estate magnate Potter Palmer and his wife, Bertha, are buried in twin sarcophagi inside an Ionic-column-lined Greek temple, the largest monument in Graceland; Louis Sullivan himself is entombed beneath a rectangular granite stone, with a large bronze medallion that he designed; and modern architect Ludwig Mies van der Rohe rests beneath a flat, black granite marker built by his grandson, Dirk Lohan, also an architect.

The **Sleepy Hollow Cemetery**, on a landscaped hillside not far from Monument Square in Concord, Massachusetts, is chockablock with ambience and ancient headstones. On its silent, shaded Authors' Ridge, many of Concord's 19th-century literary lions—Louisa May Alcott, Nathaniel Hawthorne, Henry David Thoreau, Ralph Waldo Emerson—are buried beneath simple marble markers.

Grand Finales

Overlooking the Farmington River in the old town of Farmington, Connecticut, **Riverside Cemetery** is known as New Cemetery, though it dates from 1838. Among those interred here are William Gillette, a Broadway actor famous for his Sherlock Holmes portrayal; Sarah Porter, founder of nearby Miss Porter's School, whose most notable alumna was Jacqueline Onassis; Lambert Hitchcock, creator of the Hitchcock chair; and Foone, a Sierra Leone native, who as a member of the *Amistad* slave ship mutiny was defended by John Quincy Adams and acquitted in 1841. Also buried here are Anna Roosevelt Cole, sister of President Theodore Roosevelt, and Winchell Smith, a playwright who lived just across the street and who persuaded Lillian Gish to come to Farmington to film *Way Down East*.

Just inside the gate of the **Westminster Burying Ground,** Baltimore's oldest cemetery, are the twice-moved remains of local resident Edgar Allan Poe. The original gravesite contained a statue of a raven ("Quoth the Raven, 'Nevermore' "), but nevermore; the current one has a bronze bust of Poe set into a slender six-foot-high white marble marker with only his name and dates on the bottom. On the same monument are the names of his wife, Virginia Clemm, and her mother, Maria.

The Plots Thicken

Right next to the Old Dutch Church in the New York suburb of North Tarrytown is **Sleepy Hollow Cemetery**, a historic graveyard where Washington Irving (whose plain marble marker lies behind a fence and hemlock hedge), Andrew Carnegie, and Walter Chrysler are buried. Here, too, the ghostly spirits of Irving's creations,

Icahbod Crane and the Headless Horseman, still seem to linger among the timeworn gravestones. The largest monument, on one of the highest points of ground, belongs to local resident William Rockefeller, brother of John D. Rockefeller Sr. On a circular plot behind a yew hedge, the square mausoleum, made of huge blocks of granite, was considered very modern for its time (1921).

The beautifully kept 400-acre grounds of **Woodlawn Cemetery** in the Bronx, New York, have long been the final home of well-known and moneyed New Yorkers, such as Roland Macy (founder of the department store), F. W. Woolworth, Duke Ellington, and Bat Masterson (whose final years were spent as a New York reporter and whose epitaph omits his checkered past, saying only that everybody loved him. Uh-huh).

Must-see graves include those of New York City mayor Fiorello La Guardia, nicknamed the Little Flower, whose gray granite rectangle has (surprise) a little flower etched on top, and of Herman Melville, whose unright marble gravestone has a blank scroll (he was not famous when he died) with a border of etched ivy that seems to reach out to the ivy carved into his wife's adjoining headstone.

Famous Last Words

Flat, palm- and pine-studded **Hollywood Memorial Park Cemetery** in Hollywood is smaller and less famous than Forest Lawn in Glendale (satirized by Evelyn Waugh in *The Loved One*), but it has more early stars—this is where Rudolph Valentino, among others, is buried. A map lists the celebrity sites, set among the curved roads and ponds.

Most ostentatious: the sunken reflecting pond with water lilies in front of the Douglas Fairbanks Sr. sarcophagus, which bears his profile in bas-relief. Runner-up for pretension? Tyrone Power's white marble bench, one side of which is a giant book with the masks of comedy and tragedy; on the bench is the "Good night, sweet prince" quote from *Hamlet*. Most insignificant: John Huston's, a glitzy but tiny plaque (shame on you, Anjelica). Predictably large-scale: Cecil B. DeMille's family mausoleum. Most touching: The graves of Janet Gaynor and her first husband, Adrian, which have two cypress trees and a red rose bush planted between them.

And then there's my all-time favorite memorial, in **Beth Olam Cemetery**, a section of Hollywood Memorial. A simple marble stone for Mel Blanc, master of many cartoon voices, reads THAT'S ALL, FOLKS.

Cemeteries are a change of venue for Patricia Brooks, who usually covers food and travel.

We Can Help Children Grieve:

A Child-Oriented Model for Memorializing

Linda Ellen Goldman

On a family vacation Andrew died suddenly of a rare virus. Family and friends were shocked by this unexpected death. Andrew was six years old and had just completed kindergarten. The shock of his death needed to be recognized and processed before the overwhelming feeling of loss for Andrew could be honored. A special child-oriented memorial service was a vehicle for expression of this complicated grief.

Preparing the community and school

Andrew's parents wrote a letter explaining the facts of Andrew's death and the events surrounding his illness. It was mailed to every parent of a child at Andrew's school before Andrew's parents returned home from the vacation. The head of Andrew's school included with this letter an additional letter with information and resources on children and grief. Prior to the opening of school, the faculty met and discussed appropriate ways to work with children and their grief. Counseling was available to children at school.

Preparing concerned parents

A meeting was held at Andrew's school for all concerned parents and faculty. Information and appropriate

Parents and children need to know the facts about a loss. This information lessens fear and creates a foundation from which to grieve.

resources were presented on how young children grieve. Adults expressed their own feelings, fears, and vulnerabilities, and they shared information about how Andrew's death was affecting the children. Parents were given suggestions about how to help the children grieve and prepare them for the memorial service planned for Andrew. The ideas included the following:

1. Give the facts of Andrew's death.

2. Share your feelings of grief.

3. Allow your children to express their feelings and to commemorate Andrew through drawings and stories.

4. Describe what will happen at the memorial service.

5. Invite your child to join you in coming to the service, but don't insist that she come.

6. Explain that children can participate if they feel like it by telling a story about Andrew or something special they remember. They can share artwork or poetry or join in singing. They do not have to participate if they don't feel like it.

7. Tell your child that there will be people there he knows.

8. Be prepared to leave with your child if she feels uncomfortable.

9. Let your children know that people may be sad and cry and *they* themselves may be sad and cry. That's OK. They may not feel sad and may not cry. That's OK, too.

10. Read resources written for parents, such as those mentioned at the end of this article.

11. Read to children to help prepare them and to answer questions—see the suggested books [in the box "Books to Read"].

12. Encourage your children to ask questions.

Preparing the memorial service

While Andrew's parents went through all the pain, anguish, and stages of deep personal grief to be expected under such tragic circumstances, they summoned their love for their son Andrew to help them create a loving tribute to his life. In so doing, their own grief process

From *Young Children*, September 1996, pp. 69-73. © 1996 by the National Association for the Education of Young Children (NAEYC). Reprinted by permission.

We can define death to the young child in the following way: "When someone dies his or her body stops working. No matter how hard the doctors and nurses try, they can't make the body work again. Usually people die when they are very, very, very old or very, very, very sick, or when something so bad has happened to someone that the doctors and nurses can't make the body work anymore."

The child's view of death

1. Young children ages three through six often think that **death is reversible,** and they imagine that their loved one will return after death.

Joey, age four, asked his mom, "Why can't God bring our baby back from heaven, give him back to the doctors, and then the doctors can fix him and send him home?"

2. Alice, age three, sat at her mother's funeral and whispered to her dad, "I bet Mom is sleeping in God's bed right now." Children believe that **death is sleep.**

3. Five-year-olds **may ask for facts and details of the death.** "How did Megan die? Who was with her? Where did she go?"

4. They may also **ask about the nature of death and what happens after someone dies.** "Can Megan see me?" "What does she have for dinner?" and "Can she watch TV in heaven?"

5. Three- to five-year-olds often **take language literally** and many common clichés confuse young children, inhibiting their ability to grieve. The following are a few inappropriate clichés:

"God loved Grandpa so much that he took him with him to heaven." (Three-year-old Tom thinks, "Why doesn't God love me?")

"Mom's watching over me." (Five-year-old Alice thinks, "I can't do anything without Mom seeing me.")

"Dad went on a long trip." (Four-year-old Susan questions, "Why didn't he take me?")

"Grandma went to sleep." (Three-year-old Sam wonders, "Will I die when I go to sleep, too?")

Alex, age four, began to have terrifying nightmares after the death of his alcoholic dad. His grandmother was telling him that "Dad is watching over you in heaven," and Alex was very frightened. His dad had been punitive and physically abusive. Alex visualized him being able to see and hear everything because he had taken his grandmother's words literally.

6. Magical thinking and egocentricity is another component of the young child's view of death. Five-year-old Joshua began bed-wetting after his older sister Karen was killed by a drunk driver. He had become clingy and fearful and had refused to play with other children. One night before bed he confided to his mom,

"I know it's my fault that Karen died. We had a fight that day, and I told her I hated her; she was a bad sister, and I wished she was dead. I know my words made her die!"

Children often feel that their thoughts and words can magically cause things to happen. This was a perfect opportunity for Mom to explain the facts to Josh about how his sister died.

"Your sister was killed by a drunk man in a car accident. Your words did not cause her death. Karen knows you love her, and I know we will miss her very much."

was enriched as was the grief process of all others who were involved with the memorial service.

Andrew's parents prepared a very child-oriented memorial service to celebrate Andrew's life as well as to commemorate his death. They told other parents what the ceremony would be like, so that these parents, in turn, could tell their children what to expect. A notice also was put in the school newspaper.

So many times at the Center for Loss and Grief Therapy, I have received calls from parents asking if children should come to a funeral or memorial service. Breaking this silence on children and funerals and memorial services by *including children* is an idea whose time has come. The memorial service and funeral can become a shared family experience. To include young children in these experiences we need to understand the young child's vision of death (see box "The child's view of death").

The memorial service

Andrew's memorial service served as a model for me of what is possible when parents choose to commemorate and honor the dignity of their child's life, with a true respect for all children.

While there certainly was sadness, the service held a warmth and invited an openness that allowed children of all ages, adult friends, family members, coworkers of Andrew's parents, school representatives, and Andrew's parents themselves to freely and spontaneously participate. People of all ages told stories, sang songs, and

Ways children can commemorate:

- Plant a flower or tree.
- Send a balloon.
- Blow bubbles.
- Light a candle.
- Say a prayer.
- Create a mural or collage about the life of the person who died.
- Make cookies or cake.
- Make a memory gift for the child's family.
- Write a poem, story, or song about the loved one who died.
- Talk into a tape recorder or make a video of memories.

read poetry acknowledging Andrew's wonderful life.

Children and adults sat on the floor. Chairs were set up in the back of the room for those who preferred them. Families were together. Children could lie down, stand up, or leave. They did not have to participate—they could if they wanted to. They could go outside or blow bubbles or play. Children made their own choices as long as the service was respected. A parent or caring adult was prepared to leave with any child who wanted to.

Children shared their thoughts, feelings, pictures, poetry, and stories. Artwork and stories were displayed on tables and walls. They told of memories and love and sorrow for their friend Andrew. Some children shared their photo collections about special times with Andrew. An-

drew's dad read memories of Andrew for a child who was hesitant to speak. Andrew's adult friends and relatives also shared memories. Andrew's class offered gifts for his parents—a quilt with each child's handprints on it and a photo album of the kindergarten year.

Community support was very meaningful. Andrew's principal spoke of his memories of Andrew. Andrew's parents shared their love for their son and experiences with him. They told funny stories about Andrew and had made a booklet of favorite poems and prayers for each family to take home. Some children's words were included. Andrew's good friend Chris, age seven, wrote, "Andrew is in my heart." His mom had been crying and Chris wanted to know why. She explained she was sad because she would

never be able to see Andrew again. "Don't worry," Chris replied. "I can see Andrew whenever I want, because he is always in my heart."

His teachers and friends sang many of Andrew's favorite songs. They invited the children and their families to join in if they felt comfortable. Songs included "The Earth Is Mine," "When the Rain Comes Down," "I'm Being Eaten by a Boa Constrictor," and "The Garden Song." At the very end of the service people held hands and sang "Friends, Friends."

After the service

After the service the children were invited to make commemorations of Andrew if they wanted. There was a crafts table where children could draw pictures, write let-

Four-year-old Mary was sad at school one day and explained to her teacher that she missed her dog Lucky who was recently killed by a car. Her teacher handed her a toy telephone and suggested she call him and tell him how she feels. Mary sat down, dialed a number, and began speaking. "I love you, Lucky. I miss you so much. I hope you are OK and having fun and that God plays ball with you every day."

ters, or share stories about Andrew. Bubbles were provided. Children could take them outside to blow in remembrance of Andrew.

"Memory bags" were given to each child who attended—bags filled with treats (like stickers and a piece of candy) that Andrew's parents felt he would have liked to give to his friends. The room was filled with photos of Andrew and his fam-

ily and friends, Andrew's artwork, and the artwork of Andrew's friends. The children could walk through the room freely and experience Andrew's life visually. Andrew's favorite toys and books were on display.

The children who attended Andrew's memorial service appeared to gain a great gift, the gift of inner strength. Participating with adults in

a community remembrance of their friend gave them a way to honor Andrew's life. Knowing how to honor Andrew's life gives these children a way to value and respect their own lives. We hope this will help them be a little better prepared for other life and death experiences they will face. For sadly, sooner or later, we all must face the ending of a life.

Books to Read

For teachers and parents

Breaking the Silence: A Guide to Help Children with Complicated Grief by Linda Goldman. 1996. Washington, DC: Taylor & Francis. For adults to help children with *complicated* grief issues of suicide, homicide, AIDS, violence, and abuse. It includes guidelines for educators, national resources, an annotated bibliography, and a chapter on a child-oriented memorial service.

Good Grief: Helping Groups of Children When a Friend Dies by Sandra Fox. 1988. Boston: New England Association for the Education of Young Children. A pioneering book that is an excellent source of information for adults working with children whose friends have died. Defines death for young children with clarity and simplicity.

The Grieving Child by Helen Fitzgerald. 1992. New York: Simon & Schuster. A comprehensive guide for parents to use in helping children with their grief. It is written clearly, in a very practical style, and with many useful suggestions.

Life and Loss: A Guide to Help Grieving Children by Linda Goldman. 1994. Washington, DC: Taylor & Francis. A resource for working with children and *normal* grief. It provides practical in-

formation, resources, hands-on activities, and an annotated bibliography.

Thank You for Coming to Say Good-Bye by Janice Roberts and Joy Johnson. 1994. Omaha, NE: Centering Corporation. An excellent source of information to help caring adults involve children in funeral services.

For children

Aardy Aardvark Finds Hope by Donna O'Toole. 1988. Burnesville, NC: Mt. Rainbow Publications. (ages 5–8). In this story of grief for young children, animals are used to show the pain, sadness, and hope that is felt after the death of a loved one.

About Dying by Sarah Stein. 1974. New York: Walker & Co. (ages 3–6). Contains a simple text and photographs to help young children understand death and memorializing.

The Frog Family's Baby Dies by Jerri Oehler. 1978. Durham, NC: Duke University Medical Center. (ages 3–6). A coloring book for very young children discussing feelings after a death in the family.

So Much to Think About by Fred Rogers. 1991. Pittsburgh, PA: Family Communications, Inc. (ages 3–6). An excellent activity book for young children that allows them hands-on ways to commemorate the death of someone they have loved.

Tell Me Papa by Joy and Marv Johnson. 1990. Omaha, NE: Centering Corpora-

Andrew

tion. (ages 5–8). A book that talks in very simple and clear language about death, funerals, and how children feel about both.

You Hold Me and I'll Hold You by Jo Carson. 1992. New York: Orchard. (ages 5–8). A simple story for young children about a young girl's feelings of wanting to hold and be held at a memorial service.

Young children learn through play and grieve through play. Role-playing, puppets, artwork, clay, and sand-table work are a few of the many ways they can imagine, pretend, and engage in meaningful activities that allow them to act out or project their grief feelings without having to directly verbalize them.

Young children need to know the facts of death in an age-appropriate way. They usually imagine far worse and have a sense that they are being lied to when they are not told the truth.

For further reading

Essa, E.L., & C.I. Murray. 1994. Research in review. Young children's understanding and experience with death. *Young Children* 49 (4): 74–81.

Furman, E. 1990. Plant a potato—learn about life (and death). *Young Children* 46 (1): 15–20.

Hofschield, K. 1991. The gift of a butterfly. *Young Children* 46 (3): 3–6.

MacIsaac, P., & S. King. 1989. What did you do with Sophie, teacher? *Young Children* 44 (2): 37–38.

Riley, S.S. 1989. Pilgrimage to Elmwood cemetery. *Young Children* 44(2): 33–36.

Linda Ellen Goldman, M.S., a certified grief counselor and certified grief educator specializing in working with children and grief, is codirector of counseling for children at the Center for Loss and Grief Therapy in Kensington, Maryland. She is the author of two books on helping children with grief issues, a frequent lecturer, and private-practice therapist. In addition, she is a member of the continuing education faculty of the University of Maryland School of Social Work and a consultant to Head Start.

Children's Voices

The following excerpts reflect the thoughts, feelings, and memories of children who knew and loved Andrew. They appeared in a booklet made for Andrew's first anniversary memorial, entitled *"We Remember Andrew."*

This is a drawing that Andrew made at age four-and-a-half on one of his favorite themes: a knight with a sword.

Elyssa

"Andrew, you were a good friend. When we played the chace [chase] game it was really fun. One day Paige came over and she said that you dide [died]. I did not want to bleav [believe] her but my Mom came into my room She got a letter and said that is was tror [true]. You were such a good friend. I wish you were here your teacher wood [would] be Sharan. You wood [would] be with me Elyssa we did so much things together. I am the one uuw [you] made up huugy [huggy] but I want to end it but nothing is the same with out you

This Pache [page] is dedicadid [dedicated] to one of my Best Friends Andrew Love Elyssa."

Christina

"One day Christina, Andrew's five-year-old cousin, and I (Andrew's mom) were driving in the car. She looked at me and sighed, 'If I only had one wish, do you know what it would be? I would wish for a machine with a button on it. When I pressed the button, it would bring kids back from being dead. Then cousin Andrew would be alive. Don't you think that's a good wish?' "

Adam

"Seven-year-olds ask difficult questions. Recently, Adam asked his mother Joanne who her best friend was. She replied that she didn't have one best friend, rather she liked this person for this reason, and that person for that reason. Then she asked Adam who his best friend was. He named a friend from the neighborhood and one from his class. Then he paused, 'And Andrew . . . I didn't mind when he called me names. In fact, I kind of liked it.' Joanne says that Adam sometimes asks if the doctors will ever find out why his friend got sick and died."

Christy

"Before the Memorial Service, Christy and his mother were talking about Andrew. He had a theory about what happened to his friend: 'When you die, your body goes to the ground and makes trees. And your dreams go to heaven and they come back and get born again in other people.' "

A Do-It-Yourself Funeral

Clyde Spivey, like more and more people, chose to bypass the American way of death.

Cynthia Fox

For 50 years the amiable Clyde Spivey favored a girl who seemed his opposite: that wild redhead Nancy Sharpe. Their childhood pastimes appeared to say it all. She picked off rattlesnakes in ponds with a sawed-off shotgun; he skipped class to stoke coals with the janitor. When Nancy was 18 and ran off with another boy, it seemed fitting that Clyde would enter the Air Force and earn a Good Conduct Medal. But he also led police on high-speed chases through three Texas counties, cruising to safety through base gates. "I was a Texas Ranger," he would joke later, with a slow smile that friends said was like "prying open an oyster" but that strangers found so Bobby Kennedyesque they would stop him on the street to shake his hand.

In an era of white gloves and bow ties, Nancy flew in the face of convention. Clyde was never far behind, which may explain why, hearing she was divorced with two children at 23, he stood in her driveway until she promised to marry him. It may also explain why, 34 years later, he stood in his living room watching a heaven-blue coffin tumble through his front door.

"Sheesh," he said when it disappeared into a back room. Moving slowly, as a result of pancreatic cancer, he tacked up a sign reading RESTRICTED AREA. "This won't be an open casket deal," he said firmly.

"No," said Nancy, "but if I get mad at you tonight, you'll have somewhere to go."

"At least it'll be closure," Clyde said.

He calmly began vacuuming the hall.

The Spiveys of Durham, N.C., had decided to do Clyde's funeral themselves, from his death to the first shovel of dirt on his grave. It was an iconoclastic choice in what has become an age of identical McEverything, but the Spiveys weren't alone. Lisa Carlson, executive director of the Funeral and Memorial Societies of America and author of *Caring for the Dead*, fields 200 calls a year from people interested in bypassing funeral homes. Some 90 casket companies selling directly to consumers have sprung up in the wake of a 1994 Federal Trade Commission ruling that bars funeral homes from penalizing customers who shop around for coffins. More and more people are taking advantage of a well-kept secret: In most states, it is legal to bury the dead without mortuaries, cemeteries or embalming.

One reason for all this is that funeral and burial costs, which average $8,000 nationwide ($5,400 for the funeral alone), have been rising 5 percent a year, partly because three megaparlors—Stewart Enterprises, the Loewen Group and Service Corporation International—now control more than a quarter of the U.S. market. (In England funeral costs average $1,650; in France they're $2,200.) The hospice movement has also stimulated interest. So has the growing realization that, as James Farrell wrote in *Inventing the American Way of Death*, "the price we pay for paying our last respects in the American way of death is the price of our personality."

Clyde had plenty of that. By age 58, there was nothing McAnything about him. When Nancy bought a computer for the local TV guide they ran from their home for 19 years, he vowed never to touch "that thing." Never did. After a triple bypass in 1987, he was at work in a week, muttering about "the most expensive trip I ever took"—the $350 ambulance ride. He liked his wife, red suspenders, Dr Pepper and leaving people guessing. A sign in his office read: IF YOU CAN'T STUN 'EM WITH YOUR BRILLIANCE, BAFFLE 'EM WITH YOUR BULLSHIT.

So when his doctor gave him one to three months to live last May, he said, "No hospitals." And when Nancy came home with tales of funeral chains that can jack up prices 1,000 percent with bizarre devices like $1,000 "sealers" (actually $35 rubber gaskets that are supposed to preserve loved ones, but which mausoleum operators say can cause them to explode), exorbitant "basic service" fees, and countless bills for everything from hairstyling ($75) to makeup ($75), his reaction was in keeping with All Things Clyde.

First he went with Nancy to a mortuary. But when he asked for the cheapest casket and got the classic answer—"Not in stock"—he helped Nancy make the loneliest decision of her life. He may have dropped a few hundred on red cowboy boots in his day, but he had never paid $75 for a haircut, and he wasn't much for getting blown up. And makeup? "What does a funeral director do but stand there looking at you, anyway? Make sure the tent poles don't fall?" After Nancy found out that North Carolina doesn't require a mortuary, Clyde said, "Let's do it ourselves," and he paid $600 for a coffin that would have cost him $2,000 in a funeral home.

Until casket day, everything had gone smoothly enough. They had battled neighbors who said it was unhealthy to deal with death this way and officials who erroneously told them it was against the law. Clyde had a moment of squeamishness ("You and some nurse are cleaning me up after? You'll drown me"), but it passed. He had fended off neighbors with a quiet "Death is a fact of life."

Today, however, something was bothering Clyde. When Nancy told a hospice nurse she feared high morphine doses because when people go on them "they're gone"—and was told he had been taking them for weeks—Clyde, ironing shirts, merely raised an eyebrow as Nancy sank into a chair. But later, in the kitchen, he observed his children: Warren, 41, Nancy's son from her first marriage, a sporadically employed construction supervisor married four times; Carole, 39, his stepdaughter, married twice, now supporting a man no one much approved of; Clyde Eric, 29, a born father as good-natured as his namesake, if wilder than his mother. While all knew that Clyde Eric had settled down when his daughter Haley was conceived, they also knew he had started partying again when told about the cancer. They all brought gifts—Warren, gospel music; Carole, a map pinpointing the star she had registered in his name; Clyde Eric, dinner fixings. Even Carole's son Jacob was there, which was something, seeing as he had stayed away when his great-grandmother died.

A week earlier, perusing the funeral album Nancy was making, Clyde had said: "My kids have me tore up. I pushed too hard. I really expected them to do better than I did." They had taken up half his ways, he thought, flying in the face of things, without taking up the other half, shouldering consequences. "And now there's this . . . We've had family meetings about the cancer, because mine never talked about death. Never saw my parents or brother die. So I'm trying to make them talk, handle things—something . . . poor babies."

Home funerals often "start as a money thing and turn into something else," Lisa Carlson says. The Natural Death Care Project of Sebastopol, Calif., which helps families make personalized caskets, calls do-it-yourself funerals journeys that can "connect the hearts of those

who are present to a universalizing whole." Clyde wasn't sure about that. Prompted by the invitation to honesty implied by the whole deal, a neighbor had nudged her children forward like a stage mother. "I'm sad you're going to die," one said. "Me too," said the other. Clyde nodded. "Yep," he replied. When more was apparently required, he added, uncomfortably, "It's too bad."

Sheesh.

And this funeral book he was supposed to write in? After weeks of deliberation, this is what he dredged up for his wife of 34 years: "I love you and I'm sorry I'm so stubborn."

Nope. He didn't know from "universalizing wholes."

He did know, however, that his kids were afraid of life. And why hadn't he been there for his parents' families in death? Had he been afraid of something too?

Since the illness, he had begun attending alcohol-free hootenannies. Banjos going at each other, no secrets and nothing to fear, just tobacco fields flat as Texas and people unexpectedly busting into clog dances everywhere. Maybe this crazy home funeral could bust them all up a bit, like that. Bring about some unexpected things.

Yet into the kitchen now came Warren, who, in a mood, had said he might miss the funeral because of a fishing tournament. In came Carole, who'd been staying away lately, admitting she was afraid of the dying, the talk. In came the jubilant baby Haley, riding Aunt Carole's hip, wearing sunglasses. Clyde tidied up his isosorbide, Toprol XL, Compazine, Valium, Advil, erythromycin—30 pills a day. The nurse had just added a 31st ritual: a swab for his neck so he could avoid death rattles at the end. Coffins, death rattles, babies holding babies. "Eaten anything?" he asked lightly, rising to make eggs.

That night, Clyde Eric, Carole and her kids read Bible verses into a tape recorder for the funeral. They went outside to smoke, their words lost in a symphony of crickets and tree frogs. "When Mama's daddy died, it was like someone grabbed the moon out of the sky," said Carole, brushing away a slug. She watched her 11-year-old look in vain through a telescope for his granddaddy's star.

A week later, a scare. Clyde threw up a cup of blood, cancer having pierced an organ. The family gathered, then scattered the next morning when Clyde serenely rose to pick up the TV guides from the printer's. In a nearby "honey pot," Clyde Eric fished for crappies and reminisced about his childhood, which involved, among other things, spray-painting cows pink.

That night, as Clyde, a practiced audience, lowered and hoisted an eyebrow, Nancy reenacted her day. Today's problem: the refusal of the Greensboro News & Record's obit desk to take hospice's word for a death. This had followed the health department's contention that it couldn't issue a death certificate if Clyde died on a weekend, and the claim of Guilford Memorial Park, the Loewen-owned cemetery where the family has prepaid plots, that the law required a funeral director. "Oh,"

Nancy said, throttling a pillow, "they're messing with the wrong redhead."

Clyde Eric had haunted the house for weeks, doing chores. Now, as he changed Haley's diapers, he went into high Spivey gear. Remember the L.A. trip? The old CB? "Tell the one about..." he said repeatedly, with his father's half-smile. Nancy threw a magazine at him and hit Clyde instead. "Now what did you do that for?" Clyde said, strapping his old Roy Rogers cap guns to his hips and soft-shoeing around the room. When he remembered an errand, his son said, "I can drive you." Clyde considered him. "Yes, Sunshine. You're always there."

"This one," Clyde said later, when asked which was the best year of his life. But at bedtime he stood in the kitchen with one arm around Nancy, his forehead touching hers as she sobbed.

August was a bad month. Warren left the house angry and didn't return. Carole stayed away a lot, frightened off again, and Clyde Eric was in turmoil: The mother of his child had left him. Clyde bought a power mower, taking pleasure in ferrying a visitor around the yard. But he also went from 360 milligrams of morphine daily to over 670, from 140 pounds to 90. One night, toward the end of the month, he began running in circles, in his underwear and his fanny pack of morphine, huddled over his fists as if racing a car around the dark house. The next day he didn't get up.

Then something unexpected: Without discussion, Clyde Eric, Jacob and the baby moved in. For the next two weeks, while Nancy was ill with bronchitis, it was the boys who tended the near-mute Clyde around the clock, regulating his morphine, carrying him to the bathroom as delicately as if leading him in a minuet. He was skeletal and uncoordinated, puppetlike, but he fought their help. They fought back. Hour after hour, he'd point above his head, a terrorized look on his face; hour after hour, Clyde Eric rushed from one room to another, changing his daughter's diapers, changing his dad's.

On September 13 they were joined by Carole, who spent a day and a night wrapped in a quilt, stroking her father's hair and talking in a bedtime-story voice. The next day, Warren came home. All searched Clyde's face, seeking evidence that he was still there. When a neighbor chirped, "Seen any angels yet, honey?" they got their answer. An eyebrow rose high on his face. "There he is!" Carole said. When Nancy came in, he pushed up his lips like a volcano: kiss.

Warren stayed with Clyde all night. The next day the hospice nurse visited, then tiptoed into Nancy's room. Nancy rushed out and lay beside her husband, pushing aside the baby dinosaur blanket covering him. The room filled with stunned family, so silent the oxygen machine was heard slurping. Clyde had died in one of the few moments he'd been alone since May.

Then another unexpected thing. The plan was for Nancy and the nurse to handle Clyde's death. But it was Warren who took his father's suit out of a closet, and Clyde Eric who hastily polished his boots. Once started, they just kept going. Warren clipped his father's eyebrows; Clyde Eric brought in a tub. Warren washed Clyde's face and chest, as Clyde Eric and Jacob held his fragile body. "Mama, we need his Sunday belt," Clyde Eric said, sending Nancy running. The boys dressed their father, placing his arms through the shirt, vest and jacket gingerly, as if not to awaken him. Warren tied his father's tie; Clyde Eric slipped the boots on. When done, all three raised paper cups to Clyde, then headed for the back room to get the coffin that had been stashed there months before. They placed it on a stand in the living room and fixed its cotton batting the way they would make a bed.

Later, they carried Clyde to the coffin. Clyde Eric cried as he folded his father's hands, then leaned over, smiling as if listening to him say something ornery. When Nancy announced that she didn't want her husband's mouth open, they tied a handkerchief around his head like a bonnet and placed a teddy bear under his chin. They closed the lid, draped it in the serviceman's American flag and stood still, looking around the house that no longer had Clyde Spivey in it, yet did.

The boys climbed into sleeping bags beside their father. "I've never seen anything like it," said the nurse as she left.

The next day, Nancy and Clyde Eric picked up a death certificate from the health department, which Nancy says had stopped objecting when told that *LIFE* was doing a story. They got it signed by the doctor, then went to the local papers, which took the obits. (The Greensboro editor had caved in after Nancy called the company that owns the paper to protest.) They gave another copy to cemetery head Merle Neal, who had agreed to a burial without a funeral director after Corrine Culbreth, executive director of the state Board of Mortuary Science, explained the law to her. "She should know better," Culbreth said. "She is a licensed funeral director."

At seven the following evening, 40 friends gathered in the Spiveys' living room. Next to the coffin, which had toys scattered at its base, was a crib with the baby dinosaur blanket crumpled inside.

The next day the men in Clyde's life loaded the coffin into a friend's van. At the cemetery, they carried it to the burial site, then sat in the tent Clyde had joked about when the whole hootenanny began. (Tent poles held.) After playing the tape of family Bible readings, Nancy grabbed a shovel and tossed a pile of dirt into the air. She looked vibrant against the McCemetery green. She was dressed in her husband's favorite color, the red of her hair.

The most complete guide to DIYs can be found in Lisa Carlson's *Caring for the Dead* (Upper Access, 1998). For more information, contact FAMSA at 800-765-0107 or www.funerals.org/famsa; R.E. Markin, author of *The Affordable Funeral*, at 757-427-0220; Father Henry Wasielewski at 602-253-6814.

A Time to Mourn

by Pat Andrus, MS, CFLE, CGC

We often say that our industry is dedicated to helping people in their time of greatest need. Yet for many who lose a loved one, that time comes days, weeks, months or even years after the funeral and burial ceremonies end. A birthday, an anniversary or simply a rainy Monday morning can bring on intense feelings of grief and depression. In response, many cemeteries and funeral homes provide aftercare services ranging from newsletter mailings to intensive counseling. Since its inception six years ago, The Mourning After Program at Martin and Castille Funeral Home in Lafayette, Louisiana, has become one of the most comprehensive and successful aftercare programs in the industry.

My day began with a 7:30 a.m. photo shoot and planning meeting for an upcoming community training event on therapeutic intervention for grieving children and teens, followed by a two-hour session with a new client whose mother died six weeks ago. Next, I headed to a local hospital for an in-service brown bag luncheon with the social workers on staff, where I discussed various skills for handling bereaved families. This was followed by a 30-minute private debriefing with one social worker struggling with reactions to the tragic death of a toddler run over as his father backed out of the family's driveway.

Next, I returned to my office, where I attended a staff meeting, proofread a flier produced for The Grief Center of Southwest Louisiana and checked the production progress of the funeral home's fall 1996 newsletter. Finally, at 3 p.m., I settled in at my computer to begin work on this article.

Since being named director of The Mourning After Program at Martin and Castille Funeral Home in 1990, I have never had a boring, routine day. I have at times felt overwhelmed and overloaded, but I have always enjoyed the diversity of my job and the challenge of finding new avenues to respond to the needs of our families and community.

The Mourning After Program

The primary purpose of The Mourning After Program is to provide education, support and referral resources to the families we serve and our community at large. It is the most extensive aftercare program in the Lafayette area; each year it serves more than 450 families as well as an additional 600 to 1,000 individuals through in-service programs, presentations and training sessions.

As coordinator, I am the only employee who is devoted full-time to the program, though all funeral home staff participate at some level. In addition, university interns play a vital role in planning and administering certain events.

Some of the primary components of the program are as follows:
• individual grief education, counseling and community referrals;
• follow-up home visits;

Reprinted with permission from *International Cemetery and Funeral Management,* October 1996, pp. 26-30. © 1996 by the International Cemetery and Funeral Association, Reston, VA 20191.

- a resource reference library;
- community outreach and grief seminars; and
- a quarterly newsletter.

Education, counseling and referrals. Educating people about the process of grief and bereavement usually is the most important part of our services. Counseling comes afterward, as we help clients define other resources and make choices for themselves. In some ways, education and counseling come together much like beaten egg whites folded into waffle batter. The two become one to make the perfect waffle. Without either part, the batter is flat and is of lesser quality and flavor.

Individuals and families grieving losses from any area of life are welcome to contact The Mourning After Program. Our families often return to us near anniversary times or when some other event triggers their old pain anew. They know they are welcome to ask questions without fear of being judged. The number of calls we receive from "outside" fluctuates with the holidays, the start of school after summer vacations or when tragedy strikes in smaller communities.

During counseling sessions, I provide a listening ear, resource information and education regarding the grief process, and I help the client define his or her needs. Primarily, people want to know they are all right and are experiencing their pain in acceptable ways. They want to know they are not going crazy even though they find themselves in a crazy situation. Reading sensitively written literature, attending seminars and support groups or watching a film on grief often provides the needed reassurance and comfort.

I usually schedule one or two visits with interested clients and then refer those with complicated or unresolved grief issues to local licensed counselors and social workers. They are responsible for making their own arrangements for private counseling with these professionals.

In addition to providing referrals through our counseling sessions, Martin and Castille produces a "Directory of Support Services for the Bereaved." This free 25-page pamphlet offers listings for support groups, educational programs, grief coun-

Jake Barber, age 4, participates in The Mourning After Program's Small Remembrances program, a children's memorial service held each December at the funeral home.

selors in private practice and a speakers bureau as well as other information. The funeral home publishes the directory as a joint project with a local hospital, which helps reduce costs. This service has proved effective in building credibility and referrals for both the funeral home and the hospital.

Home visits. In addition to providing counseling at our offices, we sometimes schedule home visits with Martin and Castille clients. This may include delivering the remaining paperwork and the death certificate or handling insurance signature requests. When possible, I take the time to discuss grief and bereavement issues, family needs and changes, and concerns regarding financial resources.

In the last several years, the number of home visits we have been able to conduct has diminished drastically due to time constraints. However, our president, vice president, funeral directors and office staff continue to screen the families we serve and recommend home visits for those they feel would find this service most beneficial. This often includes those who are ill, those who are uneasy about returning to the funeral home and those who specifically request a home visit.

Occasionally the funeral directors conduct initial home visits by delivering paperwork and the funeral register book, and they routinely make care calls by phone at regular intervals after the funeral. In addition, all families we serve receive a folder of materials that includes general grief information, special topic information specific to their loss, and introductory materials to The Mourning After Program.

Recently an elderly widow brusquely requested that the funeral home deliver her paperwork to her home as she didn't drive much and had no one to help her. She said she wanted no company cars with insignia in her driveway and was specific about the way the funeral director should act when going to see her. The executive secretary preparing her paperwork, concerned that the woman was perhaps paranoid or lived as a hermit, asked me to conduct a home visit.

Upon arriving at the woman's home, located in a prominent neighborhood, I found she had triple locks and a dog kennel guarding her entrance. At first, she refused to open the door, but after speaking with me for several minutes, she cracked it slightly. Ultimately she invited me in. We chatted for two hours in her small, cramped kitchen. To control expenses and the need for cleaning and to allow her to spend the maximum amount of time caring for her dying husband, she had closed off the remainder of the house.

This brilliant woman shared her history of world travel, university teaching and musical talents as well as her romantic marriage. She shared the pain of early childhood inadequacies and the breakdown of her family. She discussed the difficulties of having her only stepson live in a distant state and her fears of social service agencies and counselors. She described how overwhelmed she felt by her lack of control in her husband's death and her sense of guilt and helplessness in being unable to keep him alive.

By the end of our visit, she had invited me to come back, agreed she would call me to pick up groceries occasionally, complimented our funeral home services and

spoke of planning her own prearrangements with us. Our gift to her was someone who could fully listen to her, hear her pain and fear, serve as a resource and be available to her during her bereavement. Her gift to me was helping me fall asleep that night knowing my work makes a difference.

The Olive Branch Library. Our library offers a well-stocked selection of books, magazines, journals, pamphlets and VHS tapes geared toward grief management and coping with loss. We regularly add new materials, basing our selection on factors such as specific death topics, reading/listening levels, target audience age or overall usefulness to our market. Our children's materials and general grief information have proved most popular.

The Olive Branch, which is housed in the funeral home conference room, is open for use during our business hours. The public is welcome to browse through the materials, preferably with an appointment time. They can check out items of interest. Unfortunately, some items

Helping Yourself Through Grief

The Mourning After Program's newsletter, *A Comforting Voice*, provides information on Martin & Castille services as well as general grief management. The following advice on handling grief is excerpted from the spring/summer 1996 edition.

- Allow yourself plenty of time to heal. It takes much longer than we want to realize . . . months, not days, and yes, years in many instances.
- Acknowledge your losses. They are important.
- Cry if you need to cry. Sometimes arranging a special time and place eases our embarrassment about crying in public. Not all of us cry alike . . . some tears come as sobs, some as sighs, some are silent.
- Set small goals. Over and over again, set small goals. Baby steps become achievements and accomplishments.
- Exercise helps us sleep better.
- Find your sense of humor. Hang on tight!
- Keeping a diary or journal gives us a place to jot down thoughts and memories. Sometimes it may only be a reminder to do a task. Sometimes it's what I am afraid to voice aloud quite yet.
- Eating nutritiously is helpful, even though we don't have time or energy to cook. Just try to increase fruits and vegetables, pastas, rice, breads and other carbohydrates. Lower fats, gravies, sauces and desserts.
- Decrease alcohol and drug consumption. Drugs and alcohol mask the pain for awhile but cannot remove the pain from us.
- Accept and give out hugs.
- Have a physical checkup with a trusted physician. Review prescribed medications with a physician familiar with the grief process. Not all doctors truly understand the process or how to treat grief effectively.
- Water is necessary for our stressed bodies. Substitute water and/or fruit juice for caffeinated drinks. Decreasing the use of carbonated beverages eases digestion.

- Postpone major decisions such as selling your home, changing jobs, divorcing your spouse. Get some qualified guidance on major decision making.
- Consider participating in a support group. Family and friends may not understand the need to retell our story over and over.
- Tell others what you want from them: help, emotional support, time shared, etc.
- Seek spiritual guidance. Having a crisis in faith is not unusual in grief.
- Check out advice. Accepting the imperfections of others means realizing I have imperfections too. We all give and get bad advice at times.
- Expand your vocabulary of feeling words. Reach past the usual ones: bad, sad, glad and mad.
- Use music, art, philosophy, religion, gardening, games, nature walks, reading, writing and volunteer work to gain comfort, relief and understanding.
- Seek professional counseling to work on specific issues, questions, bothersome ideas, or just to sort things out. There's strength in knowledge.
- Realize suicidal thoughts are an intense reaction to the pain of bereavement. Reach out for help immediately.
- Make plans for the tough times like weekends, holidays, evenings, anniversaries, birthdays and other special occasions.
- Planning a ritual can help us release emotion around specific loss and gain a sense of closure. Rituals may be simple or elaborate, individual or group-oriented, personal or public.
- Recognize your impatience for what it is—a desire to be better. Just as it takes time for bread to bake, we must allow ourselves to rise, be punched down and rise again. Otherwise the product is hard and tasteless, never having developed fully.

—Pat Andrus

never find their way back to us in spite of phone calls and careful monitoring, so we purchase multiple editions of the most popular materials. When families contact us to request books, I usually meet and speak with them about their specific needs.

In addition to helping those who are dealing with grief, the library serves as a general education resource for the community. We see an influx of students around term-paper time each semester.

Community work. Our community work is a key ingredient in the success of Martin and Castille Funeral Home. Professionals in our community such as school counselors and hospital social workers turn to us for guidance, education and resource identification. Families often choose our funeral home based on the recommendations of such professionals or simply because they know we have The Mourning After Program.

By collaborating with other agencies, hospitals and organizations, we demonstrate our high ethical standards and achieve shared success. We hold yearly grief seminars, inviting the public to hear major speakers such as Dr. Alan Wolfelt and Dr. Rabbi Earl Grollman.

As trainer/facilitator, I regularly conduct series such as "Adjusting to Widowhood" and "When Grief Hits Home: The Death of Your Parent." I offer frequent presentations to support groups such as Widowed Persons Service groups, Compassionate Friends and church bereavement groups. In addition, I have participated in special programs for the Louisiana Ministerial Alliance; the local Older Americans Conference; university nursing, sociology and consumer health classes; and social service agency staffs. Finally, I conduct a number of in-service training sessions for nurses, social workers, police, teachers, school counselors, emergency personnel and nursing home staffs.

As a state vice president and long-time local volunteer with the Louisiana chapter of the American Heart Association, I have worked to identify ways Martin and Castille can work with this influential group to integrate programming and fundraising efforts. For example, by coordinating efforts for the more than 7,000 individuals in our Spanish-speaking community to receive free cholesterol and blood pressure screenings as well as health and nutrition lessons, I established Martin and Castille as the firm that helps them live better lives. This fits hand-in-hand with our funeral home's tag line, "Helping you through life."

Another group in which I am active is The Grief Center of Southwest Louisiana, which began in 1991 as a discussion and debriefing group for those working in the bereavement field and became incorporated in January 1996. Through this organization, Martin and Castille, Lafayette General Medical Center and the Diocese of Lafayette Office of Justice and Peace recently hosted a program to train community bereavement personnel on working with children and traumatic grief issues. The center plans to offer initial group and individual services to grieving children by early spring 1997.

The Grief Center of Southwest Louisiana builds on Martin and Castille's "Small Remembrances" program, special children's memorial services held at the funeral home in early December. "Small Remembrances" allows more than 200 children and their adult caretakers to participate in an educational lesson and candle-lighting ceremony in honor of the loss of a pet or family member through death, divorce, relocation or other causes.

Co-sponsoring events with other organizations and community groups allows everyone concerned to stretch their advertising dollars and spread the workload. Since The Mourning After Program is not an income-producing enterprise, this business-to-business networking proves highly effective in maintaining our reputation as a well-respected asset to the community. In addition, we have become involved in several co-sponsorships with leading television stations, allowing us to build a rapport with the media on both personal and professional levels.

> **People want to know they are all right and are experiencing their pain in acceptable ways. They want to know they are not going crazy even though they find themselves in a crazy situation.**

A Comforting Voice **newsletter.** The production of our quarterly newsletter is an excellent tool for reaching individuals, families, support groups and professionals. By carefully balancing articles, we repeat grief education themes through new words and formats. The newsletter also announces upcoming events, invites participation, and encourages the use of our resources.

This year we are shifting from a quarterly newsletter to Spring/Summer and Fall/Winter editions with a Special Holiday Issue. This allows us to massage our budget a bit, creates a special edition that can be used for two to three years worth of mailings and adds a new look to our six-year-old newsletter style.

Aftercare and You

Not all cemetery and funeral home aftercare programs are as extensive or involved in the community as ours has become. But if you have not already begun considering ways to offer aftercare, now is the time.

Aftercare programs can take many paths, which can be used effectively on their own or in conjunction with one another. Grief seminars, sensitive literature, support groups, bereavement education groups, counseling, newsletters, information and referral services all offer distinct possibilities for aftercare.

One thing these programs have in common is that they offer dual benefits: They help your clients while at the same time helping your business. Martin and Castille has found that name recognition and free publicity for the funeral home abound because of the work we do. The Mourning After Program—and therefore the funeral home—are recognized by mental health, social service and medical professionals as the grief experts in the region. Media interviews on specific topics such as grief during the holidays and coverage of our many community-based events provide public broadcasting of our name and services at no monetary cost.

School teachers, administrators and counselors respect our leadership and gratefully use our resource library. This in turn opens the door for me to work within their systems. After one presentation, an elementary school counselor wrote, "Thank you for coming to work with my students. I feel it helped a group of students that might not have 'tapped into' these feelings, otherwise."

Community reaction to our presentations offers clear evidence that word-of-mouth is the best form of advertising. By consistently interacting within the health fields, we receive recognition from many. We have been told we have heart . . . are wise . . . are blessings to our community . . . have shared insights . . . have responded to someone's great need . . . and offered assistance at just at the right time. This type of feedback offers benefits not only in the form of increased business but also in the form of our own professional development and gratification.

Family members and friends of the deceased often express relief in realizing their emotions and behaviors, while scary, are normal reactions to grief. One of our most moving letters came from a woman whose husband had committed suicide a year and a half earlier, leaving her to rear their two-year-old daughter. "I was laying here thinking about . . . the many times you saved my life," she wrote. "I can't thank you enough for your help. [My daughter] has been asking for her daddy, so I finally found the strength to say, 'Daddy died and he's never coming back.' That was hard but I did it."

I think Wes Castille, our vice president, expressed it best. When asked his views on the greatest benefit of The Mourning After Program to our funeral home, he answered, "Yes, it has drawn attention and recognition to us as a funeral home. More importantly, our own empathy has heightened. We have broadened our horizons for what we are about. And we have increased the public's and our own personal awareness of how grief affects our community at large."

The value of providing aftercare services far outweighs the cost and effort. It can be the highest form of marketing and public relations. The good we do in our area has led to a shift in the market share for us. In addition, while our program stays separate from preneed sales, it does present an opportunity to encourage those we serve to consider prearrangement. I am always willing to help connect clients or community persons with a funeral director, and I consistently encourage prearrangement as a wise decision and even a form of stress management.

Finally, I believe aftercare programs can help revitalize our entire industry, bringing it back full circle to one that is viewed as compassionate and life-supporting. Through aftercare, your firm has the power to help the cemetery and funeral industry become a positive force in today's society.

Pat Andrus is director of The Mourning After Program at Martin and Castille Funeral Home in Lafayette, Louisiana. She is certified as a family life educator and grief counselor.

Unit 6

Key Points to Consider

❖ Discuss how the seven stages of grieving over death can also be applied to losses through divorce, moving from one place to another, or the amputation of a limb (arm or leg). What is the relationship between time and the feelings of grief experienced within the bereavement process?

❖ Describe the four necessary tasks of mourning. What are some of the practical steps one can take in accomplishing each of these tasks? How can one assist friends in bereavement?

❖ What are the special problems encountered in the death of a child and in a perinatal death? How can one assist friends in this special type of bereavement?

❖ How can one know if one is experiencing "normal" bereavement or "abnormal" bereavement? What are some of the signs of aberrant bereavement? What could you do to assist people experiencing abnormal grief symptoms?

 **Links**   **www.dushkin.com/online/**

These sites are annotated on pages 4 and 5.

In American society many act as if the process of bereavement is completed with the culmination of public mourning related to the funeral or memorial service and the final disposition of the dead. For those in the process of grieving, the end of public mourning only serves to make the bereavement process a more individualized, subjective, and private experience. Private mourning of loss for most people, while more intense at its beginning, continues throughout their lifetime. The nature and intensity of this experience is influenced by the relationship of the mourner to the deceased, the age of the mourner, and the social context in which bereavement takes place.

This unit on bereavement begins with two general articles on the bereavement process. The first article, by Michael Leming and George Dickinson, describes and discusses the active coping strategies related to the bereavement process, disenfranchised grief, and the four tasks of bereavement. The second article, by Kenneth Doka, provides assistance for caregivers in dealing with the needs of bereaved survivors who cannot acknowledge their grief publicly. Next, an article by Charles Corr enhances and broadens the concept of disenfranchised grief in significant ways and explains that there are aspects of most losses that are indeed disenfranchised.

The fourth article, by Therese Rando ("The Increasing Prevalence of Complicated Mourning") illustrates the principles described by Leming and Dickinson by providing a critique of America's health care industry for its lack of involvement in the post-death grieving experience. This article discusses many different types of death and the respective influences upon the bereaved while suggesting strategies for active coping with grief.

The remaining four articles of this unit focus upon bereavement and coping strategies employed by diverse populations. The first of these articles, written by Linda Goldman, deals with children and bereavement and provides very practical strategies for assisting children to memorialize and mourn the deaths of significant others. The next article, by Morton Ender and Joan Hermsen, discusses the challenging task of working with bereaved families that have nontraditional family structures. Beth Becker discusses the changing and varied ways in which Americans are dealing with death in a multicultural society. She claims that some of the changes are supportive of the bereaved, while others are not. The last article, "GriefTips: Help for Those Who Mourn," provides a number of very practical coping strategies that grievers have found helpful in living with loss and bereavement.

The Grieving Process

Michael R. Leming
St. Olaf College

George E. Dickinson
College of Charleston

G rief is a very powerful emotion that is often triggered or stimulated by death. Thomas Attig makes an important distinction between grief and the grieving process. Although grief is an emotion that engenders feelings of helplessness and passivity, the process of grieving is a more complex coping process that presents challenges and opportunities for the griever and requires energy to be invested, tasks to be undertaken, and choices to be made (Attig, 1991, p. 387).

Most people believe that grieving is a diseaselike and debilitating process that renders the individual passive and helpless. According to Attig (1991, p. 389):

> It is misleading and dangerous to mistake grief for the whole of the experience of the bereaved. It is misleading because the experience is far more complex, entailing diverse emotional, physical, intellectual, spiritual, and social impacts. It is dangerous because it is precisely this aspect of the experience of the bereaved that is potentially the most frustrating and debilitating.

Death ascribes to the griever a passive social position in the bereavement role. Grief is an emotion over which the individual has no control. However, understanding that grieving is an active coping process can restore to the griever a sense of autonomy in which the process is permeated with choice and there are many areas over which the griever does have some control. . . .

Coping With Grief

The grieving process, like the dying process, is essentially a series of behaviors and attitudes related to coping with the stressful situation of changing the status of a relationship. . . . Many have attempted to understand coping with dying as a series of universal, mutually exclusive, and linear stages. However, because most will acknowledge that not all people will progress through the stages in the same manner, we will list a number of coping strategies used as people attempt to resolve the pain caused by the loss of a significant relationship.

Robert Kavanaugh (1972) identifies the following seven behaviors and feelings as part of the coping process: shock and denial, disorganization, volatile emotions, guilt, loss and loneliness, relief, and reestablishment. It is not difficult to see similarities between these behaviors and Kübler-Ross's five stages (denial, anger, bargaining, depression, and acceptance) of the dying process. According to Kavanaugh (1972, p. 23), "these seven stages do not subscribe to the logic of the head as much as to the irrational tugs of the heart—the logic of need and permission."

SHOCK AND DENIAL

Even when a significant other is expected to die, at the time of death there is often a sense in which the death is not real. For most of us our first response is, "No, this can't be true." With time our experience of shock diminishes, but we find new ways to deny the reality of death.

Some believe that denial is dysfunctional behavior for those in bereavement. However, denial not only is a common experience among the newly bereaved, but also serves positive functions in the process of adaptation. The main function of denial is to provide the bereaved with a "temporary safe place" from the ugly realities of a social world that offers only loneliness and pain.

With time the meaning of loss tends to expand, and it may be impossible for one to deal with all of the social meanings of death at once. For example, if my wife dies, not only do I lose my spouse, but also I lose my best friend, my sexual partner, the mother of my children, a source of income, the person who writes the Christmas cards, and so on. Denial can protect me from some of the magnitude of this social loss, which may be unbearable at one point in time. With denial, I can work through different aspects of my loss over time.

DISORGANIZATION

Disorganization is that stage in the bereavement process in which one may feel totally out of touch with the reality of everyday life. Some go through the 3-day time period just prior to the funeral as if on "automatic pilot" or "in a daze."

Nothing normal "makes sense," and they may feel that life has no inherent meaning. For some, death is perceived as preferable to life, which appears to be devoid of meaning.

This emotional response is also a normal experience for the newly bereaved. Confusion is normal for those whose social world has been disorganized through death. When my father died, my mother lost not only all of those things that one loses with a death of a spouse, but also her caregiving role—a social role and master status that had defined her identity in the 5 years that my father lived with cancer. It is only natural to experience confusion and social disorganization when one's social identity has been destroyed.

VOLATILE REACTIONS

Whenever one's identity and social order face the possibility of destruction, there is a natural tendency to feel angry, frustrated, helpless, and/or hurt. The volatile reactions of terror, hatred, resentment, and jealousy are often experienced as emotional manifestations of these feelings. Grieving humans are sometimes more successful at masking their feelings in socially acceptable behaviors than other animals, whose instincts cause them to go into a fit of rage when their order is threatened by external forces. However apparently dissimilar, the internal emotional experience is similar.

In working with bereaved persons over the past 15 years, I have observed that the following become objects of volatile grief reactions: God, medical personnel, funeral directors, other family members, in-laws, friends who have not experienced death in their families, and/or even the person who has died. I have always found it interesting to watch mild-mannered individuals transformed into raging and resentful persons when grieving. Some of these people have experienced physical symptoms such as migraine headaches, ulcers, neuropathy, and colitis as a result of living with these intense emotions.

GUILT

Guilt is similar to the emotional reactions discussed earlier. Guilt is anger and resentment turned in on oneself and often results in self-deprecation and depression. It typically manifests itself in statements like "If only I had . . . ," "I should have . . . ," "I could have done it differently. . . ," and "Maybe I did the wrong thing." Guilt is a normal part of the bereavement process.

From a sociological perspective, guilt can become a social mechanism to resolve the **dissonance** that people feel when unable to explain why someone else's loved one has died. Rather than view death as something that can happen at any time to any one, people can **blame the victim** of bereavement and believe that the victim of bereavement was in some way responsible for the death—"If he had been a better parent, the child might not have been hit by the car," or "If I had been married to him I might also have committed suicide," or "No wonder he died of a heart attack, her cooking would give anyone high cholesterol." Therefore, bereaved persons are some-times encouraged to feel guilt because they are subtly sanctioned by others' reactions.

LOSS AND LONELINESS

As we discussed earlier, loss and loneliness are the other side of denial. Their full sense never becomes obvious at once; rather, each day without the deceased helps us to recognize how much we needed and depended upon those persons. Social situations in which we expected them always to be present seem different now that they are gone. Holiday celebrations are also diminished by their absence. In fact, for some, most of life takes on a "something's missing" feeling. This feeling was captured in the 1960s love song "End of the World."

> Why does the world go on turning?
> Why must the sea rush to shore?
> Don't they know it's the end of the world
> 'Cause you don't love me anymore?

Loss and loneliness are often transformed into depression and sadness fed by feelings of self-pity. According to Kavanaugh (1972, p. 118), this effect is magnified by the fact that the dead loved one grows out of focus in memory—"an elf becomes a giant, a sinner becomes a saint because the grieving heart needs giants and saints to fill an expanding void." Even a formerly undesirable spouse, such as an alcoholic, is missed in a way that few can understand unless their own hearts are involved. This is a time in the grieving process when anybody is better than nobody and being alone only adds to the curse of loss and loneliness (Kavanaugh, 1972, p. 118).

Those who try to escape this experience will either turn to denial in an attempt to reject their feelings of loss or try to find surrogates—new friends at a bar, a quick remarriage, or a new pet. This escape can never be permanent, however, because loss and loneliness are a necessary part of the bereavement experience. According to Kavanaugh (1972, p. 119), the "ultimate goal in conquering loneliness" is to build a new independence or to find a new and equally viable relationship.

RELIEF

The experience of relief in the midst of the bereavement process may seem odd for some and add to their feelings of guilt. My mother found relief in the fact that my father's battle with cancer had ended, even though this end provided her with new problems. I have observed a friend's relief 6 months after her husband died. This older friend of mine was the wife of a minister, and her whole life before he died was his ministry. With time, as she built a new world of social involvements and relationships of which he was not a part, she discovered a new independent person in herself whom she perceived was a better person than she had ever been.

Although relief can give rise to feelings of guilt, like denial, it can also be experienced as a "safe place" from the pain, loss, and loneliness that are endured when one is grieving. According to Kavanaugh (1972, p. 121):

The feeling of relief does not imply any criticism for the love we lost. Instead, it is a reflection of our need for ever deeper love, our quest for someone or something always better, our search for the infinite, that best and perfect love religious people name as God.

REESTABLISHMENT

As one moves toward reestablishment of a life without the deceased, it is obvious that the process involves extensive adjustment and time, especially if the relationship was meaningful. It is likely that one may have feelings of loneliness, guilt, and disorganization at the same time and that just when one may experience a sense of relief something will happen to trigger a denial of the death. What facilitates bereavement and adjustment is fully experiencing each of these feelings as normal and realizing that it is hope (holding the grieving person together in fantasy at first) that will provide the promise of a new life filled with order, purpose, and meaning.

Reestablishment never occurs all at once. Rather, it is a goal that one realizes has been achieved long after it has occurred. In some ways it is similar to Dorothy's realization at the end of *The Wizard of Oz*—she had always possessed the magic that could return her to Kansas. And, like Dorothy, we have to experience our loss before we really appreciate the joy of investing our lives again in new relationships.

The Four Tasks of Mourning

In 1982 J. William Worden published *Grief Counseling and Grief Therapy,* which summarized the research conclusions of a National Institutes of Health study called the Omega Project (occasionally referred to as the Harvard Bereavement Study). Two of the more significant findings of this research, displaying the active nature of the grieving process, are that mourning is necessary for all persons who have experienced a loss through death and that four tasks of mourning must be accomplished before mourning can be completed and reestablishment can take place.

According to Worden (1982, p. 10), unfinished grief tasks can impair further growth and development of the individual. Furthermore, the necessity of these tasks suggests that those in bereavement must attend to "grief work" because successful grief resolution is not automatic, as Kavanaugh's (1972) stages might imply. Each bereaved person must accomplish four necessary tasks: (a) accept the reality of the loss, (b) experience the pain of grief (c) adjust to an environment in which the deceased is missing, and (d) withdraw emotional energy and reinvest it in another relationship (Worden, 1982).

ACCEPT THE REALITY OF THE LOSS

Especially in situations when death is unexpected and/or the deceased lived far away, it is difficult to conceptualize the reality of the loss. The first task of mourning is to overcome the natural denial response and realize that the person is dead and will not return.

Bereaved persons can facilitate the actualization of death in many ways. The traditional ways are to view the body, attend the funeral and committal services, and visit the place of final disposition. The following is a partial list of additional activities that can assist in making death real for grieving persons.

1. View the body at the place of death before preparation by the funeral director.
2. Talk about the deceased and the circumstances surrounding the death.
3. View photographs and personal effects of the deceased.
4. Distribute the possessions of the deceased among relatives and friends.

EXPERIENCE THE PAIN OF GRIEF

Part of coming to grips with the reality of death is experiencing the emotional and physical pain caused by the loss. Many people in the denial stage of grieving attempt to avoid pain by choosing to reject the emotions and feelings that they are experiencing. Some do this by avoiding places and circumstances that remind them of the deceased. I know of one widow who quit playing golf and quit eating at a particular restaurant because these were activities that she had enjoyed with her husband. Another widow found it extremely painful to be with her dead husband's twin, even though he and her sister-in-law were her most supportive friends.

J. William Worden (1982, pp. 13–14) cites the following case study to illustrate the performance of this task of mourning:

> One young woman minimized her loss by believing her brother was out of his dark place and into a better place after his suicide. This might have been true, but it kept her from feeling her intense anger at him for leaving her. In treatment, when she first allowed herself to feel anger, she said, "I'm angry with his behavior and not him!" Finally she was able to acknowledge this anger directly.

The problem with the avoidance strategy is that people cannot escape the pain associated with mourning. According to Bowlby (cited by Worden, 1982, p. 14), "Sooner or later, some of those who avoid all conscious grieving, break down—usually with some form of depression." Tears can afford cleansing for wounds created by loss, and fully experiencing the pain ultimately provides wonderful relief to those who suffer while eliminating long-term chronic grief.

ADJUST TO AN ENVIRONMENT IN WHICH THE DECEASED IS MISSING

The third task, practical in nature, requires the griever to take on some of the social roles performed by the deceased, or to find others who will. According to Worden (1982, p. 15), to abort this task is to become helpless by refusing to develop the skills necessary in daily living and by ultimately withdrawing from life.

I knew a woman who refused to adjust to the social environment in which she found herself after the death of her husband. He was her business partner, as well as her best and only friend. After 30 years of marriage, they had no children, and she had no close relatives. She had never learned to drive a car. Her entire social world had been controlled by her former husband. Three weeks after his funeral she went into the basement and committed suicide.

The alternative to withdrawing is assuming new social roles by taking on additional responsibilities. Extended families who always gathered at Grandma's house for Thanksgiving will be tempted to have a number of small Thanksgiving dinners after her death. The members of this family may believe that "no one can take Grandma's place." Although this may be true, members of the extended family will grieve better if someone else is willing to do Grandma's work, enabling the entire family to come together for Thanksgiving. Not to do so will cause double pain—the family will not gather, and Grandma will still be missed.

The final task of mourning is a difficult one for many because they feel disloyal or unfaithful in withdrawing emotional energy from their dead loved one. One of my family members once said that she could never love another man after her husband died. My twice-widowed aunt responded, "I once felt like that, but I now consider myself to be fortunate to have been married to two of the best men in the world."

Other people find themselves unable to reinvest in new relationships because they are unwilling to experience again the pain caused by loss. [A] quotation from John Brantner . . . provides perspective on this problem: "Only people who avoid love can avoid grief. The point is to learn from it and remain vulnerable to love."

However, those who are able to withdraw emotional energy and reinvest it in other relationships find the possibility of a newly established social life. Kavanaugh (1972, pp. 122–123) depicts this situation well with the following description.

At this point fantasies fade into constructive efforts to reach out and build anew. The phone is answered more quickly, the door as well, and meetings seem important, invitations are treasured and any social gathering becomes an opportunity rather than a curse. Mementos of the past are put away for occasional family gatherings. New clothes and new places promise dreams instead of only fears. Old friends are important for encouragement and permission to rebuild one's life. New friends can offer realistic opportunities for coming out from under the grieving mantle. With newly acquired friends, one is not a widow, widower, or survivor—just a person. Life begins again at the point of new friendships. All the rest is of yesterday, buried, unimportant to the now and tomorrow.

Disenfranchised Grief

Kenneth J. Doka

Introduction

Ever since the publication of Lindemann's classic article, "Symptomatology and Management of Acute Grief," the literature on the nature of grief and bereavement has been growing. In the few decades following this seminal study, there have been comprehensive studies of grief reactions, detailed descriptions of atypical manifestations of grief, theoretical and clinical treatments of grief reactions, and considerable research considering the myriad variables that affect grief. But most of this literature has concentrated on grief reactions in socially recognized and sanctioned roles: those of the parent, spouse, or child.

There are circumstances, however, in which a person experiences a sense of loss but does not have a socially recognized right, role, or capacity to grieve. In these cases, the grief is disenfranchised. The person suffers a loss but has little or no opportunity to mourn publicly.

Up until now, there has been little research touching directly on the phenomenon of disenfranchised grief. In her comprehensive review of grief reactions, Raphael notes the phenomenon:

> There may be other dyadic partnership relationships in adult life that show patterns similar to the conjugal ones, among them, the young couple intensely, even secretly, in love; the defacto relationships; the extramarital relationship; and the homosexual couple. ... Less intimate partnerships of close friends, working mates, and business associates, may have similar patterns of grief and mourning.

Focusing on the issues, reactions, and problems in particular populations, a number of studies have noted special difficulties that these populations have in grieving. For example, Kelly and Kimmel, in studies of aging homosexuals, have discussed the unique problems of grief in such relationships. Similarly, studies of the reactions of significant others of AIDS victims have considered bereavement. Other studies have considered the special problems of unacknowledged grief in prenatal death, [the death of] ex-spouses, therapists' reactions to a client's suicide, and pet loss. Finally, studies of families of Alzheimer's victims and mentally retarded adults also have noted distinct difficulties of these populations in encountering varied losses which are often unrecognized by others.

Others have tried to draw parallels between related unacknowledged losses. For example, in a personal account, Horn compared her loss of a heterosexual lover with a friend's loss of a homosexual partner. Doka discussed the particular problems of loss in nontraditional relationships, such as extramarital affairs, homosexual relationships, and cohabiting couples.

This article attempts to integrate the literature on such losses in order to explore the phenomenon of disenfranchised grief. It will consider both the nature of disenfranchised grief and its central paradoxical problem: the very nature of this type of grief exacerbates the problems of grief, but the usual sources of support may not be available or helpful.

The Nature of Disenfranchised Grief

Disenfranchised grief can be defined as the grief that persons experience when they incur a loss that is not or cannot be openly acknowledged, publicly mourned, or socially supported. The concept of disenfranchised grief recognizes that societies have sets of norms—in effect, "grieving rules"—that attempt to specify who, when, where, how, how long, and for whom people should grieve. These grieving rules may be codified in personnel policies. For example, a worker may be allowed a week off for the death of a spouse or child, three days for the loss of a parent or sibling. Such policies reflect the fact that each society defines who has a legitimate right to grieve, and these definitions of right correspond to relationships, primarily familial, that are socially recognized and sanctioned. In any given society these grieving rules may not correspond to the nature of attachments, the sense of loss, or the feelings of survivors. Hence the grief of these survivors is disenfranchised. In our society, this may occur for three reasons.

1. The Relationship Is Not Recognized

In our society, most attention is placed on kin-based relationships and roles. Grief may be disenfranchised in those situations in which the relationship between the bereaved and deceased is not based on recognizable kin ties. Here the closeness of other non-kin relationships may simply not be understood or appreciated. For example, Folta and Deck noted, "While all of these studies tell us that grief is a normal phenomenon, the intensity of which corresponds to the closeness of the relationship, they fail to take this (i.e., friendship) into account. The underlying assumption is that closeness of relationship exists only among spouses and/or immediate kin." The roles of lovers, friends, neighbors, foster parents, colleagues, in-laws, stepparents and stepchildren, caregivers, counselors, co-workers, and roommates (for example, in nursing homes) may be long-lasting and intensely interactive, but even though these relationships are recognized, mourners may not have full opportunity to publicly grieve a loss. At most, they might be expected to support and assist family members.

Then there are relationships that may not be publicly recognized or socially sanctioned. For example, nontraditional relationships, such as extramarital affairs, cohabitation, and homosexual relationships have tenuous public acceptance and limited legal standing, and they face negative sanctions within the larger community. Those involved in such relationships are touched by grief when the relationship is terminated by the death of the partner, but others in their world, such as children, may also experience grief that cannot be acknowledged or socially supported.

Even those whose relationships existed primarily in the past may experience grief. Ex-spouses, past lovers, or former friends may have limited contact, or they may not even engage in interaction in the present. Yet the death of that significant other can still cause a grief reaction because it brings finality to that earlier loss, ending any remaining contact or fantasy of reconciliation or reinvolvement. And again these grief feelings may be shared by others in their world such as parents and children. They too may mourn the loss of "what once was" and "what might have been." For example, in one case a twelve-year-old child of an unwed mother, never even acknowledged or seen by the father, still mourned the death of his father since it ended any possibility of a future liaison. But though loss is experienced, society as a whole may not perceive that the loss of a past relationship could or should cause any reaction.

2. The Loss Is Not Recognized

In other cases, the loss itself is not socially defined as significant. Perinatal deaths lead to strong grief reactions, yet research indicates that many significant others still perceive the loss to be relatively minor. Abortions too can constitute a serious loss, but the abortion can take place without the knowledge or sanctions of others, or even the recognition that a loss has occurred. It may very well be that the very ideologies of the abortion controversy can put the bereaved in a difficult position. Many who affirm a loss may not sanction the act of abortion, while some who sanction the act may minimize any sense of loss. Similarly, we are just becoming aware of the sense of loss that people experience in giving children up for adoption or foster care, and we have yet to be aware of the grief-related implications of surrogate motherhood.

Another loss that may not be perceived as significant is the loss of a pet. Nevertheless, the research shows strong ties between pets and humans, and profound reactions to loss.

Then there are cases in which the reality of the loss itself is not socially validated. Thanatologists have long recognized that significant losses can occur even when the object of the loss remains physically alive. Sudnow for example, discusses "social death," in which the person is alive but is treated as if dead. Examples may include those who are institutionalized or comatose. Similarly, "psychological death" has been defined as conditions in which the person lacks a consciousness of existence, such as someone who is "brain dead."

One can also speak of "psychosocial death" in which the persona of someone has changed so significantly, through mental illness, organic brain syndromes, or even significant personal transformation (such as through addiction, conversion, and so forth), that significant others perceive the person as he or she previously existed as dead. In all of these cases, spouses and others may experience a profound sense of loss, but that loss cannot be publicly acknowledged for the person is still biologically alive.

3. The Griever Is Not Recognized

Finally, there are situations in which the characteristics of the bereaved in effect disenfranchise their grief. Here the person is not socially defined as capable of grief; therefore, there is little or no social recognition of his or her sense of loss or need to mourn. Despite evidence to the contrary, both the very old and the very young are typically perceived by others as having little comprehension of or reaction to the death of a significant other. Often, then, both young children and aged adults are excluded from both discussions and rituals.

Similarly, mentally disabled persons may also be disenfranchised in grief. Although studies affirm that the mentally retarded are able to understand the concept of death and, in fact, experience grief, these reactions may not be perceived by others. Because the person is retarded or otherwise mentally disabled, others in the family may ignore his or her need to grieve. Here a teacher of the mentally disabled describes two illustrative incidences:

> In the first situation, Susie was 17 years old and away at summer camp when her father died. The family felt she wouldn't understand and that it would be better for her not to come home for the funeral. In the other situation, Francine was with her mother when she got sick. The mother was taken away by ambulance. Nobody answered her questions or told her what happened. "After all," they responded, "she's retarded."

The Special Problems of Disenfranchised Grief

Though each of the types of grief mentioned earlier may create particular difficulties and different reactions, one can legitimately speak of the special problem shared in disenfranchised grief.

The problem of disenfranchised grief can be expressed in a paradox. The very nature of disenfranchised grief creates additional problems for grief, while removing or minimizing sources of support.

Disenfranchising grief may exacerbate the problem of bereavement in a number of ways. First, the situations mentioned tend to intensify emotional reactions. Many emotions are associated with normal grief. Bereaved persons frequently experience feelings of anger, guilt, sadness and depression, loneliness, hopelessness, and numbness. These emotional reactions can be complicated when grief is disenfranchised. Although each of the situations described is in its own way unique, the literature uniformly reports how each of these disenfranchising circumstances can intensify feelings of anger, guilt, or powerlessness.

Second, both ambivalent relationships and concurrent crises have been identified in the literature as conditions that complicate grief. These conditions can often exist in many types of disenfranchised grief. For example, studies have indicated the ambivalence that can exist in cases of abortion, among ex-spouses, significant others in nontraditional roles, and among families of Alzheimer's disease victims. Similarly, the literature documents the many kinds of concurrent crises that can trouble the disenfranchised griever. For example, in cases of cohabiting couples, either heterosexual or homosexual, studies have often found that survivors experience legal and financial problems regarding inheritance, ownership, credit, or leases. Likewise, the death of a parent may leave a mentally disabled person not only bereaved but also bereft of a viable support system.

Although grief is complicated, many of the factors that facilitate mourning are not present. The bereaved may be excluded from an active role in caring for the dying. Funeral rituals, normally helpful in resolving grief, may not help here. In some cases the bereaved may be excluded from attendance. In other cases they may have no role in planning those rituals or in deciding whether even to have them. Or in cases of divorce, separation, or psychosocial death, rituals may be lacking altogether.

In addition, the very nature of the disenfranchised grief precludes social support. Often there is no recognized role in which mourners can assert the right to mourn and thus receive such support. Grief may have to remain private. Though they may have experienced an intense loss, they may not be given time off from work, have the opportunity to verbalize the loss, or receive the expressions of sympathy and support characteristic in a death. Even traditional sources of solace, such as religion, are unavailable to those whose relationships (for example, extramarital, cohabiting, homosexual, divorced) or acts (such as abortion) are condemned within that tradition.

Naturally, there are many variables that will affect both the intensity of the reaction and the availability of support. All the variables—interpersonal, psychological, social, physiological—that normally influence grief will have an impact here as well. And while there are problems common to cases of disenfranchised grief, each relationship has to be individually considered in light of the unique combinations of factors that may facilitate or impair grief resolution.

Implications

Despite the shortage of research on and attention given to the issue of disenfranchised grief, it remains a significant issue. Millions of Americans are involved in losses in which grief is effectively disenfranchised. For example, there are more than 1 million couples presently cohabiting. There are estimates that 3 percent of males and 2–3 percent of females are exclusively homosexual, with similar percentages having mixed homosexual and heterosexual encounters. There are about a million abortions a year; even though many of the women involved may not experience grief reactions, some are clearly "at risk."

Disenfranchised grief is also a growing issue. There are higher percentages of divorced people in the cohorts now aging. The AIDS crisis means that more homosexuals will experience losses in significant relationships. Even as the disease spreads within the population of intravenous drug users, it is likely to create a new class of both potential victims and disenfranchised grievers among the victims' informal liaisons and nontraditional relationships. And as Americans continue to live longer, more will suffer from severe forms of chronic brain dysfunctions. As the developmentally disabled live longer, they too will experience the grief of parental and sibling loss. In short, the proportion of disenfranchised grievers in the general population will rise rapidly in the future.

It is likely that bereavement counselors will have increased exposure to cases of disenfranchised grief. In fact, the very nature of disenfranchised grief and the unavailability of informal support make it likely that those who experience such losses will seek formal supports. Thus there is a pressing need for research that will describe the particular and unique reactions of each of the different types of losses; compare reactions and problems associated with these losses; describe the important variables affecting disenfranchised grief reactions; assess possible interventions; and discover the atypical grief reactions, such as masked or delayed grief, that might be manifested in such cases. Also needed is education sensitizing students to the many kinds of relationships and subsequent losses that people can experience and affirming that where there is loss there is grief.

KEN DOKA, PH.D., is a professor of gerontology at the College of New Rochelle in New York. He became interested in the study of death and dying quite inadvertently. Scheduled to do a practicum in a facility that housed juvenile delinquents, he discovered that his supervisor had changed the assignment. Instead, Doka found himself counseling dying children and their families at Sloan-Kettering, a major cancer hospital in New York. This experience became the basis of two graduate theses, one in sociology entitled "The Social Organization of Terminal Care in Two Pediatric Hospitals," and the other in religious studies entitled "Pastoral Counseling to Dying Children and Their Families." (Both were later published.) His doctoral program pursued another longstanding interest: the sociology of aging. In 1983, Dr. Doka accepted his present position at the College of New Rochelle where he specializes in thanatology and gerontology.

Active in the Association for Death Education and Counseling since its beginnings, Dr. Doka was elected its president in 1993. In addition to articles in scholarly journals, he is the author of *Death and Spirituality* (with John Morgan, 1993), *Living with Life-Threatening Illness* (1993) and *Disenfranchised Grief: Recognizing Hidden Sorrow* (1989), from which the following selection is excerpted. His work on disenfranchised grief began in the classroom when a graduate student commented, "If you think widows have it rough, you ought to see what happens when your ex-spouse dies."

ENHANCING THE CONCEPT OF DISENFRANCHISED GRIEF

CHARLES A. CORR, PH.D.
Southern Illinois University at Edwardsville

Abstract

Doka (1989a, p. 4) defined disenfranchised grief as "the grief that persons experience when they incur a loss that is not or cannot be openly acknowledged, publicly mourned, or socially supported." He suggested that disenfranchisement can apply to unrecognized relationships, losses, or grievers, as well as to certain types of deaths.

This article contends that disenfranchisement in bereavement may have a potentially broader scope than has been hitherto recognized. That claim is defended by exploring further the implications of disenfranchisement and by suggesting ways in which certain understandings or misunderstandings of the dynamic qualities of grief, mourning, and their outcomes may be open to disenfranchisement or may participate in disenfranchisement.

The aims of this argument are to enhance the concept of disenfranchised grief in itself and to deepen appreciation of the full range of all that is or can be experienced in bereavement.

In 1989 Doka (1989a) first proposed the concept of "disenfranchised grief." His suggestion had an immediate appeal to many and the concept of disenfranchised grief has since been widely accepted by practitioners, educators, and researchers in the field of death, dying, and bereavement. In particular, it has been applied in ways that seek to elucidate and validate the experiences of a broad range of bereaved persons.

In his initial proposal, Doka described the concept of disenfranchised grief, identified those aspects of the grief experience that he understood to have been subject to disenfranchisement, provided examples of many ways in which disenfranchisement has occurred, and indicated why attention should be paid to the concept of disenfranchised grief. This article seeks to enhance understanding of the concept of disenfranchised grief and by so doing to deepen appreciation of the full range of all that is or can be experienced in bereavement. The present analysis begins with a review of Doka's original description of the concept of disenfranchised grief. Thereafter, the inquiry is guided by two primary questions: 1) What exactly is meant by the disenfranchisement of grief?; and 2) What is or can be disenfranchised in grief? Responding to these questions may help to enrich understanding of Doka's seminal concept in particular, and of bereavement in general.

On that basis, it may also be possible for helpers to identify better ways in which to assist grievers of all types, especially those whose experiences have been disenfranchised.

Disenfranchised Grief: The Original Concept

In his original work, Doka (1989a, p. 4) defined "disenfranchised grief" as "the grief that persons experience when they incur a loss that is not or cannot be openly acknowledged, publicly mourned, or socially supported." In addition, he suggested that grief can be disenfranchised in three primary ways: 1) the relationship is not recognized; 2) the loss is not recognized; or 3) the griever is not recognized. Some comments on each of these three types of disenfranchisement may help to clarify Doka's original proposal.

Disenfranchised Relationships

Why don't you just stop crying and grieving for that person who died. He wasn't even close to you.

I just don't see why you should be so upset over the death of your ex-husband. He was a bum, you hated him, and you got rid of him years ago. Why cry over his being gone for good?

With respect to a *relationship* that is disenfranchised, Folta and Deck (1976, p. 235) have noted that "the underlying assumption is that the 'closeness of relationship' exists only among spouses and/or immediate kin." Unsuspected, past, or secret relationships may simply not be publicly recognized or socially sanctioned. Disenfranchised relationships can include associations which are well-accepted in theory but not appreciated in practice or in particular instances, such as those between friends, colleagues, in-laws, ex-spouses, or former lovers. Disenfranchised relationships may also include nontraditional liaisons such as those involving extra-marital affairs and homosexual relationships. In referring to these as instances of disenfranchised grief, the implication is that such relationships have often been or may be deemed by society to be an insufficient or inappropriate foundation for grief.

Disenfranchised Losses

> Why do you keep on moaning over your miscarriage? It wasn't really a baby yet. And you already have four children. You could even have more if you want to.

> Stop crying over that dead cat! He was just an animal. I bet that cat wouldn't have been upset if you had been the one to die. If you stop crying. I'll buy you a new kitten.

In the case of a *loss* which is disenfranchised, the focus of the disenfranchisement appears to arise from a failure or unwillingness on the part of society to recognize that certain types of events do involve real losses. For example, until quite recently and perhaps still today in many segments of society, perinatal deaths, losses associated with elective abortion, or losses of body parts have been disenfranchised. Similarly, the death of a pet is often unappreciated by those outside the relationship. And society is only beginning to learn about grief which occurs when dementia blots out an individual's personality in such a way or to such a degree that significant others perceive the person to be psychosocially dead, even though biological life continues. As one husband said of his spouse with advanced Alzheimer's disease, "I am medically separated from my wife—even though she is still alive and we are not divorced." To say that loss arising from a "medical separation" of this type is disenfranchised is to note that society does not acknowledge it to be sufficient to justify grief—or at least not sufficient to justify grief of the type that society associates with a physical death.

Disenfranchised Grievers

> I don't know why that old guy in Room 203 keeps moaning and whimpering about the death of his loud-mouthed daughter who used to visit him every week. With his poor memory and other mental problems, he hardly even knew when his daughter came to visit anyway.

> I told Johnnie he should grow up, be a man, and stop whining about his grandfather's death. He's too young to really remember much about his grandfather or even to understand what death really means.

In the case of a disenfranchised *griever*, disenfranchisement mainly has to do with certain individuals to whom the socially-recognized status of griever is not attached. For example, it is often asserted or at least suggested that young children, the very old, and those who are mentally disabled are either incapable of grief or are individuals who do not have a need to grieve. In this case, disenfranchisement applies not to a relationship or to a loss, but to the individual survivor whose status as a leading actor or protagonist in the human drama of bereavement is not recognized or appreciated.

Disenfranchising Deaths

> That teenager who killed himself must not have had all his marbles. His family is probably all screwed up, too. Don't be sorry for them. Just stay away from them.

> It's just too bad that actor died of AIDS. God punished him for having all that sex. And now his boyfriends will probably wind up with all his money. They sure don't need us to feel sorry for them.

In his original concept, Doka (1989a) added that some types of deaths in themselves may be "disenfranchising." He offered as examples deaths involving suicide or AIDS. The point seems to have been that our society is repelled or turns away from certain types of death, mainly because their complexities are not well understood or because they are associated with a high degree of social stigma. As a result, the character of the death seems to disenfranchise what otherwise might have been expected to follow in its aftermath. But not all societies at all points in time would or have disenfranchised deaths associated with suicide or AIDS. In other words, what is disenfranchised in one social context may not be disenfranchised in another social context. This clearly recalls Doka's fundamental point that disenfranchised grief is always founded on a specific society's attitudes and values.

Why Pay Attention to Disenfranchised Grief?

The purpose of drawing attention to the meaning of disenfranchised grief and to the ways in which it can be implemented can be seen in Doka's (1989a, p. 7) observation that, "The very nature of disenfranchised grief creates additional problems of grief, while removing or minimizing sources of support." Additional problems arise that go beyond the usual difficulties in grief because disenfranchised grief typically involves intensified emotional reactions (for example, anger, guilt, or powerlessness), ambivalent relationships (as in some cases of abortion or some associations between ex-spouses), and concurrent crises (such as those involving legal and financial problems). In circumstances of disenfranchised grief there is an absence of customary sources of support because society's attitudes make unavailable factors that usually facilitate mourning (for instance, the existence of funeral rituals or possibilities for helping to take part in such rituals) and opportunities to obtain assistance from others (for example, by speaking about the loss, receiving expressions of sympathy, taking time off from work, or finding solace within a religious tradition).

Clearly, issues associated with disenfranchised grief deserve attention. They indicate that social outlooks often embody a judgmental element (whether explicitly articulated or not) and the short-term concerns of the group when dealing with some bereaved persons. That is, societies which disenfranchise grief appear to act on specific values or principles at the expense of an overarching interest in the welfare of all of their members. In these ways, disenfranchised grief can be seen to be an important phenomenon. It is also a phenomenon that is lived out in different ways in different societies, easily observed by those who pay attention to social practices, and hurtful to individual members of society if not to society itself. For all of these reasons, it is worth exploring further what is meant by saying that some grief is disenfranchised and what is or can be disenfranchised in grief.

What is Meant by Saying That Some Grief is Disenfranchised?

As has been noted, grief always occurs within a particular social or cultural context. The concept of disenfranchised grief recognizes that in various spoken and unspoken ways social and cultural communities may deny recognition, legitimation, or support to the grief experienced by individuals, families, and small groups.

It is important to recognize that the grief under discussion here is not merely silent, unnoticed, or forgotten. Any griever may keep silent about or decide not to reveal to the larger society the fact of his or her grief, or some of its specific aspects. Failing to disclose or communicate to others what one is experiencing in grief does not of itself mean that such grief is or would be disenfranchised. Society might be fully prepared to recognize, legitimize, and support grief that an individual, for whatever reason, holds in privacy and does not share.

Further, even when an individual is willing to share his or her grief, some grief experiences may still go unnoticed or be forgotten by society. Thus, Gyulay (1975) wrote of grandparents following the death of a grandchild as "forgotten grievers." She meant that all too often attention associated with the death of a child is focused on the child's parents or siblings to the exclusion of grandparents. In fact, however, bereaved grandparents often find themselves grieving both the death of their grandchild and the loss experienced by an adult who is simultaneously their own child (or son/daughter-in-law) and the child's parent (Hamilton, 1978). Typically, when this two-fold grief of grandparents is brought to the attention of members of society, it is not disenfranchised but acknowledged and respected.

In short, the concept of disenfranchised grief goes beyond the situation of mere unawareness of grief to suggest a more or less active process of disavowal, renunciation, and rejection. Not surprisingly, the word "disenfranchise" takes its origin from the term "enfranchise," which has two basic historical meanings: 1) "To admit to freedom, set free (a slave or serf)";

and 2) "To admit to municipal or political privileges" (*Oxford English Dictionary,* 1989, Vol. 5, p. 246). In the most familiar sense of this term, to enfranchise is to set an individual free from his or her prior condition by admitting that person to the electoral franchise or granting permission to vote for representatives in a government. Disenfranchisement applies to those who are not accorded a social franchise extended by society to individuals who are admitted to full participation in the community.

A more contemporary meaning of enfranchisement is to be granted a franchise or license to offer for sale locally some national or international product or service. For example, one might purchase or be awarded a franchise to sell a certain brand of fast food or automobile, or to advertise one's local motel as a member of a national chain of motels. Often one has to earn or somehow pay for the use of a franchise, and there may also be obligations to uphold certain service standards or to deliver a product of a certain type in a certain way. When the use of a franchise has not been earned or implemented properly, it may come into dispute or even be withdrawn by those in authority. In all of these examples, it is the permission to behave in a certain way (to vote, to act as a franchisee or agent of a franchise holder) that is central to both enfranchisement and disenfranchisement.

In the case of bereavement, enfranchisement applies in particular to those who are recognized by society as grievers. These are individuals who are free to acknowledge their losses openly, mourn those losses publicly, and receive support from others—at least within that society's accepted limits. Disenfranchised grief goes beyond the boundaries of what is regarded as socially-accepted grief. It is therefore denied the legitimacy and freedom that comes with social sanction and approval (Doka, 1989b; Pine et al., 1990).

What is or Can Be Disenfranchised in Grief?

Bereavement

Doka is clearly correct in recognizing that disenfranchisement can apply to relationships, losses, and grievers. These are, in fact, the three key *structural elements* that define the meaning of the term "bereavement." Thus, what Doka has really defined is "disenfranchised bereavement." For that reason, it may help to begin our exploration of how disenfranchisement applies to grief by reminding ourselves of how we understand the root concept of bereavement.

The word "bereavement" is widely understood to designate the objective situation of one who has experienced a significant loss. If there were no significant person or object to which an individual was attached, there would be no bereavement. For example, when a parent threatens to take away from a child a much-disliked serving of spinach as a "punishment" for the child's refusal to clean his or her plate at dinner, the child is not likely to experience a loss or to grieve. Further, if the object were a significant one to the child, but the child perceived (as a result of previous parental behavior patterns) that the threatened loss would not come about in fact, again there would be no bereavement or grief. Finally, if there were no individual to grieve a loss—as when someone threatens to or actually does take away a significant object, but the threat and the loss are not effectively communicated to the individual to whom they would presumably have been directed—again there is no bereavement or grief. A griever is effectively absent when the threat is merely an empty gesture made in his or her absence or when, for some other reason, there is no awareness or experience of a significant loss—as during the period between the death of a loved one in a far-off land and the communication of that fact to the survivor.

In short, the noun "bereavement" and the adjective "bereaved" only apply to situations and individuals in which there exists an experience such that one believes oneself to have been deprived of some important person or object. Both "bereavement" and "bereaved" (there is no present participial form, "bereaving," in standard English today) are words that derive from a verb not often used today in colloquial English. That word is "reave"; it means "to despoil, rob, or forcibly deprive" (*Oxford English Dictionary*, 1989, Vol. 13, p. 295). In short, a bereaved person is one who has been deprived, robbed, plundered, or stripped of something. This indicates that the stolen person or object was a valued one, and suggests that the deprivation has harmed or done violence to the bereaved person. In our society, all too many bereaved persons can testify that dismissal or minimization of the importance of their losses are familiar components of the experience of survivors, with or without added burdens arising from disenfranchisement.

We could explore further each of the central elements identified by Doka in describing his concept of disenfranchised grief. Such an exploration might produce: 1) a rich and varied portrait of the many types of *relationships* in which humans participate, including those fundamental relationships called "attachments" which serve to satisfy the basic needs of human beings; 2) a panorama of *losses* which may affect relationships involving human beings—some permanent, others temporary, some final, others reversible; and/or 3) a list of many different types of *grievers*. If we did this, it would become apparent (among other things) that loss by death is but one category of loss, and that certain types or modes of death are more likely to be disenfranchised than others. And we might also learn that while disenfranchising the bereaved involves costs of different types for individuals and societies themselves, enfranchising the disenfranchised might also involve costs of other types (Davidowitz & Myrick, 1984; Kamerman, 1993).

All of the above are ways to enrich appreciation of the concept of disenfranchised grief. Most involve simply accepting the conceptual scheme as it was originally proposed by Doka and applying it to specific types of relationships, losses, and grievers. Applications of this type have been prominent in written reports and conference presentations in recent years (e.g., Becker, 1997; Kaczmarek & Backlund, 1991; Schwebach & Thornton, 1992; Thornton, Robertson, & Mlecko, 1991; Zupanick, 1994).

In this article, it seems more useful to try to enhance or enlarge the concept of disenfranchised grief by examining it critically in relationship to the *dynamic components* of the bereavement experience, especially as it is related to grief, mourning, and their outcomes.

Grief

> Stop feeling that way! You'll be better off if you just pack up all those bad feelings and throw them away with the garbage.

In reactions to being "reaved" or to perceiving themselves as having been "reaved," those who have suffered that experience typically react to what has happened to them. In normal circumstances, one would be surprised if they did not do so. Failure to react would seem to imply that the lost person or object was actually not much prized by the bereaved individual, that the survivor is unaware of his or her loss, or that other factors intervene. "Grief" is the reaction to loss. The term arises from the grave or heavy weight that presses on persons who are burdened by loss (*Oxford English Dictionary*, 1989, Vol. 6, pp. 834–835).

Reactions to loss are disenfranchised when they—in whole or in part; in themselves or in their expression—are not recognized, legitimated, or supported by society. How many times have grieving persons been told: "Don't feel that way"; "Try not to think those thoughts"; "Don't say those things (about God, or the doctor, or the person who caused the death)"; "You shouldn't act like that just because someone you loved died." Sometimes any reaction is judged to be inappropriate; in other circumstances, some reactions are accepted while others are rejected. In some cases, it is the existence of the reaction that is disenfranchised; in other examples, it is only the expression of the reaction that meets with disapproval. Through what amounts to a kind of "oppressive toleration" society often presses a griever to hold private his or her grief reaction in order not to trouble or disturb others by bringing it out into the open or expressing it in certain ways. The effect of any or all of these practices is to disenfranchise either some aspects of the grief or some modes in which they are manifested.

Grief as Emotions?

> I can understand why you're feeling upset about your mother's death. You can be sad if you want to. But you've got to start eating again and getting a good night's sleep.

> My co-worker used to be a such a great guy. But ever since his younger sister died, he comes to work and sometimes it's like he's wandering around in a fog and not concentrating on the job. I told him today that he needs to pull himself together and get focused on his work again.

> My friend was always such a cheery person at the Senior Citizen's Center. But ever since her grandchild died, she keeps asking all those difficult questions about why God let such a bad thing happen to an innocent child. I told her that it was OK to be sad, but she just had to accept God's will and stop questioning it.

In each of these examples, feelings of grief are legitimized but other aspects of the grief reaction are disenfranchised. One might also argue that something very much like this form of disenfranchisement can be found in much of the professional literature on bereavement. For example, quite often grief is described or defined as "the emotional reaction to loss." On its face, a definition of this type is at once both obvious and inadequate. Clearly, bereaved persons may or do react emotionally to loss; equally so, they may not or do not merely react emotionally to loss. Careless, unintentional, or deliberate restriction of the meaning of grief to its emotional components is an unrecognized form of disenfranchisement of the full grief experience.

In this connection, Elias (1991) reminded readers that, "Broadly speaking, emotions have three components, a somatic, a behavioral and a feeling component" (p. 177). As a result, "the term *emotion,* even in professional discussions, is used with two different meanings. It is used in a wider and in a narrower sense at the same time. In the wider sense the term *emotion* is applied to a reaction pattern which involves the whole organism in its somatic, its feeling and its behavioral aspects. . . . In its narrower sense the term *emotion* refers to the feeling component of the syndrome only" (Elias, 1991, p. 119).

The importance of feelings in the overall grief reaction to loss is undeniable. Equally undeniable is the importance of other aspects of the grief reaction. These include somatic or physical sensations and behaviors or behavioral disturbances, as Elias has indicated, as well as matters involving cognitive, social, and spiritual functioning. Establishing a comprehensive list of all of these aspects of the grief reaction to loss is not of primary importance here. What is central is the recognition that human beings may and indeed are likely to react to important losses in their lives with their whole selves, not just with some narrowly-defined aspect of their humanity. Failure to describe grief in a holistic way dismisses and devalues its richness and breadth.

Grief as Symptoms?

As a psychiatrist and her son-in-law, I tried to talk to your mother about your father's death. She refused and got upset after I told her that her unwillingness to discuss with me her reactions to the death was a classic symptom of pathological grief. She said she had talked to her sister and just didn't want to talk to you or me or her other children about it.

Sadness and crying are two of the main symptoms of grief. Whenever we identify them, we should refer the individual for therapy.

Another form of depicting or categorizing grief in a limiting and negative way involves the use of the language of *symptoms* to designate both complicated and uncomplicated grief. In principal, grief is a natural and healthy reaction to loss. There can be unhealthy reactions to loss. One of these would be a failure to react in any way to the loss of a significant person or object in our lives. However, most grief reactions are not complicated or unhealthy. They are appropriate reactions to the loss one has experienced. In cases of uncomplicated grief—which constitute the vast majority of all bereavement experiences—we ought to speak of signs, or manifestations, or

expressions of grief. And we ought to avoid the term "symptoms" in relationship to grief, unless we consciously intend to use the language of illness to indicate some form of aberrant or unhealthy reaction to loss. When we use the language of symptoms to describe all expressions of grief, we have pathologized grief and invalidated or disenfranchised its fundamental soundness as the human reaction to loss.

Mourning

OK, we've had our grief ever since Kerri died. Now that the funeral is over, that's it. There's nothing more we can do and nothing more we need to do. So, let's just put all this behind us and forget it.

Many aspects of what is called grief in bereavement are essentially reactive. They seek to push away the hurt of the loss with denial, or turn back upon it with anger, or reply to its implacability with sadness. Much of this is like a defensive reflex. But there is more to most bereavement experiences than this. The other central element in a healthy bereavement experience is in the effort to find some way to live with the loss, with our grief reactions to that loss, and with the new challenges that are associated with the loss. As Weisman (1984, p. 36) observed, coping "is positive in approach; defending is negative." In brief, coping identifies the efforts that we make to manage perceived stressors in our lives (Lazarus & Folkman, 1984). In the vocabulary of bereavement, this is "mourning"—the attempt to manage or learn to live with one's bereavement. Through mourning grievers endeavor to incorporate their losses and grief into healthy ongoing living.

If we fail to distinguish between grief and mourning in appropriate ways, we run the risk of ignoring the differences between reacting and coping, between seeking to defend or push away our loss and grief, and attempting to embrace those experiences and incorporate them into our lives. This is another form of disenfranchisement insofar as it blurs distinctions between two central aspects of bereavement, misconceives what is involved in mourning an important loss, and refuses to acknowledge and support both grief and mourning.

At the simplest level, the efforts that one makes to cope with loss and grief in mourning are frequently not understood for what they are and thus are not valued by society. For example, a griever will be told not to go over the details of the accident again and again, as if such filling in of the stark outlines of a death is not an essential part of the process of *realization* or making real in one's internal, psychic world what is already real in the external, objective world (Parkes, 1996). Another familiar way of disenfranchising mourning occurs when a bereaved person is advised that the proper way to manage a loss is simply to "put it behind you" or "get beyond it." This assumes that one can simply hop over a stressful event in life, ignore the unwelcome interruption, and go on living without being affected by what has happened. Sometimes, bereaved survivors are even counseled to "forget" the deceased person as if he or she had not been a significant part of their lives. None of these are appropriate elements in constructive mourning.

Note that mourning is a present-tense, participial word. As such, it indicates action or activities of the type expressed by verbs. In the language of nouns, this is "grief work" (a phrase first coined by Lindemann in 1944). Lindemann understood "grief work" in a specific way, but the central point is that the grief work at the heart of mourning is an active, effortful attempt to manage what bereavement has brought into one's life (Attig, 1991, 1996).

Moreover, since the consequences of bereavement typically include both primary and secondary losses, as well as grief and new challenges, there is much to cope with in the whole of one's mourning. Indeed, contrasting loss and grief with the new challenges of bereavement could be said to require an oscillation between "loss-oriented" and "restoration-oriented" processes in mourning (Stroebe & Schut, 1995).

In other words, in his or her mourning a bereaved person is faced with the tasks of integrating into his or her life three major elements: 1) the primary and secondary losses that he or she has experienced, 2) the grief reactions provoked by those losses; and 3) the new challenges involved in living without the deceased person. For example, if my spouse should die I would be obliged to mourn or try to learn to live in healthy ways with her loss (the fact that she has been taken away from me constituting my primary loss), with the secondary losses associated with her death (e.g., being deprived of her company or being without her guidance in some practical matters), with my grief reactions to those losses (e.g., my anger over what has been done to me or my sadness at the apparent barrenness of the life that is now left to me), and with my new situation in life (e.g., after years of marriage I may be unclear how to function as a newfound single person). If any aspect of my losses, grief, or new challenges is disenfranchised, then my efforts to mourn or cope with those aspects of my bereavement will also be disenfranchised.

Mourning:
Interpersonal and Intrapersonal Dimensions

Because each human being is both a particular individual and a social creature or a member of a community, mourning has two complementary forms or aspects. It is both an outward, public, or *interpersonal* process—the overt, visible, and characteristically shared, public efforts to cope with or manage loss and associated grief reactions—and an internal, private, or *intrapersonal* process—an individual's inward struggles to cope with or manage loss and the grief reactions to that loss. Each of these dimensions of mourning deserves recognition and respect. Much of what has already been noted here about mourning applies to its intrapersonal dimensions, but disenfranchisement is also frequently associated with the interpersonal aspects of mourning.

Interpersonal Dimensions of Mourning

Don't keep on talking about how he died. It's not going to make any difference or bring him back. Nobody wants to be around you when you keep going on about it.

What's the point of having a funeral, anyhow? Couldn't they just bury their child privately and leave us out of it? I don't want to get dragged into it.

Many people in contemporary society are unwilling to take part in the public or *interpersonal* rituals of mourning. Some of this has to do with a certain weakness or shallowness in many interpersonal relationships in contemporary society and a loosening of the bonds that formerly bound together families, neighbors, church groups, and other small communities. But it also appears to be linked to a discomfort with public ritual and open expression of strong feelings. Good funeral and memorial rituals are essentially designed to assist human beings in their need to engage in three post-death tasks: 1) to dispose of dead bodies appropriately; 2) to make real the implications of death; and 3) to work toward social reintegration and healthful ongoing living (Corr, Nabe, & Corr, 1994). Without indicating how these tasks will otherwise be met, many act as if society and individuals should do away with all public expressions of mourning. Young people in our society frequently state that when they die no one should be sad and that money that would otherwise be spent for a funeral should only be used for a party. Thoughts like this disenfranchise full appreciation of grief and the needs of individuals to mourn their losses within communities of fellow grievers.

This disenfranchisement of the interpersonal dimensions of mourning is not typical of all individuals in our society and is unacceptable to many ethnic or religious groups. Similarly, it does not apply to rituals following the deaths of public figures (e.g., a president) or very prominent persons (e.g., certain celebrities). In these instances, as well as in the very formal rituals of the armed forces which mandate specific conduct and ceremonial practice in a context of death and bereavement, or the informal but growing practice of members of sports teams wearing black bands on their uniforms or dedicating a game to the memory of someone who has died, the interpersonal needs of a community cry out for expression and guidance in public mourning practices.

In fact, formal or informal rituals—which are a prominent example of the interpersonal dimension of mourning—have been created by human beings as a means of helping to bring order into their lives in times of disorder and social disruption. Thus, Margaret Mead (1973, pp. 89–90) wrote: "I know of no people for whom the fact of death is not critical, and who have no ritual by which to deal with it." Bereavement rituals are intended precisely to give social recognition, legitimation, and support in times of loss and grief. Specific rituals may fall out of favor and no longer serve these purposes for the society as a whole or for some of its members. But to assume that such rituals can simply be abandoned without replacement, that society can satisfactorily conduct its affairs and serve its members without any ritual whatsoever in times of death, is to misconceive the needs of human beings and expose the dangers involved in disenfranchising mourning. As Staples (1994, p. 255) suggested, "The rituals of grief and burial bear the dead away. Cheat those rituals and you risk keeping the dead with you always in forms that you mightn't like. Choose carefully the funerals you miss."

Intrapersonal Dimensions of Mourning

> I was proud of her at the funeral. She was so brave and she never cried. But now she's always crying and sometimes she just seems to be preoccupied with her inner feelings. I think she's just chewing on her grief like some kind of undigested food and simply won't let go of it. Last week, I told her that there were times when we all understood it was appropriate to grieve. But she's got to get over it and she just can't keep on gnawing at it when she thinks she's alone.

> Why does she keep going back to the cemetary on the anniversary of her husband's death? That's morbid for her to keep on stirring up those feelings over and over again. She doesn't talk much to anyone else about it, but I think she needs to get on with her life without this behavior.

Some authors (e.g., *Oxford English Dictionary,* 1989, Vol. 10, pp. 19–20) seem to restrict the use of the term "mourning" to the expression of sorrow or grief, especially those expressions involving ceremony or ritual. For example, there is a traditional language that uses phrases like "wearing mourning" to refer to dressing in certain ways (e.g., in black or dark-colored garments) as a public expression of one's status as a bereaved person. Despite its historical justification, limiting the term mourning in this way leaves us without a term for the *intrapersonal* processes of coping with loss and grief.

Other authors (e.g., Wolfelt, 1996) maintain and emphasize the distinction between the intrapersonal and interpersonal dimensions of bereavement by using the term "grieving" for the former and reserving the term "mourning" for the latter. Again, there is justification for some linguistic distinction between intrapersonal and interpersonal aspects of coping with loss and grief. But the central point for our purposes is that this last distinction is a linguistic effort to fill out what is involved in both the intrapersonal and interpersonal realms when bereaved persons strive to cope with loss and grief. In this way, linguistic distinctions between intrapersonal and interpersonal aspects of mourning work to expand or enhance what is involved in coping with loss and grief, not to restrict or disenfranchise selected aspects of that coping.

Mourning: Outcomes

> It's been almost three weeks and she's still not finished with her grieving. I told her she had to forget him and get on with her new life.

> We invited John to come on a blind date with us and Mary's cousin, but he refused. Mary told him that he's got to stop wallowing in tears. He needs to get over his first wife and start looking around for someone new. Six months is long enough to mourn.

A final arena for possible disenfranchisement in bereavement relates to assumptions about the *outcomes* of mourning. This has been touched on above. If mourning is a process of coping with loss and grief, we can rightly ask: What are the results which it strives to achieve? Many would say "recovery," "completion," or "resolution." Each of these terms appears to imply a fixed endpoint for mourning, a final closure after which there is no more grieving and mourning. "Recovery," is perhaps the least satisfactory of the three terms, because it also seems to suggest that grief is a bad situation like a disease or a wound from which one must rescue or reclaim oneself (Osterweis, Solomon, & Green, 1984; Rando, 1993). Recovery is often implied in metaphors of "healing" from grief; talking in this way may otherwise be quite helpful, but it tends to suggest a time at which one will be done with healing and after which one will apparently be back to one's former self essentially unchanged by the bereavement experience.

It has been argued earlier that it is not desirable to use symptom language to interpret grief and to impose disease models upon healthy experiences in bereavement. To that we can add here that there are no fixed endpoints in mourning. One can never simply go back to a pre-bereavement mode of living after a significant loss. In fact, there is ample evidence, for many at least, that mourning continues in some form for the remainder of one's life. Interpretations to the contrary disenfranchise processes related to loss and grief which take place after the assumed endpoint or completion of mourning. They also disenfranchise the life-changing power of significant losses and the ongoing need to continue to cope with loss, grief, and new challenges in life. The misconception that grief and mourning should be over in a short time or at some predefined point is what leads to the familiar experience of many bereaved persons that over time their grief appears to become disenfranchised (Lundberg, Thornton, & Robertson, 1987).

There are, in fact, different outcomes experienced by different individuals who are bereaved. That is not surprising. Individuals who live their lives in different ways may be expected to cope with loss and grief in different ways, and to come to different results in their coping work. Research by Martinson and her colleagues (McClowry, Davies, May, Kulenkamp, & Martinson, 1987) studied bereaved parents and other family members (mainly siblings) seven to nine years after the death of a child. Results suggested that different individuals and different families dealt with the "empty space" in their lives in different ways. Some worked diligently to "get over it," that is, to put the loss behind them and go on with their lives. Others sought to "fill the space" by turning their focus toward what they perceived as some constructive direction. This type of effort to find some positive meaning in an otherwise horrible event might be illustrated by those bereaved after automobile accidents associated with the use of alcoholic beverages who throw themselves into campaigns to prevent intoxicated drivers from driving motor vehicles or to take such drivers off the road when they have been identified. A third outcome identified in this research was that of "keeping the connection." This appeared in bereaved persons who struggled to maintain a place in their lives for the deceased individual, vividly illustrated by the mother who insists that she has two sons, despite her full awareness that one of them has died (e.g., Wagner, 1994).

The important point in this research is not to argue for one or the other of these three outcomes in mourning, or even to suggest that they are the only possible outcomes. The point is that mourning is a process of acknowledging the reality of a death, experiencing the grief associated with that loss, learning to live without the deceased, and restructuring one's relationship to the deceased in order that that relationship can continue to be honored even while the survivor goes on living in a healthy and productive way (Worden, 1991). This process can be carried out in different ways and it can be expected to have somewhat different results for different individuals. As one astute psychologist observed, it is not the time that one has to use but the use that one makes of the time that one has that makes all the difference in bereavement, grief, and mourning (S. J. Fleming, personal communication, 9/28/95).

Three widows in my own experience acted out their mourning in different ways. One removed her wedding ring after the death of her husband. She said, "I am no longer married to him." Another kept her wedding ring on the third finger of her left hand. She said, "We are still connected." A third removed her husband's wedding ring before his body was buried and had it refashioned along with her own wedding ring into a new ring which she wore on her right hand. She said, "I now have a new relationship with my deceased husband."

These and other possible variations identify alternative courses in bereavement and mourning. In each case, metaphors of healing or resolution are partly correct insofar as the survivor has found a constructive way in which to go forward with his or her life. The intensity of the bereaved person's grief may have abated, but many continue to experience grief and reoccurrences of mourning in some degree, in some forms, and at some times. Grief may no longer consume them as it seemed to do immediately after their loss. They have "gotten through" some difficult times in bereavement, but they are not simply "over" their grief. In fact, many bereaved persons report that their grief and mourning never completely end.

Outsiders must take care not to invalidate or disenfranchise the ongoing grief and mourning of the bereaved, as well as their healthy connectedness to the deceased, by speaking too facilely of closure and completion (Klass, Silverman, & Nickman, 1996; Silverman, Nickman, & Worden, 1992). Such language may speak not primarily about bereavement but about the time at which a helper judges that his or her role as a counselor or therapist is no longer required. Thus, when a bereaved child decides to leave one of the support groups at The Dougy Center in Portland, Oregon (because, as was once said, "he or she now has better things to do with his or her time"), he or she is given a drawstring pouch containing several small stones (Corr and the Staff of The Dougy Center, 1991). Most of the stones in the pouch are polished and thus serve to symbolize what the child has achieved in coping with loss and grief; at least one is left in a rough state to represent the unfinished work that always remains in bereavement.

Conclusion

What have we learned from this reflection on the concept of disenfranchised grief? First, it is a concept with immediate appeal. It resonates with the experiences of many bereaved

persons and of many clinicians and scholars who have sought to understand experiences of bereavement or tried to be of assistance to bereaved persons. Second, disenfranchisement involves more than merely overlooking or forgetting to take note of certain types of bereavement and grief. It is more active than that in its nature and more determined in its messages, even if they are often conveyed in subtle and unspoken ways. Whatever is disenfranchised in grief is not free to experience or to express itself. It is prohibited, tied down, not sanctioned, and not supported by society.

Third, as Doka (1989a) originally pointed out, disenfranchisement can apply to any or all of the key structural elements in bereavement—relationships, losses, and grievers—as well as to certain forms of death. However, as this article has made clear, disenfranchisement can also be associated with the full range of the various reactions to loss (grief) and their expression, the processes of coping with or striving to manage loss, grief, and the new challenges which they entail (mourning), both the intrapersonal and the interpersonal dimensions of those processes, and various ways of living out their implications. In the aftermath of a death, the possible scope of disenfranchisement is not confined merely to the structural elements of bereavement or to grief understood in a kind of global way; it can extend to every aspect or dimension of the experience of bereavement and be applied to all of the dynamics of grief and mourning.

Enhancing our understanding of the concept of disenfranchised grief can contribute to improved appreciation of its breadth and depth. This same effort also provides an added way of drawing out some of the implications of the underlying concepts of bereavement, grief, and mourning. Further, attention to the enhanced concept of disenfranchised grief reminds helpers of the sensitivities they need to keep in mind in order not to devalue or rule out of bounds important aspects of the experiences of bereaved persons.

A caring society ought not incorporate within its death system—either formally or informally—thoughts, attitudes, behaviors, or values that communicate to bereaved persons inappropriate or unjustified messages such as: "Your relationship with the deceased person did not count in our eyes"; "Your loss was not really a significant one"; "You are not a person who should be grieving this loss"; "We do not recognize some aspects of your grief" or "Your grief is not acceptable to us in some ways"; "Your grief is in itself a symptom of psychic disorder or lack of mental health;" "Your mourning has lasted too long"; "You are mourning in ways that are publicly or socially unacceptable"; "You should not continue to mourn inside yourself in these ways"; or "Your mourning should be finished and over with by now."

Rather than the perspectives described in the previous paragraph, a caring society ought to respect the complexities and the individuality of each bereavement experience. While remaining sensitive to the deficits and excesses that define complicated mourning in a relatively small percentage of bereavement experiences (Rando, 1993), a caring society and its members ought to appreciate that healthy grief honors cherished relationships and that constructive mourning is essential for those who are striving to live in productive and meaningful ways in the aftermath of loss. Consider how different our society would be if it listened to and acted on comments such as the following from Frank (1991), who wrote: "Professionals talk too much about adjustment. I want to emphasize mourning as affirmation. ... To grieve well is to value what you have lost. When you value even the feeling of loss, you value life itself, and you begin to live again" (pp. 40–41).

REFERENCES

Attig, T. (1991). The importance of conceiving of grief as an active process. *Death Studies, 15,* 385–393.

Attig, T. (1996). *How we grieve: Relearning the world.* New York: Oxford University Press.

Becker, S. M. (1997, 26 June). *Disenfranchised grief and the experience of loss after environmental accidents.* Paper presented at the meeting of the Association for Death Education and Counseling and the 5th International Conference on Grief and Bereavement in Contemporary Society, Washington, DC.

Corr, C. A., and the Staff of The Dougy Center. (1991). Support for grieving children: The Dougy Center and the hospice philosophy. *The American Journal of Hospice and Palliative Care, 8*(4), 23–27.

Corr, C. A., Nabe, C. M., & Corr, D. M. (1994). A task-based approach for understanding and evaluating funeral practices. *Thanatos, 19*(2), 10–15.

Davidowitz, M., & Myrick, R. D. (1984). Responding to the bereaved: An analysis of "helping" statements. *Death Education, 8,* 1–10.

Doka, K. J. (1989a). Disenfranchised grief. In K. J. Doka (Ed.), *Disenfranchised grief: Recognizing hidden sorrow* (pp. 3–11). Lexington, MA: Lexington Books.

Doka, K. J. (Ed.) (1989b). *Disenfranchised grief: Recognizing hidden sorrow.* Lexington, MA: Lexington Books.

Elias, N. (1991). On human beings and their emotions: A process-sociological essay. In M. Featherstone, M. Hepworth, & B. S. Turner (Eds.), *The body: Social process and cultural theory* (pp. 103–125). London: Sage.

Folta, J. R., & Deck, E. S. (1976). Grief, the funeral, and the friend. In V. R. Pine, A. H. Kutscher, D. Peretz, R. C. Slater, R. DeBellis, R. J. Volk, & D. J. Cherico (Eds.), *Acute grief and the funeral* (pp. 231–240). Springfield, IL: Charles C. Thomas.

Frank, A. W. (1991). *At the will of the body: Reflections on illness.* Boston: Houghton Mifflin.

Gyulay, J. E. (1975). The forgotten grievers. *American Journal of Nursing, 75,* 1476–1479.

Hamilton, J. (1978). Grandparents as grievers. In O. J. Z. Sahler (Ed.), *The child and death* (pp. 219–225). St. Louis, MO: C. V. Mosby.

Kaczmarek, M. G., & Backlund, B. A. (1991). Disenfranchised grief: The loss of an adolescent romantic relationship. *Adolescence, 26,* 253–259.

Kamerman, J. (1993). Latent functions of enfranchising the disenfranchised griever. *Death Studies, 17,* 281–287.

Klass, D., Silverman, P. R., & Nickman, S. L. (Eds.) (1996). *Continuing bonds: New understanding of grief.* Washington, DC: Taylor & Francis.

Lazarus, R. S., & Folkman, S. (1984). *Stress, appraisal, and coping.* New York: Springer.

Lindemann, E. (1944). Symptomatology and management of acute grief. *American Journal of Psychiatry, 101,* 141–148.

Lundberg, K. J., Thornton, G., & Robertson, D. U. (1987). Personal and social rejection of the bereaved. In C. A. Corr & R. A. Pacholski (Eds.), *Death: Completion and discovery* (pp. 61–70). Lakewood, OH: Association for Death Education and Counseling.

McClowry, S. G., Davies, E. B., May, K. A., Kulenkamp, E. J., & Martinson, I. M. (1987). The empty space phenomenon: The process of grief in the bereaved family. *Death Studies, 11,* 361–374.

Mead, M. (1973). Ritual and social crisis. In J. D. Shaughnessy (Ed.), *The roots of ritual* (pp. 87–101). Grand Rapids, MI: Eerdmans.

Osterweis, M., Solomon, F., & Green, M. (Eds.) (1984). *Bereavement: Reactions, consequences, and care.* Washington, DC: National Academy Press.

The Oxford English Dictionary (1989). J. A. Simpson & E. S. C. Weiner (Eds.). 2nd ed.; 20 vols; Oxford: Clarendon Press.

Parkes, C. M. (1996). *Bereavement: Studies of grief in adult life* (3rd ed.). New York: Routledge.

Pine, V. R., Margolis, O. S., Doka, K., Kutscher, A. H., Schaefer, D. J., Siegel, M-E., & Cherico, D. J. (Eds.) (1990). *Unrecognized and unsanctioned grief: The nature and counseling of unacknowledged loss.* Springfield, IL: Charles C Thomas.

Rando, T. A. (1993). *Treatment of complicated mourning.* Champaign, IL: Research Press.

Schwebach, I., & Thornton, G. (1992, 6 March). *Disenfranchised grief in mentally retarded and mentally ill populations.* Paper presented at the meeting of the Association for Death Education and Counseling, Boston.

Silverman, P. R., Nickman, S., & Worden, J. W. (1992). Detachment revisited: The child's reconstruction of a dead parent. *American Journal of Orthopsychiatry, 62,* 494–503.

Staples, B. (1994). *Parallel time: Growing up in black and white.* New York: Pantheon.

Stroebe, M. S., & Schut, H. (1995, June 29). *The dual process model of coping with loss.* Paper presented at the meeting of the International Work Group on Death, Dying, and Bereavement, Oxford, England.

Thornton, G., Robertson, D. U., & Mlecko, M. L. (1991). Disenfranchised grief and evaluations of social support by college students. *Death Studies, 15,* 355–362.

Wagner, S. (1994). *The Andrew poems.* Lubbock, TX: Texas Tech University Press.

Weisman, A. D. (1984). *The coping capacity: On the nature of being mortal.* New York: Human Sciences Press.

Wolfelt, A. D. (1996). *Healing the bereaved child: Grief gardening, growth through grief and other touchstones for caregivers.* Fort Collins, CO: Companion Press.

Worden, J. W. (1991). *Grief counseling and grief therapy: A handbook for the mental health practitioner* (2nd ed.). New York: Springer.

Zupanick, C. E. (1994). Adult children of dysfunctional families: Treatment from a disenfranchised grief perspective. *Death Studies, 18,* 183–195.

THE INCREASING PREVALENCE OF COMPLICATED MOURNING: THE ONSLAUGHT IS JUST BEGINNING*

Therese A. Rando, Ph.D.

Warwick, Rhode Island

ABSTRACT

In this article, complicated mourning is operationalized in relation to the six "R" processes of mourning and its seven high-risk factors are identified. The main thesis is that the prevalence of complicated mourning is increasing today due to a number of contemporary sociocultural and technological trends which have influenced 1) today's types of death; 2) the characteristics of personal relationships severed by today's deaths; and 3) the personality and resources of today's mourner. Additionally, specific problems in both the mental health profession and the field of thanatology further escalate complicated mourning by preventing or interfering with requisite treatment. Thus, complicated mourning is on the rise at the precise time when caregivers are unprepared and limited in their abilities to respond. New treatment policies and models are mandated as a consequence.

In the 1990s, the mental health profession (a term herein broadly used to encompass any caregiver whose work places him/her in the position of ministering to the mental health needs of another) and the thanatological community are at a crucial crossroads. Current sociocultural and technological trends in American society are directly increasing the prevalence of complicated mourning at the precise point in time at which the mental health profession is particularly both unprepared and limited in its abilities to respond to the needs created. Thanatology has a pivotal role to play in identifying this crisis, delineating the problems to be addressed, and advocating for the development of new policies, models, approaches, and treatments appropriate to today's grim realities. Failure of either profession to recognize these realities is bound to result not only in inadequate care for those who require it, but to place our society at greater risk for the serious sequelae known to emanate from untreated complicated mourning [1].

After a brief review of complicated mourning, this article will: 1) identify the high-risk factors for complicated mourning; 2) delineate the sociocultural and technological trends ex-

acerbating these factors, which in turn increase the prevalence of complicated mourning; 3) indicate the problems inherent in the mental health profession that interfere with proper response to complicated mourning and to its escalation; and 4) point out the pitfalls for addressing complicated mourning that reside in the field of thanatology today. The focus on this article is restricted to raising awareness of the problem and discussing its determinants.

COMPLICATED MOURNING

Historically, there have been three main difficulties in defining complicated mourning. The first stems from the imprecise and inconsistent terminology employed. The very same grief and mourning phenomena have been described at various times and by various authors as "pathological," "neurotic," "maladaptive," "unresolved," "abnormal," "dysfunctional," or "deviant," just to name some of the designations used. Communication has been hampered by a lack of semantic agreement and consensual validation. This author's preference is for the term "complicated mourning." Such a term suggests that mourning is a series of processes which in some way have become complicated, with the implication being that what has become complicated can be uncomplicated. It avoids the pejorative tone of many of the other terms. Additionally, there is no insinuation of pathology in the mourner. Heretofore, complications typically have been construed to arise from the deficits of the person experiencing the bereavement. The term "complicated" avoids the assumption that the complications necessarily stem from the mourner him or herself. This is quite crucial because it is now well-documented that there are some circumstances of death and some post-death variables that in and of themselves complicate mourning regardless of the premorbid psychological health of the mourner.

A second difficulty stems from the lack of objective criteria for what constitutes complicated mourning. Unlike the analogous medical situation in which the determination of pathology is more readily discerned and defined (e.g., the diagnosis of a broken bone usually can be easily agreed upon by several physicians following viewing of an x-ray), the phenomena in mourning tend not to be so concrete or unarguable. For instance, a woman hearing her deceased husband's voice in some circumstances is quite appropriate, whereas in others it reflects gross pathology.

The third and related difficulty is found because mourning is so highly idiosyncratic. It is determined by a constellation of thirty-three sets of factors circumscribing the loss and its circumstances, the mourner, and the social support received. No determination of abnormality technically ever can be made without taking into consideration the sets of factors known to influence any response to loss [2]. What may be an appropriate response in one circumstance for an individual mourner may be a highly pathological response for a different mourner in other circumstances. For this reason, it appears most helpful to look at complications in the mourning processes themselves rather than at particular symptomatology.

With this as a premise, complicated mourning can be said to be present when, taking into consideration the amount of time since the death, there is a compromise, distortion, or failure of one or more of the six "R" processes of mourning [1]. The six "R" processes of mourning necessary for healthy accommodation of any loss are:

1. Recognize the loss
   • Acknowledge the death
   • Understand the death
2. React to the separation
   • Experience the pain
   • Feel, identify, accept, and give some form of expression to all the psychological reactions to the loss
   • Identify and mourn secondary losses
3. Recollect and reexperience the deceased and the relationship
   • Review and remember realistically
   • Revive and reexperience the feelings
4. Relinquish the old attachments to the deceased and the old assumptive world
5. Readjust to move adaptively into the new world without forgetting the old
   • Revise the old assumptive world
   • Develop a new relationship with the deceased
   • Adopt new ways of being in the world
   • Form a new identity
6. Reinvest

In all forms of complicated mourning, there are attempts to do two things: 1) to deny, repress, or avoid aspects of the loss, its pain, and the full realization of its implications for the mourner; and 2) to hold onto, and avoid relinquishing, the lost loved one. These attempts, or some variation thereof, are what cause the complications in the "R" processes of mourning.

Complicated mourning may take any one or combination of four forms: symptoms, syndromes, mental or physical disorder, or death [1].

Complicated mourning symptoms refer to any psychological, behavioral, social, or physical symptom—alone or in combination—which in context reveals some dimension of compromise, distortion, or failure of one or more of the six "R" processes of mourning. They are of insufficient number, intensity, and duration, or of different type, than are required to meet the criteria for any of the other three forms of complicated mourning discussed below.

There are seven complicated mourning syndromes into which a constellation of complicated mourning symptoms may coalesce. They may occur independently or concurrently with one another. Only if the symptoms comprising them meet the criteria for the specific syndrome is there said to be a complicated mourning syndrome present. If only some of the symptoms are present, or there is a combination of symptoms from several of the syndromes but they fail to meet the criteria for a particular complicated mourning syndrome, then they are considered complicated mourning symptoms. The reader should be advised that a syndrome is not necessarily more pathological than a group of symptoms which clusters together but does not fit the description of one of the complicated mourning syndromes. Sometimes just a few complicated mourning symptoms—depending upon which they are—can be far more serious than the complicated mourning syndromes. With the exception of death, severity is not determined by the form of complicated mourning.

The seven syndromes of complicated mourning include three syndromes with problems in expression (i.e., absent mourning, delayed mourning and inhibited mourning); three syndromes with skewed aspects (i.e., distorted mourning of the extremely angry or guilty types, conflicted mourning, and unanticipated mourning); and the syndrome with a problem in ending (i.e., chronic mourning).

The third form that complicated mourning may take is of a diagnosable mental or physical disorder. This would include any DSM-III-R [3] diagnosis of a mental disorder or any recognized physical disorder that results from or is associated with a compromise, distortion, or failure of one or more of the six "R" processes of mourning. Death is the fourth form which complicated mourning may take. The death may be consciously chosen (i.e., suicide) or it may stem from the immediate results of a complicated mourning reaction (e.g., an automobile crash resulting from the complicated mourning symptom of driving at excessive speed) or the long-term results of a complicated mourning reaction (e.g., cirrhosis of the liver secondary to mourning-related alcoholism). The latter two types of death may or may not be subintentioned on the part of the mourner.

GENERIC HIGH-RISK FACTORS FOR COMPLICATED MOURNING

Clinical and empirical evidence reveals that there are seven generic high-risk factors which can predispose any individual to have complication in mourning [1]. These can be divided into two categories: factors associated with the specific death and factors associated with antecedent and subsequent variables.

Factors associated with the death which are known especially to complicate mourning include: 1) a sudden and unanticipated death, especially when it is traumatic, violent, mutilating, or random; 2) death from an overly-lengthy illness; 3) loss of a child; and 4) the mourner's perception of preventability. Antecedent and subsequent variables that tend to complicate mourning include: 1) premorbid relationship with the deceased which has been markedly angry or ambivalent or markedly dependent; 2) the mourner's prior or concurrent mental health problems and/or unaccommodated losses and stresses; and 3) the mourner's perceived lack of social support.

To the extent that any bereaved individual is characterized by one or more of these factors, that individual can be said to be at risk for the development of complications in one or more of the six "R" processes of mourning, and hence at risk for complicated mourning.

SOCIOCULTURAL AND TECHNOLOGICAL TRENDS EXACERBATING THE HIGH-RISK FACTORS AND INCREASING THE PREVALENCE OF COMPLICATED MOURNING

Social change, medical advances, and shifting political realities have spawned the recent trends that have complicated healthy grief and mourning.

Social change, occurring at an increasingly rapid rate, encompasses such processes as urbanization; industrialization; increasing technicalization; secularization and deritualization (particularly the trend to omit funeral or memorial services and not to view the body); greater social mobility; social reorganization (specifically a decline in—if not a breakdown of—the nuclear family, increases in single parent and blended families, and the relative exclusion of the aged and dying); rising societal, interpersonal, and institutional violence (physical, sexual, and psychological); and unemployment, poverty, and economic problems. Consequences include social alienation; senses of personal helplessness and hopelessness; parental absence and neglect of children; larger societal discrepancies between the "haves" and the "have nots"; and epidemic drug and alcohol abuse, physical and sexual abuse of children and those without power (e.g., women and the elderly), and availability of guns. All of these sequelae have tended to increase violence even more, to sever or severely damage the links between children and adults, and to expose individuals to more traumatic and unnatural deaths.

Medical advances have culminated in lengthier chronic illnesses, and increased age spans, altered mortality rates, and intensified bioethical dilemmas. These trends, plus those involving social change, accompany contemporary political realities of increasing incidence of terrorism, assassination, political torture, and genocide, which get played out against the ever-present possibility of ecological disaster, nuclear holocaust, and megadeath to impact dramatically and undeniably on today's mourner [4–6].

VIOLENCE: A PARTICULARLY MALIGNANT TREND

Any commentary on present-day trends would be negligent if it did not elaborate somewhat upon the phenomenon of violence in today's society. Violence contributes significantly to the increasing prevalence of complicated mourning, and is associated with most of its generic high-risk factors. One crime index offense occurs every two seconds in the United States, with one violent crime occurring every nineteen seconds [7]. Violent crime has risen to the extent that in April 1991 Attorney General Richard Thornburgh issued the statement that "a citizen of this country is today more likely to be the victim of a violent crime than of an automobile accident" [8]. The U.S. Department of Justice estimates that five out of six of today's twelve-year-olds will become victims of violent crime during their lifetimes [9], with estimates for the lifetime chance of becoming a victim of homicide in the United States ranging from one out of 133 to one out of 153 depending upon the source of the statistics [10]. One category of homicide—murder by juvenile—is increasing so rapidly that it is now being termed "epidemic" by psychologist and attorney Charles Ewing [11], an authority on child perpetrators of homicide.

Other types of crime and victimization are on the rise in the United States. The National Victim Center Overview of Crime and Victimization in America [12] provides some of the horrifying statistics:

- Wife-beating results in more injuries that require medical treatment than rape, auto accidents, and muggings combined.
- More than one out of every 200 senior citizens is the victim of a violent crime each year, making a total of 155,000 elderly Americans who are attacked, robbed, assaulted, and murdered every year—435 each day.
- New York City has reported an eighty percent increase in hate-motivated crimes since 1986, with seventy percent of them perpetrated by those under age nineteen.
- One in three women will be sexually assaulted during her lifetime.
- Every forty-seven seconds a child is abused or neglected.

Certainly, society not only condones, but escalates, violence. Books, movies, music videos, and songs perpetuate the belief that violence is not merely acceptable, but exciting. Books focusing on real-life serial killers; escalating movie violence associated with anatomically precise and sexually explicit images; and music portraying hostility against women, murder, and necrophilia are routine. According to Thomas Radecki, Research Director for the National Coalition on Television Violence, by the age of 18 the average American child will have seen 200,000 violent acts on television, including 40,000 murders [13]. Children's programming now averages twenty-five violent acts per hour, which is up fifty percent from that in the early 1980s [14]. The recently popular children's movie, *Teenage Mutant Ninja Turtles,* had a total of 194 acts of violence primarily committed by the "heroes" of the film, which was the most violent film ever to be given a "PG" rating [15]. In the week of March 11, 1990, *America's Funniest Home Videos* became the highest-rated series on television. Some of the stories on that program that viewers found particularly amusing included a child getting hit in the face with a shovel, seven women falling off a bench, a man getting hit by a glider, and a child bicycling into a tree [15]. All of this provides serious concerns given the twenty-year research of Leonard Eron and L. Rowell Huesmann, who found that children who watch significant amounts of TV violence at the age of eight were consistently more likely to commit violent crimes or engage in spouse abuse at age thirty [13]. These researchers determined that heavy exposure to media violence is one of the major causes of aggressive behavior, crime, and violence in society.

Other forms of violence are increasing as well. Reports of abused and neglected children continue to rise. They reached 2.5 million in 1990, an increase of 30.7 percent since 1986, and 117 percent in the past decade [16]. One out of three girls, and one out of seven boys, are sexually abused by the time they reach eighteen [17]. In the United States, when random studies are conducted without the inclusion of high-risk groups, one in eight husbands has been physically aggressive with his wife in the preceding twelve months [18]. At least 2,000,000 women are severely and aggressively assaulted by their partners in any twelve-month period [18]. It is a myth that what has been termed "intimate violence" is confined to mentally disturbed individuals. While ten percent of offenders do sustain some form of psychopathology, ninety percent of offenders do not look any different than the "normal" individual [19].

SEQUELAE OF THE TRENDS PREDISPOSING TO COMPLICATED MOURNING

As a result of all the aforementioned sociocultural and technological trends, there have been changes in three main areas which have significantly increased the prevalence of complicated mourning:

1. the types of death occurring today
2. the characteristics of personal relationships that are severed by today's deaths
3. the personality and resources of today's mourner.

Each of these adversely impacts in one or more ways upon one or more of the high-risk factors for complicated mourning, thereby increasing its prevalence.

TYPES OF DEATH OCCURRING TODAY

Contemporary American society is witnessing the increase in three types of death known to be at high risk for complicated mourning: 1) sudden and unanticipated deaths, especially if they are traumatic (i.e., characterized not only by suddenness

and lack of anticipation, but violence, mutilation, and destruction; preventability and/or randomness; multiple death; or the mourner's personal encounter with death [20]; 2) deaths that result from excessively lengthy chronic illnesses; and 3) deaths of children. Each of these deaths presents the survivors with issues known to compromise the "R" processes of mourning, hence each circumstance is a high-risk factor for complicated mourning.

Sudden and Unanticipated Traumatic Deaths

Sudden and unanticipated traumatic deaths stem primarily from four main causes: 1) accidents; 2) technological advances; 3) increasing rates of homicide and the escalating violence and pathology of perpetrators; and 4) higher suicide rates. Although mortality rates for children and youth in the United States have decreased since 1900, the large proportion of deaths from external causes—injuries, homicide, and suicide—distinguishes mortality at ages one to nineteen from that at other ages; with external causes of death accounting for about ten percent of the deaths of children and youth in 1900 and rising to 64 percent in 1985 [21].

Current trends reveal that "accidents"—a term covering most deaths from motor vehicle crashes, falls, poisoning, drowning, fire, suffocation, and firearms—are the leading cause of death among all persons aged one to thirty-seven and represent the fourth leading cause of death among persons of all ages [22]. On the average, there are eleven accidental deaths and approximately 1,030 disabling injuries every hour during the year [22]. Accidents are the single most common type of horrendous death for persons of any age, bringing deaths which are "premature, torturous, and without redeeming value" [23].

Technological advances simultaneously have both decreased the proportion of natural deaths that occur and increased the proportion of sudden and unanticipated traumatic deaths. For instance, substantial improvements in biomedical technology have culminated in higher survival rates from illnesses which previously would have been fatal. This leaves individuals alive longer to be susceptible to unnatural death. Additionally, the increase in unnatural death is due to greater current exposure to technology, machinery, motor vehicles, airplanes, chemicals, firearms, weapon systems, and so forth that put human beings at greater risk for unnatural death. For example, prior to the advent of the airplane, a crash of a horse and buggy could claim far fewer lives and be less mutilating to the bodies than the crash of a DC-10.

The third reason for the increase in sudden and unanticipated traumatic deaths stems from the increasing rates of homicide and the escalating violence and pathology of those who perpetrate these crimes upon others. The increase in actual homicide incidence; the rising percentage of serial killers; and the types of violence perpetrated before, during, and after the final homicidal act suggest that there are sicker individuals doing sicker things. More than ever before, homicide may be marked by cult or ritual killing, thrill killing, random killing, drive-by shootings, and accompanied by predeath torture and postdeath defilement. The increasing pathology of those who commit violent crimes may be seen as the result of the previously mentioned sociocultural trends, especially but not exclusively the individual's decreasing social connections and sense of power; fewer social prohibitions, and increasing societal violence. It reflects the increasing number of individuals with impaired psychological development, characterized often by an absent conscience, low frustration tolerance, poor impulse control, inability to delay gratification or modulate aggression, a sense of deprivation and entitlement, and notably poor attachment bonds and pathological patterns of relationships.

The fourth reason for the increase in sudden and unanticipated traumatic deaths follows from the higher suicide rates currently found in Western society. As above, these types of death appear to derive from all of the aforementioned trends contributing to complicated mourning in general.

The reader will note that most of the sudden and unanticipated traumatic deaths in this category also are preventable. Given that the perception of preventability is a high-risk factor predisposing to complicated mourning, to the extent that a mourner maintains this perception as an element in his or her mourning of the death that individual sustains a greater chance for experiencing complications in the process.

Long-Term Chronic Illness Death

This type of death is increasing in frequency because of biomedical and technological advances that can combat disease and forestall cessation of life. Consequently, today's illnesses are longer in duration than ever before. However, it has been well-documented that there are significant problems for survivors when a loved one's terminal illness persists for too long [24]. These illnesses often present loved ones with inherent difficulties that eventually complicate their postdeath bereavement and expose them to situations and dilemmas previously unheard of when patients died sooner and/or without becoming the focus for bioethical debates around the use of machinery and the prolongation of life without quality. With the increase in the Human Immunodeficiency Virus (HIV) and Acquired Immunodeficiency Syndrome (AIDS), significant multidimensional stresses arise which engender those known to complicate mourning in anyone (e.g., anger, ambivalence, guilt, stigmatization, social disenfranchisement, problems obtaining required health care, and so forth). The fact that an individual may be positive for the HIV virus for an exceptionally long period of time prior to developing the often long-term, multiproblemic, and idiosyncratic course of their particular version of AIDS, with all of its vicissitudes, gives new meaning these days to the stresses of long-term chronic illness.

Parental Loss of a Child

In earlier years, by the time an adult child died, his or her parents would have been long deceased. Today, with increases in lifespan and advances in medical technology, parents are permitted to survive long enough to witness the deaths of the adult children they used to predecease. Clinically and empirically, it is well-known that significant problematic issues are associated with the parental loss of a child—issues which when

compared to those generated by other losses appear to make this loss the most difficult with which to cope [25]. These problematic issues and complicated mourning are now visited upon older parents who remain alive to experience the death of their adult child. There is even some suggestion that additional stresses are added to the normal burdens of parental bereavement when the child is an adult in his or her own right [26]. It is a uniquely contemporary trend, therefore, that associated with all of today's deaths are a greater percentage of parents who, because of medical advancements, are alive to be placed in the high-risk situation for complicated mourning upon the death of their adult child. This is a population that can be excepted to increase, and consequently swell the numbers of complicated mourners as well.

CHARACTERISTICS OF PERSONAL RELATIONSHIPS SEVERED BY TODAY'S DEATHS

As a consequence of societal trends, there has been an increase in conflicted and dependent relationships in our society. Both types are high-risk factors when they characterize the mourner's premorbid relationship with the deceased [1]. With more of these types of relationships than ever before, there is a relative increase in the prevalence of complicated mourning, which is predisposed to develop after the death of one with whom the mourner has had this type of bond.

In 1957, Edmond Volkart offered a classic discussion of why death in the American family tends to cause greater psychological impact than in other cultures, specifically causing the family to be uniquely vulnerable to bereavement [6]. The reasons he delineated are even more salient today, and are part of the trends already cited above. Among other trends, he noted that the limited range of interaction in the American family fosters unusually intense emotional involvement as compared to other societies, and that there is an exclusivity of relationships in the American family. Both trends breed overidentification and overdependence among family members, which in turn engender ambivalence, repressed hostility, and guilt that create greater potential for complications after the death. Adding fuel to this fire is the societal expectation that grief expression concentrates on feelings and expression of loss. There is a failure both to recognize and to provide channels for hostility, guilt, and ambivalence.

Problematic relationships are on the rise in our society for other reasons as well. Quite importantly, there is an overall increase in sexual and physical abuse of children, as well as other adults. Research repeatedly documents the malignant intrapsychic and interpersonal sequelae of abuse and victimization [27, 28]. This leaves the victim susceptible to complications in mourning not only because of the myriad symptomatology and biopsychosocial issues they caused, but typically with significant amounts of the anger, ambivalence, and/or dependence known to complicate any individual's mourning. In addition, the victimization may interfere with the mourner permitting him or herself to mourn the death of the perpetrator—an often necessary task that many victims resist because of inaccurate beliefs about mourning in general and/or misconstruals of what their specifically mourning the perpetrator's death may mean [1]. This only further victimizes the person through the consequences of incomplete mourning.

These forms of victimization are not the only experiences which give rise to the conflicted and dependent relationships identified as predisposing to complicated mourning. Individuals raised in families with one or more alcoholic parents or a parent who is an adult child of an alcoholic (ACOA), or with one or more parents who are psychologically impaired, rigid in beliefs, compulsive in behaviors, codependent, absent, neglectful, or chronically ill are vulnerable too. As sociocultural trends escalate these scenarios, relationships characterized by anger, ambivalence, and dependency will become prevalent, and complicated mourning will, in turn, become more frequent.

THE PERSONALITY AND RESOURCES OF TODAY'S MOURNER

Current trends suggest that the personality and resources of today's mourner leave that individual compromised in mourning for three reasons. First, given the trends previously discussed, the personalities and mental health of today's mourners are often more impaired. These impaired persons—who themselves frequently sustain poor attachment bonds with their own parents because of these trends—typically effect intergenerational transmission of these deficits via the inadequate parenting provided to their own children and the unhealthy experiences those children undergo. Clinically, one sees more often these days impaired superego development, lower level personality organization, narcissistic behavior, character disorder, and poor impulse control. Given that one's personality and previous and current states of mental health are critical factors influencing any mourner's ability to address mourning successfully, a trend towards relatively more impairment in this area has implications for greater numbers of people being added to the rolls of complicated mourners.

Another liability for a mourner is the existence of unaccommodated prior or concurrent losses or stresses. In this regard, a second reason for the increased prevalence of complicated mourning comes from the presence of more loss and stress in the life of today's mourner as compared to times in the past. To the extent that contemporary sociocultural trends bring relatively more losses and stresses for a person, both prior to a given death (e.g., parents' divorce) and concomitant with it (e.g., unemployment), today's mourner is relatively more disadvantaged given his or her increased exposure to these high-risk factors.

The third reason for increased complications in mourning arises from the compromise of the mourner's resources. Disenfranchised mourning [29] is on the rise, and the consequent perceived lack of social support it stimulates is a high-risk factor for complicated mourning. It is quite evident that conditions in contemporary American society promote all three of the main reasons for social disenfranchisement during mourn-

ing, i.e., invalidation of the loss, the lost relationship, or the mourner [29]. Examples of unrecognized losses that are increasing in today's society include abortions, adoptions, the deaths of pets, and the inherent losses of those with Alzheimer's disease. Cases of the second type of disenfranchised loss that are on the increase include relationships that are not based on kin ties, or are not socially sanctioned (e.g., gay or lesbian relationships, extramarital affairs), or those that existed primarily in the past (e.g., former spouses or in-laws). Increasingly prevalent situations where the mourner is unrecognized can be found when the mourner is elderly, mentally handicapped, or a child. The more society creates, maintains, or permits individuals to be disenfranchised in their mourning, the more those individuals are at risk for complicated mourning given that disenfranchisement is so intimately linked with the high-risk factor of the mourner's perception of lack of social support.

PROBLEMS INHERENT IN THE MENTAL HEALTH PROFESSION WHICH INTERFERE WITH PROPER RESPONSE TO COMPLICATED MOURNING AND TO ITS ESCALATION

There are three serious problems inherent in mental health today that interfere with the profession's response to complicated mourning and its escalation. Each one contributes to increasing the prevalence of complicated mourning either by facilitating misdiagnosis and/or hampering requisite treatment. The three problems are: 1) lack of an appropriate diagnostic category in the DSM-III-R; 2) insufficient knowledge about grief, mourning, and bereavement in general; and 3) decreased funds for and increased restrictions upon contemporary mental health services.

In the DSM-III-R, there is the lack of a diagnostic category for anything but the most basic uncomplicated grief, with the criteria even for this being significantly unrealistic for duration and symptomatology in light of today's data on uncomplicated grief and mourning. If they want to treat a mourning individual, mental health clinicians are often forced to utilize other diagnoses, many of which have clinical implications that are unacceptable. Other diagnoses that clinicians employ to justify treatment and to incorporate more fully the symptomatology of the bereaved individual frequently include one of the depressive, anxiety, or adjustment disorders; brief reactive psychosis; or one of the V code diagnoses.

The second area of problems in the mental health profession is the shocking insufficiency of knowledge about grief and bereavement in general. Mental health professionals tend, as does the general public, to have inappropriate expectations and unrealistic attitudes about grief and mourning, and to believe in and promote the myths and stereotypes known to pervade society at large. These not only do not help, but actually harm bereaved individuals given that they are used to (a) set the standards against which the bereaved individual is evaluated, (b) determine the assistance and support provided and/or judged to be needed, and (c) support unwarranted diagnoses of failure and pathology [30]. Yet, the problem is not all in *mis*information. Too many clinicians actually do not even know that they lack the requisite information they must possess if they want to treat a bereaved person successfully. Without a doubt, the majority of clinicians know an insufficient amount about uncomplicated grief and mourning; and of those who do know an adequate amount, only a fraction of them know enough about complicated mourning. Clinician lack of information and misinformation is the major cause of iatrogenesis in the treatment of grief and mourning.

An overall decrease in funds permitted and an increase in third-party payer insurance restrictions mark contemporary mental health services and constitute the third problem in the field adding to the prevalence of complicated mourning. These changes occur at a time when it not only is becoming more clearly documented that uncomplicated grief and mourning is more associated with psychiatric distress than previously recognized [31] and that it persists for longer duration [32], but precisely when the incidence of complicated mourning is increasing and demanding more extensive treatment for higher proportions of the bereaved. Consequently, at the exact point in time that the mental health community will have more bereaved individuals with greater complicated mourning requiring treatment for longer periods of time, mental health services will be increasingly subjected to limitations, preapprovals, third-party reviews by persons ignorant of the area, short-term models, and forced usage of inappropriate diagnostic classification. This scenario demands that the mental health professional working with the bereaved find new policies models, approaches, and treatments which are appropriate to these serious realities. Failing to do so, the future is frightening as the current system simply is not equipped to respond to the coming onslaught of complicated mourners.

THE PITFALLS FOR ADDRESSING COMPLICATED MOURNING RESIDING IN THE FIELD OF THANATOLOGY TODAY

It is unfortunate, but true: Thanatologists are contributing to the rising prevalence of complicated mourning as are contemporary sociocultural and technological trends and the mental health profession. While it is not in the purview of this article to discuss at length the myriad problems inherent in our own field of thanatology that contribute to complicated mourning, it must be noted:

- A significant amount of caregivers lack adequate clinical information about uncomplicated grief and mourning, e.g., the "normal" psychiatric complications of uncomplicated grief and mourning.
- Many thanatologists, in their effort to promote the naturalness of grief and mourning and to depathologize the way they construe it to have been medicalized, maintain an insufficient understanding of complicated grief and mourning.

- There is nonexistent, or at the very least woefully insufficient, assessment conducted by caregivers who assume that the grief and mourning they observe must be related exclusively to the particular death closest in time and who do not place the individual's responses within the context of his or her entire life prior to evaluating them.
- The phenomenon of "throwing the baby out with the bathwater" has occurred regarding medication in bereavement. Out of a concern that a mourner not be inappropriately medicated as had been done so often in the past, caregivers today often fail to send mourners for medication evaluations that are desperately needed, e.g., antianxiety medication following traumatic deaths.
- The research in the field has not been sufficiently longitudinal and has overfocused on certain populations (e.g., widows), leaving findings that are not generalizable over time for many types of mourners, especially complicated mourners.
- Caregivers do not always recognize that any work as a grief or mourning counselor or therapist must overlay a basic foundation of training in mental health intervention in general. While education in thanatology, good intentions, and/or previous experience with loss may be appropriate credentials for the individual facilitating uncomplicated grief and mourning (e.g., a facilitator of a mutual help group for the bereaved), this is not sufficient for that person offering counseling or therapy.
- Given that thanatology itself is a "specialty area," thanatologists often fail to recognize that the field encompasses a number of "subspecialty areas," each of which has its own data base and treatment requirements, i.e., all mourners are not alike and caregivers must recognize and respond to the differences inherent in different loss situations (e.g., loss of a child versus loss of a spouse or sudden and unanticipated death versus an expected chronic illness death).
- Clinicians working with the dying and the bereaved are subject to countertransference phenomena, stress reactions, codependency, "vicarious traumatization" [33], and burnout.

This constitutes a brief, and by no means exhaustive, listing of the types of pitfalls into which a thanatologist may fall. Each "fall" has the potential for compromising the mourning of the bereaved individual and in that regard has the potential for increasing the prevalence of complicated mourning today.

CONCLUSION

This article has discussed the causes and forms of complicated mourning, and has delineated the seven high-risk factors known to predispose to it. The purpose has been to illustrate how current sociocultural and technological trends are exacerbating these factors, thereby significantly increasing the prevalence of complicated mourning today. Problems both in the mental health profession and in the field of thanatology further contribute by preventing or interfering with requisite intervention. It is imperative that these grim realities be recognized in order that appropriate policies, models, approaches, and treatments be developed to respond to the individual and societal needs created by complicated mourning and its sequelae.

*This article is adapted from a keynote address of the same name presented at the 13th Annual Conference of the Association for Death Education and Counseling, Duluth, Minnesota, April 26–28, 1991 and from the author's book, *Treatment of Complicated Mourning,* Research Press, Champaign, Illinois, 1993.

REFERENCES

1. T. Rando, *Treatment of Complicated Mourning,* Research Press, Champaign, Illinois, 1993.

2. T. Rando, *Grief, Dying, and Death: Clinical Interventions for Caregivers,* Research Press, Champaign, Illinois, 1984.

3. American Psychiatric Association, *Diagnostic and Statistical Manual of Mental Disorders,* (3rd ed. rev.), Washington, D.C., 1987.

4. H. Feifel, The Meaning of Death in American Society: Implications for Education, in *Death Education: Preparation for Living,* B. Green and D. Irish (eds.), Schenkman, Cambridge, Massachusetts, 1971.

5. R. Lifton, *Death in Life: Survivors of Hiroshima,* Random House, New York, 1968.

6. E. Volkart (with collaboration of S. Michael), Bereavement and Mental Health, in *Explorations in Social Psychiatry,* A. Leighton, J. Clausen, and R. Wilson (eds.), Basic Books, New York, 1957.

7. Federal Bureau of Investigation, U.S. Department of Justice, *Uniform Crime Reports for the United States,* U.S. Government Printing Office, Washington, D.C., 1990.

8. Violent Crimes up 10%, *Providence Journal,* pp. A1 and A6, April 29, 1991.

9. National Victim Center, *America Speaks Out: Citizens' Attitudes about Victims' Rights and Violence,* (Executive Summary), Fort Worth, Texas, 1991.

10. Bureau of Justice Statistics Special Report, *The Risk of Violent Crime,* (NCJ-97119), U.S. Department of Justice, Washington, D.C., May 1985.

11. Killing by Kids "Epidemic" Forecast, *APA Monitor,* pp. 1 and 31, April, 1991.

12. National Victim Center, *National Victim Center Overview of Crime and Victimization in America,* Fort Worth, Texas, 1991.

13. Violence in Our Culture, *Newsweek,* pp. 46–52, April 1, 1991.

14. J. Patterson and P. Kim, *The Day America Told the Truth,* Prentice Hall Press, New York, 1991.

15. National Victim Center, *Crime, Safety and You!,* 1:3, 1990.

16. Children's Defense Fund Memo on the Family Preservation Act, Washington, D.C., July 2, 1991.

17. E. Bass and L. Davis, *The Courage to Heal: A Guide for Women Survivors of Child Sexual Abuse,* Harper and Row Publishers, New York, 1988.

18. A. Brown, *"Women's Roles" and Responses to Violence by Intimates: Hard Choices for Women Living in a Violent Society,* paper presented at the conference on "Trauma and Victimization: Understanding and Healing Survivors" sponsored by the University of Connecticut Center for Professional Development, Vernon, Connecticut, September 27–28, 1991.

19. R. Gelles, *The Roots, Context, and Causes of Family Violence,* paper presented at the conference on "Trauma and Victimization: Understanding and Healing Survivors" sponsored by the University of Connecticut Center for Professional Development, Vernon, Connecticut, September 27–28, 1991.

20. T. Rando, Complications in Mourning Traumatic Death, in *Death, Dying and Bereavement,* I. Corless, B. Germino, and M. Pittman-Lindeman (eds.), Jones and Bartlett Publishers, Inc., Boston, (in press).

21. L. Fingerhut and J. Kleinman, Mortality Among Children and Youth, *American Journal of Public Health, 79,* pp. 899–901, 1989.

22. National Safety Council, *Accident Facts, 1991 Edition,* Chicago, 1991.

23. M. Dixon and H. Clearwater, Accidents, in *Horrendous Death, Health, and Well-Being,* D. Leviton (ed.), Hemisphere Publishing Corporation, New York, 1991.

24. T. Rando (ed.) *Loss and Anticipatory Grief,* Lexington Books, Lexington, Massachusetts, 1986.

25. T. Rando (ed.), *Parental Loss of a Child,* Research Press, Champaign, Illinois, 1986.

26. T. Rando, Death of an Adult Child, in *Parental Loss of a Child,* T. Rando, (ed.), Research Press, Champaign, Illinois, 1986.

27. C. Courtois, *Healing the Incest Wound: Adult Survivors in Therapy,* Norton, New York, 1988.

28. F. Ochberg (ed.), *Post-Traumatic Therapy and Victims of Violence,* Brunner/Mazel, New York, 1988.

29. K. Doka (ed.), *Disenfranchised Grief: Recognizing Hidden Sorrow,* Lexington Books, Lexington, Massachusetts, 1989.

30. T. Rando, *Grieving: How To Go On Living When Someone You Love Dies,* Lexington Books, Lexington, Massachusetts, 1988.

31. S. Jacobs and K. Kim, Psychiatric Complications of Bereavement, *Psychiatric Annals, 20,* pp. 314–317, 1990.

32. S. Zisook and S. Shuchter, Time Course of Spousal Bereavement, *General Hospital Psychiatry, 7,* pp. 95–100, 1985.

33. I. McCann and L. Pearlman, Vicarious Traumatization: A Framework for Understanding the Psychological Effects of Working with Victims, *Journal of Traumatic Stress, 3,* pp. 131–149, 1990.

Children Grieve Too

Lessons in how to support children through a normal, healthy grief process

by Linda Goldman

Certified Grief Therapist and Grief Educator
Center for Loss and Grief Therapy
Kensington, Maryland

Learning how to deal with grieving children will help parents, teachers, and students exist in a more healthy living and learning environment. The complex relationship between loss issues and a young child's ability to function in and out of the classroom needs to be addressed in a new and fresh way. We need to see children's grief, and our own, as on ongoing life process that is approachable through words, activities, and nonverbal communication. This understanding can enable Head Start centers to create a safe environment for parents, teachers, and children to acknowledge and process difficult feelings.

The prevailing myth that Head Start children are too young to understand grief and loss issues seems outdated. If children are capable of love, they are certainly capable of feeling grief. We, as Head Start parents and educators, can model our own grief as a teaching tool for young children, allowing them to express thoughts and feelings of sadness, anger, fear and frustration. As role models, we need to be in touch with our own grief in order to help grieving children heal.

Young children continually process and incorporate a large part of their physical world. They are influenced by how adults around them act and react to this world. Children will process and incorporate the reactions of

From *Children and Families,* Spring 1997, pp. 22-31. Reprinted by permission of the author and the National Head Start Association. © 1997.

Drawing is a great way to relay unacknowledged feelings. This picture was drawn by 7-year-old Sara who has AIDS. This picture illustrates her hope that after she dies, she can be in heaven with her mother, who also has AIDS.

Head Start parents and teachers into their own grief. The Head Start community serves as a model for the children when it expresses sadness that a teacher died, anger that a friend has cancer, fear that a school was vandalized, and frustration that there is no cure for AIDS.

This article will show you how to help a grieving child, and in turn help Head Start educators create a more effective learning environment for the entire school community. Grief issues can create trauma in children that can inhibit learning and development, resulting in larger numbers of our children having social and academic difficulties in and out of school. Children's experiences in the preschool years lay the foundation for their ability, openness, and readiness to learn. School systems need to identify, work with, and meet the needs of children faced with these life-changing situations.

Normal grief symptoms

Before we can help children with their grief issues, we need to understand how grief affects all of us. The death of a parent, sibling, friend, or teacher greatly impacts kids and grownups. Shame and guilt often accompany the death of a loved one, with adults and children fearing they in some way caused the death. Isolation and loneliness sometimes follow a death. People who are grieving often feel that they are not understood and that they are different from others.

In addition to death, members of the Head Start community may grieve losses in other life circumstances. Moving to a new state, learning that a beloved teacher is retiring, or losing a favorite doll are typical examples of nondeath losses that can create great stress and anxiety. Normal grief may involve feelings of numbness, rage, deep sadness, overwhelmed states of emotion, regression, panic, and difficulties eating and sleeping. Time appears to stand still, and adults and children experience forever the loss of life as they knew it before the grief experience.

Normal signs of grief for children

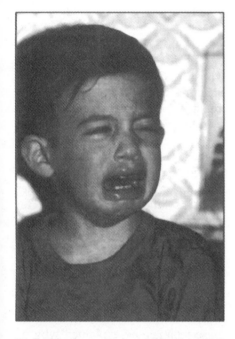

It's healthy for a grieving child to cry. Children need to feel their sadness and feel free to express it.

In addition to normal grief issues, there are special considerations that apply specifically to kids. Understanding their unique method of grieving can enable Head Start personnel to gain a greater depth of understanding for a grieving child. There appears to be a direct relationship between the intensity of children's grief and loss issues and their ability to learn and grow. Children experience decreased capacity to concentrate if they experience an extreme trauma, such as witnessing their mom's murder. If they cannot or will not speak about this event, the trauma begins a long episode of blocked energy, and this block often results in an inability to learn.

A grieving child often is misdiagnosed as learning disabled or as having Attention Deficit Disorder. The unresolved grief continues and grows unaddressed throughout the child's education. Children may become hyperactive, easily distracted, or impulsive. These behaviors are often misinterpreted as emotional or learning problems instead of being viewed as a cry for help. Head Start teachers and educators need to become familiar with normal grief symptoms in order to more accurately identify problem areas.

Young children are often preoccupied with death, and they worry excessively about their own health and the health of those around them. Four-year-old Tommy, whose baby sister Ann had died, asked his mom every night, "Am I going to die too?" "If our baby Ann went to heaven, can I go with her?" The young child often speaks of the person that died in the present and maintains a continuous and ongoing relationship with the deceased. Alice, a 6-year-old, used her toy telephone to call her mom who had died and tell her about the school day. "I miss you, Mommy. I'm showing you my art project while we talk. I love you!"

Adam, a 5-year-old, began imitating his dad's gestures after he died. Adam patted his dog, Muffin, saying, "You're a good girl, Muffin" just the way his dad used to do. Imitating a loved one who died is a normal sign of grief. Children often feel the presence of a mom or dad who has died. Mary, a 4-year-old preschooler, told me she felt her mom was with her whenever she saw a butterfly and that the butterfly was a messenger saying, "I love you."

Parents, teachers, educators, and caring adults can reduce anxieties for children and their families by normalizing common thoughts and feelings. For example, adults can assure children that it is a normal grief response to worry about their own health after a loved one dies. It's normal to fear death after a parent dies in a car crash. And it's also normal to want to seek revenge after the

Normal Signs of Grief

Adults and children need to be aware of normal signs of grief. When educators and parents see signs of grief, they can ensure that children get the help and support they need. And when children learn normal signs of grief, they can share similar ways of expressing thoughts and feelings with other grieving children. The following are common responses to grief. Children may:

- Tell and retell their stories.
- Become preoccupied with death or their own health and that of a surviving parent or guardian.
- Speak of dead loved one in the present.
- Feel the presence of a loved one.
- Imitate and idolize a loved one who died.
- Become the class clown or the class bully.
- Withdraw from other children.
- Show an inability to concentrate and have a tendency to daydream.
- Experience nightmares, manifest bedwetting, or regress and become clingy.
- Complain of stomachaches and headaches.

murder of a family member. Normalizing grief responses will help minimize the stress level that often accompanies these new and scary feelings.

The young child's view of death

Piaget, a French educator whose thoughts have greatly influenced the world of grief therapy for children, explains that young children be-tween the ages of 2 and 7 are categorized as part of the preoperational stage of cognitive development. This state is marked by magical thinking, egocentricity, reversibility, and causality.

Kids imagine their words have magical powers, and so they often feel that they are in some way responsible for tragedies. Ashley and Roxanne are sisters, ages 4 and 7. After a tremendous argument over a stuffed animal, Ashley screamed at her sister, "I hate you, and I wish you were dead!" She tore Roxanne's stuffed toy to bits. The next night, Roxanne was killed in a car accident. Ashley blamed herself, saying over and over that she knew her words made her sister die.

In a similar example, Charlie yelled at his older brother, "I hate you. I wish you were dead!" Charlie was haunted with the idea that this wish created his brother's fatal ski accident. Charlie's egocentric perception made him see himself at the center of the universe, capable of creating and destroying the world around him just by willing it.

Molly, a 6-year-old first grader whose dad died in an automobile accident, visualized death as reversible and believed that her dad was going to come back. She wrote a letter to her dad, addressed it to heaven, and put it in the mail. She waited and waited to receive a letter back, even though she knew her dad was killed in a car crash. Her age-appropriate belief in causality caused her to question in her mind: "Is Dad not writing back because I didn't get a good report card?"

Brian was a 3-year-old whose thinking convinced him that he had killed his dad. When he confided these feelings, he explained why he thought that he had murdered his dad. "My dad picked me up the night he had his heart attack. If he hadn't done that, he wouldn't have died. It's all my fault." Brian needed to understand that his dad's heart attack was caused by being overweight and smoking cigarettes, not his driving to pick up Brian.

Memory books are a collection of drawings and writings that allow a child to re-experience memories and share thoughts and feelings in a safe way. This picture is from the memory book of Tommy, a 5-year-old. The large figure in the center is his Uncle John, whom Tommy had not seen in three years. The picture helped Tommy's grief therapist realize that the child had been lacking male support since his father's death four years earlier.

Clichés that inhibit the grief process

Many times, children take language literally. They need direct and simple language explaining death. When defining death for the young child we could say, "Death is when the body stops working. Usually people die when they are very, very old, or very, very, very sick, or their bodies are so injured that the doctors and nurses can't make their bodies work again." The following examples show how children misunderstand clichés:

- "Mom said they put our dog Lucky to sleep. Will I die when I go to sleep too?" questions 4-year-old Sam.
- "Grandpa went to heaven." Alice thought, "Why can't I go too?"
- "Do you think Dad is watching over me?" Kevin asked. "I hope not. That's too embarrassing."
- Five-year-old Mary wondered, "Grandma said God loved Grandpa so much he took him to heaven. Doesn't God love me that much?"

Children take these clichés so literally that sometimes their limited understanding can produce tragic events. Tanya was a 6-year-old whose mom had AIDS. Tanya heard adults repeatedly say her mom was "going to be with the angels," Tanya decided she wanted to be with the angels too and, so, after telling her older cousins she was "going to be with Mom," she walked in front of a moving train. Experts debate whether this death was suicide. The sad truth is that Tanya probably took the cliché literally, thinking that she would be with the angels and her mom. Like most children her age, she also probably assumed that her and her mom's deaths would be reversible.

Ways to help the grieving child

Grieving children must feel heard and understood. Many sensitive issues will arise, and feelings of worry, sadness, rage, terror, shame, abandonment, and self-hatred will emerge. The Head Start community needs to create a safe environment to meet the needs of all grieving children. Children must feel secure and free to express their thoughts and feelings, and feel listened to in the process.

Letter writing is an excellent activity to help grieving children express unrecognized feelings. This letter by 5-year-old Ashley clarified her perception that her mother was buried in the ground, but she was still alive.

Amy, who was a 5-year-old client in grief therapy, expressed great anger at her teacher Mrs. Jones for failing to acknowledge the death of Amy's dad. After her first week of school, Amy had bravely told Mrs. Jones that her father had died of cancer. Mrs. Jones never responded to her, and Amy waited and waited for a reply.

Every child is unique, and so is their grief. Too often, adults try to prescribe to children what they should think and feel, instead of allowing children to tell us what they think and feel.

Usually, it is a good idea to encourage children to share pictures of deceased loved ones in order to open a dialogue and allow the expression of memories. Adam refused to bring into grief therapy a picture of his dad after he died, but he said he would later. Six months later, when he was ready, Adam appeared with a picture of his dad and him playing baseball. This behavior is typical, and it shows how important it is to respect a grieving child and wait until the child is ready to show a picture and share memories of a loved one who has died.

When children can express previously hidden emotions, they gain a greater understanding of themselves and allow adults to be more in touch with what is going on in their grief process. So often, children need to tell their story over and over. Using tools such as drawing, writing, role-playing, and re-enactment, children can safely project feelings and thoughts about their loss.

Grief feelings and thoughts are continual and ever-changing. Sometimes, they arrive without warning, and children may feel unprepared for their enormity in a school setting. Create an understanding with the grieving child that allows her or him to go to a safe place outside the classroom when these unexpected situations occur, without needing to explain why in front of classmates. Also, allowing visits to the school nurse reassures children that they and their family are okay.

Memory work is used in grief therapy to enable children to tell about a person who died and open discussion. Memory books are a collection of drawings and writings that allow a child to re-experience memories and share thoughts and feelings in a safe way. Kids can tell about how their family was before their dad died, and how their family appears to them after dad died.

A 5-year-old named Ryan created a page in his memory book explaining feelings before his dad died. He drew and wrote about his dad yelling at him to "Go to bed!" and wrote his response of "Help me." Ryan used his memory book page as a tool to understand his relationship with his dad, discovering the anger and fear he felt toward his father before he was murdered. These unresolved feelings had made the grief process more difficult by stifling feelings. This page in his memory book allowed Ryan to discover hidden feelings, see his grief, and bring his difficult relationship out in the open.

Tommy was another 5-year-old whose memory book revealed a great absence of men in his life. When asked to draw his family now (four years after his father's death), he drew his Uncle John in the center of his picture watching him play on the playground. Tommy's mother was shocked by the placement of Tommy's uncle, because Tommy hadn't seen his Uncle John for almost three years. The loss of any significant men since his dad's death

---

Do's and Don'ts
for Adults Responding to Grieving Children

How parents and educators respond to a child's grief has a great impact on the child's ability to heal. Maintaining direct, honest, age-appropriate communication allows children to process thoughts and feelings at their own rate and comfort level.

Do:
- Keep the sense of security real for children.
- Maintain consistent routines.
- Prepare children for what will come (death, funeral, feelings).
- Use age-appropriate, clear, truthful language, because young children take words literally.
- Familiarize yourself with the normal symptoms of grief.
- Become a role model for grieving children.
- Validate children's feelings.
- Promote continuing communication with family.
- Allow children to call home if needed during the school day, and allow them to leave the room without having to give explanations.
- Create a safe person or place for children to go to during the school day to discuss feelings comfortably.
- Keep explanations brief and to the point. Repeat if needed, and ask the children to repeat what they think they heard to verify their understanding.
- Remember that children grieve differently.
- Realize many children grieve through play.
- Encourage children to say good-bye to a loved one who has died.

Don't:
- Force or expect children to verbalize feelings about their loss.
- Use clichés that children could take literally.
- Tell children their feelings are wrong.
- Suggest to children that they will get over their grief.
- Assume that children are not grieving if they don't show their feelings.

Phone play is one of many tools adults can use to encourage children to say good-bye to a loved one who has died.

emerged as a central issue for Tommy through the use of his memory book. With this knowledge, a new support group of men could be formed in Tommy's life. This male support group included a Big Brother, a coach as mentor in sports activities, and more frequent visits with Uncle John.

Another memory book page illustrates the worries in words and drawing of 6-year-old Alice. She explains that she worries about her family and that they are sad. "This is a picture of what I worry about," she says and shares a drawing of her family at the grave of her father. When questioned, she explained that one of her worries was that her surviving family wouldn't have enough money to stay in their house and they may have to move. This memory book page served as a vehicle to establish that Alice was worrying and to explore what those worries were.

Letter writing is another tool that allows children to express unrecognized feelings. Ashley, a 5-year-old kindergartener, came into grief therapy on Mother's Day, very angry that no one had mentioned the death of her mom. She was encouraged to write a letter to her mom. The letter clarified Ashley's perception that her mom was still alive but buried in the ground. In the letter, Ashley maintained an ongoing relationship with her mom, wondering what she would buy her for Mother's Day. Children's magical thinking can hold two contradictory concepts together. Ashley knew that her mom's body was no longer working, yet she believed that her mother would be coming back.

Drawing is a great way to allow small children to relay unacknowledged feelings. Kids can draw pictures of how they visualized their loved one dying, the hospital or fu-

neral scene, or their image of where their loved one is now. Seven-year-old Sara has AIDS and so does her mom. Sara drew a picture of herself and her Mom in heaven, expressing her own and her mom's imagined death, and the hope they could be together in heaven.

Remember, it's healthy for a grieving child to cry. Children need to feel their sadness and feel free to express it. So often, well-meaning adults tend to inhibit tears, perhaps because we feel helpless when we see a young child cry, or perhaps it reminds us of our own sadness. Children are given messages such as "Don't cry, you need to be grown up!" "Boys don't cry, you need to be the man of the house now," and "Your dad wouldn't have wanted you to cry." These messages shut off tears and halt the natural grief process. Tears may be upsetting for an adult to see, but healthy for the child to experience.

What we can mention . . .

Too many children face losses in the form of sudden fatal accidents and deaths due to illness, suicide, homicide, and AIDS. There are also many nondeath related issues that have a similar or same effect on children. Loss of family stability from separation and divorce, violence and abuse, unemployment, multiple moves, parental imprisonment, and family alcohol and drug addiction are a few of the many grief issues impacting young children. In forming an open Head Start environment for exploring these life circumstances, it is helpful to remember that what we can mention, we can manage. If we, as caring and educated adults, are incapable of discussing an important and universal life issue, how then are children to learn what to think? Who will model such thoughts for them?

If Head Start professionals and parents can provide grief vocabulary, resources, and crisis and educational interventions, they will create a loss and grief program for young children that allows a safe experi-

---

Grief Activities for the Young Child

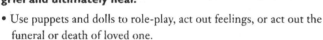

Following are hands-on activities that parents and teachers can use with grieving children to help them express their grief and ultimately heal.

- Use puppets and dolls to role-play, act out feelings, or act out the funeral or death of loved one.

- Use a sandtable or a dollhouse to re-enact the death or funeral of a loved one.

- Make memory books or memory boxes to allow children a physical way to store and hold memories.

- Use a tape recorder or punching bag as a vehicle to release feelings.

- Draw pictures that describe stories, dreams, and happenings surrounding a death.

- Use clay as a vehicle to re-create feelings and also as a means to work through feelings kinesthetically.

- Play music such as Hap Palmer's feelings song to open discussion about how kids feel.

- Read books about death (see the Books about Death and Grieving sidebar with this article).

- Display props such as toy telephones, ambulances, baby bottles, sunglasses, and doctor kits to promote creative fantasy for the young child.

- Have children draw their bodies and show where they feel happy, sad, angry, worried, or scared. Choose colors to tell about feelings.

- Have children write letters to a loved one who has died in order to understand their age-appropriate beliefs and perceptions.

ence of these deep and difficult life issues. Head Start centers can become a bridge of communication between the world of fear, isolation, and loneliness to the world of truth, compassion, and dignity for grieving children.

Linda Goldman specializes in working with children and grief. She is the author of two books on helping children with grief issues, Life and Loss: A Guide to Help Grieving Children *and* Breaking the Silence: A Guide to Help Children With Complicated Grief: Suicide, Homicide, AIDS, Violence, and Abuse. *Goldman is a consultant to Head Start, and she conducts workshops for school systems and universities to educate caring adults to respond to children's loss issues. Write her with questions or comments at the Center for Loss and Grief Therapy, 10400 Connecticut Avenue, Suite 514, Kensington, MD 20895. FAX: 301-656-4350.*

Photographs and illustrations are reprinted from Life and Loss: A Guide to Help Grieving Children *and* Breaking the Silence: A Guide to Help Children with Complicated Grief: Suicide, Homicide, AIDS, Violence, and Abuse *with permission from Taylor & Francis, publisher.*

Books about Death and Grieving

For teachers and parents:

Breaking the Silence: A Guide to Help Children With Complicated Grief: Suicide, Homicide, AIDS, Violence, and Abuse by Linda Goldman. 1996. Washington, DC: Taylor & Francis. A clearly written guide for adults to help children with complicated grief issues. It includes guidelines for educators, national resources, and an annotated bibliography.

Death in the Classroom by Kathleen Cassini and Jacqueline Rogers. 1990. Cincinnati, OH: Griefwork of Cincinnati. An informative teacher's textbook and resource guide that sensitively confronts ways to work in the classroom with death.

Grief Comes to Class by Majel Gliko-Braden. 1992. Omaha, NE: Centering Corp. A practical book designed to help teachers and parents assist bereaved children.

Life and Loss: A Guide to Help Grieving Children by Linda Goldman. 1994. Washington, DC: Taylor & Francis. A resource for working with children and grief. It provides practical information, resources, hands-on activities, a model of a good-bye visit for children, and an annotated bibliography.

For children:

About Dying by Sarah Stein. 1974. New York: Walker & Co. (ages 3-6). This book contains simple text and photographs to help young children understand death and provide ways to help them participate in commemorating.

The Frog Family's Baby Dies by Jerri Oehler. 1978. Durham, NC: Duke University Medical Center (ages 3-6). A coloring book explaining and answering questions about death for the young child.

When Someone Very Special Dies by Marge Heegaard. 1988. Minneapolis, MN: Woodland Press (ages 4-7). An excellent workbook for young children that uses artwork and journaling to allow them to understand and express their grief.

Where's Jess? by Joy and Marv Johnson. 1982. Omaha, NE: Centering Corporation (ages 4-6). A book for young children that answers their questions and expresses their feelings when a sibling dies.

WORKING WITH THE BEREAVED: U. S. ARMY EXPERIENCES WITH NONTRADITIONAL FAMILIES

This paper uses a postmodern family perspective to examine the interaction between Army Casualty Assistance Officers (CAOs) and the families of deceased soldiers. The data we examine are open-ended survey responses of CAOs (N = 188) who assisted bereaved families of soldiers killed in three unrelated air disasters. Five themes emerged from our analysis of the qualitative responses: postmodern family structures, contested definitions of "significant other," language, diversity, and emotion. These themes appear to be related to the difficult demands associated with bereavement work. We argue that the experiences of the CAO are comparable to the experiences of others who may work with the bereaved (e.g., police, officers, medical workers, and disaster workers) when working in similar familial contexts.

MORTEN G. ENDER

Department of Sociology, University of North Dakota, Grand Forks, North Dakota, USA

JOAN M. HERMSEN

Department of Sociology, University of Maryland, College Park, Maryland, USA

Families in the United States are undergoing significant changes. Of particular note is the increase in varied, nontraditional household and family arrangements. Family scholars have recently highlighted the importance of recognizing the presence of these families and incorporating such recognition into both interactions with families and research on families (Bernardes, 1993; Fine, 1993). Theorizing on, as well as the documentation of, nontraditional families is burgeoning (see, for example, Cherlin, 1992; Thorne & Yalom, 1992). However, applied research focusing on nontraditional families is rather limited.

This paper answers the call for research that acknowledges the presence of nontraditional families and seeks a more complete understanding of the influence of nontraditional families on other aspects of social life. In particular, this paper describes the nontraditionality of the bereaved families encountered by Army Casualty Assistance Officers (CAOs) and the five emergent themes related to assisting nontraditional families. Using the qualitative responses from surveys of CAOs, we highlight an array of family arrangements and the subsequent complexity of bereavement work interaction. Further, we illustrate how nontraditional family arrangements challenge those called on to provide assistance in times of family crisis.

Although this study contributes to a growing body of research on military casualty workers (Bartone, 1987; Bartone & Ender, 1994; Ender, 1991; Rosenbaum & Ballard, 1990), the results are applicable to a variety of disaster, crisis intervention, bereavement, and emergency service workers. Hospice workers (Murphy & Perry, 1988), health care workers (Vachon, 1987), AIDS caregivers (Pearlin, Semple, & Turner, 1988), and rescue workers (Wright, Ursano, Bartone, & Ingraham, 1990) are some professionals who provide direct assistance; firefighters (Fullerton, McCarroll, Ursano, & Wright, 1992), paramedics (Palmer, 1983), police officers (Eth, Baron, & Pynoos, 1987; Hall, 1982, Hendricks, 1984), teachers (Cullinan, 1990), and coroners (Charmaz, 1975) might provide indirect assistance to families in times of crisis.

Army Casualty Assistance Officer

The CAO is either an active duty, reserve, or retired senior-level noncommissioned officer or officer temporarily assigned to a family of a recently fallen soldier. CAOs provide short- and long-term personal affairs assistance to the families following the death of a soldier. According to the *Casualty Assistance Handbook* (Department of the Army, 1985), a CAO is "charged by the Secretary of the Army to render all reasonable assistance necessary to settle the personal affairs of a deceased [Army] member" (p. 3). Tasks might include acquiring financial assistance, making funeral arrangements, organizing and administering personal belongings, and assisting the family with relocation and privilege cards. Although the bulk of CAO responsibilities are clearly outlined and instrumental in nature, the socioemotional demands placed on the CAO by the bereaved, him/herself, coworkers, and the media, among others, are unmistakable and require significant attention (Bartone, 1987; Ender, 1991). In short, the CAO crosses the military organizational boundary into the family domain to settle the deceased soldier's personal affairs (Bartone & Ender, 1994). The role of CAO can range from subordinate to liaison to full representative on behalf of the family, depending on the family's request. A typical CAO assignment is approximately 2 weeks. Some cases, depending on the nature of the death, can last 6 months or longer.

Next of Kin

All U. S. Army soldiers are required to complete and periodically update a Record of Emergency Data card (Department of Defense, 1986).[1] The card states:

> This extremely important form is to be used by you to show the names and addresses of your spouse, children, parents, and any other person(s) you would like notified if you become a casualty, *and,* to designate beneficiaries for certain benefits if you die. (p. 1)

The card remains on file with Headquarters, Department of the Army, Casualty Affairs and Memorial Operations Centers, Alexandria, Virginia and, upon a soldier's death, identifies for the CAO who was notified of the death[2] and who will receive gratuities, allotments, and other death "benefits." The Army refers to official next of kin as either primary or secondary next of kin to distinguish

the former as the immediate family members of soldiers (e.g., spouses and children of married soldiers or parents of single soldiers) from the latter as the less immediate family members (e.g., parents of married soldiers or siblings of single soldiers). Significant strides have been made across the history of Army Casualty Affairs to accommodate varied family members and today the Army officially recognizes secondary next of kin, if they are identified as such by the soldier on his/her data card (Bartone & Ender, 1994). However, while a name on a Record of Emergency Data card may define the official next of kin, this form does not delineate the emotional or "salient" next of kin. And although they may not be officially listed as next of kin, these family members are likely to emerge during the caregiving process, obliging the CAO to extend formal and informal assistance to them as the CAO is outside the organization boundary and has some flexibility in adjusting to the demands of the role (Bartone, 1987).

"New" Families

The dominant ideology in the discourse on family in the United States has been that of the traditional nuclear or modern family which has typically been equated with "the family" (Scanzoni & Marsiglio, 1993). This view of the modern family developed out of the work of sociologists such as Talcott Parsons and Ernest Burgess (Cheal, 1993), who argued that families functioned as organized units with periodic states of disorganization. In terms of family definitions, deviations from the traditional nuclear family, according to functionalists, would be limited, short lived, and dysfunctional relative to the larger society.

Contemporary scholars are recognizing, however, that social organization is not as completely patterned as previously thought. Greater variety in form, structure, and meaning is now found in various institutional realms, and yet is not considered dysfunctional. This emerging social condition has been labeled "postmodern" (Harvey, 1990). The institution of the family aptly reflects the postmodern description.

Judith Stacey's work, *Brave New Families* (1991), is an example of scholarship addressing the "new families." She adopts a postmodern view to describe the diverse, fluid, and unresolved nature of family arrangements. The label "postmodern family" becomes a sensitizing concept, signaling the "contested, ambivalent, and undecided character of contemporary gender and kinship arrangements" (p. 17).

Given the increasing alternative family forms in the military (Segal & Harris, 1993), we would expect some military families to be postmodern. Further, we suggest that the postmodern military family may be a source of conflict for CAOs if these officers are ideologically lodged in a modern view of "family."[3]

Methods

This study used a naturalistic approach. This methodology is especially appropriate as it allows the interaction in the bereavement context to emerge from the perspective of all the participants involved. The strength of a qualitative methodology that appreciates a postmodern sensibility is the ability to consider vague and difficult phenomena such as feelings, emotions, personal experience, and subjective perceptions (Denzin & Lincoln, 1994; Rosenau, 1992). This approach facilitates flexibility in manipulating the methodological complexities imposed by language, texts, and method. Although some readers might consider this approach "messy,"[4] it is precisely this open-ended, processional, and holistic feature that sensitizes the reader to the experiences of different CAOs and families in the bereavement work interaction.

Sample

CAOs participating in this study were those assigned to contact the families of victims killed in one of three separate and unrelated air disasters in three countries. Two of the disasters were accidents and the other was ruled a terrorist bombing. The data were collected by researchers at the Walter Reed Army Institute of Research between 1985 and 1990. Of the

240 CAOs involved in the three crashes, 78% ($N = 188$) responded to the survey.

Measures

The three pencil-and-paper surveys included demographic and open-ended questions. The open-ended questions solicited from the respondents a chronology and their understanding of the experience. For example, one question asked the CAO to describe the first week of the assignment. The remaining questions followed this general, open-ended pattern. Questions centered around task performance, coping, attitudes toward CAO duty, and recommendations for future CAO work. CAOs provided handwritten responses to the open-ended questions. In this way, the qualitative approach allowed the interaction to emerge from the perspective of the participants. Responses were transcribed electronically and collated onto a master word processing file.

Procedures

The components of the data analysis model (i.e., data examination, data reduction, data display, and conclusions) are interactive rather than linear (Miles & Huberman, 1994). In other words, the qualitative methods provide a cyclical and continuous process of analysis. For example, tentative conclusions are drawn, followed by further data examination. In data reduction, pattern codes are used as an analysis strategy. Pattern codes are inferential codes that identify an emergent theme for the analyst similar to factor-analytic devices used in statistical analysis. We each read the master file separately and assigned pattern codes. For example, our first-level coding involved identifying situations in the master data file involving nontraditional and extended family arrangements (e.g., "divorced mother," "illegitimate daughter," or "great uncle"). In this case, a specific or subtheme file was created with an electronic "cut and paste" feature found on most word processors. The second-level strategy involved analysis of the subtheme files for emergent salient patterns such as "emotion." With all files, pattern codes were discussed among the analysts for inconsistencies. Discussions centered on reaching consensus on all patterned codes and themes. By the final analysis, we identified five noteworthy and salient themes—postmodern or nontraditional family types, contested definitions of "significant other," language, diversity, and emotion.

Results

Of the 188 CAOs in our sample, 95% were male and 80% were married. The modal number of family members officially assisted by a CAO was two, with 70% of the CAOs officially assisting two to four family members. Sixty percent of the respondents said it was their first CAO experience. Below we address the five themes that emerged from the written responses.

The Postmodern Military Family

Of the 188 CAOs in the sample, 36% ($n = 68$) discussed families in some detail in response to questions even though the open-ended questions did not solicit family-related information. In addition, the results of the pattern code analysis indicate a very wide array of families encountered by the CAOs. We coded 20 of these 68 next of kin encounters as primary and the remaining 42 as secondary. The prominence of references to secondary or ancillary next of kin in the CAO responses suggests some military families can be described as postmodern.

CAO interaction with extended family members (e.g., parents of married soldiers, siblings) was frequent. One CAO worked with a married soldier's family and stated:

> . . . the family consisted of surviving mother and six sisters that reside in the states of Superior, Olympia, and Majestica.[5] The widow resided locally in Glacier with two children—a stepdaughter, 12, and a natural son, 9 months. There was an ex-wife (service member) stationed in Fort Smith with a natural son, 9.

Another soldier commented, "There was the widow and the soldier's mother and father were divorced. Each was a separate family. Thus there were three families drastically affected and needed assistance." CAOs encountered a host of additional ancillary next of kin. Among them were separated, divorced, and remarried parents, aunts and uncles, siblings, unwed and wed mothers of children of deceased soldiers, fiancées, grandparents, other extended family members, close family friends, and neighbors.

All of the people had a relative degree of significance for the deceased soldier that cannot be determined by traditional definitions. The blurred boundaries between primary and ancillary next of kin support the postmodern character of the families encountered. As discussed below, we suggest that these fluid boundaries can be representative of contested definitions of "significant other."

Contested Definitions of "Significant Others"

As outsiders, CAOs in this study were cognizant of the problems of defining or elucidating modern perceptions of family boundaries. Again, the Army recognizes that others outside the immediate family of primary next of kin such as secondary next of kin need and deserve assistance. However, we found that traditional designations of "significant other" are contested; that is, "unofficial family" outside the official designations may maintain that they, too, deserve some definition of official next of kin. In the words of one CAO, "More care should be taken in identifying the next of kin. There was doubt who the 'real' next of kin was the day before the funeral." CAOs noted interaction with not only the official next of kin as defined by the Army (and by the deceased soldier) but also the self-defined unofficial next of kin. Furthermore, among both official and unofficial next of kin, there may be competing perceptions of who is the principal significant other. For example, a CAO acknowledged the contested definitions of "significant other" in this way:

> Unlike the widow, the mother was never satisfied that enough was being done. She felt that I should be her CAO rather than for the widow. She resented me talking to the widow before her.

The contested definitions of "significant other" are often accompanied by a host of negative emotions by the self-defined significant other. Being left out of the official care-receiving circle may suggest (correctly or not) to the ancillary next of kin that he/she was not important to the deceased soldier:

> On the drive back from taking the biological mother to the airport to attend the memorial service, the stepfather started crying, wanting to know why he couldn't go [to the memorial services] for free too since he had raised the boy since he was 8 years old.

The next of kin determination process was also addressed by numerous CAOs. In particular, problems in identifying the official next of kin were noted. These problems were primarily due to inaccurate information, delayed receipt of information, or complications such as ages of next of kin. The following comments by a CAO illustrate the above point:

> My first mission was to determine the true next of kin. The divorce became final while the soldier was in the Sinai so that meant his 2-year-old daughter was the sole heiress. However, his mother was the primary adult next of kin.

A second frequently noted problem that arose from the contested definitions of "significant other" was related to the disposition of service benefits. A CAO made this point by saying:

> His mother didn't get his SGLI [Serviceman's Group Life Insurance] but I feel that's who that soldier wanted to get his money and who needed it most. He had put her as his beneficiary in his original request, but when the unit updated their emergency record cards during the predeployment preparations someone probably told him to put it "By Law" in a rush and as it turned out, he had an illegitimate child, and the child's mother got the money.

And as further stated by another CAO:

> I was also required to work with both sets of parents who were divorced and both had remarried. The natural mother could not understand why she had no say in the funeral arrangements, entitlements and other benefits.

The contested definitions of "significant other" give a CAO latitude in subverting the bureaucratic definition of "real," "primary," or "significant" next of kin. Although a CAO must provide assistance to the official next of kin, s/he may also extend support to persons who emerge as significant others and/or to those whom the official next of kin allow into the assistance network.[6]

Language

Language forces a particular perspective on a social situation. When describing their experiences, some CAOs used specific language in their responses that emphasized traditional family formations. For example, one CAO confided:

> My case was not like the "normal" one. [The deceased] had an illegitimate daughter, 4 years old still living with her mother . . . to complicate it even more, [the deceased's] mother and father were divorced. . . .

The above statement by the CAO illustrates the prevailing cultural belief that a family is a stable, nuclear, modern family. The family encountered in this case was not "normal" because of the "illegitimate daughter" and divorced parents. Thus, it seems the CAO who entered this situation found a family who did not fit with his idea of family. This can be contrasted with another CAO who noted, "I had a very simple case—parents with a 12-year-old daughter."

In addition, the language highlighted the use of the nonnormative and potentially stigmatizing label "illegitimate" when speaking of particular children. Application of such a label suggests that the traditional modern family of "legitimate" children is the referent for the soldier. As one soldier said, "I was placed in a situation to support the deceased's family and each one of his illegitimate children's families." And another:

> Coping with the family's anger and frustration was the hardest part of being a CAO. They wanted answers and results now. Sometime later, when it was determined that the deceased's illegitimate son was to be the primary beneficiary, more anger and frustration was directed toward me from brothers, sisters, and other family members and friends.

In this case, the illegitimate son appears not to be viewed as a "family member" by the deceased's brothers and sisters. The presence of an illegitimate son places additional stress on the CAO as s/he must cope with the anger expressed by the remaining family members.

Diversity

CAOs noted 11 incidents relating to issues of ethnicity, race, and/or gender as they assisted their families. The diversity comments focused on the dual purpose of easing the bereavement work of the CAO and increasing the comfort level of the recipients. Both recognizing and confronting diversity challenges in the bereavement interaction were evident in the responses of the CAOs. Furthermore, in commenting on suggestions for improving the assistance process, some CAOs offered ideas about dealing with the ethnic and racial diversity that may be encountered when assisting families. For example, recognizing racial diversity, one CAO noted, "It was almost as if I became one of their direct family members, even though they were black and I am white." And in the words of another CAO, "I assisted a rural black family and I am a black officer. Affirmative action aside, I think this helped me build a good relationship with the family."

CAOs adopted strategies to address the diversity encountered, with the primary focus remaining on providing adequate assistance to the family of the deceased. Recognizing and acting on the diversity encountered is a way for the CAO to ensure a more sensitive, accurate assistance experience. An example of a CAO meeting the challenges of racial diversity follows: "A black NCO [noncommissioned officer] requested to assist me as I, being white, did not want there to be a failure to communicate on my part or the widow's."

For some CAOs, diversity was viewed as a barrier to successful assistance. A particular problem noted by some CAOs was an inability to communicate effectively because of differences in native language.[7] Thus, whereas the information to pass on may itself be difficult to explain and comprehend, the process of exchange may become even more tenuous when differing languages are involved. As stated by one CAO, "Next, I became physically and emotionally drained because I was dealing with a Korean mother and wife that knew very little English." This is contrasted with a positive and common-language experience of a CAO's though the language was not English: "I speak Spanish so it was easy for me to understand the widow and family."

Suggestions by CAOs for confronting diversity centered on whom to assign to which families, with the common idea being that CAOs should resemble the families they are to serve to the deceased soldier they are to represent. Although the rationale for his suggestion remains unstated, a CAO's following comments argue for the homogeneity of CAO and deceased soldier: "I was a CAO for the family of a deceased female soldier. In the future I think it may help if the CAO would have also have been a female."

To sum, CAOs are not only encountering diverse families but they are also interacting with families that are racially and/or ethnically different from their own families of origin. Diverse families offer a unique challenge to CAOs in the assistance process.

Emotion

CAO duty may be one of the most demanding of "emotion work" occupations defined by Hochschild (1983). The assistance process of the CAOs involves not only managing the administrative affairs of the deceased soldier's next of kin but also coping with a complex of emotions experienced by themselves (e.g., they may have been a work colleague or neighbor of the deceased soldier) and by a host of survivors who surround the deceased. Comments made by the CAOs indirectly highlight the emotional nature of the bereavement work. The emotions described include those experienced by the CAO and those the CAO projected onto the persons they assisted. That is, the emotions can be described as those felt versus those encountered. Irrespective of the source of emotion, Hochschild notes that emotion workers who must suppress emotions are likely to become alienated from their true feelings.

The emotions felt by the CAOs included, anger, love, frustration, depression, and embarrassment. The following comments by a CAO capture some of this emotion: "I was initially somewhat resentful that I had to deal with the death of someone else's loved one that I didn't even know; however, I got over this later...." Another CAO stated, "The most difficult part of being a CAO was the anger I had when I saw the family members taking advantage of the mother and her newly acquired insurance money." A CAO summed up the emotions of those in the survivor network by stating, "Some people admired me as a soldier and some hated me for being a part of the military machine that snuffed the life of their friend." And as further suggested by another CAO:

The most difficult part of being a CAO is dealing with the feelings of the family. Such as knowing when to try to lift their spirits and when to show sympathy and compassion when they're feeling down.

The death of a young soldier during peacetime virtually assures that the situation will be emotionally charged. And the emotion-laden words used to describe the assistance encounter suggest that emotions are far from absent in this process. Some emotions felt by the CAO and by the survivors are products of the postmodern family arrangements and add a dynamic to the tasks of CAOs and to the experiences of the families. Failing to acknowledge the legitimacy of postmodern family characteristics may increase the intensity of emotions experienced by CAOs, survivors, and others involved in the process.

Discussion and Conclusions

Families in the United States have undergone significant structural changes. The characteristics of these families appear to have an impact on bereavement work. In the present study, the responses of the CAOs to open-ended survey questions highlight the postmodern character of the families encountered. Furthermore, interaction with the bereaved revealed four additional themes that also reflect postmodern processes. The themes include contested definitions of "significant other," language, diversity, and emotions. Two themes—contested definitions and diversity—are based in the emerging postmodern family whereas the theme of language reflects the bias toward modern family formulations.

The responses of the CAOs suggest that providing assistance in these postmodern contexts may have created additional pressures in their helper role. Although all CAOs endeavor to perform their role admirably and with sincere concern for the families, the unexpected encounter with fluid, diverse, changing, and emotionally demanding social contexts challenges the CAO in different and unanticipated ways.

We suggest that the five themes highlighted above point to the need for personal and organizational adaptation that can facilitate bereavement work and contribute to the caregiving process. In the present case, if CAOs are further informed, through CAO manuals and training, that the next of kin they are likely to encounter may be from diverse and fluid families, with nontraditional levels of commitments to the deceased, the initial shock and accompanying strain may not be as pronounced. In addition, Record of Emergency Data cards could be expanded for greater flexibility in determining the significant others of a soldier. Finally, a debriefing program should be implemented not only to benefit the individual CAO but also to inform other CAOs of the friends and family they may encounter in future CAO assignments.

Manuals are an initial step in the appropriate direction. While the CAO handbook clearly outlines step by step the instrumental tasks necessary to complete the duty, it provides virtually no insight to the range of families the CAO will be called on to assist. At a minimum, the manual could include a section that provides information on personal biases associated with caregiving, a range of "typical" family profiles, and research-based information on each family type profiled. For example, research indicates that fictive kin—non-blood kin who relationally define themselves as family—are important to African American and Native American families (Dilworth-Anderson, Burton, & Turner, 1993).

Training, at many levels, is recommended. The results warrant that ROTC, junior officer, and senior noncommissioned officer training academies recognize that addressing the changing form and nature of families, with special emphasis on the military family, would make an effective contribution to bereavement work processes.[8] For example, the United States Military Academy at West Point offers an undergraduate course in the sociology of the family; however, the course is not required for all cadets. University ROTC programs and other in-service academies and schools should incorporate mandatory human service, family, or death and dying information sessions into their programs. In addition, an audiovisual aid, including information about the entire casualty process, including the role of soldiers, CAOs, coworkers, family members, friends, and the media, could be made available to all local-level commanders throughout the Army. These policy recommendations are consistent with research findings in police work (Hall, 1982), the U. S. Navy (Phillips, 1988), and especially the U. S. Air Force (Rosenbaum & Ballard, 1990).

The Record of Emergency Data cards should provide for ample opportunity to list and designate the others significant to the soldier, including primary, secondary, and fictive kin. The card should also request the soldier to identify for the CAO special familial circumstances (e.g., medical problems and language requirements) and soldier/family confidentiality should also be completely assured. The casualty system could better cope with changes in the soldier's family if the system were automated and regularly updated.

Finally, a mandatory group-debriefing program at a neutral location and sponsored by the headquarters of the Casualty Affairs and Memorial Operations Center in conjunction with clinical workers and program evaluators should be implemented to assist CAOs after completing the duty. We emphasize the mandatory, group, and location nature of the assignment as research indicates that self-referral, although organizationally

available, is generally avoided due to fears about being fired and ridiculed among soldiers (McCarroll, Ursano, Wright, & Fullerton, 1993) and fears about "loss of face" among police officers (Eth et al., 1987). Other "masculine dominated" organizations may want to consider this strategy. In addition to the opportunities for personal consultation, sharing the diversity of experiences with other CAOs and the Army will serve to improve the casualty assistance process in the future.[9] Finally, social science evaluators can gain unique and much needed insights into the bereavement process as the complexities of interaction will emerge from the perspective of the various participants.

No longer can a common set of cultural understandings be assumed. Rather, helpers may now be asked to perform their duties in terrains and contexts that are very diverse linguistically, culturally, racially, emotionally, and sexually. The failure to address the postmodern family during the bereavement process may contribute further to feelings of victimization on the part of the deceased soldier's family. In addition, unintended insensitivity rooted in ideological family preferences and/or unawareness based on a lack of appropriate information can potentially prevent the CAO from coping effectively with an emotionally intense and structurally unique family situation. On the other hand, an informed CAO, flexible in ability to cope with unique and potentially conflicting needs of a complex family, may find him/herself better able to meet all the demands of the role.[10]

There is no indication that postmodern family arrangements are waning ("The Changing American Household," 1993). Moreover, the military family is often influenced by the larger society and the recent debate over homosexuals in the armed forces suggests more change is forthcoming (Scott & Stanley, 1994). The Army, as an organization, is in the forefront of being committed to those affected by death and has altered its policies accordingly (Bartone & Ender, 1994).[11] An increased awareness of family changes in the postmodern context should benefit military casualty workers, the Army, and families affected

by death. Other organization workers such as coroners, police officers, hospice workers, health care workers, and even commercial industries (e.g., airline, railroad, and chemical) should be cognizant of the uniqueness and variation of the families they may be required to assist in the face of trauma.

References

Bartone, P. (1987, October). *Boundary crossers: The role of the family assistance officers in the Gander disaster.* Paper presented at the biannual meeting of the Inter-University Seminar on Armed Forces and Society, Chicago, IL.

Bartone, P., & Ender, M. G. (1994). Organizational responses to death in the military. *Death Studies, 18,* 25–39.

Bernardes, J. (1993). Responsibilities in studying postmodern families. *Journal of Family Issues, 14,* 35–49.

The changing American household. (1993, July). *American Demographics Desk Reference Series, No. 3,* 2–3.

Charmaz, K. (1975). The coroner's strategies for announcing death. *Urban Life, 4,* 296–316.

Cheal, D. (1993). Unity and difference in postmodern families. *Journal of Family Issues, 14,* 5–19.

Cherlin, A. (1992). *Marriage, divorce, remarriage.* Cambridge, MA: Harvard University Press.

Cullinan, A. L. (1990). Teachers' death anxiety, ability to cope with death, and perceived ability to aid bereaved students. *Death Studies, 14,* 147–160.

Denzin, N. K., & Lincoln, Y. S. (1994). Introduction: Entering the field of qualitative research. In N. K. Denzin & Y. S. Lincoln (Eds.), *The handbook for qualitative methods* (pp. 1–18). Thousand Oaks, CA: Sage.

Department of the Army. (1985). *Casualty assistance handbook* (Pamphlet No. 608–33). Washington, DC: Superintendent of Documents, U. S. Government Printing Office.

Department of Defense. (1986). *Record of emergency data: DD form 93 (160–135).* Washington, DC: Superintendent of Documents, U. S. Government Printing Office.

Dilworth-Anderson, P., Burton, L. M., & Turner, W. L. (1993). The importance of values in the study of culturally diverse families. *Family Relations: Journal of Applied Family and Child Studies, 42,* 238–242.

Ender, M. (1991). *Associated strains of a temporary role: The case of the army casualty assistance officer.* Unpublished master's thesis, University of Maryland, College Park.

Eth, S., Baron, D., & Pynoos, R. (1987). Death notification. *Bulletin of the American Academy of Psychiatry and the Law, 15,* 275–281.

Fine, M. (1993). Current approaches to understanding diversity: An overview of the special issue. *Family Relations: Journal of Applied Family and Child Studies, 42,* 235–237.

Fullerton, C., McCarroll, J., Ursano, R., & Wright, K. (1992). Psychological responses of rescue workers: Fire fighters and trauma. *American Journal of Orthopsychiatry, 62,* 371–378.

Hall, M. (1982). Law enforcement officers and death notification: A plea for relevant education. *Journal of Police Science and Administration, 10,* 189–193.

Harvey, D. (1990). *The condition of postmodernity: An enquiry into the origins of cultural change.* Cambridge, MA: Blackwell.

Hendricks, J. (1984). Death notification: The theory and practice of informing survivors. *Journal of Police Science and Administration, 12,* 109–116.

Hochschild, A. (1983). *The managed heart: Commercialization of human feelings.* Berkeley, CA: University of California Press.

Marcus, G. E. (1994). What comes (just) after "post"? The case of ethnography. In N. K. Denzin & Y. S. Lincoln (Eds.), *The handbook for qualitative methods* (pp. 563–574). Thousand Oaks, CA: Sage.

McCarroll, J. E., Ursano, R. J., Wright, K. M., & Fullerton, C. S. (1993). Handling bodies after violent death: Strategies for coping. *American Journal of Orthopsychiatry, 63,* 209–214.

Miles, M., & Huberman, A. (1994). *Qualitative data analysis: A expanded sourcebook.* Beverly Hills, CA: Sage.

Murphy, P., & Perry, K. (1988). Hidden grievers. *Death Studies, 12,* 451–462.

Palmer, C. (1983). A note about paramedics' strategies for dealing with death and dying. *Journal of Occupational Psychology, 56,* 83–86.

Pearlin, L., Semple, S., & Turner, H. (1988). Stress of AIDS caregiving: A preliminary overview of the issues. *Death Studies, 12,* 501–518.

Phillips, R. J. (1988). *Breaking the news: A proactive ministry to the casualty and assistance call officers of the United States Navy.* Unpublished master's thesis, Princeton Theological Seminary, Princeton, NJ.

Raphael, B. (1986). Victims and helpers. In B. Raphael (Ed.), *When disaster strikes: How individuals and communities cope with catastrophe* (pp. 222–244). New York: Basic Books.

Rosenau, P. (1992). *Post-modernism and the social sciences: Insights, inroads and intrusions.* Princeton, NJ: Princeton University Press.

Rosenbaum, S. D., & Ballard, J. A. (1990). Educating Air Force mortuary officers. *Death Studies, 14,* 135–145.

Rosenberg, M., & McCullough, B. (1981). Mattering: Inferred significance and mental health among adolescents. *Research in Community and Mental Health, 2,* 163–182.

Scanzoni, J., & Marsiglio, W. (1993). New action theory and contemporary families. *Journal of Family Issues, 14,* 105–132.

Scott, W., & Stanley, S. (Eds.). (1994). *Gays and lesbians in the military: Issues, concerns and contrasts.* New York: Aldine de Gruyter.

Segal, M., & Harris, J. (1993). *What we know about army families* (No. DAA L03–86–D–0001). Alexandria, VA: U. S. Army Research Institute for the Behavioral and Social Sciences.

Stacey, J. (1991). *Brave new families: Stories of domestic upheaval in late twentieth century America.* New York: Basic Books.

Thorne, B., & Yalom, M. (Eds.). (1992). *Rethinking the family: Some feminist questions.* New York: Longman.

Vachon, M. (1987). *Occupational stress in the care of the critically ill, the dying and the bereaved.* New York: Hemisphere.

Wright, K., Ursano, R., Bartone, P., & Ingraham, L. (1990). The shared experience of catastrophe: An expanded classification of the disaster community. *American Journal of Orthopsychiatry, 60,* 35–42.

Notes

1. In the absence of a card or the soldier indicating "By Law" on the card, the order for next of kin is spouse, eldest child, father, mother.

2. A notification officer notifies the primary next of kin face to face within 24 h of the death. The CAO first meets with the next of kin after the official notification of death has been served.

3. As Raphael (1986) notes with regard to disaster workers, "each [helper] brings his own special wish to assist, his own drive to succor, his own personality and past life experience, and most importantly, his own perceptions of what is needed and what he will do" (p. 229). We suggest that to the degree that life experience and personal perceptions of what constitutes "family" suggest a nuclear, modern family arrangement, the CAO may have difficulty caring for and meeting the needs of the family that does not fit this model. Like their military peers, police officers, rescue workers, and other professionals perform their duties from within an organizational context and also may be influenced by the dominant social ideology of the family. Although our data cannot directly assess CAOs' attitudes and perceptions regarding the diversity of families they assisted, our data do suggest that the nontraditional families were central in CAOs' reflections on their experiences.

4. For an in-depth discussion of "messy texts" or "worlds apart cultural criticism" and post-postmodern methods, we refer the reader to Marcus (1994).

5. Fictitious names are used. The original names were deleted in transcription to protect participant confidentiality.

6. Contested definitions of "significant other" raise further issues—for example, the degree to which we feel we matter to others, or "mattering" (Rosenberg & McCullough, 1981). The CAO is asked to determine who mattered to the soldier (beyond the formal next of kin) and to whom the soldier mattered, and these individuals thus may receive informal assistance. This practice indicates a recognition that this latter group of persons may have emotional needs to be addressed.

7. Linguists, if available, may accompany CAOs in English-as-a-Second-Language situations.

8. When asked openly how they coped with the demands of CAO duty, a handful of CAOs noted completing baccalaureate degrees in sociology and psychology or having taken a course in these disciplines.

9. For example, two of the three air disasters in the present study included very-high-profile media exposure and lengthy body identification processes. These features added a host of other people and new dimensions to the caregiving process.

10. Indeed, although not empirically examined, experienced CAOs (i.e., more than one experience as a CAO) in the study appear to recognize this element and appear to cope well with the duty. This suggests that on-the-job training in a postmodern context is evident. However, most CAOs perform the duty once in a military career and may never have the opportunity to build on their experiences as CAOs (Ender, 1991).

11. The deaths of U. S. soldiers from friendly fire during the Persian Gulf War were the impetus for further congressional modifications in the casualty notification system, including access to detailed information for family members, a doubling of death gratuities and Service Member Life Insurance (SGLI) policies, and more-timely notification.

Received 8 August 1995; accepted 28 April 1996.

The study is based on data collected by the Department of Military Psychiatry, Walter Reed Army Institute of Research, Washington, DC. The data were collected under the research protocol *Job Stress, Coping and Burnout in Army Casualty Operations Workers,* Paul T. Bartone, principal investigator and currently with the U. S. Army Medical Research Unit—Europe, Heidelberg, Germany. Additional financial support provided by the Fellowship Office, Graduate Studies and Research, University of Maryland at College Park.

The authors wish to thank Richard Brown, Doris Durand, Ken Kammeyer, Eddie McCarroll, Leora Rosen, Joe Rothberg, and two anonymous reviewers for their thoughtful comments on earlier versions of this manuscript.

An earlier draft of this paper was presented at the Eastern Sociological Society annual meeting, Baltimore, Maryland, March, 1994.

Address correspondence to Morten G. Ender, Department of Sociology, University of North Dakota, Grand Forks, ND 58202, USA. E-mail: ender@prairie.nodak.edu

MOURNING
IN AMERICA

*The ways that Americans deal with death
are changing. Some developments are
supportive of the bereaved; others are not.*

When Pat and Anna Gillis were growing up in Lowell, Massachusetts, in the 1960s, the two sisters were inseparable. They were a familiar sight in their close-knit neighborhood, going to Catholic school each weekday, to the public library on Saturdays, and to church on Sundays. Pat was often shy, but would follow Anna into new situations, peppering her with questions the whole way, confident her big sister would know the answers.

But in adolescence, Pat began to pull away from Anna, spiraling downward into substance abuse. She struggled with addiction for 20 years, until finally at age 34 she stopped using drugs. For the next two years, Pat focused on repairing frayed relationships with her family, being a better mother to her two young sons, and healing from her troubled past. Just as she was doing better, she died suddenly in her sleep last Halloween.

Anna was devastated by the loss of her only sibling. "I feel like an egg whose insides have been blown out," says the Bethesda, Maryland, writer and editor. "I look okay from the outside, but if someone squeezed me, I'd crumble."

Anna is among the estimated eight million people in the United States each year who lose a loved one. And while bereavement is one of the most profound and universal experiences of our lives, far too often people feel isolated in their grief, unsupported by those around them, and unprepared for the depth of their sorrow.

Throughout human history all cultures have created ways to honor the dead and help those who mourn. Neanderthals living more than 35,000 years ago buried their dead with cornflower, grape hyacinths, and hollyhocks. In the Himalayas, the grave of a Neanderthal child was ringed with wild goat horns. Later, the Cro-Magnons adorned their dead with elaborate necklaces of ivory beads. The bodies of ancient Egyptians were mummified and buried with favorite objects.

"All cultures have a belief about the soul or spirit that continues on beyond the physical form," says psychologist Carol Wogrin, director of the Bereavement Studies Program at Mount Ida College near Boston. "All cultures have a belief in treatment and disposal of the body and all have mourning practices. The specific content of those beliefs, though, varies tremendously."

Wogrin and other bereavement experts are concerned that today Americans are abandoning longheld customs. Until recent times, death was a familiar and intimate part of life. People typically died at home, often at a young age. The body was prepared and buried by family members or close friends. Funerals were performed by ministers who could speak with personal knowledge about the deceased. Food was brought to the bereaved family and those in mourning wore black or draped their doorways in black crepe.

But these traditions are fast disappearing. Death often occurs in a hospital or nursing home, where it is viewed not as an inevitable part of life but as a failure of medical technology. Family members often never see the body, but simply call the mortuary. Like Anna Gillis, people frequently live far from their hometowns and extended families. Once the funeral is over, the bereaved return to their routines and to friends, colleagues, or pastors who never knew their loved one.

In the book *Grief Ministry, Helping Others Mourn,* coauthor Donna Reilly Williams contrasts the American way of dying with what she witnessed in an African hospital. When a person died, drums began to beat in the hospital courtyard. Soon a pickup truck arrived, filled with family and friends from the village where the person had lived. For four hours, the group surrounded the bed, singing hymns, praying, eating, and lovingly holding and stroking the body. Even though patients were waiting in the hall for a bed, the hospital staff viewed this time of mourning as intrinsic to patient care.

Our culture tends to be uncomfortable with such displays of intense feelings. Some believe our inability to cope well with death is not a modern affliction but one rooted in our national psyche. "It's the old pioneering psychology [that] you have to be tough," says Vamik D. Volkan, professor of psychiatry at University of Virginia. "We do a lot more denial and repression of emotions than many other cultures," he says. In the traditional Turkish Cypriot culture, he points out, mourners went through the streets, screaming their pain and anger at the deceased for leaving them. In the Maori culture of New Zealand, bereaved family members cut their breasts to express their loss or subjected themselves to ritualized beatings by others. These customs, which seem strange

From *Common Boundary*, May/June 1999, pp. 20, 22-26. © 1999 by Common Boundary. Reprinted by permission.

The strangest thing about grief is the way it bites you when you're not paying attention. . . . Odd little things knock you completely flat.
—*Anna Gillis*

to us, Volkan says, gave mourners an outlet for normal feelings of guilt and anger that accompany their grief.

Practitioners of some Eastern religions, such as Tibetan Buddhism, focus a great deal of attention on what they view as the cycle of life and death. The actions Buddhists take in life are believed to influence the direction they will take as they pass through death into rebirth. "We think about death a lot—its inevitability and its unpredictability," says Konchog Norbu, who converted to Tibetan Buddhism eight years ago and is a monk at Kunzang Palyul Choling Buddhist temple in Poolesville, Maryland. "Based on its inevitability, we consider it prudent spiritual practice to prepare ahead of time."

Accepting the inevitability of death, discussing it openly, and giving the bereaved ongoing comfort can prevent long-term emotional and physical turmoil. Mourners can be helped immensely by participating in meaningful rituals and having the opportunity to talk about their loved one as time passes. But the value of this kind of support is often not understood in our society.

Lee Pollak directs a bereavement center at the Jewish Family and Children's Services Agency in San Francisco. The hardest part of her job is recruiting people to participate in support groups and other programs offered at the center. "Many think they should be able to go it alone and that they don't need support or education," she says. "They think everyone suffers, and it's acknowledging that you're weak to get help."

The Ways of Grief

Grief, though universal, is at the same time very individual. "The more complicated the relationship was in life, the more complicated in death," says Pollak. Take the death of a spouse when a marriage was fraught with problems. "At death, what comes up are all the disappointments of dreams that didn't come true, the lost op-

portunities, the unresolved passion of those angry feelings that have no place to go," says Pollak. "It says a lot for trying to resolve issues, if possible, during life."

Some losses are easier to accept. The "best" death seems to be when our loved one is ill or quite elderly and the relationship among family members is strong and caring. Nothing is left unsaid, whether words of love or forgiveness. This was the case for Kathleen Phelan, a Dominican sister in Washington, D. C., whose mother, Ada, was a widow suffering from Alzheimer's disease. "She was a tiny, strong-hearted, gritty little thing," says Kathleen. Although Ada no longer recognized her, Kathleen traveled across the country as often as she could to visit her mother in a San Diego nursing home. Ada held on for years, through many broken bones and severe dementia, but finally succumbed three days after Christmas in 1997.

When death was approaching, Kathleen was able to be there. She searched for words to comfort her mother. "I knew my father was still alive in her mind," she says. "So I leaned over and whispered, 'Soon you'll be dancing with Ned.' She looked over at me, and her eyes opened up. I will never forget the luminous smile that came across her face. It was almost as if she were looking right through me to those people who were in her deepest memory." Even as she grieves for her mother, Kathleen knows Ada's suffering is over and that is a great relief. It was, she says, "like opening a window."

For people such as Lynne and Todd Waymon, who lost their only child in a car accident, no such consolation can be found. The Waymons were living what they describe as a "charmed life" before their son's death. They both have fulfilling work, Todd as a professor at the local community college and Lynne as a self-employed speaker and writer. They have a loving marriage, are actively involved in their community, and were devoted to 16-year-old Matthew, whom they'd adopted from India as a baby. Matthew was a handsome and good-natured young man, an avid soccer player with a large circle of friends. The Waymon's house was a gathering place, with teenagers slouching on the wide front porch, helping themselves to food from the refrigerator, and watching sports on big-screen television.

On a hot July day in 1998, Matt headed off to summer school with his buddies. On the way home, his close friend, who was driving too fast, lost control of the car. The car flipped, fatally crushing a 40-year-old father of 3 in his pickup truck, and killing Matt and Irn Williams, another boy in the car.

The depth of the Waymons's grief and shock was almost unbearable. "The future is destroyed," says Lynne, as she and Todd, five months after the accident, sit in their living room surrounded by pictures and mementos of Matt. "Our whole frame of reference had to do with being proud of him and watching him walk into the future knowing he was going to fall in love, go to college. We were so involved with his life, probably overly involved," Lynne adds, smiling sadly.

Anna Gillis, too, was shaken to the core by her sister's death. "The strangest thing about grief is the way it bites you when you're not paying attention," she says. "Odd little things knock you completely flat." Soon after Pat's death, Anna was hiking in the woods with her husband when she was suddenly jolted by a memory of youthful autumns: Pat and she anxiously waiting outdoors for their father to come home from work to take them out for Halloween.

As the memory hit her, Anna says, "I burst into what I can only describe as keening. It was positively primal; it came from deep inside and I just wailed." Anna, who is half Irish American and half Argentinean, was reminded of the banshees of Irish legend. "I always thought the wailing of the banshees sounded weird. Now it sounds incredibly healthy," she says. "Instead of wailing, those who lose a loved one go around trying to be dignified all the time. In fact, the grief is ready to explode inside them."

Finding Meaning in Ritual

As intensely painful as grief can be, pioneers in the field of bereavement counseling find that much can be done to ease this difficult journey. Having a meaningful service of farewell; receiving practical support from friends, neighbors, and employers; honoring loved ones at special times throughout the year; and acknowledging the long-term nature of the grieving process can bring real comfort to those in pain.

Every faith has rituals that often correspond to the psychological stages of grief. One of the most developed traditions comes from Judaism, which has detailed laws and customs, from the moment of death through a year of observances. Jews do not believe in cremation or in embalming the body for viewing, which they see as disrespectful of the deceased. The funeral and burial take place as soon as possible, followed by a week-long Shiva, during which the bereaved receive visitors at home. Throughout the year, special prayers from the congregation offer consolation to mourners. "From a psychotherapeutic point of view, Judaism has a very functional attitude towards death," says Pollack. "It focuses on a year's worth of activities to mark a loss, with a number of different rituals that mirror what we know are clinical needs."

Islamic mourning practices are similar. In the Arab Islamic tradition, services are held at the mosque. The body is ceremonially washed, wrapped in white, and buried as soon as possible. For three days, mourners stay at home to receive visitors who recite a passage from the Koran when they arrive. Forty days later a special time of remembrance is held.

In Tibetan Buddhism, the focus is on helping the dying person rather than on comforting those left behind. If death is anticipated, the community drops everything and begins round-the-clock prayer. The teacher or lama is nearby, helping the person negotiate the process of death. "The whole idea is to have somebody die in a very conducive spiritual environment," says Konchog. "If we feel everything has been done for the person that's died, there isn't so much grief."

For people closely tied to religious communities, the rituals and customs—no matter what they are—can be comforting. Even those who have abandoned their childhood faith can find the traditions consoling. But without strong ties to a community, people can be isolated in their grief. Increasingly, funeral directors find themselves dealing with clients they've never met who have no traditions or religious practices on which to draw. "We're less likely to know the people with whom we're working when they come in our front door," says O. Duane Weeks, director of the New England Institute of Funeral Service Education at Mount Ida College. "We have an hour or so to get them to trust us with this very important thing that needs to be really good and really special."

Weeks identifies two parallel changes going on in American attitudes toward funerals. On the one hand, a growing number of people opt for no rituals whatsoever, a change that Weeks finds troubling. On the other hand, there is a positive movement toward services in which mourners ask to be active rather than passive participants.

In the Catholic church, for example, families are more likely to be personalized. When Ada Phelan died, Kathleen found the pastor open to her ideas for the liturgy. Joined by sisters from her congregation, she selected music, Scriptural passages, and prayers of petition. At the service, she welcomed mourners and told them of her mother's life.

"The liturgy for me was very consoling and intimate," she says. In contrast, when she lost her father 25 years ago, her input was not welcome. "To me, my mother's funeral was a celebration of the two of them."

Anna Gillis delivered the eulogy at her sister's funeral. "I wanted people to remember what was best about my sister," she says. This was especially important to Anna since her sister's former substance abuse was well known in the community. Anna

We think about death a lot—its inevitability and its unpredictability. . . . Based on its inevitability, we consider it prudent spiritual practice to prepare ahead of time. —Konchog Norbu, Buddhist monk

spoke of Pat's kind-hearted nature, her sense of humor, her generosity and curiosity. "Giving the eulogy felt like a proper goodbye," she says. "You've publicly stated, this person is dead but I want to remember them. It was a way for me to make my amends publicly for anything I may have said about her. It was also a gift to my parents and to my nephews."

On the other end of the spectrum are those who see no value in having a service. "A high percentage of the people I meet believe that the memorial service or funeral depends on the wishes of the deceased," says Don Montagna, leader of the Washington Ethical Society in Washington, D. C. "I tell them the memorial service is not for the dead, but for those who suffer the loss. The purpose is to honor our loved ones and the important role they played in our lives. We're also sending a message to ourselves—we could drop dead tomorrow. Do we really want no one to look up from his workbench?"

Just as long-held customs can be deeply consoling, so too can newly created practices. At the nonsectarian Saint Francis Center in Washington, D. C., rituals are seen as crucial to the grieving process. The center counsels people suffering all sorts of loss, not only the death of a loved one but divorce, incarceration of a parent, and illness. Among the center's programs are support groups for inner-city children who have lost multiple family members to violence, AIDS, accidents, and natural death.

"We help people develop their own rituals if they don't have institutionalized ones," says Saint Francis Center executive director Robert Washington. People are encouraged to plant trees, for example, or to make "memory boxes," which have been found to be especially meaningful for children. Inside the box go strands of hair, rings, and photographs. "On specifically designated occasions, they open up the box and reminisce," says Washington.

When young Matthew Waymon died, his friends seemed to know instinctively the power of ritual. They began by bringing flowers and handmade posters to the accident site. For several days they maintained a vigil there, a safe haven where normally tough-talking boys felt free to weep, to hold each other, and to say that they loved each other, words they wish they'd said to Matt but never had. Several later got tattoos dedicated to their friend. They also attended his memorial service, where 800 people came to pay tribute to Matt and honor the Waymons's loss. Matt was described by a leader of the Ethical Society, to which the Waymons belong, as having "a wonderful sense of tease and fun and play. He was someone who was different, who was unfailingly kind, and who stood for good." Most moving were the young people who were introduced to the crowd as Matt's "heart friends." The teenagers, looking awkward in suits and ties, struggled to put words to their grief. "You could count on Matt to help you out. He was as good at listening as he was at talking," said one boy. "Everybody says Matt's gone, but I don't believe it," said another. "You see all these people here? If everybody loves him the way they do, he's not gone. He's still inside of us." Such testimonials, tearfully given, bring ongoing comfort to his family.

Social Support

"In my fog, I was aware that a lot of people were doing a lot of things for Todd and me and that made me feel very taken care of," says Lynne Waymon of the immediate aftermath of her son's death. Being members of the Ethical Society gave them a supportive community that brought food, helped make arrangements, and cushioned them in their sorrow. But before long, the phone began to ring less. "The world has gone on," Lynne says. "Your world, though, has a whole different calendar: before and after."

The actions or inaction of friends, coworkers, and medical staff play an important role in how people move through the grieving process. Workplaces, through supportive attitudes and policies, can help ease a person's suffering. Typically, only three days are allowed off from work even for the death of a close family member. "Workplaces are shooting themselves in the foot to think people can come back and be productive in that short a time," says Washington. "There are ways they can honor the grief that both help the person and allow them to be more productive—giving them a lighter work load, more time off, or shorter work weeks for a while."

Todd Waymon found that a supportive environment allowed him to return to teaching sooner than expected. Rather than burying his grief, Todd began the first day by sharing his loss with his students. "I told them if I'm late, if I break down crying, you'll understand." By creating an emotional bond, his students, in turn, were more open with him about their own private tribulations.

Perhaps the most precious gift to a grieving person is the opportunity to share stories of their loved one. The Waymons long to hear anecdotes about their son. One friend who didn't have the chance to know Matt invites Lynne to "tell me a Matthew story," a gesture she deeply appreciates.

Conversely, what is most hurtful is a failure to acknowledge the loss. "The main thing I notice is many people's inability to act," says Lynne. "The best ones say 'I don't know what to say.' The worst ones say nothing." She recalls one colleague who, like the Waymons, had adopted her child. Lynne assumed this friend in particular would identify with her loss. Yet when she came to Lynne's home on business, shortly after Matthew's death, she never expressed a word of sympathy.

"I wish there were more guidelines," says Lynne. "It's all so hush-hush and secret and difficult to talk about." Saying the wrong thing, such as "It was God's will" or "Everyone goes through it," can be hurtful. So too can acting uncomfortable if the bereaved person starts to cry. "People say, 'I'm so sorry I made you sad,'" says Lynne. "It's ridiculous. I am sad. The best thing to do is let me talk about it." Her husband agrees. "I have a thousand gallons of tears to shed," he says, "and I want to get on with it."

Kathleen Phelan feels her grieving was made more difficult by the staff of the nursing home where her mother had lived for nine years, the last two at $10,000 a month. Ada died on the weekend, and no social workers or administrators were available to offer professional services or to assist with necessary logistics. In fact, the home never acknowledged her mother's death. "No one came to the funeral or sent flowers or even a card," she says. After the funeral, when Kathleen came to pack her mother's belongings, her room had already been given to another patient, and all of Ada's worldly belongings were in four large garbage bags. A year later, the memory still angers and hurts Kathleen.

A Long Journey

There is no timetable for grief, and the journey is filled with peaks and valleys. Just when you feel you're getting better, a fresh wave of pain pulls you back. Finding ongoing ways to honor your loved one, experience the grief, and still carry on with life can be difficult.

I knew my father was still alive in her mind. . . . So I leaned over and whispered, "Soon you'll be dancing with Ned." She looked over at me, and her eyes opened up. I will never forget the luminous smile that came across her face.
—Kathleen Phelan

When people feel they have exhausted their own resources, they sometimes seek help from a grief counselor or bereavement center. The Saint Francis Center helps people to grieve "more efficiently and effectively," says Washington. For example, a mother with young children who has lost her husband cannot afford to stop functioning. Counselors might urge her to set aside a time each evening, once the children are in bed, to play music that reminds her of her husband, think about him, cry, and then to put it away. "The important thing is to help them open up their pain which is easy, but also learn how to close it down," he says.

Anna Gillis found comfort in a support group at the center. "I'm physically detached from the places and people who would be able to best help me get over my grief," she says. In the support group, she is able both to share her sorrow and to console others in turn.

Creative expression—keeping a journal, writing poetry, painting, dancing—is also healing. Lynne Waymon took up singing in a chorus as a way to bring a spark of joy into her life as well as refocus her attention. "I have to think real hard to figure out these alto parts, and it feels good because my mind is so destroyed," she says. "I enjoy the concentration a lot." Also, she and Todd each find it helpful keeping a journal. Writing down her feelings calms Lynne when she can't stop crying. For Todd, the journal is a record of his emotional journey.

"Grief has an absolutely transformative power," says Volkan. When we lose someone, he says, we lose what they give us, whether it's love, economic security, or guidance. Taking on these functions ourselves or being open to new ways of finding them can be an enriching experience. For some people, the bereavement process can bring a new appreciation for life, for their relationships, and for the world around them. There is a sense of joining in a universal experience and feeling more strongly connected to the rest of humanity.

"I've learned that grieving is a part of life, part of the experience of being human," says Anna Gillis. "I can't bear now to hear people speak ill of others—you don't know if you'll have them tomorrow. It's made me feel a lot more compassionate in general."

Pollak believes the language of grief should be changed. Grief is not something we "get over," or even "heal from," as if it were an illness, but rather a journey to a new stage of life. "The goal is not forgetting and it's not resolving," she says. "It's reconciling yourself to that loss and discovering some kind of spiritual meaning [in it]. You will always have a relationship with the person who has died, but the relationship is different. That is your quest—to discover that relationship."

This transformative power of grief has been experienced time and again by Don Montagna of the Washington Ethical Society. When he began his career, he dreaded conducting memorial services but now he appreciates the opportunity to be involved in such experiences. "The purpose of the ceremony is to purify, to keep the person's spirit alive," he says. "We let go of anything mundane or trivial, and we forgive the negative."

He urges the bereaved to not just go through the motions at the service but to experience fully what has been lost. He first meets privately with family members to learn as much as he can about the loved one's life—the historical conditions in which they lived, their family background, education, career, relationships, warts and all. In some cases, dark secrets emerge, and survivors are guided toward a path of forgiveness. "If you recognize your parent made a mistake, you don't clean it up and say it doesn't matter. You have to say, 'I'll find better ways to manage my kids. Thanks, Dad, for teaching me this,'" says Montagna.

In every ceremony, those who attend are asked to silently reflect on a quality they most treasure about the deceased. "We get clear about what was the really special way that person had of being," he says. "We recognize that what we most appreciated is what we yearn and grieve for. By choosing one quality and making it stronger in ourselves, we fan the flames and keep the spirit of our loved one alive. If you do that, you really feel not only the importance of that person, but your connection to the whole human web."

Beth Baker is a Tokoma Park, Maryland, writer and a contributing editor to Common Boundary.

Grief Tips
Help for Those Who Mourn

James E. Miller

Following are many ideas to help people who are mourning a loved one's death. Different kinds of losses dictate different responses, so not all of these ideas will suit everyone. Likewise, no two people grieve alike—what works for one may not work for another. Treat this list for what it is: a gathering of assorted suggestions that various people have tried with success. Perhaps what helped them through their grief will help you. The emphasis here is upon specific, practical ideas.

Talk regularly with a friend.
Talking with another about what you think and feel is one of the best things you can do for yourself. It helps relieve some of the pressure you may feel, it can give you a sense of perspective, and it keeps you in touch with others. Look for someone who's a good listener and a caring soul. Then speak what's on your mind and in your heart. If this feels one-sided, let that be okay for this period of your life. Chances are the other person will find meaning in what they're doing. And the time will come when you'll have the chance to be a good listener for someone else. You'll be a better listener then if you're a good talker now.

Walk.
Go for walks outside every day if you can. Don't overdo it, but walk briskly enough that it feels invigorating. Sometimes try walking slowly enough you can look carefully at whatever you want to see. Observe what nature has to offer you, what it can teach you. Enjoy as much as you're able the sights and the sounds that come your way. If you like, walk with another.

Carry or wear a linking object.
Carry something in your pocket or purse that reminds you of the one who died—a keepsake they gave you perhaps, or a small object they once carried or used, or a memento you select for just this purpose. You might wear a piece of their jewelry in the same way. Whenever you want, reach for or gaze upon this object and remember what it signifies.

Visit the grave.
Not all people prefer to do this. But if it feels right to you, then do so. Don't let others convince you this is a morbid thing to do. Spend whatever time feels right there. Stand or sit in the quietness and do what comes naturally: be silent or talk, breathe deeply or cry, recollect or pray. You may wish to add your distinctive touch to the gravesite—straighten it a bit, or add little signs of your love.

Create a memory book.
Compile photographs which document your loved one's life. Arrange them into some sort of order so they tell a story. Add other elements if you want: diplomas, newspaper clippings, awards, accomplishments, reminders of significant events. Put all this in a special binder and keep it out for people to look at if they wish. Go through it on your own if you desire. Reminisce as you do so.

Recall your dreams.
Your dreams often have important things to say about your feelings and about your relationship with the one who died. Your dreams may be scary or sad, especially early on. They may seem weird or crazy to you. You may find that your loved one appears in your dreams. Accept your dreams for what they are and see what you can learn from them. No one knows that better than you.

Tell people what helps you and what doesn't.
People around you may not understand what you need. So tell them. If hearing your loved one's name spoken aloud by others feels good, say so. If you need more time alone, or assistance with chores you're unable to complete, or an occasional hug, be honest. People can't read your mind, so you'll have to speak it.

Write things down.
Most people who are grieving become more forgetful than usual. So help yourself remember what you want by keeping track of it on paper or with whatever system works best for you. This may include writing down things you want to preserve about the person who has died.

Ask for a copy of the memorial service.
If the funeral liturgy or memorial service held special meaning for you because of what was spoken or read, ask for the words. Whoever participated in that ritual will feel gratified that what they prepared was appreciated. Turn to these words whenever you want. Some people find these thoughts provide even more help weeks and months after the service.

Remember the serenity prayer.
There is a prayer attributed to theologian Reinhold Niebuhr, but it's actually an ancient German prayer. It has brought comfort and support to many who have suffered various kinds of afflictions. Perhaps it will help you. The prayer goes, God, grant me the serenity to accept the things I cannot change, courage to change the things I can, and wisdom to know one from the other. Great truth is contained here. Call these words to mind when you need their direction.

Plant something living as a memorial.
Plant a flower, a bush, or a tree in memory of the one who died. Or plant several things. Do this ceremonially if you wish, perhaps with others present. If you do this planting where you live, you can watch it grow and change day by day, season by season. You can even make it a part of special times of remembrance in the future.

Plan at least one thing you'll do each day.
Even if your grief is very painful and your energy very low, plan to complete at least one thing each day, even if it's a small thing. Then follow through with your plan, day after day. Don't feel you have to keep busy all day long; that can become awfully tiring and even counterproductive. Just help yourself feel that you're not entirely at the mercy of this overwhelming experience—there are some things you can do to help you through this time.

Spend time in your loved one's space.
If it's what you want to do, you may sit in the other's favorite chair, or lie in their bed, or just stand in their room or among their possessions. Do this if it brings you comfort. But don't do it if it feels too awkward. You'll know quickly enough what's right for you.

Journal.
Write out your thoughts and feelings. Do this whenever you feel the urge, but do it at least several times a week, if not several times a day. Don't censor what you write—be just as honest as you can. In time, go back through your writings and notice how you're changing and growing. Write about that, too.

Rest.
Grieving is hard work. So do what's best for you: get your rest. Take naps if you wish. Lie down from time to time. Relax in a comfortable chair. Pace yourself so you have interludes in which you can replenish yourself. Give yourself plenty of permission to take things easy.

Purchase something soft to sleep with.
A teddy bear is a favorite choice for some. But there are other options. Select something that feels warm and cuddly. Then, whatever your age, cuddle it.

Write the person who died.
Write letters or other messages to your loved one, thoughts you wish you could express if they were present. And who

knows but what they're not present in some way? Preserve what you write in your journal if you wish, or on stationery, or on your computer. Or, if you wish, discard what you've written after awhile. You'll find this urge to write the other will eventually leave you, but for awhile it can be a real release for you, as well as a real connection.

Get a physical.
It's wise to get a physical examination within a few months after the death. But it's also an assuring thing to do. Chances are good you'll experience various physical reactions when you're grieving. It's helpful to make sure that your body is acting normally, whatever normal may be for you. Your physician can be an important ally at this time of your life.

Get physical.
Exercise. Flex your muscles. Stretch your body. Expand your lungs. It will help you feel better. It really will.

Consider a support group.
Spending time with a small group of people who have undergone a similar life experience can be very therapeutic. You can discover how natural your feelings are. You can learn from the experiences and the ideas of others. You can find backing as you make the changes you must. Support groups are not for everyone, of course. But many people have come to swear by them. You won't know unless you try.

If you're alone, and if you like animals, get a pet.
The attention and affection a pet provides may help you adapt to the loss of the attention and affection you're experiencing after this significant person has died. Pets can also be fun to play with. Certain pets offer you a sense of personal security, too, if that is important to you.

Light a candle at mealtime.
Especially if you eat alone, but even if you don't, consider lighting a taper at the table in memory of your loved one. Pause to remember them as you light it. Keep them nearby in this time of sustenance. You might light a candle at other times as well—as you sit alone in the evening, for instance.

Donate their possessions meaningfully.
Whether you give your loved one's personal possessions to someone you know or to a stranger, find ways to pass these things along so that others might benefit from them. Family members or friends might like to receive keepsakes. They or others might deserve tools or utensils or books or sporting equipment. Philanthropic organizations can put clothes to good use. Some wish to do this quickly following the death, while others wish to wait awhile.

Create a memory area at home.
In a space that feels appropriate, arrange a small tableau that honors the person: a framed photograph or two, perhaps a prized possession or award, or something they created, or something they loved. This might be placed on a small table,

or a mantel, or a desk. Some people like to use a grouping of candles, representing not just the person who died but others who have died as well. In that case, a variety of candles can be arranged, each representing a unique life.

Drink water.
Grieving people can easily become dehydrated. Crying can naturally lead to that. And with your normal routines turned upside down, you may simply not drink as much or as regularly as you did before this death. Make this one way you care for yourself.

Use your hands.
Sometimes there's value in doing repetitive things with your hands, something you don't have to think about very much because it becomes second nature. Knitting and crocheting are like that. So are carving, woodworking, polishing, solving jigsaw puzzles, painting, braiding, shoveling, washing, and countless other activities.

Give yourself respites from your grief.
Just because you're grieving doesn't mean you must always be feeling sad or forlorn. There's value in sometimes consciously deciding that you'll think about something else for awhile, or that you'll do something you've always enjoyed doing. Sometimes this happens naturally and it's only later you realize that your grief has taken a back seat. Let it. This is not an indication you love that person any less, or that you're forgetting them. It's a sign that you're human and you need relief from the unrelenting pressure. It can also be a healthy sign you're healing.

See a grief counselor.
If you're concerned about how you're feeling and how well you're adapting, make an appointment with a counselor who specializes in grief. Often you'll learn what you need, both about grief and about yourself as a griever, in only a few sessions. Ask questions of the counselor before you sign on: What specific training does he or she have? What accreditation? A person who is a family therapist or a psychologist doesn't necessarily understand the unique issues of someone in grief.

Begin your day with your loved one.
If your grief is young, you'll probably wake up thinking of that person anyway. So why not decide that you'll include her or him from the start? Focus this time in a positive way. Bring to your mind fulfilling memories. Recall lessons this person taught you, gifts he or she gave you. Think about how you can spend your day in ways that would be in keeping with your loved one's best self, and with your best self. Then carry that best self with you through your day.

Invite someone to be your telephone buddy.
If your grief and sadness hit you especially hard at times and you have no one nearby to turn to, ask someone you trust to be your telephone buddy. Ask their permission for you to call them whenever you feel you're at loose ends, day or night. Then put

their number beside your phone and call them if you need them. Don't abuse this privilege, of course. And covenant that someday it will be payback time—someday you'll make yourself available to help someone else in the same way you've been helped. That will help you accept the care you're receiving.

Avoid certain people if you must.
No one likes to be unfriendly or cold. But if there are people in your life who make it very difficult for you to do your grieving, then do what you can to stay out of their way. Some people may lecture you, or belittle you, or antagonize you, either knowingly or unknowingly. Take care of your health during your grief, including your emotional health. If that means protecting yourself from others for awhile, then do so.

Structure alone time.
You may have your full share of alone time, in which case you'll want to ignore this suggestion. But if you're often among family, friends, and colleagues, make sure you also have time all by yourself. A large part of the grieving process involves what goes on inside yourself—your thoughts, your feelings, your memories, your hopes and dreams. So allow yourself the opportunity to go inside so you can grow inside.

Listen to music.
Choose music you believe will help you at a given moment, whether it's contemporary or ancient, instrumental or vocal, secular or religious. Let the sounds surround you and soothe you. Take this music with you, if you wish, as you go about your day.

Create your own music.
Play an instrument. Sing a song. Or just hum. Use your music to express what you feel, to unite you with others, to focus on your hope.

Do something your loved one would enjoy.
Remember the one who died in your own unique way. One widowed woman has a special sourkraut meal once a year. She doesn't like this tangy dish herself, but it was her husband's favorite, and she finds solace in remembering him in that way. There are probably a hundred different things you could do that once brought meaning or satisfaction to the one you loved. The meaning and satisfaction don't have to end with the death of that person.

Write stories about your loved one.
Recreate those events you don't want to forget. Write them out in detail—when and where they occurred, who was there, what happened, what the results were. Describe everything as well as you can. Add dialogue if you wish. Make an entire collection of stories. It will help you today and it will become a valuable resource for yourself and others in the future.

Screen your entertainment.
Some TV shows and movies are best not viewed when you're deep in grief. The same goes for certain books or articles. If

you have any question, do a bit of research before you find yourself in the midst of an experience which brings up too many feelings for you to handle comfortably. For example, if your loved one recently died of cancer, you can do without reliving that experience on a 30-foot movie screen.

Read practical books and articles on grief.
Reading is a great way to find your way through this round-about experience. Steer clear of those books that are like text-books for professionals. They won't offer you the undergirding you need. Go for the ones that speak to you directly and honestly as a person in mourning. It will probably help to read shorter books and more succinct articles—your power of concentration is likely to be diminished.

Engage your soul.
You'll want to do this your own way. Some people meditate, some pray, and some spend time alone in nature. Some worship with a congregation and others do it on their own. Many grieving people begin to sense that all of us, living and dead, are connected on a spiritual level in a way that defies easy understanding. Include your soul as you grow through your grief.

Change some things.
As soon as it seems right, alter some things in your home to make clear this significant change that has occurred. Rearrange a room or replace a piece of furniture or give away certain items that will never again be used in your home. This does not mean to remove all signs of the one who died. It does mean not treating your home or your loved one's room as a shrine which cannot be altered in anyway.

Plan ahead for special days.
Birthdays, anniversaries, holidays, and other special events can be difficult times, especially for the first year or two. Give thought beforehand to how you will handle those days. Do things a little differently than you used to, as a way of acknowledging this change in your life. But also be sure to invoke that person's presence and memory somehow during the day. If you don't include that person in some way, you'll spend too much of your energy acting as if nothing has been changed with that day, knowing full well that much has changed.

Allow yourself to laugh.
Sometimes something funny will happen to you, just like it used to. Sometimes you'll recall something hilarious that happened in the past. When that happens, go ahead and laugh if it feels funny to you. You won't be desecrating your loved one's memory. You'll be consecrating their love of life, and your own, too.

Allow yourself to cry.
Crying goes naturally with grief. Tears well up and fall even when you least expect them. Subdued sniffles can become racking sobs on a moment's notice. It may feel awkward to you, but this is not unusual for a person in your situation. A good rule of thumb is this: if you feel like crying, then cry.

If not, then don't. Some grieving people seldom cry—it's just their way.

Talk to the other one.
If it helps, you might talk with the one who died as you drive alone in your car, or as you stand beside the grave, or as you screw up your courage to make an important decision. This talking might be out loud, or under your breath. Either way, it's the same: you're simply wishing the other was with you so you could talk things over, and for the moment you're doing the best you can to continue that conversation. This inclination to converse will eventually go away, when the time is right.

Donate in the other's name.
Honor the other's memory and spirit by giving a gift or gifts to a cause the other would appreciate. World hunger? A favorite charity? A local fund-raiser? A building project? Extend that person's influence even farther.

Create or commission a memory quilt.
Sew or invite others to sew with you. Or hire someone to sew for you. However you get it completed, put together a wall hanging or a bedroom quilt that remembers the important life events of the one who died. Take your time doing this. Make it what it is: a labor of love.

Take a yoga class.
People of almost any age can do yoga. More than conditioning your body, it helps you relax and focus your mind. It can be woven into a practice of meditation. It's a gentle art for that time in your life when you deserve gentleness all around you.

Plant yourself in nature.
Dig a flower garden and keep it in color as long as possible. Dig a vegetable garden and stay close to it until frost. Walk in forests and put your hands on trees. Collect leaves and wild-flowers. Watch firsthand how rivers and lakes and oceans behave. Look up at the stars and don't just wonder—hope.

Connect on the Internet.
If you're computer savvy, search the Internet. You'll find many resources for people in grief, as well as the opportunity to chat with fellow grievers. You can link up with others without leaving your home. You'll also find much more to expand your horizons as a person who is beginning to grow.

Speak to a clergyperson.
If you're searching for answers to the larger questions about life and death, religion and spirituality, consider talking with a representative of your faith, or even another's faith. Consider becoming a spiritual friend with another and making your time of grieving a time of personal exploring.

Read how others have responded to a loved one's death.
You may feel that your own grief is all you can handle. But if you'd like to look at the ways others have done it, try C. S. Lewis's *A Grief Observed,* Lynn Caine's *Widow,* John Bram-

blett's *When Good-Bye Is Forever,* or Nicholas Wolterstorff's *Lament for a Son.* There are many others. Check with a counselor or a librarian.

Learn about your loved one from others.
Listen to the stories others have to tell about the one who died, both stories you're familiar with and those you've never heard before. Spend time with their friends or schoolmates or colleagues. Invite them into your home. Solicit the writings of others. Preserve whatever you find out. Celebrate your time together.

Take a day off.
When the mood is just right, take a one-day vacation. Do whatever you want, or don't do whatever you want. Travel somewhere or stay inside by yourself. Be very active or don't do anything at all. Just make it your day, whatever that means for you.

Invite someone to give you feedback.
Select someone you trust, preferably someone familiar with the workings of grief, to give you their reaction when you ask for it. If you want to check out how clearly you're thinking, how accurately you're remembering, how effectively you're coping, go to that person. Pose your questions, then listen to their responses. What you choose to do with that information will be up to you.

Vent your anger rather than hold it in.
You may feel awkward being angry when you're grieving, but anger is a common reaction. The expression holds true: anger is best out floatin' rather than in bloatin'. Even if you feel a bit ashamed as you do it, find ways to get it out of your system. Yell, even if it's in an empty house. Cry. Hit something soft. Throw eggs at something hard. Vacuum up a storm. Resist the temptation to be proper.

Give thanks every day.
Whatever has happened to you, you still have things to be thankful for. Perhaps it's your memories, your remaining family, your support, your work, your own health—all sorts of things. Draw your attention to those parts of life that are worth appreciating, then appreciate them.

Monitor signs of dependency.
While it's normal to become more dependent upon others for awhile immediately after a death, it will not be helpful to continue in that role long-term. Watch for signs that you're prolonging your need for assistance. Congratulate yourself when you do things for yourself.

Give yourself rewards.
Be kind to yourself in your grief. Do those things for yourself that you really enjoy, perhaps at the end of a long day, or in the midst of a lonely time. Treat yourself to a favorite meal or delicacy. Get a massage. Buy some flowers. Do something frivolous that makes you feel good. Then soak up those moments as fully as you can.

Eat healthy.
Your diet affects how you think and feel as well as how your body acts. Eat balanced meals. Eat even if you're not hungry. Eat regular meals rather than just snacking. Avoid too much fat.

Take up a new hobby.
Try something you've never tried before. Expand your horizons. Do what you want to do, not what someone else may have wanted for you. Learn. Be open to meeting new people. Associate this part of your life with who you're becoming, rather than who you've been.

Do something to help someone else.
Step out of your own problems from time to time and devote your attention to someone else. Offer a gift or your service. Do this for yourself as much as for the other. Feel good about your worth.

Honor your funnybone.
Watch a comedy on TV. View a funny movie. Read humorous books or articles. Savor jokes. When you're able to laugh, you encourage your healing.

Write down your lessons.
Your grief experience will have much to teach you. From time to time reflect upon what it is you're learning. State it as plainly as you're able. Carry those lessons with you as you go about your days.

GriefTips are intended for use by people in mourning. They're also intended to be the collected wisdom of people who have experienced mourning first-hand. I encourage you to add your own GriefTip along with any words of explanation you choose. Include your email address so I can show you the edited version of your idea before it's entered here as the latest GriefTip. Your name will appear if you desire. Just request it. (http://www.opn.com/willowgreen/tips.html)

34, 37–38, 40, 41; cost of, 18, 19–22, 150–151; in different religious traditions, 139–142; do-it-yourself movement for, 150–152; fads in, 142; function of, 130–132

G

Gillis, Anna, 200, 201, 202, 203
"good death," 14
Graceland Cemetery, in Chicago, Illinois, 143–144
grief: advice coping with, 155, 204–208; children and, 144–149, 185–192; counseling, 94, 153–154, 177–179, 180; definition of, 130; disenfranchised, 164–167, 168–176, 177–184; process of, 160–163, 177–179, 180; resolution of, 130–131; work of, 162, 163
Grimm, Brothers, 41, 42–43
guilt: as aspect of grief, 131, 161, 162, 178, 181; of children, 37; within patient-physician relationship, 71–72

H

harpists, music-therapy project and, 12–13
Head Start programs, children's grief and, 185–192
health care fraud, 86–87
health proxies, 77–78, 101, 106
heart disease, 58
Hemlock Society, 58, 118
"higher-brain" criterion of death, 26–28, 30
Hinduism, funeral traditions in, 139–140
HIV. See AIDS
Hollywood Memorial Park Cemetery, in Hollywood, California, 144
home, dying at, 58, 60–61
home health aides, 16
homicides, 58, 179, 180
homosexual relationships, bereavement in, 164, 165, 167, 182
hospice care, 16–17, 39, 41, 45, 60–61, 67, 92, 93, 94, 95, 101, 115, 151; for children, 47–48; home funerals and, 150, 151–152; in nursing homes, 83–89; religion and spirituality in, 64–65
hospitals: care in, 58–59; deaths in, 14–15, 39, 58, 60–61
Humphrey, Derek, 58

I

insurance, long-term care and, 54, 55
intensive care units, 60, 61; "psychosis" of, 60
Islam, funeral traditions in, 140

J

Janeway, James, 41
Japan, 113
John Hopkins University, 14, 16
Judaism, 140, 201

K

Kevorkian, Jack, 58, 61, 97, 99, 102, 113, 114
Klagsbrun, Samuel, 125–126
Kübler-Ross, Elizabeth, 40, 122–127; 160

L

life-sustaining treatment. See euthanasia
listening, 82
literature, children's themes of death in, 39–46
"Little Mermaid, The," 44
"Little Red Riding Hood," 39, 42–43
Little Women, 40
"living dead," 134
living wills, 58, 118, 119
Loewen Group, 22–23, 150, 151
loneliness, as part of grief process, 161, 162
long-term care, 53–54
long-term care residents, end-of-life care and, 76

M

magical thinking, about death, 36, 146, 188, 191
Maori culture, bereavement in, 200–201
Massachusetts Medical Society, 99
Medicaid, 54, 85–86
medical advances, life expectancy and, 99, 179
medical impotence, 81–82
medical school training, dying patients and, 14–15, 16, 61, 106
Medicare, 84, 85–86
memorial services, child-oriented, 145–149
memory books, 190–191
memory boxes, 202
mental health professionals, complicated mourning and, 177–184
Mitford, Jessica, 19, 22, 23, 58, 61
Modern Maturity, 51
Montagna, Don, 202, 203
Moody, Raymond, 126
Morse, Melvin, 126
mortuary schools, 22
mourning, 172–175, 200–203. See also bereavement; disenfranchised grief
Mourning After Program, The, 153–157
music therapy, 12–13
Muslims. See Islam

N

National Funeral Directors Association, 18, 20–21, 22, 23, 133
National Hospice Organization, 16
National Institutes of Health, 25–26, 162
Natural Death Care Project, 23, 151
Neanderthals, 200
near-death experiences, 124
Netherlands, physician-assisted suicide in, 68, 71, 103, 113, 114
neurodegenerative disorders, 106
Nietzsche, Friedrich, 69
Nuland, Sherwin, 126
nursing homes: death in, 39, 61; hospice care in, 83–89; long-term care in, 53–55
nurses: assisted suicide and, 69; interactions with families, 60

O

Office of Inspector General (OUG), health care fraud and, 86–87
Omega Project, 162
On Death and Dying (Kübler-Ross), 122, 124
Open Society Institute Project on Death in America, 75
organ donation, 16, 24–31, 110–111
Osler, William, 14
out-of-body experiences, 124

P

pain management, 14–17, 75, 77, 78, 113; assisted suicide and, 68, 70–71, 72, 92–95, 97, 105, 106–107, 115
palliative care, pediatric, 47–48. See also end-of-life care; hospice care; pain management
Parsis, burial rites of, 139
Patient Self-Determination Act, 100
Pauzé Tombstone Fund, 22
pediatric palliative care, 47–48
perinatal deaths, 165
permanent vegetative states, 26, 27, 28–29, 30, 113
Perrault, Charles, 41–43
pets, death of, 147, 166, 182
Phelan, Kathleen, 201, 202, 203
physician-assisted suicide (PAS), 14, 15, 30, 58, 61, 62, 64, 68–74, 76, 92–98, 118; argument against, 104–109; argument for, 99–103; international views of, 113–117. See also euthanasia
planning for death, 58–61
Pollack, Lee, 201, 203
poverty, 179
President's Commission for the Study of Ethical Problems in Medicine and Biomedical and Behavioral Research, 24, 26, 27, 30
private funerals, 131

Test Your Knowledge Form

We encourage you to photocopy and use this page as a tool to assess how the articles in **Annual Editions** expand on the information in your textbook. By reflecting on the articles you will gain enhanced text information. You can also access this useful form on a product's book support Web site at ***http://www.dushkin.com/ online/.***

NAME: _____ DATE: _____

TITLE AND NUMBER OF ARTICLE: _____

BRIEFLY STATE THE MAIN IDEA OF THIS ARTICLE: _____

LIST THREE IMPORTANT FACTS THAT THE AUTHOR USES TO SUPPORT THE MAIN IDEA:

WHAT INFORMATION OR IDEAS DISCUSSED IN THIS ARTICLE ARE ALSO DISCUSSED IN YOUR TEXTBOOK OR OTHER READINGS THAT YOU HAVE DONE? LIST THE TEXTBOOK CHAPTERS AND PAGE NUMBERS:

LIST ANY EXAMPLES OF BIAS OR FAULTY REASONING THAT YOU FOUND IN THE ARTICLE:

LIST ANY NEW TERMS/CONCEPTS THAT WERE DISCUSSED IN THE ARTICLE, AND WRITE A SHORT DEFINITION: